THE ACADEMIC SCRIBBLERS

REVISED EDITION

THE ACADEMIC SCRIBBLERS

THIRD EDITION

WILLIAM BREIT

Trinity University

ROGER L. RANSOM

University of California, Riverside

With a new foreword
by Robert M. Solow

PRINCETON UNIVERSITY PRESS

PRINCETON, NEW JERSEY

Originally published by Holt, Rinehart and Winston; second edition
published by The Dryden Press, an imprint of Harcourt Brace & Company.
Third edition, and first Princeton Paperback printing, with a new foreword
by Robert M. Solow and a new afterword by the authors, 1998

Quotations in Chapter 11 from the *New Industrial State,* Third Edition,
Revised, by John Kenneth Galbraith copyright © 1967, 1971, 1978 by
John Kenneth Galbraith are reprinted by permission of Houghton Mifflin
Company (published in the British Commonwealth and Empire by Andre
Deutsch, Limited).
Quotations in Chapter 11 from *Economics and the Public Purpose* by
John Kenneth Galbraith are copyright © 1973 by John Kenneth
Galbraith. Reprinted by permission of Houghton Mifflin Company
(published in the British Commonwealth and Empire by Andre Deutsch,
Limited).
Art reference for drawing of Thorstein Veblen courtesy the Bettmann
Archive. Art reference for drawing of Alvin H. Hansen courtesy of United
Press International and Wide World Photos. Art reference for drawing of
Edward H. Chamberlin courtesy of Wide World Photos.

Library of Congress Cataloging-in-Publication Data

Breit, William.
    The academic scribblers / William Breit, Roger L. Ransom ; with a
new foreword by Robert M. Solow. — 3rd ed.
        p.   cm.
    Originally published: Chicago : Dryden Press, c1982. With a new
foreword and with a new afterword by the authors.
    Includes bibliographical references and index.
    ISBN 0-691-05986-1 (pbk. : alk. paper)
    1. Economics—History—20th century.   2. Economists—Biography.
3. Economics—United States—History—20th century.   4. Economists—
United States—Biography.   I. Ransom, Roger L., 1938– . II. Title.
HB87.B72   1998
330′.092′2—dc21   98-25286

Princeton University Press books are printed on acid-free paper and meet
the guidelines for permanence and durability of the Committee on
Production Guidelines for Book Longevity of the Council on Library
Resources

http://pup.princeton.edu

Printed in the United States of America

10 9 8 7 6 5 4 3 2 1

... The ideas of economists and political philosophers, both when they are right and when they are wrong, are more powerful than is commonly understood. Indeed the world is ruled by little else. Practical men, who believe themselves to be quite exempt from any intellectual influences, are usually the slaves of some defunct economist. Madmen in authority, who hear voices in the air, are distilling their frenzy from some academic scribbler of a few years back.

—*John Maynard Keynes*

CONTENTS

FOREWORD

ROBERT M. SOLOW

William Breit and Roger L. Ransom write out of conviction that serious economic ideas are important for the making and understanding of economic policy. If they are right, and I think they are, then it must also be important that serious citizens understand not only the potted conclusions of economic analysis, but also something about the reasoning and observation that lead up to them. Because economics is not cut-and-dried, this kind of understanding would be a necessary basis for intelligent policy debate. All that sounds obvious. But there are at least three persistent and ubiquitous booby traps in the way of this nice view of the relation between ideas and action.

The first, and least important, is the natural tendency for academic economists to write for each other, to care about the good opinion of professional colleagues, and therefore to pursue their own version of art for art's sake. The outcome can be extravagant assumptions, virtuoso technique, and results of very dubious relevance to real issues of economic policy. I say that this tendency is natural because any practitioner of a craft wants to impress the masters of the guild. (Why shouldn't economic upstarts try to upstage Paul Samuelson the way other trumpet players used to try with Louis Armstrong?) I think this tendency is not so important precisely because the cast of characters in Breit and Ransom shows that there are plenty of academic economists who remain interested in understanding everyday economic life and economic policy, and are prepared to turn their professional apparatus in that direction. As long as that is so, all those technical flourishes keep people sharp, and sometimes hit pay dirt.

The second booby trap in the path of intelligent policy debate is the sound bite. Economics is complicated; significant and useful propositions do not come easy. Even stating clearly what is currently

going on out there can be difficult. It is a fair guess that no significant and useful proposition, along with the necessary qualifications,
can be stated adequately in twenty-five words or less. But that is all
the opening the profession normally gets for commenting on controversial questions of economic policy. (Other complicated subjects get
the same treatment; but we are talking about economics, not ge-
netics.) The result is that what most people hear or read are slogans,
buzzwords, and jargon. Whose fault is that? Partly the profession's,
but the odds are stacked against it.

The third booby trap is the prevalence of pundits who know nothing of economics, but make up for that with confidence. They have
neither any carefully earned understanding of the way the economy
works, nor any grasp at all of what serious economics is about. But
they have opinions, and flamboyantly advertised opinion sells. I put
some blame on the profession for not caring enough about clarity
and persuasiveness. But it is hard to resist a sort of intellectual
Gresham's Law: bad talk drives out good. Pandering beats logic every
time. This does not excuse academics for evading the obligation to
speak for rigor.

The Academic Scribblers would like to be a partial antidote. The
authors' goal, bless their hearts, is to make basic economic ideas
clear and interesting. One way to lighten and brighten the way is to
say something about the lives of protagonists themselves, all major
figures in the Anglo-American mainstream. (Well, Veblen is neither
Anglo American nor mainstream, but he is too good to miss.) There
is some danger in this device; the personality of the inventor adds
nothing to the truth or falsity of a statement about economics. But
Breit and Ransom do not push it too far. They do not try to turn
economists into rock stars (which would make turning brass into
gold look like child's play). Maybe knowing a little about the thinker
helps one to pay attention to the thought. But it is the thought that
matters.

Economics is a strange sort of discipline. The booby traps I mentioned often make it sound as if it is all just a matter of opinion. That
is not so. Economics is not a Science with a capital *S*. It lacks the
experimental method as a way of testing hypotheses. And it feels the
lack keenly because its hypotheses are about individuals, groups, and
social institutions whose behavior changes from time to time. But it
is possible to think logically about economic life, and to respect facts,
and that is what the academic scribblers and their colleagues try to
do.

Differences of opinion arise often, as the reader will learn. There
are always differences of opinion at the cutting edge of a science,
even in chemistry, say. But they last longer in economics (Oh Lord,
do they last longer) and there are reasons for that. As already mentioned, rival theories cannot be put to an experimental test. All there
is to observe is history, and history does not conduct experiments;
too many things are always happening at once. The inferences that

can be made from history are always uncertain, always disputable, if only because different scholars are observing different snippets of a complicated reality. You can't even count on a long and undisturbed run of history, because the "laws" of behavior change and evolve.

Excuses, excuses. But the point is not to provide excuses. It is to alert the reader to the nature of the intellectual enterprise engaged in by the heroes of this book. The questions you should ask about them are roughly these. Do they ask you to believe incredible things about actors in the marketplace? If not, do they reason logically from the things they ask you to believe? If so, are their conclusions contradicted by any facts we know? If not, pay attention: you may learn something interesting and valuable.

PREFACE

This book attempts primarily to capture within the confines of a single
volume the most elusive game of all: contemporary economic thought.
We undertake this safari through the thickets of modern controversy
because of our deep conviction that economics students and intelligent
laymen should know more about the individuals whose theories have
come to rule their world. The recent observation of Professor A. W.
Coats seems particularly encouraging: "Studies of recent economic
thought and policy are especially important because the economists'
direct influence has latterly been much greater than in most earlier
times... [W]e urgently need more research into these questions, if only
to advance the education of historians, whose notions of the nature and
influence of economic ideas are lamentably deficient."

We have attempted to limit the range of our journey in two major
ways: (1) The study is largely restricted to the ideas of American
economists and (2) we have traced the development of the ideas which
have had or are likely to have impact on economic policy. Where
non-Americans are discussed in any detail, it is in order to form the
backdrop for the American arena of controversy.

Among the most difficult tasks confronting us was the selection of
quarry to be included in the study. The writers chosen represent
virtually every prominent viewpoint in the American economics profession today. Each of them was, moreover, influential in shaping these
views. Because we set out to explore carefully only certain areas of
economic thought, many names and topics are omitted from the story.
In part this is because of our primary emphasis on policy. Our discussion neglects many of the important technical developments of contemporary economic theory—such areas as mathematical growth models, general equilibrium models, statistical inference, or econometrics.
We fully recognize the importance of these developments in providing
sophisticated building blocks with which to construct economic policy.

We remain convinced, however, that men, not models, are the ultimate determinants of policy. For those who find these omissions serious, we hope that, in spite of the limitations of our approach, we have conveyed some of the diversity, richness, and profundity of contemporary American economic thought.

From the very beginning of the collaboration we determined that it should be, in every sense, a joint project. Although initial responsibility for the several chapters was divided between the two authors, we were able to gain coordination by periodic meetings at the University of Virginia and at the University of California at Berkeley, where we were visiting members of the faculty during the summer quarter of 1968. Both authors consider the thinkers included in this volume to be important economists, but the reader will doubtless detect certain lapses from impartiality. Nevertheless, we believe that each of us helped serve as a check on any over- or underenthusiasm of the other.

Many of our friends and colleagues listened to our ideas and offered helpful advice. We cannot list all of them here, but we want especially to thank James M. Buchanan, William Patton Culbertson, Kenneth G. Elzinga, S. Herbert Frankel, Ivan C. Johnson, John M. Letiche, Roland N. McKean, and Leland B. Yeager for their encouragement and patience. The research assistance of Joseph E. Camp is also gratefully acknowledged, as is a timely subvention from the University of Virginia's Research Committee on Summer Grants.

Over the past several years the students in Breit's seminar in economic thought at the University of Virginia have provided a forum that aided greatly in the development of this work. We must mention, in particular, Evelyn Glazier, Richard Higgins, Joseph Jadlow, Roger Spencer, Robert Tollison, and George Trivoli. Both authors also experimented with parts of this book at the undergraduate level. The enthusiasm of nonspecialists toward the issues raised was a steady source of encouragement.

Moreover, we are deeply indebted to Mrs. Betty H. Tillman. Her ability to turn our illegible script into an acceptable manuscript was astonishing.

In the preparation of this work, we contacted the living economists included within it, and some of them we bothered continually. Nevertheless, each of them seemed willing to come to our assistance when needed. We hope they will not be too disappointed by the result.

December 1970

Charlottesville, Virginia   *William Breit*

Riverside, California   *Roger L. Ransom*

PREFACE

TO THE SECOND EDITION

With all the wisdom hindsight allows, it is evident that the first edition of *The Academic Scribblers* appeared at a watershed moment in the history of contemporary economic thought. The time was precisely right for a summing up of the achievements of those who had shown the way toward the solution of the most pressing economic problems of recent decades. The story was told in terms of the clash between what we called the "new economics" and the "new neoclassicism." The new economics encompassed those economists who had been influenced by the critics of neoclassical economic thought and who counseled activist, interventionist policies to bring about a more efficient and equitable operation of the competitive capitalist system. The new neoclassicism comprised those thinkers who, reaching back to the insights of neoclassical thought for support, developed new theories and arguments for what Henry Simons called "a positive program for laissez faire." At the time of the first edition, the new economics was clearly in the ascendancy in terms of influence and prestige; its chief weapons were the tools provided by John Maynard Keynes and his followers. Under its programs, the economy after World War II, performed better than it had in recent memory. As one observer of that period has put it:

> By the mid-1960's not only was the level of affluence unprecedented in human history, but business cycles seemed to have been licked. Every year times were better; downturns seemed consigned to history. Economists proclaimed themselves the high priests of social engineering, claiming in their Keynesian wisdom credit for the sustained boom.[1]

---

[1] James W. Dean, "The Dissolution of the Keynesian Consensus," *The Public Interest* (Special Edition, 1980), p. 21.

Of course, there was much controversy among economists over the reasons for the smooth functioning of the system in its post-Depression phase. And the new neoclassicists sensed much danger ahead and offered Cassandra-like warnings. Nevertheless, economists of both schools were imbued with a solid confidence in the ability of their science to show the way toward highly satisfactory performance. More important, others shared this certitude. Starting in 1969, economists became the first social scientists eligible to be awarded the prestigious Nobel Prize. They appeared with regularity on the covers of news magazines, were quoted in articles in the daily press, testified before congressional committees seeking their opinions and prognostications; and a few even managed to get on the television talk-show circuit. Indeed, two of the subjects of this book hosted television series devoted to economics in the 1970s.

To slightly modify Euripides, "Whom the gods would destroy, they first make great." The experience of persistently high levels of inflation accompanied by deep unemployment during the ensuing decade brought economists their severest test since the Great Depression. "Stagflation," which had already appeared on the scene and was discussed in the first edition of this book, turned out to be a highly intractable problem with far more traumatic consequences for economics than either we—or our fellow economists—had foreseen. The Keynesian nostrums no longer seemed to work, and the 1970s witnessed a dramatic reversal in the fortunes of policy activists. It was a period in which the new neoclassicism made dramatic and impressive inroads into public consciousness. The term *monetarism* used to describe Milton Friedman's macroeconomics (which did not even appear once in the first edition of this book) became as familiar as the term *Keynesianism*, with which it was almost always contrasted.

Moreover, the "rational expectations" revolution in macroeconomic thinking, with its implication that systematic economic policy cannot outsmart human ingenuity even in the short run, led to a sort of nihilism, especially among a younger generation of theorists. Their views are not entirely shared by either Paul Samuelson or Milton Friedman, although this new way of thinking has some connections with the work of both. Furthermore, another development within the new neoclassicism—dubbed "supply-side economics"—began to receive a great deal of attention and had an almost immediate effect on policy formulation. These new developments are discussed in the pages to follow.

Those pages have been changed considerably in order to clarify the ideas and disputes surrounding the stagflation conundrum and the emerging consensus that there is no reliable trade-off between inflation and unemployment. It will be seen that the solutions offered are as diverse as the style in which the arguments are presented. In this edition of *The Academic Scribblers*, as in the first, a main theme is that style and personality are ultimately decisive in the art of persuasion. The glittering linguistic virtuosity of a John Kenneth Galbraith is a much more important weapon than empirical evidence in gaining respect for his positions. And the ice-cold logic of a Friedman, Samuelson, or Lerner commands assent from those who perceive that an argument which is beautiful might very well be true.

Since the first edition appeared, two of the economists included have died. Both Alvin H. Hansen and Frank H. Knight had largely withdrawn from the arena of economic debates by 1970; but their influence survived, and it survives their deaths. The chapters devoted to these two men remain in place with only slight emendations.

In pondering the revision of this work, we gave considerable thought to the question of which, if any, new academic scribblers had emerged who might warrant treatment in a separate chapter. We concluded (with some surprise not unmixed with relief) that no single figure had achieved the prominence and influence in so many facets of economics as had the subjects of the first edition. There are some scholars within hailing distance of greatness in that regard who, in a few more years, might earn a niche in our gallery. Their names will appear in our story but in chapters mainly devoted to the achievements of others. And there are economists who would have cynosure status at any meeting of the American Economic Association whose names will not appear here at all. That is because they have remained far above the squalid temptation of offering counsel on matters of economic policy.

Our purpose remains unchanged: to study contemporary American economic theorists who have had a policy impact. We have attempted to convey the essential facts of their lives and to explore the nature of their contributions. Four of the chapters have been substantially rewritten, and new matter has been added to most of the others. We have also taken this opportunity to eliminate certain errors in the first edition. We hope that the volume, thus freshened up, will continue to be of use to the general reader as well as the specialist.

Our debts to others remain cosmopolitan, and each of us has his own list. Breit is especially thankful for the prodding and encouragement of his friend and partner in other ventures, Kenneth G. Elzinga, who kept insisting that the first edition deserved a successor. Discussions with other colleagues, Edgar K. Browning, Clark Nardinelli, Herbert Stein, and Ronald Warren, led to improvements in the final version. Ransom acknowledges the influence of Richard Sutch, with whom he has been working for the past decade, and the numerous discussions with E. K. Hunt, who was a colleague at Riverside during the turbulent years of the 1970s.

Most of all, we owe thanks to the subjects of the book, who were kind enough to respond to our inquiries. Whenever we called upon them for aid, they never failed us. They are, of course, in no way responsible for the views we express, but without their help, the book would show a great many more blunders than now adorn it.

December 1981

Charlottesville, Virginia   *William Breit*

Riverside, California   *Roger L. Ransom*

1

INTRODUCTION

A few years ago a distinguished national magazine asked the following questions of some twenty-seven historians, economists, political scientists, educators, and philosophers:

1.   What books published during the past four decades most significantly altered the direction of our society?
2.   Which may have a substantial impact on public thought and action in the years ahead?

Although the participants represented wide areas of interests and were invited to submit as many titles as they desired, the book cited most often would scarcely be expected to attract a large reading public and would most certainly not be a likely candidate for sale to a motion picture studio. It was *The General Theory of Employment Interest and Money* by John Maynard Keynes. Among those who voted for it were a political columnist, a philosopher, two historians, a political scientist, and over a half-dozen other representatives of the intelligentsia. This wide-ranging agreement on the importance of a work by an English economist would probably be surprising to the general public, which might have expected the result to favor such authors as Toynbee, Kinsey, or Marshall McLuhan.

And yet, by almost any standard of influence, the choice seems unerringly right. For this work truly has left its mark on our times as has no other single volume, even leading one writer to christen the period since World War II as "The Age of Keynes." The widely held notion of the necessity for a strongly interventionist state to maintain full employment was unquestionably established in large part by this work.

It would be superficial, of course, to suggest that the "new economics" of post-World War II America is simply the product of one man's ideas. The new economics encompasses much recent theoretical analysis which implies that laissez-faire under free competition will lead neither to an efficient nor to full employment of resources. These ideas involve not only Keynes's concept of inadequate demand but also the wastes of competition, the irrationality of the consumer, and divergencies between private and social interests. Such considerations ostensibly lead to the conclusion that free-market capitalism is viable only with the help of an activist government stepping in to maintain demand; to provide goods and services neglected by befuddled, ignorant, or wrong-headed consumers; and generally to levy the taxes and provide the subsidies that would bring about the maximum degree of economic welfare. Keynes was, in the main, silent on such topics as advertising, excess capacity, waste, pollution, congestion, and inadequate provision of public services. Yet these problems are coming to play just as important a role in the exercise of economic policy as is the maintenance of adequate demand. Although August Heckscher has called Keynes's book "the prophetic work which laid the basis for the economics of the welfare state,"[1] others must share in this accomplishment.

But if the general public is only slightly familiar with the name of Keynes, it is even less aware of the names of other economists who helped provide the rationale for the interventionist economic policy of our times. As we shall show, the writings of Thorstein Veblen, Arthur Cecil Pigou, and Edward H. Chamberlin taken together have probably had at least as much influence as Keynes in setting the tone for economic policy in the second half of the twentieth century. These men, along with Keynes, were to shape the thought and policy prescriptions of some of the most influential economists of our time: Alvin H. Hansen, Paul A. Samuelson, Abba P. Lerner, and John Kenneth Galbraith. It will be demonstrated that contemporary economic thought and policy run largely in terms of the arguments and tools provided by these economists.

Yet there is another story to be told in this volume. Revolutions have their counterrevolutions, and upheavals in economic thought are no exception. In American economics the counterrevolution has been led by three important scholars, who happen to have been associated with the University of Chicago. These economists have presented ideas intended to clarify the meaning of neoclassical economics—the body of thought with largely laissez-faire policy implications which was the accepted doctrine before the strictures of Veblen, Pigou, Chamberlin, and Keynes tended to cast it into disrepute. In so doing, they extended, refined, and drew new implications from these theories in attempting to rebut the interventionist themes of the new economics. It is important that the contributions of Frank Knight, Henry Simons, and Milton Friedman be understood. We shall, therefore, describe some of the intellectual and empirical work associated with these counterrevolutionaries, who have attempted to see economic problems more from the standpoint of pure economic theory and less from that of the

---

[1]   Cited in Rochelle Girson, "Mutations in the Body Politic," *Saturday Review*, 29 August 1964, p. 74.

political process. The clash and conflicts between the new economists and the new neoclassicists constitute the subject matter of this study. As will probably become clear, whichever school of thought gains ascendancy in the calculable future will be decided as much by the force of its adherents' personalities as by the logic and elegance of their arguments.

It was Keynes who wrote the words about the "academic scribblers" which we have quoted on the frontispiece and which gave this book its title. In the final sentence of his *magnum opus* Keynes warned, "it is ideas, not vested interests, which are dangerous for good or evil." This book is about those academic scribblers who, for good or evil, are influencing the agitators, civil servants, and politicians who will shape economic events today and tomorrow.

Part One

The Pillars of Neoclassical Economics

THE INTELLECTUAL GANTRY OF NEOCLASSICAL ECONOMIC POLICY

The economist, like everyone else, must concern himself with the ultimate aims of man.

Alfred Marshall

The policy conclusions dominating the reasoning of most economists during the first 40 years of the twentieth century followed from the logic of what is known as neoclassical economic thought. The date 1871 is used to mark the beginning of this way of thinking about economic problems. In that year two books appeared—one in England, one in Austria—which deviated sharply from the mainstream of classical economics. The Englishman was William Stanley Jevons and the Austrian was Carl Menger.[1] Working independently, they simultaneously discovered (or "rediscovered")[2] a way of thinking which subsequently came to be known as "marginalism." The basic logic of this approach gave to the analysis of political economy a degree of systematization unrivaled by the earlier classical writers. In so doing it marked the transition from "political economy" to "economics." The suffix "-ics" is significant, for it decisively arrayed economics along with such subjects

---

[1] William Stanley Jevons, *The Theory of Political Economy*, 5th ed. (New York: Kelley & Millman, 1957). Original edition, 1871; Carl Menger, *Principles of Economics* (Glencoe, Ill.: Free Press, reprinted 1950). Original edition, 1871.

[2] Most of the elements of the neoclassical approach were already contained in the work of H. H. Gossen in a book which he published in 1854. This book, almost completely neglected, was soon withdrawn from circulation by the disappointed author. Others, (Cournot, Dupuit, Longfield, Senior, and Von Thünen) also were precursors of some aspects of neoclassical thought, but did not develop anything like the systematic presentation of Gossen, Jevons, and Menger. The subject of "lost discoveries" is a fascinating topic all to itself.

as mathematics and physics, as having a rigor equal to the formal and physical sciences.

The Scope and Method of Neoclassical Economics

Neoclassical theory is distinguished from classical doctrine by significant changes in both scope and method. The shift in scope involved a redefinition of the economic problem; the methodological change was the introduction of marginal analysis.

The classical economists saw the economic problem as being essentially "dynamic." The measure of economic welfare to Adam Smith and his followers was the quantity of output. But output was a function of the quantity of labor available and its productivity. The question they presumed to answer was: How can the capital stock be augmented and markets widened so as to increase the productivity of labor, physical output, and, therefore, welfare? The neoclassical economists, on the other hand, conceived the economic problem as the attempt to get an optimal result by allocating a *given* quantity of scarce resources among competing uses. Scarcity became the central problem of economics. Jevons stated the problem as follows:

> Given, a certain population, with various needs and powers of production, in possession of certain lands and other sources of material; required, the mode of employing their labour which will maximize the utility of the produce.[3]

Thus, there was a marked shift from a concern over the dynamic problem of growth to a concern over the static problem of efficiency.[4]

Perhaps the most striking feature of neoclassical economics is its concern with changes which involve a slight increase or decrease in the stock of anything under consideration. The meaning and significance of this technique were so well stated by one of the school's leading adherents, Philip H. Wicksteed, that it is worth quoting at length.

> . . . The marginal service rendered to us by any commodity is that service which we should have to forego if the supply of the commodity in question were slightly contracted; our marginal desire for more of anything is measured by the significance of a slight increment added at the margin of our present store. And the importance of this service, or the urgency of this desire, depends . . . on the quantity we already possess. If we possess, or have just consumed, so much of a thing that our desire for more is languid, then additions at the margin have little value to us; but if we possess, or have consumed so little that we are keenly desirous of more, then marginal additions have a high value for us . . . . Thus by increasing our supply of anything we reduce its

---

[3] Jevons, *The Theory of Political Economy*, p. 267. Note that he desires to maximize the *utility* of the produce, not the physical output itself.

[4] A detailed and excellent discussion of the difference between the classical and neoclassical view of the economic problem is to be found in Hla Myint, *Theories of Welfare Economics* (New York: Augustus M. Kelley, 1962).

marginal significance and lower the place of an extra unit on our scale of preferences; and suitable additions to our supply will bring it down to any value you please. Thus, whatever the price of any commodity that the housewife finds in the market may be, so long as its marginal significance to her is higher than that price, she will buy; but the very act of putting herself in possession of an increased stock reduces its marginal significance, and the more she buys the lower it becomes. The amount that brings it into coincidence with the market price is the amount she will buy.[5]

The assumption that the utility of a good declined as its stock increased meant that the process described by Wicksteed was an equilibrating one. As the stock of a good changes, the value of additional units changes, thus creating a situation where the marginal value is just equal to the price.

This tool enabled the neoclassical writers to solve a problem which beset classical economic thought from Adam Smith onward, namely the paradox of value, or the "diamond-water paradox." Adam Smith had reasoned that since water has greater utility (that is, is more useful) than diamonds, and yet diamonds are more expensive than water, utility could not be a determinant of price. Marginal analysis made it blindingly clear that the key factor in the determination of price is the *marginal significance* of having slightly more or less of the item. Although the total utility of water is doubtlessly greater than the total utility of diamonds, the marginal utility of diamonds is very high (because the stock of diamonds is relatively low), while the marginal utility of water is low (because the stock of water is plentiful). In this fashion, the neoclassicists introduced the role of demand as an important determinant of price.

The Emergence of Economic Man:
Consumer Sovereignty

The fact of scarcity creates a necessity for choice and a careful comparing of alternatives. Accordingly, a new view of human nature came into focus in the writings of neoclassical economists. The individual is imagined in a constant process of delicately balancing his marginal expenditures and marginal utilities. This rational, calculating human, who emerges most clearly in the pages of Menger's *Grundsatze*, also appears in most of the works of neoclassical writers, including Jevons, Pareto, and Wicksteed.[6] The significance of the notion of the "economic

---

[5]   Philip H. Wicksteed, *The Common Sense of Political Economy*, vol. 1 (London: Routledge & Kegan Paul, 1957), pp. 40-41.

[6]   The individual so described has gone by many names in the literature. We refer to him as *economic man*, a term introduced by Pareto. Of course these economists were purposely abstracting from other aspects of man's behavior. That man is multi-motivated was probably understood by all of them. Nevertheless, as Frank H. Knight has complained, ". . . if Menger was aware of the many other men who walk about and variously 'perform in the same skin' as the creature who merely uses means to satisfy needs . . . his *Grundsatze* gives no evidence of the fact." Frank H. Knight, "Introduction to Carl Menger" in Menger, *Principles of Economics*, p. 16.

man" is that it provided a rationale for the doctrine of *consumer sovereignty*. This concept implies that, as Adam Smith put it,

> Consumption is the sole end and purpose of all production; and the interest of the producer ought to be attended to, only in so far as it may be necessary for promoting that of the consumer.[7]

Consumer sovereignty provided one of the cornerstones in supporting the laissez-faire policy prescription of neoclassicism. For, granted the maximization of utility as the problem, marginal calculations as the tool, and economic man as the actor, the state has little or no role to play. Standards are set by economizing consumers and scarce resources allocated so as to maximize welfare. The specific refinement made in the consumer demand criterion for production is in the concept of cost. Cost is ultimately determined by consumer evaluations. In considering how much of any commodity should be produced, the relevant question is whether it will cover the costs of production. Here again, the use of "margins" comes into play. An increase in the consumption of a commodity by a consumer represents an increase in his welfare or benefit. However, it involves a withdrawal of resources from the production of something else. This means a decrease in the benefit (and hence a cost) to the would-be consumers of the alternative commodity. As long as the benefit is greater than the cost, production of the item in question should be expanded, and where the cost is greater than the benefit, the production should be contracted. The appropriate output is reached where the additional benefit is precisely equal to the additional cost, or, as the economist says, where marginal benefit equals marginal cost. At this point, neither an expansion nor contraction of output can increase welfare. But what mechanism guarantees this felicitous result? The answer lies in the neoclassical doctrine of perfect competition.

The Doctrine of Perfect Competition

As in the case of the consumer demand criterion of welfare, the doctrine of perfect competition was already implicit in classical economics. But precision is the keynote of neoclassicism, and thus the doctrine was refined and elaborated. In its refined neoclassical form, there are three major conditions for perfect competition. These are worth listing formally:

1. *Perfect Knowledge.* This assures that in a given market at a given time, there will be only one price for identical commodities, and no scope for higgling.
2. *Large Numbers.* This assures that no producer or consumer has any

---

[7] Adam Smith, *An Inquiry into the Nature and Causes of the Wealth of Nations*, 5th ed. (New York: Random House, 1937), p. 635. The idea was implicit in classical and neoclassical thought. The term consumer sovereignty was not Smith's, but was introduced into the literature surprisingly late—in 1934—by Professor W. H. Hutt.

appreciable effect on price so that both are price takers rather than price makers in all markets. (Hence, collusion among buyers and sellers is ruled out.)

3. *Homogeneous Products.* This assures that the products of an industry are perfectly substitutable for one another.

Granted the above mentioned conditions, it should be obvious that the competitive firm can sell any output it desires at the given market price. With even a slight increase in price, it would lose all its customers.

The doctrine of perfect competition is the required corollary of the doctrine of consumer sovereignty. This is true for two reasons. First, only under perfect competition is there a guarantee that the entrepreneur, in the quest for profit, will submit to the will of the consumer. Second, perfect competition assures ideal output, in the sense that marginal benefit is always equated with marginal cost. As we have seen, for the consumer the price of an item is the measure of the importance of an additional cost incurred in producing an extra unit of output. The rationality of the economizing consumer induces him to equate his marginal evaluation of the item to its price. But we can see that the conditions of competition will induce the producer to equate marginal cost to marginal revenue. Since marginal revenue is the addition to total revenue from selling one more unit of product, under perfect competition (where the firm is a price taker), it is also precisely equal to the price of the output. So the producer will expand as long as price is above marginal cost, since the excess of price above marginal cost represents the extra profit that can be made by producing more units. By similar logic, if marginal cost exceeds price, the entrepreneur will reduce output. Thus, the producer as an economic man is motivated, under perfectly competitive conditions, to equate price with marginal cost. With consumers and producers so motivated, the conditions of competition create an equilibrium where marginal costs always equal marginal benefits. From a social viewpoint, economic efficiency (or welfare) is then maximized.[8] In short, freedom of choice and competition are the best instruments for promoting the welfare of society. But was there any guarantee that this solution would provide employment for all resources in the economy? This question was answered by Say's Law.

Say's Law and Full Employment Equilibrium

The classical conclusion of automatic full employment rested upon Say's Law of Markets—stated crudely as "Supply creates its own demand." The fact that inadequate demand could be a cause of unemploy-

---

[8] There is an additional happy property of perfect competition, which, for our purposes, we need not consider. Under perfect competition, the division of output among firms will be optimal; that is, output will be produced at minimum possible total cost. The proof of this proposition is handled nicely in Tibor Scitovsky, *Welfare and Competition* (Chicago, Ill.: Richard D. Irwin, 1951), p. 151.

ment, given the insatiability of human wants, was inconceivable. For if human wants are insatiable, then the money for which men work will be used to help satisfy these wants. Supply will always generate sufficient demand to clear the market through the circular flow of payments from suppliers to consumers or investors. No money would be hoarded, and hence all payments returned to the system in the form of purchases of goods. Saving was possible; however, all money saved was invested, since the interest rate would adjust in such a fashion as to induce any idle funds into the market for capital goods. Shifts in demand might create temporary gluts in markets; however, these would be adjusted through the movements of wages and prices for each market.

The neoclassical economists refined the explanation of Say's Law by showing the determination of the level of real output through marginal analysis. The American economist John Bates Clark stated this explicitly in his *Distribution of Wealth* published in 1899. Following from the reasoning of the argument regarding the firm's output, it is clear that the producer will never want to offer a worker a wage greater than the value of the added output his labor can produce. Assume that the entrepreneur is hiring additional workers to work with a fixed stock of capital. Under the principle of diminishing marginal productivity, a point is eventually reached where each additional worker adds less to the total product than the preceding worker. The problem is, how many workers will the firm hire? If the firm is attempting to maximize profits under conditions of perfect competition, the firm will add additional workers until the wage paid to the last worker (and therefore all preceding workers, on the assumption that each additional worker is equally skilled) is just equal to the value of the marginal product. This is precisely the same condition as saying that price equals marginal cost.

To prove this, we must ask, what is the marginal cost of adding an additional worker? It is the wage rate that is paid to him divided by the amount that he adds to the total product. For example, if the wage rate is $45 and the worker adds 15 units of output, what is the marginal cost of hiring this worker? It is clearly 45 divided by 15, or $3, because the marginal cost is defined as the addition to total cost of adding only *one* unit of output. If the wage rate is $75 and the worker adds 15 units of output, the marginal cost is $5, and so on.

Assume that the firm, operating in a perfectly competitive market, finds that it can receive $8 per unit of output, and the wage rate is $40. How many workers will the firm hire and how much output will the firm produce? The firm will continue to hire workers and increase output until the last worker adds 5 units of output. For only at this point does the price of the output ($8) equal the marginal cost of the output (40/5). In other words, the firm will hire workers up to the point where the wage rate is equal to the *value* of the marginal product, that is, price times the marginal product. Or the marginal product equals the real wage (the money wage deflated by the price level). In symbols:

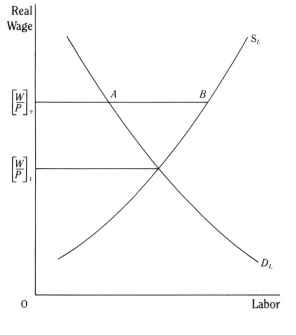

Figure 2.1

If	$P = MC$	(Price equals marginal cost)
and	$MC = W/MP$	(Marginal cost equals the money wage rate divided by the marginal product)
then	$P = W/MP$	(Price equals the money wage divided by the marginal product)
and	$W = P(MP)$	(The money wage rate equals the value of the marginal product)
then	$MP = \dfrac{W}{P}$	(The marginal product equals the real wage)

Clark applied this reasoning not only to labor markets but to markets for all factors of production. His conclusion was that under perfect competition each factor would inexorably receive a return precisely equal to its contribution. For a factor's contribution to the product was its marginal product, and Clark could demonstrate that each factor would receive a wage equal to the value of this marginal product.

This analysis of the demand for labor, combined with the neoclassical view that the supply of labor is a function of the real wage rate, provides a sophisticated explanation for Say's Law. Full employment is realized where the supply curve of labor cuts the demand curve. In Figure 2.1 we have measured the real wage rate on the vertical axis and the amount of labor on the horizontal axis. The demand curve for labor is given by the curve D_L, and in accordance with Clark's analysis, shows for each quantity of labor the marginal product associated with each worker. The greater the number of workers hired, the lower the marginal product of all workers. On the vertical axis we measure the real wage rate. The curve thus shows, for each real wage rate, the quantity of workers that would be demanded.

The supply curve of labor is represented by curve S_L. It was usually assumed that the greater the real wage rate, the greater the number of workers willing to work. The intersection of the two curves thus gives the uniquely determined point of employment and the average real wage rate corresponding to that volume of employment. This is a position of full employment since there is neither a surplus nor a shortage of labor. If the real wage were to be pushed up to $(W/P)_2$, there would be unemployment in the amount AB. But this could only be temporary since the surplus laborers would bargain to push wages down again to $(W/P)_1$ by cutting money wages. Only an absence of perfect competition, or government interference in the form of minimum wage laws, could cause permanent unemployment by not allowing wages to reach the level at which the two curves intersect. So full employment is the result of a perfectly competitive economy in all factor markets.

The reader should note that a cut in money wages was the same thing as a cut in real wages because the price level remained unchanged. The level of money wages did not determine the price level. Rather it was the price level that determined the level of money wages. Then what determined the price level? The answer to this final question was provided by the *quantity theory of money*, which was accepted by virtually every neoclassical writer.

Quantity Theory of Money

Although there were a number of variants of the quantity theory, all of them centered upon the assertion that there was a rough proportionality between changes in the stock of money and changes in the general level of prices in the economy.[9]

The neoclassicists made a fundamental distinction between the *real value* of money and the *nominal value* of money. The real value of money must be expressed in terms of how much a unit of money can buy in the market place; the nominal value of money is expressed in the unit of account (such as a dollar). Quantity theorists insisted that people act to maintain some level of *real balances*, without regard to the nominal value of these holdings.

---

[9] The roots of the quantity theory go well into the seventeenth century. The earliest formulations argued for the existence of a strict proportionality: a 10 percent increase in the money stock would cause a 10 percent increase in prices. Later writers such as David Hume pointed out some qualifications to such a conclusion. The reader interested in the development of this theory might profitably consult M. Friedman's comments in "Money: The Quantity Theory," *The International Encyclopedia of Social Sciences* (New York: Macmillan Co. and The Free Press, 1968), pp. 432-47. The present discussion draws heavily from Friedman's exposition.

To see how this behavior affects expenditures, consider the case in which an increase in the stock of money has left people with money balances which—in real terms—they consider to be too large. People will then wish to dispose of their "excess" real balances by increasing expenditures. But, for one person to reduce his money holdings, someone else must increase his, for the nominal stock of money does not change for the community as a whole. Thus, attempts to lower holdings of money will generate an increase in expenditures. Prices will be bid up, lowering the value of a unit of money. With a fall in the value of money, larger nominal balances will be required to meet the desired level of real balances. Pressures to continue expansion of expenditures will be eased. In fact, if there is no change in output, prices will have to rise by exactly enough to make the larger nominal money balances just equal in real terms to the initially desired level of real balances. If rising expenditures elicited an increase in income (production), it would also relieve the pressure to adjust money balances. With higher incomes, people would desire larger holdings in real terms. Both circumstances—a fall in the value of money as prices rise, or a rise in real income—return the system to equilibrium. Obviously, the argument can be reversed for a situation in which real balances are less than the desired level.

These relationships between money, prices, and real income can be expressed through the circular flow of payments in the economy. Two explanations are commonly associated with the neoclassical school: the *transactions approach* of the American economist Irving Fisher, and the *cash-balances approach* of the economists at Cambridge, England.[10] Fisher reasoned that since each transaction in the economy consisted of a price coupled with some good or service, the total value of all transactions could be expressed as the product of some "average price" (P) times the number of transactions (T). At the same time, the sum of all payments in the economy must total the amount of money (M) times the *velocity* of money (V), which indicated the number of times a unit of money "turned over." He could then express the flow of payments in the economy as:

$$MV = PT \qquad (2.1)$$

where V, the transactions velocity, is defined as $\dfrac{PT}{M}$.

Fisher's equation of exchange is nothing more than an accounting identity, given his definition of velocity. To make the equation a useful analytical device, velocity must be viewed as a *behavioral* variable. This is the essence of the quantity theory; for if velocity is stable (or at least predictable), then the relation of the stock of money to income and

---

[10] A third explanation was that of Knut Wicksell, a Swedish economist who wrote at the turn of the century. Wicksell's writing was not as widely read as Fisher or the Cambridge group. It is interesting to note that the "Keynesian" writers today point to Wicksell as the example of the quantity theory, for he came closest to anticipating some of the later developments.

prices is immediately apparent. The cash-balance approach to the circular flow identity recognizes the crucial role of velocity. The Cambridge group reformulated Equation (2.1) and stated the relationship of money to prices using *income* rather than transactions, and replacing Fisher's *V* with an expression representing the desire of people to hold money balances.[11] They expressed the circular flow of payments as:

$$M = kPy \qquad (2.2)$$

Where y is the level of real income, and k is the ratio of money balances to income: M/Py. The demand for cash balances is therefore the reciprocal of velocity. The two are like opposite ends of a seesaw; a rise in the demand for money is tantamount to a decline in the velocity of circulation.

The cash-balances analysis best represents the neoclassical statement of monetary theory by men such as Alfred Marshall and A. C. Pigou. Indeed, it was Pigou's statement of the theory which John Maynard Keynes chose as the stereotype for his assault on neoclassical thought in 1936. The cash-balances equation (2.2), like Fisher's equation (2.1), clearly shows the manner in which money affects prices and income. It says nothing, however, about the equilibrium level of real income in the economy. Given a flexible price level, *any* level of real income (y) can be made consistent with *any* nominal supply of money; people must simply adjust their money balances to bring the real balances to the desired levels. The determination of output, as we have already seen, was left to the interaction of supply and demand in the factor markets of the economy; the quantity theory saw to it that the flows of money payments would automatically let supply create its own demand. Nonetheless, the monetary theory of the neoclassical writers did stress the powerful influence which the level of the money supply could exert on the level of expenditures. And this, they pointed out, meant that the monetary actions of a central bank could have substantial influences on the levels of prices and money income in the economy. Money *was* important.

All these ideas were to find their clearest expression in the writings of one man who can be taken as the exemplar of neoclassical economic thought—*Alfred Marshall.*

---

[11] The expression for total transactions (*T*) in Equation (2.1) proved elusive when attempting to empirically study the quantity theory. The development of national income accounts made the use of income rather than transactions more useful. Fisher's equation would then be:
$$MV = PY$$
where *Y* is total physical output of the economy. Note that the velocity in this equation is income velocity, not transactions velocity.

3

ALFRED MARSHALL

EXEMPLAR OF NEOCLASSICAL
ECONOMIC THOUGHT

... I was led to attach great importance to the fact that our observations of nature, in the moral as in the physical world, relate not so much to aggregate quantities, as to increments of quantities, and that in particular the demand for a thing is a continuous function, of which the "marginal" increment is, in stable equilibrium, balanced against the corresponding increment of its costs of production. It is not easy to get a clear view of Continuity in this aspect without the aid . . . of diagrams.

Alfred Marshall

If one name in the history of economic thought is synonymous with the neoclassical approach—incorporating into one system the chief pillars of neoclassicism—it is that of Alfred Marshall. Marshallian economics came to represent the very best in this new approach to the subject. His great book, *Principles of Economics*, first published in 1890, went through eight editions before Marshall's death in 1924. It became the standard work of reference in the field for thousands of economics students. His work is thought of today as the most orthodox of neoclassicism; yet, as we shall show, it contained the germs of the destruction of the neoclassical model.

However, it is chiefly noted for Marshall's ingenious demonstration of how both costs of production through the supply side of the market (the older classical cost-of-production approach to value) and marginal utility through the demand side of the market (the new subjective utility approach) interacted to determine relative prices. Of course, he was not the first to see the relation between supply and demand in price determination. But he was the one who most effectively synthesized the approaches, showed many of the implications of the analysis, and fashioned many of the analytical instruments that came to make up the economists' toolbox. The present subject matter of price theory in terms of its methodology, divisions, terminology, and the conclusions regarding the implication of various economic policies, does not deviate in its essentials from those Marshall developed. The modern conception of the demand curve, the elasticity of demand, the nature of consumer's surplus, the use of long-run and short-run analysis, quasirent, partial equilibrium, and comparative statics—all owe much to this pioneering genius of the science of economics. Furthermore, he shares with Jevons the distinction of having developed the technique of marginal analysis.

Alfred Marshall was born in 1842, only nineteen years after the death of David Ricardo and eight years after the death of Malthus. He studied at Cambridge, where his interests ran primarily to mathematics; but he also had a deep interest in philosophy, especially the works of Kant and Hegel. When still a young man, he wandered around the Alps carrying on his back, not mountain climbing equipment, but a knapsack of books. Reaching a suitable spot he would settle down next to a rock and study the *Critique of Pure Reason*. Eventually he decided that on deep metaphysical questions mankind could never hope to know more than a very little, so he turned to the study of ethics. His decision to move into economics resulted from a vacation in which he "visited the poorest quarters of several cities and walked through one street after another, looking at the faces of the poorest people. Next, I resolved to make as thorough a study as I could of Political Economy."[1] It was on vacations that Marshall seemed to reach the high points of his life. His vacation walks in the Alps gave him a love for the outdoors, and until the end of his life he always did his best thinking in the open air. When he taught at Oxford, his study was in a garden; and at Cambridge he worked on an open balcony. When he visited in Palermo, he worked on the roof of a quiet hotel. It was while he sat on the roof of his hotel in Palermo, shaded by a bathcover awning in 1881, that he hit on the idea of elasticity. He was, we are told by Mrs. Marshall, "highly delighted with it."[2]

In 1877, he married his pupil Mary Paley, with whom he collaborated on his first book, *The Economics of Industry*. His first academic post after his marriage was at Bristol, and, in 1884, he was named Professor of Political Economy at Cambridge, holding this chair for twenty-three years. His growing fame as an economist drew large throngs of students to his classroom, but his style was best suited to small groups and he did his best to discourage attendance. One of his students provided the following reminiscence of his classroom effect.

---

[1] J. M. Keynes, "Alfred Marshall, 1842-1924," in *Memorials of Alfred Marshall*, ed. A. C. Pigou (New York: Kelley & Millman, 1956), p. 10. (Hereafter this volume of collected memorials will be cited as *Memorials*.) Marshall's early career as an economist and his initial economic writings are discussed in J. K. Whitaker, *The Early Economic Writings of Alfred Marshall, 1867–1890*, 2 vols. (New York: Macmillan Co. and The Free Press, 1975).

[2] Keynes, p. 45 n.

Memory still recaptures the man coming into his room . . . his head bent forward as if in thought, mounting his platform with a little fluster of manner, leaning on his desk, his hands clasped in front of him, his blue eyes lit up, now talking easily, now chuckling over some story, now questioning his class, now pausing impressively, with rapt expression, his eyes in a far corner of the room, now speaking in solemn prophetic tones of some problem of the future—the feeding of India, the prospect of England maintaining her greatness, the banishment of poverty from the world.

He had a singular power of illustration. His mind was stored with facts . . . . He dived into the remote past, or drew on recent statistics, on letters in the papers, on some play then being performed, on his own observation. He was never out of touch with life . . . . Occasionally he invited questions or remarks, but few people were ever bold enough to speak under Marshall's intent and expectant gaze.[3]

He retired from teaching in 1908 in order to devote his life to writing, but continued to live in Cambridge in the house that he built in Madingley Road called "Balliol Croft." It was here that he died in 1924, within two weeks of his 82nd birthday.[4]

Marshall's conception of economic science is indicated by the Latin motto inscribed on the title page of his magnum opus: *Natura non facit saltum*, meaning "nature makes no leaps." He regarded his analysis as being akin to the Darwinian approach in biology and his work is imbued with biological analogies.[5] Throughout his *Principles*, Marshall's objective was to discover the continuities and regularities in economic activities and to measure them.

He took pains to point out his assumptions to his reader and was always keenly aware that the conditions he posited exist solely in a particular institutional framework. The regularities he sought will appear in a largely laissez-faire competitive economy inhabited by utility-maximizing consumers and profit-maximizing producers. The environment is one of full employment guaranteed by the smooth workings of Say's Law and the quantity theory. Of course, Marshall was careful to point out the multi-motivated facets of man's behavior. But he felt that for purposes of abstraction, it is necessary to reduce these motives to a common denominator. The chief group of motives can be measured in terms of money since so large a part of man's actions is involved in the pursuit of a livelihood—that is, in "the ordinary business of life." And although Marshall claimed to eschew any simple explanation of human nature, it is man dominated by acquisitive characteristics that is of central concern. The end result is virtually

---

[3]   E. A. Benians, "Reminiscences," *Memorials*, pp. 78-79.

[4]   For further details of Marshall's life, the reader should consult C. W. Guillebaud, "Editorial Introduction," in Alfred Marshall, *Principles of Economics*, 9th variorum ed., vol. 1 (New York: Macmillan Co., 1961), pp. 3-6; Keynes, pp. 1-65; and A. C. Pigou, "In Memorium: Alfred Marshall," *Memorials*, pp. 81-90.

[5]   See Alfred Marshall, "Mechanical and Biological Analogies in Economics," reprinted in *Memorials*, (1898), pp. 312-18.

indistinguishable from the economic man of Jevons and Menger. For while man is motivated by many impulses and often acts irrationally, the actions of individuals in their economic life are most rational and measurable, for their actions are registered in price. To Marshall, therefore, economic laws were simply generalizations about human behavior, which can be measured in terms of money. If it is to be scientific, economics must limit its scope to phenomena that have a price measurement. Hence, value and distribution theory must be its central core. On the basis of the regularities that can be measured, predictions can be made about future events, with only a small margin of error.

It was Marshall's genius to see the limitations inherent in his analysis, to hedge and qualify his statements, and to anticipate criticism. One can find almost anything one looks for in the work. And though his *Principles* was the apogee of neoclassicism, it contained an explicit suggestion of a case for government intervention that went beyond anything allowed for by his neoclassical peers. For he experimented with the possibility of improving welfare through a scheme of taxes and subsidies to industries under certain conditions. In so doing he developed a notion that has proved very fruitful in welfare economics— the concept of *consumer's surplus*.

Consumer's surplus is the difference between how much a consumer pays for a commodity and how much he would have been willing to pay rather than do without it. This surplus is an index of well-being. If we could measure it accurately, we would have a test of the amount of welfare our economy generates for consumers. All that would be required is a list of the maximum prices a consumer would be willing to pay for each unit of a good, compared with the price he actually pays. We saw in the discussion of the equilibrium mechanism operative in the consumer market that the marginal utility of a good declines as its stock increases. When translated into a schedule of maximum prices that a consumer would pay for a commodity, this would (when plotted) show a curve going downward and to the right. Measuring price on the vertical axis, and quantity demanded on the horizontal axis, as in Figure 3.1, a demand curve is depicted showing the maximum prices a consumer would pay for various units of a good. We can now use this artifice to show consumer's surplus. In our diagram, consumer's surplus at price P for Q units of commodity X would be represented by the triangular area ABP.[6] Such an area would exist for the consumer in competitive markets where he is a price-taker for the commodities he purchases. Under competition, producers sell all units of their com-

---

[6] This area is only an approximation to consumer's surplus unless we make the Marshallian assumption that the marginal utility of money is constant. Marshall assumed that such a small amount of money is spent on each commodity that changes in money's marginal utility can be ignored. Only under this assumption is the area under the demand curve and above the price line precisely the amount of consumer's surplus. On the more technical aspects of consumer's surplus, the interested reader can profitably consult George J. Stigler, *The Theory of Price*, 3rd ed. (New York: Macmillan Co., 1966), pp. 78-81.

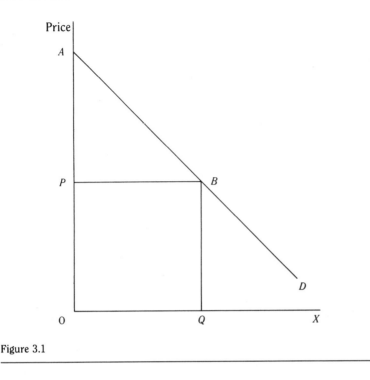

Figure 3.1

modities for a price that just equals the marginal cost of the *last* unit. If the producer could somehow monopolize the industry and force each consumer to pay the maximum price for each unit rather than do without it, then all the consumer's surplus would be diverted to the monopolist. Indeed, it is just this ability of the monopolist to compel a consumer to travel down the demand curve that is one of the major objections of welfare economists to imperfect markets. For if we accept the doctrine of consumer sovereignty, and take the consumer's well-being as our criterion for welfare, then our goal is to maximize consumer's surplus. Neoclassical welfare economics as developed by Marshall made this criterion explicit.

Now we require only one more Marshallian concept, which, when combined with consumer's surplus analysis, will allow us to see why Marshall was led to suggest a break with the laissez-faire policy conclusions of neoclassicism. This is the notion of *average costs*. Average cost is the total cost of production divided by the number of units of output. In the long run, a firm may produce under conditions of increasing cost (the usual assumption of neoclassical economics), constant average costs, or decreasing average costs, depending on the existence of what Marshall called "external economies" in the industry in which the firm operates. Such economies are beyond the control of the firm. They depend upon the size of the industry, economy, or world markets. The existence of decreasing average costs was an historical fact, and it was associated with increases in the size of firms and industries. Marshall was searching for an explanation of this phenomenon, but he wanted an explanation that would reconcile the observed existence of decreasing average costs with the existence of perfect competition. It was the doctrine of external economies that enabled Marshall to effect this reconciliation. To Marshall, external economies arise from the "neighborhood effects" of concentrating large numbers of small businesses in the same locality. This concentration leads to a cross-fertilization of ideas, the development of subsidiary and complimentary industries, and the availability of specialized labor. Furthermore, the development of communication and transportation facilities also leads to cost reductions for the industry, and they are examples of external economies. There are, of course, other reasons why a firm's average costs might fall as it expands. Marshall summarized these reasons under the term "internal economies," and he minimized their importance. Internal economies are cost-reducing factors that result from an expansion of the firm's size, enabling it to achieve greater advantages of large scale production. These economies do not result from the general expansion of the industry or economy as in the case of external economies. Here Marshall noted the ability of an expanding firm to use larger and more efficient machines, to get quantity discounts on large purchases, to enjoy a more extensive division of labor, and to hire better managerial talent. Marshall also noted that easier credit terms were usually available for the larger firm, thus effecting lower average costs for capital.

With all these advantages arising from internal economies, the continued viability of the small firm, and hence of competitive markets, comes into question. But Marshall was optimistic on this subject. Empirical evidence showed the weaker firms continued to exist in most industries along with the stronger ones, indicating that the latter could not expand their size and output indefinitely. Marshall explained this continued existence of competition in the presence of internal economies on the grounds that few entrepreneurs could be guaranteed a perpetuation of exceptionally skillful management through their heirs. The mortality of the great entrepreneurs maintained free competition. It is in this discussion of the coexistence of decreasing costs and competition that Marshall makes greatest use of his biological analogies. The background for the entire discussion is a uniquely Marshallian concept—namely, the *representative firm*. In turning our attention to an individual firm, Marshall cautions that one must be careful to select a representative firm; that is a "normal" firm, which has had a fairly long life, fair success, managed with normal ability, and with normal access to external and internal economies. He uses the biological analogy of trees in the forest and compares the life cycle of trees to the life cycle of entrepreneurs. Just as trees, business firms grow to maturity and decay. In its early phases of growth, a firm enjoys internal economies; in its later phases, the economies are offset by diseconomies, which limit its ability to experience decreasing costs. Just as no one tree will ever take over a forest, no one firm can expand indefinitely and thereby dominate an entire industry.[7]

But Marshall was not completely satisfied with this explanation and so he added another factor—the possibility of a falling demand curve. If the firm has a partial monopoly position, then the perfectly horizontal demand curve facing the firm under perfectly competitive conditions is no longer applicable. This would mean that price would fall more rapidly than the firm's average costs, thus limiting the firm's expansion. Note that this falling demand curve is incompatible with the assumption of perfect competition.

In effect, Marshall explained the existence of perfect competition with decreasing costs by the simple expedient of assuming it away. For this reason, his suggestion of a falling demand curve was ignored and, as we shall see in Chapter 6, was only rediscovered in the 1930's. Ironically, it was then used to undermine, rather than bolster, one of the key neoclassical pillars.

Although Marshall minimized the importance of internal economies, he strongly emphasized the existence of external economies of scale. As we have seen, this means that each firm in an industry benefits from the general expansion of the industry or economy. But all benefit together. No one firm has any particular advantage over any other in the process. Given the mortality of the able entrepreneurs and the lack of equally competent heirs, the individual firm is limited in its isolated expansion. But all firms in the industry are the beneficiaries of reduced costs resulting from general economic growth. In that way, Marshall ingeniously (or some would say disingenuously)[8] reconciled perfect competition with the historical evidence of decreasing costs.

If, in fact, there are industries that operate under decreasing average cost conditions because of net external economies, then a possible basis exists for government intervention, which will increase welfare by increasing consumer's surplus. That is, the state might be able to increase consumer welfare by taxing industries operating under increasing cost conditions (where the tax receipts are greater than the loss in consumer's surplus), using the revenue to subsidize decreasing cost industries (where the subsidy is less than the gain in consumer's surplus). It will prove instructive to examine the simple geometry of this proposition.[9]

---

[7] See Marshall, *Principles*, pp. 315-16.

[8] As we have already noted, Marshall had to abandon a rigorous definition of perfect competition. His notion of the mortal entrepreneur replaced by inferior talent disrupts a model in which, by definition, resources are presumed to remain constant, and the notion of a perfectly elastic demand curve is abandoned when the existence of quantity discounts is admitted into the model. Why should a firm offer quantity discounts if it can sell unlimited quantities at the prevailing competitive market price? On this, see George J. Stigler, *Production and Distribution Theories* (New York: Macmillan Co., 1941), p. 82.

[9] The reader uninterested in the purely technical geometry of Marshall's analysis at this point can omit the discussion in the next two paragraphs without cutting the thread of the general argument.

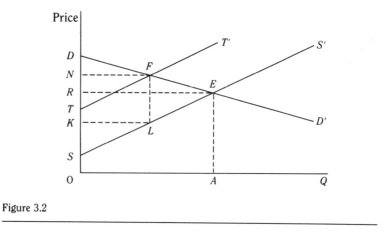

Figure 3.2

First, let us examine the case of an increasing cost industry, depicted in Figure 3.2. The fact that this industry operates under increasing costs is represented by the industry supply curve *SS'*, which goes upward and to the right. This curve is intersected by industry demand curve *DD'* going downward and to the right. In equilibrium the industry produces output *OA* and sells it at price *OR*. Consumer's surplus is the area of the triangle *DER*. Now let us impose a tax on this industry of amount *ST*. That is, each unit of output is now produced at an increased cost of *ST* per unit, and this fact is represented by the supply curve *TT'* lying above *SS'* by the amount of the per unit tax of *ST*. Note that the curve *TT'* now intersects demand curve *DD'* at *F*. Consumer's surplus has clearly been reduced by the amount *NREF*. But in this particular case, the receipts from the tax are *NFLK*, which are greater than the loss in consumer's surplus of *NREF*. So the tax receipts are greater than the loss in consumer's surplus.

Now let us see what happens if we use these tax receipts to subsidize a decreasing cost industry, as depicted in Figure 3.3. Here the industry's supply curve *SS'* slopes downward and to the right, indicating the presence of decreasing costs. In equilibrium, the industry produces the amount *OA* and sells it for price *OR*. Consumer's surplus is *DER*. Granting a subsidy to this industry of *ST* per unit of output reduces the supply curve or costs of production per unit of output in the amount *ST*, and the new supply curve is *TT'*. But note that consumer's surplus has been increased by the amount *NREF*, since the firm has expanded output from *OA* to *OB*. This is clearly greater than the total cost of the subsidy, *NKLF*. Through this expedient, therefore, consumer's surplus has been increased.

Marshall himself considered the above demonstration of rather slight importance. He recognized that his "proof" of the efficacy of government intervention was purely geometrical and depended on the slopes of the curves. Also, it was characteristic of his general reticence to break with the neoclassical model that he noted that indirect effects

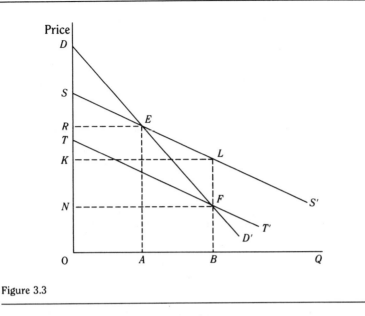

Figure 3.3

of taxes and subsidies could more than offset any gains in welfare to be made through their use. "These conclusions," he warned, "do not by themselves afford a valid ground for government interference . . . . Much remains to be done . . . in order to discover what are the limits of the work that society can . . . do towards turning the economic actions of individuals into those channels in which they will add the most to the sum total of happiness."[10]

Hints at the direction of economic analysis and policy in the years immediately following Marshall already were contained in his *Principles*. Marshall's suggestion of the downward-sloping demand curve as an explanation of the limits of the firm's expansion would have led directly to Chamberlin's monopolistic competition revolution in economics, if its full implications had been then understood. As we shall see, this upheaval had enormous impact on economic attitudes and policy prescriptions, especially in the 1950's and 1960's. Marshall's concept of externalities, although limited to a discussion of pecuniary and technological effects, was picked up by his pupil A. C. Pigou, whose modification of it led to far-reaching implications regarding government intervention. Pigou also was to develop the Marshallian tax and subsidy scheme into elaborate proposals for modifying the neoclassical approach to economic problems. These in turn were also to have their major impact on policy in the 1960's. Moreover, Marshall's insistence on the view that economic science must proceed on a basis of continuity, on the assumption that "nature makes no leaps" in the Darwinian sense, was to become the watchword of the American institutionalists,

---

[10] Marshall, *Principles*, pp. 315-16.

who followed Thorstein Veblen in insisting that economics must become an "evolutionary science." Economics must rid itself of the
pre-Darwinian view of the economic man with inborn and specially
endowed propensities for rational calculation. Translated into the economic ideas of the 1960's, the doctrine of consumer rationality was to
come under increasing fire, with all the implications for policy that
discarding the presumption of consumer sovereignty would entail.
And, finally, Keynes was later to make Marshall's full employment
model only a special case of a general theory of employment. The
magnitude of the influence of Keynes's work on later economists and
policy makers was to be unparalleled in the entire history of economic
thought.

But we are getting ahead of our story. Marshall himself was dimly
aware of the cataclysm that lay in store. In 1915, in a letter to one of his
former students, he wrote:

> . . . A thousand years hence (1920-1970) will, I expect, be *the* time for
> historians. It drives me wild to think of it. I believe it will make my
> poor *Principles*, with a lot of poor comrades, into waste paper. The
> more I think of it, the less I can guess what the world will be like fifty
> years hence.[11]

What the world of economic theory and policy became in those 50 years
is the subject matter of the chapters that follow.

---

[11] Keynes, pp. 487-90.

Part Two

THE ECLIPSE OF NEOCLASSICAL ECONOMICS

4

THORSTEIN VEBLEN

THE ABROGATION OF
CONSUMER SOVEREIGNTY

> . . . History records more frequent and more spectacular instances
> of the triumph of imbecile institutions over life and culture than of
> peoples who have by force of instinctive insight saved themselves
> alive out of a desperately precarious institutional situation, such
> as now . . . faces the peoples of Christendom.
>
> *Thorstein Veblen*

The foundations of neoclassical economic science, as outlined in the
preceding chapters, are, the reader will possibly agree, formidable.
Upon them was constructed a social science second to none in rigor or
esthetic qualities. The use of the tool of "margins" made the apparatus
susceptible to manipulation by Euclidian geometry and the differential
calculus. It was not long before the time and effort required for proficiency in its highly specialized vocabulary and theoretical techniques
restricted the serious study of the economy to the trained specialist.
After 1871, the subject emerged from relative obscurity and close
association with theology, to a highly professional status.[1]

Nevertheless it has always been the case that the received view of
economics has had its detractors, who have, in the main, willingly
accepted the theoretical apparatus, but used it to turn it on itself. Karl
Marx, for example, accepted the tools of classical economics. He simply
took it as his task to draw their logical extension. Others, such as the
influential American writer, Henry George, suggested heretical policy
proposals from the most orthodox of doctrine: Ricardian differential
rent theory.

---

[1] Cf. John B. Parrish, "Rise of Economics as an Academic Discipline: The Formative Years to 1900,"
Southern Economic Journal 34 (July 1967): 1-16.

With the neoclassical critics, this acceptance of method and scope was even more complete. Some only claimed to be refining the existing apparatus and, in so doing, asserted they had made its predecessors obsolete. This was true of A. C. Pigou and Edward Chamberlin. Or, as in the case of J. M. Keynes, they have rejected a part of the apparatus while retaining much of the whole. In what follows, we shall see examples of each of these.

But Thorstein Veblen is, in this, as in all else that came within his vision, unique. Reaching intellectual awareness in the heyday of the neoclassical revolution, Veblen was to become its most fervid and, in many ways, most misunderstood, critic. His biting satire and shrewdly perceptive idioms set a standard and style for critical discourse that was not soon reached again by professional economists.

To understand Veblen is to understand the roots of many of the ideas and attitudes of the disenchanted generation of young people who emerged in the 1960's. A photograph of him at the age of 47 shows a heavily moustached man, looking much like the portraits of Mark Twain: his long hair parted in the middle, leaning back in his chair holding a lighted cigarette between the thumb and forefinger of his left hand. Cigarettes were his one extravagance; they were supplied to him by one of his former students and cost 3½ cents each. According to Joseph Dorfman,[2] his living quarters were furnished with objects of his own making. His furniture consisted of chairs and tables constructed of dry goods boxes, which he covered with burlap. The ritual of making beds was considered a waste of energy, so the covers were merely drawn down over the foot of the bed so that they could be drawn up without much effort at night. A similar attitude prevailed with regard to other mundane household chores. Dishes were washed only when the cupboard was bare of such utensils. As each implement was used it was stacked in a tub, and when the total supply was exhausted the hose was turned on them.

His appearance was generally shoddy. A vivid picture of his demeanor is provided by one of his students: "The first time I saw him, ambling along the Quad, with a slouch hat pulled down over his brow, with coat and trousers 'hanging'; with untrimmed hair and moustache creating a general unkempt appearance, I thought he was a tramp."[3] The most obvious traits were a shaggy head of hair and a frizzly beard. Student reminiscences tell of his cast-off-like clothing, his collar several times too large, and a coat and vest that rarely matched. He had a fondness for safety pins: his watch was attached to a piece of black ribbon which was pinned to the front of his vest; and when he sat down in front of his class and drew up his trouser legs, "his sturdy woolen hose was revealed to be held up by equally sturdy safety pins."[4] In a photograph taken of him in

---

[2] Joseph Dorfman, *Thorstein Veblen and His America* (New York: Viking Press, 1934). This book is the definitive, full-length study of Veblen's life and works and is the source of most of the material on Veblen's life in this chapter.

[3] Dorfman, p. 274.

[4] Dorfman, p. 313.

1920 (reproduced as the frontispiece of Dorfman's book) two safety pins can be seen, one attached to the top of his vest, perhaps to be used as a spare in the event of an unforeseen contingency, the other keeping the ends of his collar neatly in place.[5]

He led a life that became legendary with every economist having his favorite "Veblen story." His attractiveness to many American intellectuals and students doubtlessly derives in part from his anti-Establishment sentiments and style, his refusal to conform to the conventional modes of conduct, and his general sense of helplessness.[6] Many of the film heroes of the long-haired youth of American campuses are admired for the very traits that Veblen possessed. When students applaud W. C. Fields's or the Marx Brothers' high-camp flouting of middle-class conventions (shocking uppity dowagers, putting things over on stuffed shirts), they are approving the irreverent attitudes that Veblen affected.

Born to Norwegian immigrants in 1857 on a farm in Wisconsin, Veblen was seven years old when the family moved to Minnesota. Later he attended Carleton College in Northfield. It was characteristic of his father's old world authoritarianism that young Thorstein was never consulted on his choice of school. He first learned that he was to enter Carleton when the family buggy deposited him there. It was at Carleton that Veblen came into contact with economics, at the hands of one of its most distinguished neoclassists—John Bates Clark. At this time, Clark was working out the principles of his approach to marginal productivity theory of factor prices. Clark, alone among the members of the faculty, liked Veblen. He considered him the most acute thinker among his students, in spite of the fact that at weekly public declamation exercises Veblen delivered papers defending cannibalism and drunkards.

It was at Carleton that Veblen met the girl who was later to become his first wife, Ellen Rolfe, the niece of the president of Carleton, and the daughter of one of the first families of the Midwest. After graduation, Veblen entered Johns Hopkins University where he studied philosophy and political economy. One of his teachers was Charles Sanders Peirce and a fellow student was John Dewey, both of whom helped found that distinctly American school of philosophy known as pragmatism. But Veblen was disappointed with Hopkins and stayed less than a year. He then entered Yale, studied under William Graham Sumner, and took his Ph.D. in philosophy in 1884. But he was unable to obtain an

---

[5]   In this, ironically, Veblen was a forerunner of leisure-class fashions. He would doubtlessly have gotten wry amusement from the fact that safety pin-type collar pins later became quite stylish, often being made of 14-karat gold. And, as C. E. Ayres has suggested, Veblen was a "charter member of the do-it-yourself club," having deep respect for mechanical ability and even the simplest skills. C. E. Ayres, "Veblen's Theory of Instincts Reconsidered" in D. Dowd, ed., *Thorstein Veblen: A Critical Reappraisal* (Ithaca, N. Y.: Cornell University Press, 1958), p. 28.

[6]   Veblen's anti-Establishment attitude even led him to reject the highest honor that can be given by the American economics profession: the nomination to the presidency of the American Economic Association. In 1925, when the chairman of the nominating committee offered the presidency to Veblen (on condition that Veblen join the association and agree to deliver a presidential address) Veblen refused the offer with the comment, "They didn't offer it to me when I needed it." See Dorfman, p. 492.

academic position. College teachers with a philosophical bent were ordinarily chosen from the ranks of divinity students. So Veblen returned as a failure to his hometown community, where he was to remain seven years.

During this period he read avidly. In Dorfman's words:

> As one pile of books disappeared, he promptly secured another. For days all that one could see of him was the top of his head at the garret window. For intellectual companionship he had his remarkably keen father. He told Ellen Rolfe upon his return from Yale that he had never met his father's intellectual equal. When Veblen was puzzled over some economic problem, he would go out and follow along by his father's plough to talk it over with him. When the day's work was done, Thomas Veblen would leisurely discuss abstruse topics with his son while they smoked.[7]

Veblen and Ellen Rolfe were married four years after his return from Yale. But Veblen still found it impossible to get an academic post notwithstanding his Ph.D., his wife's connections, and letters of recommendation from John Bates Clark. Finally, a family council decided that Veblen should reenter academic work if only as a student. His "inactive" period of seven years was difficult to explain to university administrators, and the idea was that he should register at a respectable university and make a fresh start. He decided to enter the field of economics at Cornell University. The chairman of the department was J. Laurence Laughlin, a leading exponent of neoclassical economics. Wearing a coon-skin cap and corduroy trousers, Veblen entered Laughlin's study in Ithaca and announced simply, "I am Thorstein Veblen." That was the first Cornell University knew of his intention to enter. But Laughlin was impressed by the strange young man and was able to secure a special fellowship for him. Veblen remained at Cornell one year, and when Laughlin was appointed head of the economics department at the new University of Chicago, one of the conditions of his acceptance was that he could bring Veblen with him. Veblen was then thirty-five years old.

At Chicago, Veblen pursued his keen interest in anthropology and induced his better students to read extensively in such works. It was this study that led to his dissatisfaction with a major pillar of neoclassical economics. He wrote the following to one of his students at this time:

> As for the anthropological reading, which I have inveigled you into, I do not know that it will be of much direct use, but it should be of some use in the sense of an acquaintance with mankind. Not that man as viewed by the anthropologist is any more—perhaps he is less—human than man as we see him in everyday life and in commercial life; but the anthropological survey should give a view of man in perspective and more in the generic than is ordinarily attained by the

---

[7]   Dorfman, p. 57.

classical economists, and should give added breath and sobriety to the concept of "the economic man."[8]

When he was forty-two years old he published his first major work, a volume that contained the essence of the arguments he was to make against the classical model of the economy for the rest of his life. The book was called *The Theory of the Leisure Class* and almost immediately catapulted Veblen into fame.[9] Its literary style, as Veblen himself remarked, was polysyllabic. Readers believed him to be a satirist of the most penetrating sort and aficionados of language sought him out to address their literary clubs. But Veblen always refused. For he was disappointed at the popularity of the work, since he felt that those who praised it most highly had misunderstood its message. Veblen coined many new phrases which were to become part of the vocabulary, words like "conspicuous consumption," "the higher learning," "captains of industry." Not until John Kenneth Galbraith's "affluent society" and "conventional wisdom" did another economist leave his imprint on the language. Dorfman has pointed out that "overnight the language on the university campus changed, and it was said that those who read Veblen could be distinguished by their speech."[10] His old mentor John Bates Clark was delighted at his success and claimed that Veblen had fulfilled his promise.

The Veblenian Dichotomy

The book itself carries out a theme that Veblen had inaugurated in some of his earlier papers on economics. In them he had developed his hunch, derived from his anthropological studies, that every society can be characterized in terms of a dichotomy between those aspects that are dynamic and those that are static. The dynamic qualities of a culture are those that contribute to what he termed "the life process," while those that were static were inhibitory of human life and work. To Veblen, the dynamic aspect was closely related to those activities in which problems were solved through the use of tools, modern science, and matter-of-fact thinking. It is clear that Veblen identifies these activities with the "economic life process," which was "still in great measure awaiting theoretical formulation."[11] An inquiry into this economic life process would deal with the process of cumulative change in society which results from changes in technology—"the methods of dealing with the material means of life." The keynote of all Veblen's thinking was that

---

[8]   Dorfman, pp. 132-33.

[9]   Thorstein Veblen, *The Theory of the Leisure Class* (New York: New American Press, 1953). Originally published in 1899.

[10] Dorfman, p. 197.

[11] Thorstein Veblen, "Why Is Economics Not an Evolutionary Science?," *The Place of Science in Modern Civilisation* (New York: Russell & Russell, 1961), p. 70. (The volume is hereafter cited as *The Place of Science.*)

such tool-using; technological activities derived from man's "instinct of workmanship," "idle curiosity," and the "parental bent." These created a desire within the human breast to see in all human effort and enjoyment an enhancement of life.

The other aspect of culture was represented by those activities which were of an essentially "ceremonial" character. When Veblen speaks of ceremonial behavior, he is talking about the authoritarian, taboo-ridden, emotion-fraught aspect of behavior which is contrary to the life process and is static by its very nature. These activities of man derived their sanction not from their ability to solve pressing problems, but simply because they are ancient and therefore honorable. The institutions of society have a binding force that derives from the past and are resistant to change because they are linked to the "dawn history" of the tribe. It is from hereditary status that all taboos derive their sanction. Veblen's study of anthropology and of Darwin convinced him that this aspect of behavior (characterized by superstition, teleological thought processes, ritualistic activities) can be projected back to the beginning of human organization, in which certain relationships among men were imbedded in the mores, which the people of the community accept as right and good and which have a tendency to gain priority in order, rank, and importance in social questions.

Just as the "technological" forces were represented by the workmanship proclivity in man's instinctive makeup, the "ceremonial" processes are representative of an opposing instinct, an acquisitive "sportsmanlike" propensity in man. It is the clash of opposing instincts in man's nature that has given rise to the dichotomization of culture into dynamic and static elements—that aspect of social life in which tools and instruments are used and that other aspect pervaded by folklore, mana, and mystic potencies.

With this dichotomy, Veblen dissected all behavior and institutions. In his *Theory of the Leisure Class*, Veblen analyzed the consumption patterns of our modern society and found the dichotomy in clear and unequivocal form.

Yet neoclassical economic theory made no such distinction. For in the received doctrine, one kind of expenditure is no less legitimate than any other. An additional dollar spent on the purchase of a diamond bracelet or package of cigarettes is no different in terms of welfare, and therefore efficiency, from an additional dollar spent on insulin by a diabetic. As long as the additional utilities per dollar spent on the items are equated, welfare is maximized. From the point of view of the individual consumer and from the point of view of economic science, there is no question of "waste."

But Veblen rejected the neoclassical notion of the economic man carefully equating his utilities. Furthermore he believed that waste is an economic factor which can be analyzed and about which much can be said of a scientific sort. It is only because economics is not an evolutionary science that the neoclassical preconception of man's behavior could have come to dominate the analysis. This framework sees man as an isolated datum, an island of satisfaction. Consumers are supposedly competing for consumer goods by equating their marginal evaluations to prices, and factors of production are moving to the manufacture of those goods and services for which consumers have valued the factors' marginal product highest.

If economic science was couched in Darwinian cause-and-effect terms, the static ceremonial elements of consumer behavior would be recognized. For habit and convention, emulation and display, emotion and superstitious irrationality make up much of the motive for consumption.

> Not only is the individual's conduct hedged about and directed by his habitual relations to his fellows in the group, but these relations, being of an institutional character, vary as the institutional scene varies. The wants and desires, the end and aim, the ways and means, the amplitude and drift of the individual's conduct are functions of an institutional variable that is of a highly complex and wholly unstable character.[12]

The neoclassical notion of economic man is based on the psychology of hedonism—the view that man is motivated by the pursuit of pleasure maximization in an isolated state of nature. Veblen's caricature of neoclassical theory's economic man is one of the most quoted examples of his witty, sardonic style.

> The hedonistic conception of man is that of a lightning calculator of pleasures and pains, who oscillates like a homogeneous globule of desire of happiness under the impulse of stimuli that shift him about the area, but leave him intact. He has neither antecedent nor consequent. He is an isolated, definitive human datum, in stable equilibrium except for the buffets of impinging forces that displace him in one direction or another. Self-imposed in elemental space, he spins symmetrically about his own spiritual axis until the parallelogram of forces bears down upon him, whereupon he follows the line of the resultant. When the force of the impact is spent, he comes to rest, a self-contained globule of desire as before.[13]

The Veblenian dichotomy was utilized to show that the neoclassical principles that were outlined in the preceding chapters are not really useful in determining welfare from the point of view of the "life process." For the present enjoyment of goods by a consumer depends not so much on rational calculation as on the consumption patterns of others, habit, and the desire for emulative display and conspicuous consumption. Moreover, to Veblen such consumption is wasteful in the sense that it does not serve human life. This judgment is a value judgment, but one that has a scientific basis in the "instinct of workmanship." The competitive advantage of one consumer over another

---

Thorstein Veblen, "The Limitations of Marginal Utility," *The Place of Science*, pp. 242-43.

[13] Thorstein Veblen, "Why is Economics Not an Evolutionary Science?," *The Place of Science*, pp. 73-74.

does not satisfy this instinctual craving in man, who must see in all human activities "usefulness" from the point of view of being generically human. Competitive expenditure does not, therefore, have the approval of conscience and does not square with the notion that consumption must result in a net gain in the fullness of life. So an expenditure is waste if the custom or institution on which it rests can be traced to invidious pecuniary comparisons. Instead of standards in consumption being set by considerations of this life process, they have, through a "contamination" of the instinct of workmanship, come to be determined by the usage of those next above in reputability. This means that ultimately all standards are set by the wealthy leisure class.

In this way, Veblen showed that man's sense of beauty is set by wastefulness. The perversion of man's technological proclivity by culture is such that the less well adaptable is an object to its ostensible use, the more beautiful it is. Thus, for example, a machine-made spoon of aluminum has a brute efficiency as compared to a hand-wrought spoon of silver. The latter is conspicuously wasteful and therefore more beautiful. So our sense of costliness masquerades under the name of beauty.

> The high gloss of a gentleman's hat or of a patent leather shoe has no more intrinsic beauty than a similarly high gloss on a threadbare sleeve; and yet there is no question but that all well-bred people . . . instinctively and unaffectedly cleave to the one as a phenomenon of great beauty and eschew the other as offensive to every sense to which it can appeal.[14]

The End of Consumer Sovereignty

What Veblen has done, of course, is to bring into question the whole notion of consumer sovereignty. Once it is recognized that the utility a consumer receives depends on the consumption patterns of others, or that consumer satisfaction depends on habitual patterns of behavior, or that culture has so perverted man's instinct of workmanship that he does not know what is good for him, then the view that laissez-faire brings about the maximization of welfare in consumption does not necessarily follow.

If a consumer buys an expensive automobile only in order to receive utility from the emulation of one's neighbors, the individual might be better off if there were a simultaneous restriction of consumption by everyone. Moreover, if his conspicuous consumption of expensive jewelry causes deep dissatisfaction to envious persons, the price paid for the jewels does not reflect the reduction in satisfaction that others have experienced. So under such circumstances relative prices are not a reliable guide to relative satisfactions. This means that the interferences with laissez-faire by the state might increase satisfaction by, for

---

[14] Veblen, *The Theory of the Leisure Class*, p. 97.

example, taxing the purchase of jewelry and compensating those who lose satisfaction from seeing others display their jewelry. When there are external diseconomies in consumption, to allow the allocation of resources at the dictates of consumers no longer can be guaranteed to maximize satisfaction. Thus Veblen, in making economic man into social man upset the policy implications of neoclassical consumption theory.

Veblen's emphasis on the role of conspicuous consumption in the economic order is one of his most enduring contributions to social science. His was the age when tycoons such as Cornelius Vanderbilt, Henry Clay Frick, and J. Pierpont Morgan displayed their wealth through private railway cars, yachts, and fantastic palaces serving as family residences. Although the system of vulgar display described by Veblen has disappeared for the most part (to some extent a victim of Veblenian ridicule), it has been replaced in our own time by conspicuous consumption in slightly altered forms. As John Brooks has recently suggested, there is a rising form of American conspicuous waste in which the state of being rich and powerful is boasted through "parody and display"; one's wealth is flaunted, but at the same time the display must make clear that the conspicuous consumer posesses "irony and wit."[15] Updating Veblen's diagnosis of leisure-class consumption, Brooks points to the snob appeal of the Conrad Watch Company's *Delirium I* timepiece, advertised as the world's thinnest watch, with a thickness of one-sixteenth of an inch and a pricetag of $4,400. He also points to the flaunting of commercial and industrial objects in the home-furnishing style called "high-tech," in which pipes and support posts are exposed, bookcases are constructed of commercial steel shelving, lighting is provided by factory lamps, and the furniture is upholstered with movers' blankets; and he notes the use of the telephone beeper, which, by beeping during social occasions, conspicuously demonstrates the user's importance.

Veblen went even further in applying the dichotomy in his later critiques of the market economy. In *The Theory of Business Enterprise*,[16] he carried his distinction between "industrial and pecuniary employments" into the distinction between making goods and making money. And in a series of articles published in 1908, he developed the dichotomy into the distinction between industrial processes and business activities. In his book and essays, he made the point that gain from a business investment is often in direct proportion to its retarding effect on the life process of the community. The institution of ownership gives the owner of industrial technology not only the right of use of the economy's material equipment but also the right of abuse and neglect. Such destructive behavior affords an income to the investor, which, like any other income, can be capitalized. This gain can be

---

[15] See John Brooks, "The New Snobbery: How to Show Off in America," *The Atlantic Monthly* 247 (January 1981): 37-48.

[16] Thorstein Veblen, *The Theory of Business Enterprise* (New York: Charles Scribner's Sons, 1904).

realized through the "advised idleness" of the industrial plant, a method which does nothing to enhance the livelihood or satisfy the desires of the community. So we find as a common trait of modern life the "capitalization of inefficiency" through misdirecting the industrial process, preventing efficiency, and inhibiting output.

Moreover, a great many enterprises do not have to rely on nonproduction for these dubious benefits. Such establishments as racetracks, saloons, and gambling houses derive their profits for their owners through activities that are suggestive of probable net detriment to mankind.[17]

Furthermore, a large amount of technological equipment is engaged in manufacturing products in which disserviceability is mingled with waste. For example, goods of fashion, proprietary articles, sophisticated household supplies, and advertising enterprise; all of these draw their profits from "skilled mandacity," owing their value to a perverse use of the technology employed. Capital, therefore, is of two kinds: industrial capital, which is technologically serviceable, and ceremonial capital, which is valued in terms of the income which it yields to its owner. The community's evaluation of the latter determines its worth, and so a vast amount of effort is put into advertising in order to influence a favorable consideration. Thus the main interest of the entrepreneur is in making money, not in making goods. And the making of money is often in direct proportion to the amount of disturbance and sabotage to industrial processes that the entrepreneur can create.[18]

Veblen believed that the domination of life and work by business enterprise and industrial sabotage was a transitory phenomenon. For the machine process inculcated into individuals a matter-of-fact, cause-and-effect way of thinking incompatible with ceremony and superstition. As a new breed of highly trained and specially gifted experts becomes more and more essential to the operation of business enterprise, "these expert men, technologists, engineers, or whatever name may best suit them, make up the indispensable General Staff of the industrial system; and without their immediate and unremitting guidance and correction the industrial system will not work."[19]

These technological experts will ultimately develop a sense of "class-consciousness" that will lead them to see that the waste and confusion resulting from the management of industrial processes by absentee owners and financial managers could be eliminated by a general strike and the establishment of a "soviet of technicians" who would take no account of absentee ownership. ". . . [T]here is the patent fact that such a thing as a general strike of the technological specialists in industry need involve no more than a minute fraction of one percent of the population; yet it would swiftly bring a collapse of the old order and

---

[17] Thorstein Veblen, "On the Nature of Capital," *The Place of Science*, p. 358.

[18] Veblen's analysis of "sabotage" is developed most completely in his *The Engineers and the Price System* (New York: Viking Press, 1921), especially Chapter 1.

[19] Veblen, *The Engineers*, p. 69.

sweep the timeworn fabric of finance and absentee sabotage into the discard for good and all."[20]

Veblen's academic career probably was not bolstered by his unorthodox views on business culture. What is more, his lack of discretion in his personal affairs and various amatory scandals involving female students made his position with university administrators untenable. He moved from Chicago to Stanford to the University of Missouri and eventually to The New School for Social Research. Notwithstanding his international reputation, he never rose above the rank of associate professor.

When he retired to his cabin near Palo Alto, he was lonely and neglected. His finances were in a parlous state. Ill health and an uneasy state of mind plagued him in his final days. On August 3, 1929, he died, knowing that he had not set economics on what he considered the right track. But his influence on succeeding generations of economists was to become evermore pronounced, culminating in the mid-twentieth century in the writings of Galbraith, where Veblen's conspicuous consumers and efficiency experts were to reappear in a form and at a time that seemed eminently ripe for them. David Riesman has summarized Veblen's contribution to social science.

> Whatever our debt to the theories Veblen developed, I think we are all in his debt for his way of thinking. Irreverent and catty to the very end, he avoided becoming a substantial citizen, which he defined as one who owns much property. He died insolvent. But the intangible assets that have come down to us, his books and his personal style, have still the power over us that Veblen was all too inclined to disparage: the power of ideas and of personality.[21]

---

[20] Veblen, *The Engineers*, pp. 81-82.

[21] David Riesman, *Thorstein Veblen, A Critical Interpretation* (New York: Charles Scribner's Sons, 1953), p. 208.

5

Arthur Cecil Pigou

EXTERNALITIES IN
PRODUCTION

Wonder, Carlyle declared, is the beginning of philosophy. It is not
wonder, but rather the social enthusiasm which revolts from the
sordidness of mean streets and the joylessness of withered lives,
that is the beginning of economic science.

A. C. Pigou

Thorstein Veblen's earliest impact was on a generation of young American economists and social scientists who called for radical experi-
mentation and restructuring of property relationships during the Great
Depression. Some of them were to prove influential in the New Deal and
indeed were to take the name for Roosevelt's administration from
Veblen's own works.[1] The early Veblenians took as their text the *Engineers and the Price System*, calling for a rule of the engineers and
technocrats to bring order out of the chaos of the Great Depression.

As we shall see, John Maynard Keynes's message at this period was
equally dramatic. He attempted to show how the capitalist system could
be saved from its greatest threat—the revolution of the unemployed
masses—through extensive governmental spending policies. While
Veblen was working out his ideas on the "imbecile institutions" of the
market economy, John Maynard Keynes was studying under a man who
was working on problems which seemed less spectacular, but were

---

[1] Disciples of Veblen are generally considered to be members of a school of economic thought called
"institutionalism." The label is misleading since it identifies this school with the nontechnological
forces which they consider inhibitory of progress, rather than with the technological forces which
they consider crucial in contributing to human well-being. But no terms that alternatively have
been suggested ("instrumentalism," "technologism") have gained wide usage. Without doubt, the
leading institutionalists in the Veblenian tradition are John Kenneth Galbraith and C. E. Ayres.
Ayres's work is noteworthy for being explicitly and avowedly indebted to Veblen, and because it
contains a theoretical framework for understanding this approach to the study of the economy. See
C. E. Ayres, *The Theory of Economic Progress* (New York: Schocken Books, 1962), and C. E. Ayres,
Toward a Reasonable Society (Austin: University of Texas Press, 1961).

ultimately to prove just as challenging as Keynes's and Veblen's policies for the survival of the free enterprise system. For no one had yet shown a satisfactory resolution of the conflict between privacy and freedom. To this Cambridge economist, the belching chimneys and car exhausts that contaminate our air, blacken our laundry, and burn our eyes; the waste materials of our fully employed factories that pollute our streams and rivers, killing our fish and wildlife; and the noise of our blaring auto horns and high-powered stereos, disturbing the nightly tranquility of our crowded neighborhoods, were par excellence the weak link in the neoclassical logic of unfettered individualism.

The economist who considered these disturbing problems in their explicit form and jarred the complacency with which the policy implications of neoclassicism were held was one of the most paradoxical figures in the history of economics. He had the rather odd name of Pigou, but his personality and eccentricities were well suited to the oddness of his name. In truth, there were two Pigous in the professional career of one individual. On the one hand, he was a leading exemplar of the neoclassical school of thought. Indeed, John Maynard Keynes was to use Pigou as the epitome of the neoclassical viewpoint on full employment analysis, which Keynes would set out to annihilate. Pigou himself struck back by referring to Keynes's *General Theory* as "this macedoine of misrepresentations."[2] And to many younger students of economics, Pigou's name is inextricably linked with the "Pigou effect," an argument in answer to Keynes that attempted to rehabilitate neoclassical employment theory by demonstrating its logical completeness under the classical assumptions of wage and price flexibility.

On the other hand, Pigou must be credited with having pioneered the contemporary concern with the untoward social consequences of private actions, and hence with one chief aspect of the contemporary attack on the laissez-faire model. Pigou raised his disturbing questions as early as 1912 in his book *Wealth and Welfare*.[3] Economists were to wait almost a half-century before realizing that the issues Pigou had grappled with were among the most important facing an opulent economy, indeed were to threaten the very legitimacy of the system. But few economists then understood the nature of the breakthrough in analysis that Pigou had made. The critics of capitalism, until Pigou, had questioned the stability of the system itself and argued for alternative systems of economic order. Frank Knight, alone among the reviewers of Pigou's first edition of *The Economics of Welfare* in 1920,[4] noted the significant fact that Pigou had shifted the debate from the choice between alternative systems of economic order, to the methods of changing and improving the already functioning system. Professor Harry Johnson, in his touching obituary for Pigou, comments that

---

[2] It is characteristic of his objectivity of mind that he was later to change his appraisal of Keynes, although he had been deeply offended.

[3] A. C. Pigou, *Wealth and Welfare* (London: Macmillan & Co., 1912).

[4] A. C. Pigou, *Economics of Welfare*, 4th ed. (London: Macmillan & Co., 1932).

Pigou's analysis, in shifting the argument from revolutionary change to the methods of improving the existing system, "was at once its originality, in the period when Pigou first developed it, and its obvious limitation during the troubled inter-war period which followed its publication. Now that the Keynesian Revolution has been digested, and the political divisions of the thirties and forties have been reconciled in a system of welfare capitalism, economists are becoming increasingly occupied with policy problems of the kind with which Pigou was concerned, and in whose analysis he was the pioneer."[5] John Kenneth Galbraith later was to make us critically aware of the "unevenness of our blessings," popularizing many of the problems Pigou clearly foresaw almost a half-century before anyone else was to take notice.

One of the strangest men in a science noted for its curious personalities, Pigou's character went through an extreme transformation. In his early days he was a gay, joke-loving, social, hospitable bachelor, but he later turned into a rather eccentric recluse. His lifelong friend and colleague, C. R. Fay, explained the metamorphosis as follows: "World War I was a shock to him, and he was never the same afterwards." He had spent most of his vacations from Cambridge in voluntary ambulance work at the front in France, Belgium, and Italy, and was sickened by what he saw. Very early in his career, he recognized the intimate relationship between social and economic problems, reflecting a passion for both humanistic and scientific concerns. As a student, Pigou displayed a rare ability to excel in both aspects of human knowledge. At the age of twenty-four, he won prizes for two essays, the titles of which give striking evidence of the diverse concerns of the young scholar. One was called "The Causes and Effects of Changes in the Related Values of Agricultural Produce in the United Kingdom during the Last Fifty Years"; the other, "Robert Browning as a Religious Teacher." Two years earlier he had won a gold medal for English verse, with an ode on Alfred the Great. (After the war, with his change in mood, he sold the medal to aid in the relief of starving Georgians.) Upon graduating from King's College, Cambridge, he spent his time lecturing, publishing, and engaging in debate on tariff reform, an issue that was to absorb him until late in life.

A former student described Pigou's personal appearance in mid-1940's as a tall, straight figure, eccentrically garbed, glimpsed occasionally walking about the countryside or reclining in a deck chair on the grass by the porter's lodge inside King's front court. He was to remain in his deck chair during Nazi air raids as a defiance to Hitler. Pigou had a well-earned reputation for sartorial economy, appearing in the 1950's at the Marshall Library proudly attired in a pre-World War I suit.

Like many shy personalities who protect themselves by affecting a curmudgeon pose, Pigou's inconsistencies in his prejudices often

---

[5]   Harry Johnson, "Arthur Cecil Pigou, 1877-1959," *Canadian Journal of Economics and Political Science* 26 (February 1960): 155.

charmed his acquaintances and proved disarming. Claiming that they lacked the capacity for intellectual integrity, Pigou pretended that he could not tolerate women, foreigners, or politicians. But he made exceptions in each case. He compared women to "that variety of spider which acquires a mate and in due course devours him." Needless to say, Pigou remained a bachelor throughout his life. Yet, he welcomed honeymoon couples to his beautifully situated cottage. Although most foreign economists, and especially Americans, were persona non grata, he was extremely gracious to Alvin Hansen and his wife. And while he taught his undergraduates that "the main purpose of learning economics was to be able to see through the bogus economic arguments of the politicians," he listened with admiration to the speeches of Winston Churchill.[6] Pigou allowed himself to acquire a reputation for being a hermitlike recluse; yet he often invited undergraduates and faculty members to his cottage in Buttermere, taking pleasure in astonishing his visitors by awarding them his war medals for their exploits in hill walking and rock climbing.

He was a stimulating conversationalist, and much like Veblen, a rejector of ceremony in all its forms. Late in his life, when he presided over a meeting of his College in the election of a new Provost, he described the outcomes of the successive returns as though calling a horse race, to the obvious displeasure of the assembled Fellows.

At the age of thirty, when he took over the Chair of Political Economy of his beloved mentor, Alfred Marshall, he made a powerful statement of his version of what economics is about.

> If it were not for the hope that a scientific study of man's social actions may lead . . . to practical results in social improvement, I should myself . . . regard the time devoted to that study as misspent . . . . If I desired knowledge of man apart from the fruits of knowledge, I should seek it in the history of religious enthusiasm, of passion, of martyrdom and of love; I should not seek it in the marketplace.[7]

But it was to the marketplace that Pigou was to turn his cool and reflective eye.

Externalities and Market Failure

To Pigou, all was not well in the laissez-faire market. Where his neoclassical forebears and colleagues saw efficient allocation, Pigou saw waste. Where the received doctrine spelled out welfare through equating at the margin, Pigou saw that the incorrect use of margins was leading to faulty conclusions. Businessmen, in pursuing their own self-interest in the free market economy, were creating "externalities" by which they profited at society's expense, or others in society were

---

[6] D. G. Champernowne, "Arthur Cecil Pigou 1877-1959," *Royal Statistical Society Journal*, 122, pt. II (1959): 264.

[7] Johnson, "Arthur Cecil Pigou," p. 152.

profiting at their expense. In the former case, too much product from society's viewpoint was being provided; in the latter case, too little. In order to get a clear grasp of Pigou's argument, it will be necessary to examine the meaning of the term "externality," and the background of its development.

The halcyon environment guaranteed by the neoclassical economic analysis rested in part on the conclusion that, from a social viewpoint, economic welfare is maximized under laissez-faire competitive conditions. In equilibrium, marginal costs equal marginal benefits. The profit-maximizing producer is always induced to bear the cost incurred in producing an extra unit of product, while the utility-maximizing consumer will pay a price just equal to the marginal satisfaction he derives from its consumption. That is why free competition and free choice had such appeal to the neoclassical writers. What man of good will (and a sufficiently libertarian bent of mind) could complain if the costs of production and the benefits of consumption were borne entirely by the parties involved in any transaction? Since the whole is always equal to the sum of its parts, all costs and all benefits being incurred by the individuals in society precisely in proportion to their participation in production and consumption, social welfare is optimized.

But Pigou asked, what if there is a divergence between the private and the social product? That is, what if the private production of a commodity yields social benefits surpassing the purely personal satisfaction yielded to the consumer who buys it? Or, alternatively, what happens to the welfare of society under perfect competition and consumer sovereignty, if the private production of a commodity has negative, unpleasant, disturbing, or other costly effects on innocent third parties? Would not the market mechanism then fail to take the full costs and benefits of production into account? Would not too much of some goods be produced and too little of others (from society's viewpoint)? And, if so, what happens to the esteem with which we learned to view the neoclassical model?

The classical and neoclassical economists had dichotomized the economic system into rigid zones: that area where no restraints should be imposed upon private actions, and that area of extreme cases where the government could intervene. The latter cases were usually summed up under the rubrics of "monopoly" and "paternalism." To Adam Smith, there were certain enterprises such as national defense and those "public institutions, which, though they may be in the highest degree advantageous to a great society, are, however, of such a nature, that the profit could never repay the expense to any individual." But the Master was magnificently vague about the extent of such enterprises and, aside from a few remarks about those institutions that facilitate commerce and instruct the people, there was little elaboration. By the time John Stuart Mill published the very last edition of his *Principles of Political Economy*, he was thought to have been something of a socialist. Yet he still maintained that the only obvious limitation to a laissez-faire policy was in the case of minors and lunatics who were clearly incapable of knowing their own self-interest.

Pigou was not the first to demur. In 1883, a British economist and philosopher, Henry Sidgwick, had broken with the traditional approach. To Sidgwick, a clear-cut boundary did not exist between the areas of governmental action and private enterprise. He fashioned the analytical tool that Pigou was later to sharpen and refine: the distinction and possible divergencies between the private and social net products which create *externalities* or *neighborhood effects*. Sidgwick cast doubt on the proposition that in a competitive laissez-faire system, an individual's claims on wealth will always be exactly equal to his net contribution to society, a result that the neoclassical model had implied. Sidgwick, in elucidating his point, referred to the case of a lighthouse, an example that economists have used ever since to illustrate a good that must be provided collectively if it is to be provided in an amount satisfying society's desires. If a lighthouse is financed privately by a person who produces it for his own consumption, motivated perhaps solely by considerations of his own benefit, he will unintentionally provide external economies or benefits to others. This is what Sidgwick meant when he said the marginal social product may exceed the marginal private product. Since this is the case, and not being able to exclude others from the light's benefits, he may very well hope that some more altruistically minded individual will build the lighthouse, enabling him to act as a "free rider." It follows that the socially optimal number of lighthouses do not get constructed. And so Sidgwick made a case for government intervention, or collective provision of this *public good*, as later economists were to call it.

Pigou took Sidgwick's lead in this analysis, going far beyond him in developing realistic examples of externalities, and in suggesting a scheme for resolving the serious problems they pose for a free society.

To Pigou, only by eliminating the divergencies between the marginal private and marginal social products, would society's welfare be maximized. He even went so far as to assert that the chief duty of the economist is to identify and eliminate the divergencies.

In the *Economics of Welfare*, Pigou states that his aim is to show that the world of Adam Smith and neoclassical orthodoxy is indeed a dream world. Far from the economic system requiring little state action, the system has performed as well as it has *because* of governmental action. If self-interest promotes human welfare, it is only because human institutions have been designed to bring about this salubrious result. The problem is to determine what government action is still required. In Pigou's words, his task is "to bring into clearer light some of the ways in which it now is, or eventually may become, feasible for governments to control the play of economic forces in such ways as to promote the economic welfare, and through that, the total welfare, of their citizens as a whole."[8]

---

[8] Pigou, *Economics of Welfare*, pp. 129-30.

In his first example of a divergence between private and social products, Pigou refers to the case of railway engines that damage the surrounding woods and crops by emitting sparks. In such an instance, Pigou recommends that the railways should be forced to compensate the crop and forest owners whose property is damaged. Otherwise, the true output of society is incorrectly calculated. For one must reckon the "uncompensated damage" done to the owners of property who have suffered losses due to the action of others over whom they have no control. To Pigou, all that was required was a change in the liability laws requiring compensation for such damages. If the railway is not made liable, it does not take into account the real marginal costs of running an additional train. If it did so, it might in fact decide not to run the train, thus sparing the crops for the use of society. It is the lack of state action, in the form of stringent compulsory liability charges, that is the source of the divergence between private and social products.

A second case of divergence, according to Pigou, comes about because one person, in the course of rendering some service to a second person, incidentally also renders services to third parties, of such a sort that payment cannot be exacted from them.[9] The reader will note that Sidgwick's lighthouse would be an example of such an externality. Pigou chooses a case perhaps more appropriate to an industrial society. He discusses the situation in which a factory owner who, attempting to reduce the air pollution caused by the production of his firm's commodity, goes to the expense of installing a smoke-preventing device. Since he cannot, under the neoclassical laissez-faire model, receive payment for such services, it is unlikely that enough smog prevention will be provided. Thus we must violate the neoclassical policy prescription. Factory owners with chimneys belching smoke should be given bounties to encourage the installation of smokeless smoke stacks. Pigou then turned his attention to the problems of urban blight. He cast a jaundiced eye at the factories in residential areas destroying the amenities of the neighborhood. In Pigou's view, we should not let our obsession with the neoclassical model blind us to the realities of contracted airspace, the disappearing playing room for our children, and the crowded neighborhoods. For the health and efficiency of the families in our cities are being sacrificed to the ideology of the free unfettered market. Only state interference, forcing the appropriate fines and subsidies bringing marginal social and marginal private costs and benefits into equality, can right the wrongs, and bring about the results that the neoclassical model was supposed to guarantee. The rules of liability must be clear. Only the state can set the rules and enforce them. Pigou, in attacking the problems of urban blight, polluted rivers and air, and other "uncompensated damages"—problems which seem so pressing in the latter half of the twentieth century—was indeed a man ahead of his time. To those of his contemporaries calling

---

[9] Pigou, *Economics of Welfare*, p. 183. Most of this analysis had appeared in Pigou's *Wealth and Welfare* in 1912.

for violent change, his suggestion of fines and subsidies to redress the balance must surely have seemed inadequate palliatives. But Pigou persisted in believing that such governmental action, mild as it seemed to firebrand revolutionaries, was all that was needed to make the classical model relevant for the twentieth-century industrial economy. His influence was to be felt later, after the Keynesian revolution had been digested, on such economists as Hansen, Galbraith, and Samuelson. What we call the welfare state today is in no small measure the outgrowth of attitudes and policies prescribed in the *Economics of Welfare*. But if his ideas have had an impact on us, no one would have been more surprised than Pigou. More like Veblen, and less like his student Keynes, he had little hope for the power of ideas to transform our lives. A skeptical man, he stated in his presidential address to the Royal Economic Society in 1939, ". . . the hope that an advance in economic knowledge will appreciably affect actual happenings is . . . a slender one. It is not likely that there will be a market for our produce. None the less . . . we cultivate our garden. For we also follow, not thought but an impulse—the impulse to inquire—which, futile though it may prove, is at least not ignoble."[10]

---

[10] A. C. Pigou, "Reminiscences of Changes in the Economics Profession," *Economic Journal* 49 (June 1939): 221.

6

EDWARD HASTINGS
CHAMBERLIN

THE WASTES
OF COMPETITION

The force of his own merit makes his way.
Inscription under a picture of E. H. Chamberlin,
1916 Yearbook, Iowa City High School

In 1921, a graduate student at the University of Michigan wrote a paper discussing the ability of railroads to charge discriminatory rates on different classes of freight. He was puzzled why theorists such as A. C. Pigou and Frank Taussig could not agree as to the reason for such rate-making power. The student was Edward H. Chamberlin, and the ideas in the paper were sufficiently original that his professor suggested it be submitted to the *Quarterly Journal of Economics*. It was returned, as Chamberlin noted much later, "no doubt with the highly relevant comment to the effect that it needed more cultivation both intensive and extensive."[1] The details of the argument in the paper are no longer of great concern; what is important is that the young student began questioning the whole structure of value theory at that time, and a decade later, he was to initiate a major revision of economic theory.

Away from the halls of academia, the young Chamberlin hardly appeared as one who would become a true innovator in economic theory. He was, in many respects, the stereotype of the "all-around-guy." Tall, good-looking, and athletic, Chamberlin liked sports as

---

[1] The comment was written in 1961 when Chamberlin discussed "The Origins and Early Development of Monopolistic Competition Theory," *Quarterly Journal of Economics* 75 (November 1961): 517. Chamberlin's reminiscences in this article provide a very illuminating picture of the development of his ideas.

much as his books. He was not, in any sense, a "bookworm." His father had died when Edward was young, and through high school and college he worked as a reporter on the *Iowa City Citizen*. In 1916 he went to the University of Iowa, where he took up the study of accounting.[2] There he came in contact with one of the most influential of economics teachers, Frank Knight.[3] Although they were later to be bitterly opposed to each other on the issues raised by Chamberlin's work, Knight encouraged Chamberlin to teach economics and accept a post to study under Fred M. Taylor at the University of Michigan. When he went to Harvard in 1922 to get his doctorate, Chamberlin had already resolved to write his dissertation on the problems surrounding the competitive model.[4] At Harvard he found a willing supervisor in Professor Allyn Young, who was himself engaged in a debate over similar problems in the 1920's. Chamberlin's thesis was completed in 1927, and six years later its ideas were formulated into *The Theory of Monopolistic Competition*.[5]

Few economists who have achieved the prominence of E. H. Chamberlin have had their work characterized by such a single-minded purpose. Chamberlin's outstanding trait was his tenacity in pursuing a goal. He was an ambitious man who wanted to be remembered for his work in value theory. He once told a friend while working on his dissertation that he was "writing something that's going to change the theory of value." Both his tenacity and his pride are illustrated by the recollections of his lifetime friend, Howard Ellis, when the two were at Michigan, where they often argued points of theory. Ellis would feel that a debate on some theoretical point had been settled in his favor, but Chamberlin would return to the issue after several days to try a new angle of attack on the problem.

His work in value theory was not always warmly received; at one point Chamberlin was led to identify an entire "school" of economists who were ". . . distinguished by the zeal with which the theory of monopolistic competition has been attacked. . . ."[6] Through it all, he doggedly continued to cultivate his theory "intensively and extensively." A measure of the success of his effort is that almost every textbook on value theory today utilizes some elements of the Cham-

---

[2]   The class of 1916 at Iowa City High produced a second outstanding economist. Along with Chamberlin, Howard Ellis, now professor emeritus at the University of California, Berkeley, graduated and went along to the University of Iowa. Both later went on to study at Michigan and Harvard. We are indebted to Professor Ellis for reminiscences on the early years of his acquaintance with Chamberlin.

[3]   Knight's influence on his students was extraordinary, as is evidenced by the long list of prominent economists who remain his admirers today. See Chapter 12.

[4]   Joseph A. Schumpeter, commenting on Chamberlin's work, notes that it provides "a striking instance of subjective and objective originality." Joseph A. Schumpeter, *History of Economic Analysis* (New York: Oxford University Press, 1959), pp. 1150-1151n.

[5]   Edward H. Chamberlin, *The Theory of Monopolistic Competition* (Cambridge, Mass.: Harvard University Press, 1933). Chapter 3 of the initial edition was originally published in the *Quarterly Journal of Economics*; the book has subsequently gone through eight editions with additional appendices added from time to time.

[6]   Edward H. Chamberlin, "The Chicago School," in idem, *Towards a More General Theory of Value* (New York: Oxford University Press, 1957), p. 296. The irony of this is that Chamberlin's old mentor, Frank Knight, was a leading figure in this school of thought.

berlinian framework derived from the *Theory of Monopolistic Competition*.

Some of the originality of Chamberlin's work has been buried over the years (despite his own attempts to prevent it) by the fact that, six months after the appearance of *The Theory of Monopolistic Competition*, the English economist Joan Robinson published her *Economics of Imperfect Competition*.[7] Chamberlin and Robinson are usually referred to as the joint discoverers of the analysis of "imperfect" markets, a point which pained Chamberlin to no end. His attempt to distinguish his own "product" from that of Robinson became almost an obsession with him as his career wore on.[8] While his stress on this point may not have been wholly warranted, there are important differences in the two approaches, which we shall return to later.

Chamberlin need not have worried over the recognition his work received. *The Theory of Monopolistic Competition* was awarded the David A. Wells prize at Harvard in 1927 as the best thesis in economics that year. Within a decade he was promoted to full professor. In 1951, Chamberlin was elected to the David A. Wells Chair in Political Economy at Harvard, a post he held until his death in 1967.

Problems with the Neoclassical Theory of the Firm

We have already dealt with the foundations of the Marshallian theory of the firm.[9] It will be recalled that a major difficulty with the postulates of perfect competition involved the cost structure of the firm. If Marshallian "external economies" resulted in a firm realizing *increasing returns* over a very wide range of output, the firm's share of the market might ultimately become large enough to influence the industry price. One of the fundamental conditions of perfect competition—that each firm has an imperceptible influence on supply—would no longer be realized.

Marshall saw the possibility that increasing returns could make perfect competition unworkable. However, his explanations as to why the competitive markets would in fact be likely to survive were not convincing. As a result, the 1920's saw a rising rumble of discontent over the existing theory's inability to explain the case of increasing returns. Economists began to question whether the neoclassical theory of value, which recognized only two market structures—competition and monopoly—was sufficiently broad to allow a meaningful analysis of the movements of prices and output in the "real world." In large part, it

---

[7] Joan Robinson, *Economics of Imperfect Competition* (London: Macmillan & Co., 1933). A third "discoverer" of imperfect competition, Heinrich Von Stackelberg, also treated the question of imperfect markets in a highly original fashion in his *Marktform und Gleichgewicht* (Berlin: Verlag Von Julius Springer, 1943). His work has received far less attention than the other two.

[8] The extent of this preoccupation can be seen in the collection of essays, Chamberlin, *Towards a More General Theory of Value*, published in 1957. Robinson is reported to have commented at one point "I'm sorry I ruined his life."

[9] See the discussion of Marshall in Chapter 3.

was the gap left by these two "ideal" market structures which prompted the work of economists such as Chamberlin, Robinson, and Von Stackelberg.[10] Even more than with most economists of the time, Chamberlin's dissatisfaction with value theory reflected his conviction that Marshallian theory could not answer questions posed by existing market structures in the American economy. This was not surprising: "The theory of pure competition could hardly be expected to fit facts so far different from its assumptions."[11] He did not despair, however, since ". . . there is no reason why a theory cannot be formulated which will fit them."[12]

To construct such a theory, Chamberlin began with one of the few noncompetitive cases treated by earlier writers—*duopoly*, or two sellers.[13] The narrow case was easily expanded into a situation which Chamberlin termed *oligopoly*: a market with more than one seller, but one where the actions of a single seller can exert a perceptible influence on market price. The possibility that any firm might have sufficient control over supply to influence the price posed new problems for the equilibrium analysis. In pure competition, the firm paid no heed to its rival's actions since they could not affect the industry price. In oligopoly this is no longer true; therefore, the demand for any given firm's product will depend on the reactions of other firms in response to actions by the initial firm.

Earlier writers had treated this problem of "interdependence" by assuming that each firm would ignore the other firms' actions. This is clearly unrealistic; Chamberlin's solution was to assume that *every* seller "will take account of his *total* influence on price, indirect as well as direct."[14] He then concluded that the resulting equilibrium price and output would be that of a monopolist; for if each firm realizes its total effect on price, it will join with the others to maximize joint profits as a single seller.

---

[10] In 1922, J. H. Clapham questioned the relevance of the Marshallian analysis of increasing returns in his article, "Of Empty Economic Boxes," *Economic Journal* 32 (September 1922): 305-14. This touched off a long debate by both English and American economists regarding the issues of competition and costs. Robinson's *Economics of Imperfect Competition* clearly emerged from the debates in the *Economic Journal*. Chamberlin, on the other hand, insists that his work did not stem from the "increasing-returns debate." Cf. Chamberlin; "The Origins and Early Development of Monopolistic Competitive Theory." One should recall, however, that his advisor, Allyn Young, was a major participant in this controversy, and Chamberlin probably felt a good deal of "indirect" influence through him. See Paul A. Samuelson, "The Monopolistic Competition Revolution," in Robert Kuenne, *Monopolistic Competition Theory* (New York: John Wiley & Sons, 1967).

[11] Chamberlin, *Theory of Monopolistic Competition*, p. 10.

[12] Chamberlin, *Theory of Monopolistic Competition*, p. 10.

[13] A. A. Cournot provided the earliest analysis in 1838 in his *Researches into the Mathematical Principles of the Theory of Wealth*, trans. Nathaniel T. Bacon (New York: Macmillan Co., 1898). F. Y. Edgeworth was the leading neoclassicist to take up the problem in his article, "Professor Graziani on the Mathematical Theory of Monopoly," *Economic Journal* 8 (June 1898): 111-114.

[14] Chamberlin, *Theory of Monopolistic Competition*, p. 46. Given his announced objective of constructing a theory which would better fit the "facts" of the "business world," it is interesting to note that Chamberlin's treatment of the issue of interdependence is hardly more realistic than his predecessors'. Clearly, it is unlikely that every firm will be able to assess *all* the indirect and direct effects of a change in output or price. For a compressed discussion of the major theses of oligopoly, see William Breit, "Approaches to Oligopoly: An Introduction to a Symposium," *Social Science Quarterly* 49 (June 1968): 42-48.

Chamberlin's solution to the oligopoly problem is just another special case resulting from a set of assumptions regarding the reactions of a large firm to its rivals. His approach to value theory did, however, lay the foundation for a fundamental change in analysis. Marshall began his analysis with the notion of a "commodity." He termed a group of firms producing that commodity an *industry*, which he proceeded to analyze. Chamberlin shifted the emphasis away from this industry group to the study of the individual demand curve of *each firm*. He distrusted the concept of industry groups, calling such attempts a "snare and delusion" which were "in the highest degree arbitrarily drawn." Far from assisting the analysis, Chamberlin felt they drew attention away from the most important point of focus—the firm's demand curve.

To Chamberlin, the presence of either polar case—monopoly or competition—was rare; he viewed the more general case of *monopolistic competition* as the most prevalent, with instances of oligopoly arising where some firms are large enough to affect total supply.

The emphasis on quantifying market structures in the *The Theory of Monopolistic Competition* created an entirely new field of specialization in economics: "industrial organization."[15]

Product Differentiation and the Firm

Chamberlin was struck by the failure of existing theory to take account of the wide variation of products produced within any Marshallian industry. One can easily delineate a "cigarette industry," but the consumer of cigarettes has very strong opinions regarding the relative merits of Camels, Marlboros, Pall Mall, and so forth. The consumer of "automobiles" is similarly able to point out definite tastes as between the various makes and models of automobiles; he chooses among over 100 models from a single manufacturer alone. Clearly, Chamberlin reasoned, a firm is free to manipulate the "products" it sells as well as their price and level of output. In particular, the ability of most firms to "differentiate" their product from that of other firms brought a new dimension onto the decision matrix of the firm.[16] This opportunity was

---

[15] Note the comments by Joe S. Bain, "The Impact on Industrial Organization," *American Economic Review* 54 (May 1964): 28-32. An early attempt to pursue the possibilities of Chamberlin's empirical approach to market structure was Robert Triffin's *Monopolistic Competition and General Equilibrium Theory* (Cambridge, Mass.: Harvard University Press, 1940). His use of "cross elasticities," to measure the impact of a change in price by one firm through the change in output of another, pointed out the difficulties of actually measuring the interdependence between firms. The selections by Fellner and Bain in Kuenne, *Monopolistic Competition Theory*, provide a recent appraisal of the impact of *The Theory of Monopolistic Competition* on the field of industrial organization. William Fellner, "The Adaptability and Lasting Significance of the Chamberlinian Contribution," and Joe S. Bain, "Chamberlin's Impact on Microeconomic Theory," in Kuenne, *Monopolistic Competition Theory*, pp. 3-30 and pp. 147-176, respectively.

[16] While his major emphasis—particularly in *Theory of Monopolistic Competition*—was on "product differentiation," Chamberlin also saw other ways in which the "product" was an important variable in the firm's decision matrix. See Edward Chamberlin, "The Product as an Economic Variable," in idem, *Towards a More General Theory of Value*, Chapter 6, pp. 105-137.

an important option, for "virtually all products are differentiated, at least slightly."[17] The basis for differentiation is broad indeed, for it is not important that differences in products be real; they may simply be imagined by the consumer. All that matters is that consumers *behave as if* the products are not alike. If they judge the two as being different, they will presumably pay some additional sum to buy the one they like most, regardless of the actual characteristics of the goods.

The importance of product differentiation stems from the effect it has on the demand for a firm's output. We characterized the perfectly competitive firm as being a "price taker"; the price for its output is determined by the industry equilibrium, and it views price as a horizontal line such as *PP* in Figure 6.1. With a differentiated product, the firm would have a demand curve such as *dd* in Figure 6.1, since variations in the price of its "unique" product will now have some impact on the amount demanded by consumers.

Chamberlin emphasized that the degree of product differentiation can be influenced by actions of the firm; the uniqueness of its "product" can be increased through "advertising." Diagrammatically, this means that the producer will be able to move the demand curve for his "product" to the right (say to *d'd'*) by incurring "selling costs."[18] Firms can now increase their market power through advertising outlays which make consumers prefer their products to other products; the firm is no longer simply a "price taker."

In the neoclassical model, the given price to the firm and the entry or exit of firms from the industry maintained a pressure which kept each firm producing at its most efficient level of production. All "excess profits" were removed.[19] With demand to the firm downward sloping, the firm will be induced to maximize profits by producing at point *A* in Figure 6.2.[20] According to Chamberlin, this situation must be temporary, since

> the extra profit will . . . attract new competitors into the field, with a resulting shift in the demand curve, for the "product" of each seller (*DD* in Figure 6.2) will be moved to the left, since the total purchases must now be distributed among a larger number of sellers. . . . With each shift in the demand curve will come a price readjustment, . . . the process continuing until the demand curve for each "product" is tangent to its cost curve, and the area of surplus profit is wiped out.[21]

---

[17] Chamberlin, *Theory of Monopolistic Competition*, p. 57.

[18] Chamberlin uses "selling costs" and "advertising" interchangeably. He defined selling costs as those actions which try to "alter the position or shape of the demand curve for a product." Chamberlin, *Theory of Monopolistic Competition*, p. 117.

[19] See the discussion in Chapter 2.

[20] Point *A* is where the difference between average revenue (price) and average cost is greatest. This is equivalent to saying that at *A*, marginal revenue equals marginal cost. However, Chamberlin did not employ the terminology of marginal cost and revenue, preferring to work with average quantities.

[21] Chamberlin, *Theory of Monopolistic Competition*, pp. 83-84.

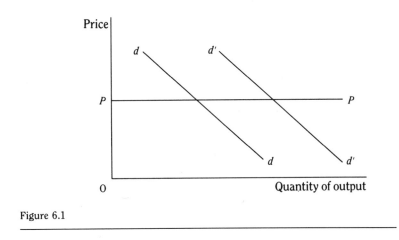

Figure 6.1

In other words, the demand *to the firm* is reduced by the entry of new firms. The firm's dream of monopoly profits is thus thwarted. Once the rate of profit is reduced back to zero (that is, a normal return), we have the situation of *dd* in Figure 6.2, with the firm now producing at *B*.[22] At *B*, all profits have disappeared. However, each firm produces less than a purely competitive firm would, for the competitive equilibrium would be at *C*—where average cost is lowest. Note the paradox; the firm at point *B* has no profits, just as if it were in a purely competitive industry. Yet the price and output are those we would expect from a monopolist. Thus Chamberlin's conclusion: monopolistic competition gives us the disadvantages of monopoly (higher price with reduced output) without giving the firm any profits. The result is the creation of excess capacity on the part of each firm. Price is no longer equated to marginal cost,[23] and the balance between the alternative costs and consumers' desires is upset. Nor is there any pressure for change, since any seller will lose by either raising or lowering price. Profits are just "normal," so there is no incentive for either new entrepreneurs to enter the market, nor existing ones to leave.

The introduction of selling cost further complicated the analysis. With free entry into the "group," excess profits cannot persist. If a firm succeeds, through advertising, in shifting its demand curve to the right, it may increase its share of the market. It will be induced to expand output, but its costs—from advertising—will increase. Although the final equilibrium is unclear, Chamberlin concluded that

---

[22] The demand curve must ultimately cease to move at *dd*, since further movements to the left would entail losses to the firms, encouraging exit from the industry. Chamberlin illustrates the relation of the firm and industry demand curves by showing a "path" which the firm demand will follow as it feels the effects of entry and exit. This is omitted from Figure 6.2 for simplicity.

[23] This must be so since the marginal cost at *B* is below the average cost. With the demand curve no longer horizontal, the "marginal revenue" will always be less than price. The firm equates marginal revenue to marginal cost, and both marginal revenue and marginal cost are less than price under monopolistic conditions. See the discussion in Chapter 2.

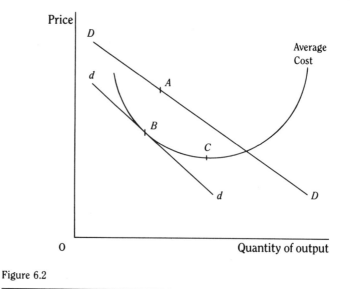

Figure 6.2

. . . it seems likely that advertising diminishes the discrepancy
between actual and most efficient scale of production. But total costs
and prices are higher. Selling costs per unit are greater than the
decrease in production costs. The resources expended to achieve this
result are therefore greater than those saved by achieving it. And, of
course, the balance of excess capacity remains.[24]

That is, the firm will move back towards (*C*) as the *dd* curve shifts to the
right, but the cost curve will shift up due to the introduction of selling
costs. In Chamberlin's view, this upward movement in costs would
offset any gains in efficiency realized by moving towards the competitive level of production.

A major appeal of the neoclassical theory of the firm was its simplicity
and its implications with regard to efficiency of production. Chamberlin's exposition in *The Theory of Monopolistic Competition* implied
that with only a slight change in assumptions—in the direction of
greater realism—the competitive solution was no longer ideal. In the
"small group" solution (oligopoly), the distortion is greater still. Here
Chamberlin concluded that the results depend on the assumptions one
makes with regard to firms' reactions in the face of interdependence; a
"general solution" does not exist. A major pillar of the neoclassical
theory was thus seriously undermined by Chamberlin's assertions.
Veblen insisted that advertising would stimulate conspicuous consumption and undermine the rationality of the consumer. This implied
that—in Veblen's terms—there is "waste." Chamberlin's point is that
even if the consumer acts rationally to adjust his expenditures accord-

---

[24] Chamberlin, *Theory of Monopolistic Competition*, p. 172.

ing to preferences for various "products," advertising leads to the development of excess capacity in the system. Chamberlin's emphasis on the analysis of the firm's demand curve removed the problems surrounding "increasing returns" and competitive industries, since the limit to the size of the firm is set by profit maximizing entrepreneurs facing a downward sloping demand curve; but, at the same time, his work challenged the relevance of the competitive model.

The Impact of Monopolistic Competition

We have concentrated our discussion on Chamberlin's analysis of monopolistic competition. One cannot adequately assess Chamberlin's contribution without some reference to Robinson's *Economics of Imperfect Competition*. There is little doubt that the two writers intended to approach the same general question: imperfect market systems.[25] Yet it is equally clear that they approached the issue from rather different viewpoints and with rather different objectives.

Chamberlin's analysis contains two major aspects which are either lacking or treated differently by Robinson: product differentiation, and his analysis of the equilibrium of the individual firm. While Robinson employed differences among products to define industries, she did not recognize product differentiation between firms *within an industry*. In this respect, she followed the neoclassical framework; the product was not a "variable" to be manipulated by the firm. Her analysis rested in large part on the Marshallian analysis of monopoly, elaborating the refinements introduced by the "increasing returns" debate of the 1920's.

In modifying the Marshallian monopoly analysis, Robinson merely redefined the Marshallian demand curve to account for the interdependence between firms.[26] She then developed a geometric presentation of the situation in which the additional cost of each unit was just balanced by the additional revenue. Robinson's "kit of analytical tools" is an excellent expository device for the general case of industry analysis. It reflects the fact that she was interested in a much broader range of investigation than Chamberlin. She viewed the world as being essentially a group of monopolists, and one of her objectives was to measure the distortion on the distribution of income generated by this power. This is a question which Chamberlin carefully avoided.[27] Her

---

[25] Furthermore, they defined the "imperfections" in quite similar terms. See the comparison of the two "problems" posed by the writers given in Triffin, *Monopolistic Competition and General Equilibrium Theory*, pp. 37-42. Triffin is still one of the best references on the subject of monopolistic competition. An excellent—and concise—exposition of the theories is provided in George Malanos, *Intermediate Economic Theory* (Philadelphia: J. B. Lippincott, 1962), pp. 501-27.

[26] This is not quite the same treatment that Chamberlin (and Stackelberg) gave to the question of interdependence. Chamberlin thought the firm would know the results of the interaction. Robinson deals with an industry where the analytical tool of a demand curve accounts for whatever result interdependence creates.

[27] See, for example, his comments with regard to "exploitation" in "Mrs. Robinson's Recent Visit to Monopolistic Competition," in idem, *Towards a More General Theory of Value*, pp. 307-12.

interest in "exploitation" led Robinson to formulate her model in far more general terms; for example, she was able to extend her reasoning to the market for factors as well as for goods and services.

On the other hand, Robinson almost completely ignored the question of the firm equilibrium in a situation of "oligopoly," or few sellers. As she herself pointed out, it was not to her purpose.[28] Her concern was with the industry, and she characterized the firm's demand curve as being a proportional fraction of the industry demand. Chamberlin was concerned with the equilibrium of the firm in oligopoly, but concluded it was not determinate. The real innovator in this area was Stackelberg, who developed the notion of rival strategies by firms in an imperfect market. However, the reactions of the firms—more than the final position of equilibrium—received the largest attention in his model.[29]

Chamberlin's discussion of the roles of advertising and product differentiation represents a major breakthrough in adjusting economic theory to the realities of the "business world," which was unanticipated by the other innovators of imperfect competition. And therein lies his unique contribution, for the discussion of selling costs and market power of advertising led to the development of a new attack on the concept of consumer sovereignty. Chamberlin himself was primarily interested in explaining the firm's attempt to monopolize the market where it had at least some influence over price. One result of this effect was the presence of "excess capacity"; the firm in monopolistic competition would not produce at the efficient level as would the competitive firm.

But Chamberlin did not view this as a wholly undesirable result; the higher prices brought about through selling costs reflect the buyers' desire for increased variety of products. This, he points out, is the basis for the curve *dd* as opposed to the curve *PP* in Figure 6.1: the difference in products is worth something to the consumer. He viewed the monopolistic competition solution, therefore as "a sort of ideal," not a reflection of misallocation.[30]

The *Theory of Monopolistic Competition* also provided fuel to those who viewed the success of advertising in influencing consumer wants as undermining the competitive system. If the firm could in fact manipulate demand, then the ability of the consumer to choose rationally between alternatives in the market would be impaired. Such arguments went well beyond the scope of Chamberlin's inquiry, following much more in the vein of Veblen. Nor is it clear that the proposals of men such as Alvin Hansen and John Kenneth Galbraith met with

---

[28] Robinson, *The Economics of Imperfect Competition*, p. 21.

[29] A more complete discussion of Stackelberg's model is included in the exposition by Malanos, *Intermediate Economic Theory*, pp. 517-27.

[30] On this point, see J. M. Cassels, "Excess Capacity and Monopolistic Competition," reprinted in William Breit and Harold M. Hochman, *Readings in Microeconomics* (New York: Holt, Rinehart, and Winston, 1968), pp. 256-66. Originally printed in *Quarterly Journal of Economics* 51 (May 1937): 426-43. For a more recent recognition of this point, see Donald Dewey, *The Theory of Imperfect Competition* (New York: Columbia University Press, 1969), p. 18.

Chamberlin's approval. His attack on the Marshallian theory of value perhaps succeeded too well. Chamberlin himself was a man of massively conservative tendencies; some of his later writings on labor could very nearly be termed reactionary. It is perhaps ironic that his most bitter detractors in the profession were those embracing the philosophy of classical liberalism.

In 1965, E. H. Chamberlin was elected Distinguished Fellow of the American Economic Association. The citation accompanying the award sums up his position in economic thought.

> It is not given to many scientists to reach into the minds of all their fellows and to influence the work of a whole generation, but the author of *Theory of Monopolistic Competition* did so.

7

JOHN MAYNARD KEYNES

UNEMPLOYMENT IN
EQUILIBRIUM

Keynes's intellect was the sharpest and clearest that I have ever known. When I argued with him, I felt that I took my life in my hands, and I seldom emerged without feeling something of a fool.

Bertrand Russell

John Maynard Keynes is the most redoubtable name in contemporary economic thought, for the upheaval in economic theory in the 1930's is usually associated with him. The appearance of his *General Theory of Employment Interest and Money* in 1936[1] marked an even sharper turning point in the development of economic thought than did the appearance of the marginal analysis of Menger and Jevons sixty-five years earlier. Keynes was a highly respected economist when he wrote the *General Theory*, and he minced no words in stating the objective of his work.

> ... The postulates of classical theory are applicable to a special case only and not to the general case, the situation which it assumes being a limiting point of the possible positions of equilibrium. Moreover, the characteristics of the special case assumed by the classical theory happen not to be those of the economic society in which we actually live, with the result that its teaching is misleading and disastrous if we attempt to apply it to the facts of experience.[2]

---

[1] John Maynard Keynes, *The General Theory of Employment Interest and Money* (New York: Harcourt, Brace and World, 1936).

[2] J. M. Keynes, *General Theory*, p. 3. We noted earlier that Keynes referred to the accepted doctrine of the period as the "classical" rather than "neoclassical" body of thought.

Few economists at the time had a stronger background from which to attack neoclassical theory than did Keynes.[3] Born in 1883, he was the son of a well-known economist, John Neville Keynes.[4] Young Keynes was educated at Eton and later Cambridge, where he received a good deal of individual instruction from both Marshall and Pigou.[5] Although Keynes's first interest was not economics, Marshall saw sufficient promise in his student to write J. N. Keynes: "Your son is doing excellent work in Economics. I have told him that I should be greatly delighted if he should decide on the career of a professional economist."[6] Keynes himself obviously thought he had learned a great deal; when he did not receive top score on a civil service exam, he remarked: "I evidently knew more about Economics than my examiners."[7]

His father's eminence as an economist notwithstanding, Keynes came into economics rather gradually; his early interests were in probability analysis and mathematics. Throughout his life, Keynes's career encompassed an extraordinary range of activities in and out of the academic life. His initial position just out of Cambridge was with the India Office for two years. Prompted by Marshall's support, he returned to Cambridge where he was finally appointed lecturer in economics in 1908. His interests remained largely outside economics; his first work in economics appeared in 1909.[8] In 1913, Keynes was appointed to the Indian Currency Commission, a post which led him into the Treasury, and eventually in 1919, to the peace conference at Versailles as the representative of the Treasury. Disgusted with the terms of the treaty, Keynes dramatically resigned his position in September 1919, and two months later published his *Economic Consequences of the Peace*.[9] The book strongly protested the imposition of large reparations on Germany and insisted that the terms of the Versailles Treaty could never be enforced. It received wide circulation and

---

[3] Most of the information in this section is taken from R. F. Harrod, *The Life of John Maynard Keynes*, 2nd ed. (New York: Harcourt, Brace and World, 1952), which is the most authoritative account of Keynes's life. Harrod was quite close to Keynes, and his biography is extremely partial to its subject. Modern readers, wishing to profit from the perspective of twenty years since Harrod's work might prefer Robert Lekachman, *The Age of Keynes* (New York: Random House, 1966). His emphasis on policy makes Lekachman's work an excellent source for the layman; however, the author is generally partial to Keynes in his treatment of the material.

[4] John Neville Keynes taught at Cambridge for many years and was a close associate of Alfred Marshall. His *Scope and Method of Political Economy* (London: Macmillan & Co. 1891) remains as an excellent statement of the domain of the professional economist today.

[5] Pigou had just received a chair at Cambridge. It is interesting to note that two of the men who launched penetrating attacks on the neoclassical system were trained and highly regarded by the most eminent of all neoclassicists, Alfred Marshall.

[6] Harrod, p. 107.

[7] Harrod, p. 121. Harrod argues that Keynes was probably correct. After all, there were very few examiners who ". . . were capable of understanding such by-play with Marshall." In the opinion of his biographer, Keynes was one of the few.

[8] The work in probability was published in 1920 as: John Maynard Keynes, *A Treatise on Probability* (Cambridge: Cambridge University Press, 1920). The economics article was published as: John Maynard Keynes, "Recent Economic Events in India," *Economic Journal* (March 1909), pp. 51-67.

[9] John Maynard Keynes, *The Economic Consequences of the Peace* (New York: Harcourt, Brace and World, 1920).

catapulted Keynes into the public spotlight, although making him quite unpopular with the government. Fortunately, he was offered the editorship of the *Economic Journal* that year—in large part due to support from Marshall. From that point on, Keynes was seldom quiet; by 1936, when the *General Theory* appeared, he was a leading authority on economic theory and policy.

In addition to his academic and government experience, Keynes was a successful financier. His activities as a speculator in the commodity, currency, and stock markets resulted in an estate of $2 million at the time of his death in 1946. As bursar of King's College, he was able to considerably enlarge the endowment.[10] He was a patron of the arts; his wife, Lydia Lopokova, was a ballerina, and at one point he financed a theater group. Nor did he confine his intellectual activities to economics. Keynes frequently engaged in discussion with the "Bloomsbury set," a collection of intellectuals in London, including such people as Lytton Strachey, Duncan Grant, Clive Bell, E. M. Forster, and Virginia Woolf. It was his contact with individuals of this caliber (some of whom he knew as a student at Cambridge) that helped shape the broad intellectual background of Keynes.

Harry Johnson, who had the experience of seeing John Maynard Keynes perform before the Political Economy Club at Cambridge, has described him in action.

> Keynes was a brilliant phenomenon: he was a sparkling man and a great experience for me. . . . Keynes sat there in an arm-chair with his legs slumped out in front of him—and he had very long legs; he was in some ways, physically, a slightly miniaturized John Kenneth Galbraith. He had some notes on the table beside him, but he never seemed to look at them. He gave us a very elegant talk, beautifully constructed, every sentence a piece of good English prose and every paragraph cadenced—just a wonderful performance. But it was in the discussion afterwards that I learned so much from him. . . . One of the secrets of his charm was that he would go out of his way to make something flattering out of what a student had said. If the student had made an absolute ass of himself, Keynes would still find something in it which he would transform into a good point. It might well be the very opposite of what the student had said; but the student was so relieved to find that he was not being cut to pieces that he was really impressed by the brilliance of what he was told he *had* said. On the other hand, when a faculty member got up . . . Keynes simply cut their heads off. No matter how ingenious what they said was, he would make nonsense of it."[11]

---

[10] Harrod relates that in 1920 Keynes was near bankruptcy; by 1946, his estate was valued at about £450,000 ($2.25 million). (Harrod, p. 297.) He enlarged the "free funds" of the college from about £30,000 ($150,000) to £380,000 (about $1.8 million). (Harrod, pp. 297, 388.)

[11] Harry G. Johnson, "Cambridge in the 1950s," in Elizabeth S. Johnson and Harry G. Johnson, *The Shadow of Keynes* (Chicago: The University of Chicago Press, 1978), pp. 132-133. This is an excellent book which attempts to relate Keynes to the Cambridge society in which he lived. Another useful source on Keynes, which gives a good sense of the range of Keynes's activities, was compiled by his nephew. See Milo Keynes, *Essays on John Maynard Keynes* (Cambridge: Cam-

Keynes and the Neoclassicists

Keynes was forever advocating policies which ran counter to the "usual" interpretation of monetary thinking; yet, in a real sense he retained much of the outlook of the neoclassical (indeed, the classical) writers. He attacked the laissez-faire policies of the earlier economists but was certainly not an advocate of government intervention. Keynes lacked the faith of his predecessors in the rationality of economic man, but he retained a strong belief in individualism, and there is not in his writings an attack on the neoclassical theory of individual choice. To the extent that the new economics of recent times has a strongly interventionist trend, it did not come directly from Keynes. Although the following remarks of the *General Theory* have been quoted frequently they are often ignored when the implications of "Keynesian" theory are brought up.

> But, above all, individualism, if it can be purged of its defects and its abuses, is the best safeguard of personal liberty in the sense that, compared with any other system, it greatly widens the field for the exercise of personal choice. It is also the best safeguard of the variety of life, which emerges precisely from this extended field of personal choice, and the loss of which is the greatest of all losses of the homogeneous or totalitarian state.[12]

With regard to his own argument for government intervention, Keynes goes on to point out that

> Whilst, therefore, the enlargement of the functions of government, involved in the task of adjusting to one another the propensity to consume and the inducement to invest, would seem . . . to be a terrific encroachment on individualism, I defend it, on the contrary, both as the only practicable means of avoiding the destruction of the existing economic forms in their entirety and as the condition of the successful functioning of individual initiative.[13]

It has been pointed out that the classical economists were interested in the shaping of "better men" through the economic process.[14] Keynes appeared to be concerned that this element was lacking in the society of the mid-twentieth century. In a letter to one of the leading adherents of classical liberalism, F. A. Hayek (commenting on the latter's *Road to Serfdom*), Keynes writes:

> What we need, therefore, in my opinion, is not a change in our economic programmes, which would only lead in practice to disillu-

---

bridge University Press, 1975). It has been reported that Keynes, by a familiar caprice of nature, was capable of emotional interest in men. His amorous activities in this regard are evidenced by his letters to Duncan Grant and Lytton Strachey. See Michael Holroyd, ed., *Lytton Strachey: A Critical Biography*, 2 vols. (New York: Holt, Rinehart, and Winston, 1968).

[12] J. M. Keynes, *General Theory*, p. 380.

[13] J. M. Keynes, *General Theory*, p. 380.

[14] See the comment by George Stigler, *Five Lectures on Economic Problems* (London: Longmans, Green & Co., 1949), p. 4.

sion with the results of your philosophy; . . . No, what we need is the
restoration of right moral thinking—a return to proper moral values
in our social philosophy. . . . Dangerous acts can be done safely in a
community which thinks and feels rightly, which would be the way to
hell if they were executed by those who think and feel wrongly.[15]

Clearly, then, Keynes does not appear to be a man antagonistic to the
free enterprise system. He was a professional economist, rigorously
trained in the neoclassical tradition, with broad experience in the
applications of that theory to practical policy. Gradually, in the context
of the problems facing Britain after World War I, he became convinced
that the policy recommendations of the old orthodoxy suffered from
serious shortcomings, and this dissatisfaction culminated in the
appearance of the *General Theory*. We need not consider the gradual
evolution of Keynes's ideas; what is important is that they represented a
direct attack on existing economic doctrine by a man already recognized as an eminent economist.[16]

We have already commented on the fact that neoclassical employment theory was largely implicit and not carefully spelled out. This
difficulty bothered Keynes when he approached the question of unemployment. The acceptance of Say's Law was so universal that Keynes
complained that "the fundamental theory underlying it has been
deemed so simple and obvious that it has received, at the most, a bare
mention."[17]

The Classical Model

Keynes called his book *The General Theory of Employment Interest
and Money*, because he felt that he had developed a truly general theory
in the sense that he could explain all levels of employment, as opposed
to the neoclassical theory which concerned itself only with the special
case of full employment. As we have seen, the classical conclusion that
the equilibrium level of employment was full employment rested mainly upon Say's Law of Markets. The cure for unemployment, in the view
of the neoclassical model (which Keynes outlined for purposes of
exposition) was to allow real wages to fall until all workers willing and
able to work would be hired. It is the relationship between the money
wage and the price level that defines the real wage, and it is the real
wage that entrepreneurs look to in deciding the amount of employment
they will offer. The possibility that inadequate demand could be the
cause of unemployment was brushed aside. For if individuals decide to
consume less of their income, they will by definition, be saving more.

---

[15] Quoted in Harrod, pp. 436-37. Friedrich A. Hayek's *The Road to Serfdom* (Chicago: University of
Chicago Press, 1944) is, by wide agreement, one of the most lucid and articulate statements of the
case against state intervention.

[16] The roots of the *General Theory* can be seen in Keynes's earlier works, particularly his *Treatise on
Money*, 2 vols. (London: Macmillan & Co., 1930). For a concise summary of the development of
Keynes's thought up to the *General Theory*, see Lekachman, Chapter 3.

[17] J. M. Keynes, *General Theory*, pp. 4-5.

The fall in consumption expenditure would mean falling profits, wages, and prices, in consumption goods industries. But the increased saving would mean a lower rate of interest and hence a greater amount of investment demanded in capital goods industries. The workers unemployed temporarily in the consumption sector would eventually be reabsorbed in the investment sector. As long as wages, prices, and interest rates are flexible and resources are mobile, then inadequate demand could not be a problem.

If looked at from the point of view of the labor market, the neoclassical model indicates that persistent unemployment could only be a result of some barrier to the fall in the money wage and, given the level of prices, some fall in the real wage. For the fact of unemployment must mean that, at the given real wage, the demand for labor is less than the amount supplied. If workers would take a cut in their money wage, this would mean a cut in their real wage. (The price level would remain constant because the quantity theory of money indicates that the price level is a function of the quantity of money alone, and not the level of money wages.) But the demand for labor and the supply of labor in the neoclassical framework are both functions of the real wage. When the real wage falls, the quantity of labor demanded increases, while the quantity of labor supplied declines. Eventually, full employment would be reached, where the quantity of labor demanded and the quantity of labor supplied were equal. Hence, any unemployment must be a result of some barrier to the fall in the real wage, namely, the refusal of workers to accept cuts in their real wage. This being the case, such unemployment was interpreted as being *voluntary unemployment*. Workers simply refused the proffer of employment at a lower real wage. All other unemployment was interpreted as *frictional*; in a complex economy, the number of jobs looking for workers and workers looking for jobs cannot always be instantaneously adjusted to each other. There are frictions or inadequate information, so that at any given time unemployment from this cause would be expected.

But Keynes introduced a new category of unemployment: *involuntary unemployment*. To Keynes, the neoclassical theory of employment was inadequate to explain this category, although it is most significant during a major depression. In order to explain the existence of involuntary unemployment, Keynes required a new theory.

The General Theory

The question that Keynes attempted to answer was: what determines the level of employment and national income at any given time? His answer was: it depends upon the volume of effective demand. Unemployment is a direct result of inadequate effective demand. A theory of effective demand stems from the realization that there are two kinds of people in our economy who do two kinds of things. One group, the workers in already existing factories and shops, produces consumer goods and services; the other group, consisting of workers employed in building new factories and machines, produces investment goods and services. The amount of employment in existing plants depends upon consumer demand, which, in turn, depends upon the disposable income or purchasing power people have. But the demand for investment goods is largely autonomous, in the sense that it is independent of purchasing power or income.

The kernel of Keynes's theory of effective demand rests on his notion of the consumption function. That is, as income increases and consumption rises, the latter increases less than does the former. Thus, the volume of investment must be constantly increased to maintain the full employment level of income. Since Keynes believed that consumption patterns are largely fixed, the level of employment, given the consumption function, depends upon investment. But the decision to invest is made independently of the decision to save. The decision to save is made by everybody together deciding how much to consume or not consume in, say, the next year. So all consumers taken together plan to save a certain amount of their income. In the meantime, businessmen are planning to invest so much for the next year. Now it would be the greatest coincidence if the amount that consumers had planned to save was precisely equal to the amount that businessmen planned to invest. And it is precisely the divergencies between these two magnitudes that ultimately determine the volume of employment.

Let us assume that the amount that businessmen plan to invest is greater than the amount that consumers plan to save. In bringing these plans to fruition, the businessmen would find, for example, that their inventories are below the desired level. They would then invest more in inventories generating an increased flow of income and employment. But as income rose in response to the high levels of consumption and investment (since one man's expenditure is another man's income), saving, which to Keynes is a function of income, would rise. And it would continue to rise until it was precisely equal to investment. At this point, anticipated saving and investment would be equal.[18] But note that it is the change in the level of income that brought the two flows into equality.

What happens if the amount that consumers plan to save is greater than the amount that businessmen plan to invest? In that case, since one man's decision not to spend means someone else getting less income, total income in the economy would decline. As inventories accumulate, businessmen cut back their investment, and workers are

---

[18] It is one of Keynes's points that *actual* saving and investment are always equal. But this is purely definitional since income is defined as being equal to consumption expenditures plus investment expenditures. And since saving is defined as the difference between income and consumption, saving equals investment. That is

$$Y = C + I$$
$$\text{since} \quad S = Y - C$$
$$\text{and} \quad I = Y - C$$
$$\text{therefore} \quad S = I$$

Unfortunately, the distinction between anticipated and actual saving and investment was not fully understood by many readers of the *General Theory*. See the discussion in Chapter 8, *infra*.

laid off. Income falls, saving falls, and eventually saving and investment will be equal again at the new lower level of income. This new lower level of income with involuntary unemployment would be an equilibrium level, since there are no forces at work to restore full employment.

But what about competition in the labor market? Would the unemployed workers take cuts in wages that would restore full employment, as the neoclassical model assumed? Not so, says Keynes. For the neoclassical model is correct only as regards the demand curve for labor, but is incorrect regarding the supply curve. That is, Keynes accepted the proposition that the demand for labor is a function of the real wage, and that in equilibrium the real wage is equal to the marginal productivity of labor, as John Bates Clark and Alfred Marshall had maintained. But the trouble was with the neoclassical postulate regarding the supply function of labor. To the neoclassical economists, the supply of labor was a function of the real wage rate. But to Keynes, workers bargain for and react to changes in money wages because they have no control over the real wage. Keynes assumed that the labor supply function has a flat portion at the established money wage rate, implying that workers refuse to take money wage cuts either because of class consciousness, or what is often referred to as the "money illusion." Thus, there can exist an unemployment in the labor market. Figure 7.1 depicts such a situation.

With a money wage of W_0 and the demand for labor (determined by the value of the marginal product) VMP_1, unemployment exists in the amount AB. To the neoclassical economists, the situation is one of disequilibrium, since the money wage would be cut to W_1, leading to full employment at N_1. To the neoclassical economist, this was true, since the money wage cut (given the price level) would mean a fall in the real wage rate and, therefore, an increase in the quantity of labor demanded and a reduction in the quantity supplied. But Keynes argued that the classical economists are incorrect even within the framework of their own models. Since money wages constitute a large proportion of marginal cost, a cut in the money wage would mean a fall in marginal costs. Since, under conditions of competition, entrepreneurs price at marginal cost, price would fall almost as much as wages. Thus, the fall in the money wage would mean a fall in the real wage, with little or no change in the volume of employment.[19] In terms of our diagram, this

---

[19] J. M. Keynes, *General Theory*, p. 12. It appears that Keynes was of two minds in this matter. By Chapter 19 of the *General Theory*, he admitted that variations in money wages might affect real wages through what has come to be called the "Keynes Effect." Because a fall in wages will be accompanied by a fall in prices, the stock of money in "real" terms increases. Assuming the nominal amount of money is constant, this lowers the rate of interest and increases investment, thereby increasing employment and income. Notwithstanding this fact, Keynes rejected the manipulation of money wage rates as a policy for increasing employment. For one thing, in capitalistic economies there is no method available to bring about a universal reduction of the money wage rate. Employers must have sufficient bargaining power to push it downward, which they may not have. What is more, even if employers had such power, wages might be reduced in one industry before another, causing great labor unrest and dissatisfaction. Also, falling prices would have adverse effects on debtors. Keynes therefore felt that manipulation of the quantity of money would be a much sounder policy to follow in the event of unemployment. J. M. Keynes, *General Theory*, pp. 257-71.

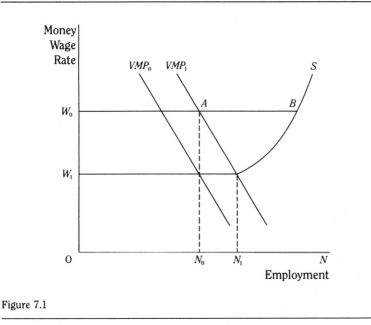

Figure 7.1

would be depicted as a fall in the value of the marginal product as prices fell, that is, a shift to the left of the VMP_1 curve to VMP_0. The volume of employment thus remains at N_0.

Thus, workers have no expedient whereby they can influence the real wage. A cut in the money wage, even within the context of the neoclassical model, means no fall in the real wage. So workers are helpless to affect the amount of employment simply by taking wage cuts. These workers are therefore involuntarily unemployed. For if the offer of employment at wage rate W_0 were made, even though it would mean a lower real wage, workers would be forthcoming, in the amount AB. In the diagram, AB is the amount of involuntary unemployment.

Keynes, in the light of his own theory of employment, would explain the sequence of events resulting from wage cuts differently. His argument was that a cut in the money wage rate would involve a fall in income and therefore in aggregate demand in money terms.[20] This would also be represented by a shift to the left of aggregate demand curve for labor, VMP_1. The lower money wage might therefore be associated with the same volume of employment as before, with unemployment in the amount $N_0 N_1$.

Keynes's Policy Prescriptions

The essence of the Keynesian policy proposals following from this analysis is that instead of waiting for the real wage to fall, monetary and

---

[20] Axel Leijonhufvud, *On Keynesian Economics and the Economics of Keynes* (New York: Oxford University Press, 1968), p. 98.

fiscal policy should be employed to increase aggregate demand. This would imply a movement to the right of the VMP_1, until it cut the labor supply function at B. Keynes pointed out that there are a number of ways open to increase aggregate demand. First, there is the possibility of increasing the nominal amount of money. As the money supply increases, interest rates would fall, investment would increase, and income would rise. The VMP_1 curve would move to the right as the price level rose, and the real wage would fall. At B, full employment would be reached. Thus in Keynes's system, "demand determines employment, and employment determines the marginal product (that is, the real wage), not the other way around."[21]

But Keynes admitted the possibility that monetary policy might not be effective in doing the job of bringing about full employment. It is here that he introduced one of his most interesting and original conceptions: the notion of liquidity preference. To Keynes, the quantity theory of money was incorrect in postulating that velocity would be constant in the face of changes in the quantity of money. For with an increase in the supply of money, the quantity of money supplied would be greater than the quantity demanded for speculative purposes at the given interest rate. This would mean that people would buy securities, thereby pushing the rate of interest down and the price of securities up. But as the rate of interest falls, there are increasing numbers of people at the margin who expect it to rise again. Hence, the quantity of money demanded will increase. It is this process that makes the community willing to hold the larger stock of money at lower interest rates. But the increase in the amount of money demanded means that velocity moves in the opposite direction from increases in the quantity of money. Keynes thus denied the simple relationship between increases in the stock of money and increases in the price level, with velocity constant, that the neoclassical model postulated.

Figure 7.2 illustrates Keynes's liquidity preference curve. It shows the quantity of money demanded at various rates of interest. As the interest rate rises from, say, r_3 to r_4, the quantity of money demanded for speculative purposes declines, since increasing numbers of speculators have come to believe that the interest rate will fall, and those who hold bonds will realize capital gains. So we can interpret a movement up the liquidity preference curve as a movement from money into bonds, and a movement down the curve as a movement from bonds into money. The actual rate of interest is determined by the demand for money for speculative balances, on one hand, and the stock of money (as supplied by the monetary authority) on the other.

It is at interest rate r_2 that monetary policy would become completely ineffective in curing a depression. For an increase in the money supply would not lower the rate of interest. The public would be willing to hold the increased money stock at r_2, since expectations are that the interest

---

[21] Alvin H. Hansen, *A Guide to Keynes* (New York: McGraw-Hill, 1953), pp. 21-22.

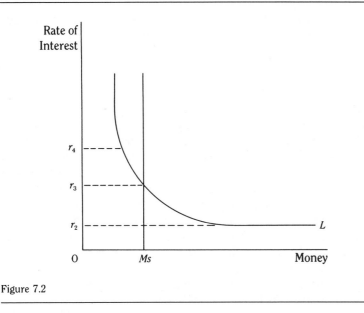

Figure 7.2

rate will rise in the future. Thus, no one is willing to hold bonds since they fear capital losses. Once this point is reached (and it should be clear that Keynes considered this situation a *very* special case occurring perhaps in the midst of a great depression), then the government must invest directly in various government projects to cure the unemployment. That is, since interest rates will not fall below this point, there is no way to get more investment from the private sector. Hence direct government investment was recommended. In such a situation, fiscal measures—government tax cutting and spending—rather than monetary measures were called for.[22]

This theory of the rate of interest is decidedly different from that of the neoclassical model. To the neoclassical economist, the rate of interest is not a monetary, but a real phenomenon. It is determined by the demand for capital (which is determined by the marginal productivity of capital) and the supply of saving (which is determined by the thrift of the community). So the rate of interest is a function of real forces: productivity and thrift. Keynes's objection to this theory is that it assumes that the volume of saving is only a function of the rate of interest and is independent of the level of income. To Keynes, saving is a function of income, and in order to determine the volume of saving, we must be able to determine the level of income. But that is precisely what

---

[22] It should be noted that Keynes also considered monetary policy ineffective in the event that private investment became highly unresponsive to changes in the rate of interest. Keynes believed that when expectations are such that businessmen have had a collapse of confidence in the economy, ". . . moderate changes in the prospective yield of capital-assets or in the rate of interest will not be associated with very great changes in the rate of investment." (J. M. Keynes, *General Theory*, p. 250.) Thus a liquidity trap is not an essential factor in making monetary policy ineffective. A highly inelastic investment demand schedule would have similar implications for policy, requiring direct government expenditures of a fiscal nature.

the neoclassical model is unable to do, since according to Keynes, that approach is only able to explain the full employment income, and not all levels of income.

The Multiplier

In working out the implications of government investment to increase the volume of employment, Keynes made effective use of a concept called the *multiplier*. Keynes borrowed this notion from his brilliant pupil, Richard Kahn.[23] It provided a tool which Keynes used to show that deficit financing could provide an increase in income, which was a multiple of the original injection of government spending. The tool itself can be derived from Keynes's concept of the *marginal propensity to consume*, that is, the change in consumption which is associated with a change in disposable income ($\Delta C/\Delta Y$). This analysis will perhaps be made clearer with an illustration.

Assume that individuals in an economy have decided to invest $100 billion. The people who receive this $100 billion will regard it as income. Assume that another $500 billion is being provided by the activities of the consumers in spending on consumption. For the economy as a whole, therefore, income is $600 billion, because we know that

$$Y = C + I \tag{7.1}$$

However, consumption is—according to Keynes's theory—a function of income. Let us assume that the marginal propensity to consume ($\Delta C/\Delta Y$) is $\frac{2}{3}$, then

$$C = a + \frac{2}{3}Y \tag{7.2}$$

but $C = 500$ when $Y = 600$

$$500 = a + \frac{2}{3}600$$
$$a = 500 - 400 \tag{7.3}$$
$$= 100$$

Thus the consumption function is

$$C = 100 + \frac{2}{3}Y \tag{7.4}$$

In equilibrium

$$Y = C + I \tag{7.5}$$

therefore

$$Y = 100 + \frac{2}{3}Y + I$$
$$Y - \frac{2}{3}Y = 100 + I \tag{7.6}$$
$$Y = \frac{1}{1 - \frac{2}{3}} (100 + I).$$

---

[23] Richard F. Kahn, "The Relation of Home Investment to Unemployment," *Economic Journal*, (June 1931), pp. 173-98.

If investment is increased by ΔI per period, this will increase the equilibrium income by ΔY

$$Y + \Delta Y = \frac{1}{1 - \frac{2}{3}} (100 + I + \Delta I)$$

$$Y + \Delta Y = \frac{1}{1 - \frac{2}{3}} (100 + I) + \frac{1}{1 - \frac{2}{3}} \Delta I \qquad (7.7)$$

$$\Delta Y = \frac{1}{1 - \frac{2}{3}} \Delta I$$

Thus, if the government decides to increase its investment by $10 billion per period, then income will increase by $10 billion multiplied by the multiplier $[1/(1 - \frac{2}{3})]$

$$\Delta Y = \frac{1}{1 - \frac{2}{3}} \ 10 \text{ billion}$$

$$= \frac{1}{\frac{1}{3}} \ 10 \text{ billion} \qquad (7.8)$$

$$= 30 \text{ billion}$$

Knowing the marginal propensity to consume ($\Delta C/\Delta Y$), we can derive the multiplier $\dfrac{1}{(1 - \Delta C/\Delta Y)}$; and knowing the multiplier, we can estimate the change in income that will result from any change in expenditure, whether it be consumption, private investment, or government. Note also that the multiplier can work in reverse. A decrease in expenditures of any kind will generate a magnified decrease in income, depending upon the marginal propensity to consume.

Later criticisms of the multiplier centered on the fact that its ultimate effect depends in part on how the government spends the extra money. It is possible that the government expenditure would merely replace what individuals were already spending, inducing them to add this amount to their savings. That is, government spending can divert private spending either into savings or into expenditures that are less attractive. Furthermore, the effect depends on where the money that the government spends comes from. As we shall see in future chapters, there might be considerable differences, depending on whether the government taxes, prints the money, or borrows from the public.

Keynes's Impact

Keynes's ideas gradually found their way into policy proposals of governments. By the end of the 1930's the New Deal was increasingly relying upon public works expenditures to cure unemployment. In 1946—a decade after the appearance of the *General Theory*—Congress passed the Full Employment Act, although it said nothing about using "Keynesian" methods to achieve the broad goals set forth in that legislation. Only gradually did government economists openly embrace the new economics. By 1964, however, the Keynesian forces had clearly triumphed when Congress passed a $14 billion tax cut.[24] With the government already running a substantial budget deficit, the main reason for the tax cut was to boost aggregate demand at a time when unemployment was felt to be excessively high. Furthermore, in arguing for the tax cut, government economists stressed the importance of fiscal policy.

The success with which Keynes was able to get his ideas accepted was in no small part due to the forcefulness with which he always stated his views. Keynes was never timid about saying what he believed, and he felt that what he said was important. As he was working on the *General Theory*, he wrote George Bernard Shaw in 1935:

> To understand *my* state of mind, however, you have to know that I believe myself to be writing a book on economic theory which will largely revolutionize—not, I suppose, at once, but in the course of the next ten years—the way the world thinks about economic problems. . . . I can't expect you or anyone else to believe this at the present stage. But for myself I don't merely hope what I say, in my own mind I'm quite sure.[25]

At the time, Shaw—and many others—were probably not convinced; fifty years later, it would appear as though Keynes may have been too pessimistic in his appraisal of the impact of his work.[26]

---

[24] Herbert Stein, *The Fiscal Revolution in America* (Chicago: University of Chicago Press, 1969), especially Chapters 15, 16, and 17.

[25] Harrod, p. 462.

[26] The complete written work of Keynes is being published for the Royal Economic Society in what will eventually amount to about thirty volumes under the general title *The Collected Writings of John Maynard Keynes* (London: Macmillan, 1971-).

Part Three

THE NEW
ECONOMICS

8

ALVIN H. HANSEN

THE AMERICAN KEYNES

> We have yet to pay proper respect to those who pioneered the
> Keynesian revolution. Everyone now takes pride in the resulting
> performance of the economy. We should take a little pride in the
> men who brought it about. . . . The debt to Alvin Hansen is especially
> great. Next only to Keynes, his is the credit for saving what even
> conservatives still call capitalism.
>
> *John Kenneth Galbraith*

The *General Theory of Employment Interest and Money* presented a
set of ideas which ultimately exerted a profound influence on the
direction of economic theory and policy. The effect, however, did not
come directly to the United States from Keynes. At the end of World
War II, much of what Keynes was arguing remained quite foreign to the
average student of economics on this side of the Atlantic. In England
his position at Cambridge and his preeminence in public life gave
Keynes access to a large and interested audience. At Cambridge he was
quickly able to attract a remarkable group of young economists—some
of them American—who defended, modified, and expanded the
theoretical constructs introduced in the *General Theory*. A substantial
number of young economists, many of them affiliated with the second
Roosevelt administration, were impressed by the force of Keynesian
arguments. However, the new economics had made scant headway into
the classrooms of American colleges.[1] In the absence of a leading

---

[1] The presence of "Keynesians" in the Roosevelt administration is not to say that the policies in that
period were, in fact, Keynesian. A letter from Keynes to President Roosevelt in February 1937, was
very cooly received by the American president. The speed with which the new economic policies
caught on in the late 1930's is discussed in Herbert Stein, *The Fiscal Revolution in America*
(Chicago: University of Chicago Press, 1969), and also in Robert Lekachman, *The Age of Keynes*
(New York: Random House, 1966). Also see the recollections of Alan Sweezy, one of Hansen's
students, "The Keynesians and Government Policy," *American Economic Review* 62 (May 1972).
Hansen's role in formulating economic policy is discussed by James Tobin, "Hansen and Public
Policy," *Quarterly Journal of Economics* 90 (February 1976): 32–37.

economist to champion the new ideas, the impact of these debates was confined to only a few places in the United States.

The delay was short-lived; by 1941, the Keynesian cause in the United States had found a champion, who had the academic stature to make himself heard throughout the profession. In that year, Professor Alvin Hansen of Harvard University published a book entitled *Fiscal Policy and Business Cycles*.[2] In this work Hansen not only supported Keynes's analysis of the macroeconomic problems of the 1930's but also presented a comprehensive scheme of *compensatory finance*, which insisted that the government should implement a continuous policy of stabilization regardless of the position of the revenues and taxes collected. Hansen's theory of compensatory finance was rooted directly in Keynes. Not content with simply presenting the theoretical arguments, Hansen went to some length to support the need for such a policy by presenting statistical evidence gathered from the preceding decade of economic performance in the United States.

Fiscal Policy and Business Cycles represented the culmination of several years of intensive research by Hansen on the problems of the 1930's. Portions of the book had appeared in professional journals, and a previous book entitled *Full Recovery or Stagnation?* had presented most of the elements that were combined into his later, more comprehensive book.[3] The style of *Fiscal Policy and Business Cycles* hardly matched Keynes's flamboyance or Veblen's biting wit. It was a straightforward, if somewhat pedantic, approach to an economic problem. As such, it hardly attracted the attention of the nonspecialist. But for the professional economist, the book was an important tract. Alvin Hansen was a leading American economist in 1941, a past president of the American Economic Association, and holder of the prestigious Littauer Chair in Political Economy at Harvard University. His comments reflected not only his own views but those of a growing group of economists (many of them products of Hansen's seminar at Harvard) who were attacking the pre-Keynesian explanations of the Depression. Hansen's presentation may have been dry, but it was also clear and concise. Henry Simons, an economist who was most certainly *not* one of Keynes's American admirers, noted the book's appearance with considerable misgiving.

> Now, from the ranks of older, distinguished economists, comes Professor Hansen to argue their Keynesian case and to espouse their cause. . . . His book is the academic apology par excellence for the inner new deal and all its works. It may well become the economic bible for that substantial company of intellectuals, following Keynes

---

[2] Alvin Hansen, *Fiscal Policy and Business Cycles* (New York: W.W. Norton, 1941).

[3] Alvin Hansen, *Full Recovery or Stagnation?* (New York: W.W. Norton, 1938). This book, which includes most of the important articles by Hansen during the years just prior to 1938, provides an excellent guide to his thinking at the time that Keynes's *General Theory* came out.

and recklessly collectivist, whose influence grows no less rapidly in academic circles than in Washington.[4]

Simons may have exaggerated the immediate impact of Hansen's book, but his appraisal that Hansen's espousal of the Keynesian cause was symptomatic of a general conversion by economists to the new orthodoxy was not so farfetched. The appearance of *Fiscal Policy and Business Cycles* is a convenient benchmark to denote an appreciable acceleration in the Keynesian movement.

When he arrived at Harvard in 1937, Hansen found an active group (at least among the students) favoring the new approach. The faculty, to be sure, was less enthusiastic. Commenting on Hansen's move from the University of Minnesota, his student Paul Samuelson observed:

> I have always hazarded the guess that Hansen received his call to Harvard by miscalculation. They did not know what they were getting. And neither did he. His 1936 review of the *General Theory* must have struck a Harvard committee as unfavorable; only Hansen remembered it as being among the most favorable reviews that Keynes received.[5]

Undaunted, Hansen pressed his inquiries into the causes of the Depression, and his contributions to the debates attracted a steady stream of first-rate graduate students to his seminar on fiscal policy. In the preface to *Fiscal Policy and Business Cycles*, he credits discussions in these seminars with providing an important stimulus towards developing his own ideas. Paul Samuelson wrote a mathematical appendix; other people who were to go on to prominence in the profession were also represented. "The great thing," Hansen later recalled, "was that we were all students trying to find our way about."[6] By the end of the thirties, there were two Cambridges advocating revolution in economic thought.

Alvin Hansen was at the very center of the American Cambridge, and he remained there for over a quarter of a century. In the formative years of the Keynesian attack, he published numerous books and articles promulgating the new economics.[7] His writing was supplemented by personal appearances whenever possible. Invited to testify before the

---

4 Henry Simons, "Hansen on Fiscal Policy," *Journal of Political Economy* 50 (April 1942): 162. We will return to Simons and his dispute with Hansen's policy recommendations in Chapter 13.

5 Paul A. Samuelson, "Hansen as a Creative Economic Theorist," *Quarterly Journal of Economics* 90 (February 1976): 29.

6 Walter Salant, "The Fiscal Policy Seminar," *Quarterly Journal of Economics* 90 (February 1976): 22. Among the economists contributing to the introduction to *Fiscal Policy and Business Cycles* were James Tobin, Paul Sweezy, and John Dunlop, each of whom credits Hansen with being a truly outstanding teacher.

7 Hansen ranks three of his books written in this era as his most important works: *Monetary Theory and Fiscal Policy* (New York: McGraw-Hill, 1949); *Business Cycles and National Income* (New York: W.W. Norton, 1951); and *A Guide to Keynes* (New York: McGraw-Hill, 1953). All of the books deal with Hansen's attempts to clarify and expand the framework of analysis sketched by Keynes.

Temporary National Economic Committee in May 1939, Hansen "used this occasion to expound the Keynesian analysis of the Great Depression from which we were still suffering."[8] The hearings resulted in public debate over the issues raised by Hansen, an outcome he obviously relished. And, of course, through it all, he continued to instill in students an eagerness to explore the implications of the new theory. He was assisted in this by a set of vigorous debates with a colleague at Harvard, John H. Williams. Williams and Hansen together taught the seminar on fiscal policy in the Graduate School of Public Administration at Harvard in the late thirties. As they debated the merits of the emerging ideas in economic theory, they profoundly shaped the thinking of a generation of students at Harvard and elsewhere.[9] There can be little doubt that Hansen had a major role in bringing the Keynesian revolution in the United States to maturity, or at least to adolescence. By the time he retired from Harvard (but not from the public scene), he had earned the title "the American Keynes."[10] When he died in June 1975 at age eighty-seven, the *New York Times* noted:

> Keynesian thinking attracted only a handful of adherents at first, but, starting in 1937 when Mr. Hansen joined the Harvard faculty, its influence spread largely as a result of his tireless exertions. He won fame (and notoriety) for his stubborn promotion of what was then considered a noxious heresy.[11]

In several ways it is ironic that Alvin Hansen should be credited with fomenting a major revolution in economic thinking, particularly a revolution which has come to be associated with a dramatic increase in the extent of government intervention in the economy. Hansen was a very conservative man, the epitome of midwestern America in the early twentieth century. Born in Viborg, South Dakota, in 1887, he grew up in an atmosphere of rural America, which left an indelible imprint on his personality and thinking. Years after he had achieved fame as a professor at Harvard, his contemporaries in Viborg still thought of him as one of them. The habits and values he learned as a child on the Dakota farmlands stayed with him wherever he went. "Dad did work steadily, constantly, evenings and weekends," one of his daughters

---

[8] Alvin Hansen, "Keynes After Thirty Years," in *Weltwirtschaftliches Archiv*, vol. 47, p. 218.

[9] For an excellent account of how Hansen and Williams ran the seminar (and an enumeration of some of the more notable students who attended it), see Salant. Another former student who provides an excellent description of the effectiveness of Hansen and Williams is Seymour E. Harris, "Alvin Hansen," in *The International Encyclopedia of the Social Sciences* (New York: Macmillan and the Free Press, 1968), p. 320. In "Keynes After Thirty Years," p. 218, Hansen termed Williams a "consistently able, fair-minded critic of Keynesian thinking."

[10] One should hasten to add that his influence has hardly been confined to the United States; Hansen's books on Keynes have been sold in all corners of the globe. At the time of his death in 1975, ten of Hansen's books had been translated into one or more languages, yielding a total of twenty-nine translations.

[11] *New York Times*, 7 June 1975.

recalled years later, "but organized his time for frequent family outings."[12]

The *Viborg Enterprise* recalled, in remembering their famous native son in 1975, that Hansen was "the first of his community to attend college."[13] After receiving his B.S. from nearby Yankton College in 1910, Hansen remained in the Dakota area as a teacher and then superintendent of schools at Lake Preston, South Dakota. Like Veblen and Keynes, Hansen did not rush to the teaching of economics; he was almost thirty when he first met classes at Brown University in the fall of 1916. Two years later he received his doctorate from the University of Wisconsin. In 1919, he joined the faculty of the University of Minnesota, where he taught for eighteen years.

Our interest in Hansen stems primarily from his extraordinary ability to place the work of Keynes in the American setting. He was, by contemporary standards, an orthodox economist in 1930. His 1927 work on the business cycle was widely accepted as a standard reference in that field.[14] He had co-authored a textbook in economics in 1928 and was well-versed in both the British neoclassicists and the Swedish writers, such as Knut Wicksell.[15] His interest in business cycles had led him to carefully study the works of John Maynard Keynes well before the appearance of the *General Theory*.

Hansen's graduate work at the University of Wisconsin was an important part of his development. He was deeply impressed by one of the few uniquely American economists John R. Commons. At a time when neoclassical theory and policy were in their heyday, Commons argued for an expansion of the functions of government. His view of the economic system, and particularly the plight of the laboring man, led him to reject the idea that free markets alone would bring about the best possible solution. Common's philosophy favored a partnership of government and the market. He did not see government as interfering in the economy; its purpose was to assist the operation of the market in a wide variety of ways. Such a view seems conventional enough today; it was not so widespread in the first three decades of this century. Hansen accepted Commons's judgment at the outset of his career. He was thus far more disposed to accept a larger government role than were most of his contemporaries.[16] At the time Hansen was studying at the University

---

[12] Quoted from a letter to Professor Rod Peterson from Mrs. Marion Therifield. We are indebted to Professor Peterson for sharing this letter with us. Richard Musgrave notes the effects of Hansen's background in his essay "Caring for the Real Problems," *Quarterly Journal of Economics* 90 (February 1976): 1-7.

[13] *Viborg Enterprise*, 12 June 1975.

[14] Alvin Hansen, *Business Cycle Theory: Development and Present Status* (Boston: Ginn & Co., 1927).

[15] Alvin Hansen and Frederic B. Garver, *Principles of Economics* (Boston: Ginn & Co., 1928).

[16] Commons's views on government action were most pronounced in his own area of economic specialization: labor. Hansen's application of the Commons legacy stands out most clearly in his early writings on Keynes and in his later writings, such as idem, *The Economic Issues of the 1960's* (New York: McGraw-Hill, 1960), or idem, *The American Economy* (New York: McGraw-Hill, 1957).

of Wisconsin, a favorite topic of economics was the business cycle. Hansen's views on this subject were significantly influenced by the work of Wesley Clair Mitchell, a student of Thorstein Veblen. Mitchell's approach to the issue of business cycles was inspired by Veblen's mistrust of orthodox economic theory. Mitchell collected massive statistical data that would, he insisted, reveal the underlying reasons for fluctuations without the need for any detailed "theory."[17] Hansen did not adopt Mitchell's distaste for theory; he did, however, incorporate Mitchell's emphasis on the need for empirical evidence to support any theoretical framework. Throughout his career he remained suspicious of models of the business cycle, in much the same spirit as his colleague at Harvard, E. H. Chamberlin, had distrusted models of perfect competition; they were simply not realistic. Herein lies another irony of Hansen's position in the history of economic ideas: he was quite antipathetic towards the mathematical formulations of macroeconomic models that blossomed after World War II. ". . . Hansen's originality may tend to be overlooked," Paul Samuelson observed, because "by 1935 economics entered into a mathematical epoch. It became easier for a camel to pass through the eye of a needle than for a nonmathematical genius to enter into the pantheon of original theorists."[18]

In today's highly specialized academic market, we would classify the Hansen of 1930 as a quantitative institutionalist with a strong interest in business cycles. By the end of the Great Depression, we would have to add the prefix "Keynesian." Hansen's peculiarly American roots in an otherwise rather orthodox background make his conversion to the new economics of considerable interest to the historian of thought. He has, fortunately, provided us with a very complete record of his thoughts in that decade between the stock market crash and the outbreak of World War II. One can see in these writings the gradual erosion of his skepticism as it gives way to enthusiastic support of the new economics.

Certainly his initial interest in Keynes is not surprising. Hansen was, after all, a leading theorist in the area of business cycles in this country. He was convinced that external forces, usually in the form of sharp fluctuations of investment, were largely responsible for business fluctuations. Already uncertain that self-correcting tendencies in a market economy would effectively counter such forces, the catastrophe of the thirties added statistical support for a view that came increasingly to dominate his thinking: an unacceptably high level of idle resources might persist over a long period of time. Keynes's vehement arguments for direct investment were certainly interesting.[19]

---

[17] See Wesley C. Mitchell, *Business Cycles* (Berkeley: University of California Press, 1913). Mitchell later found the National Bureau of Economic Research in New York, and his statistical approach to the problem of business cycles produced what are today referred to as the "leading indicators," which some economists use as a guide to the timing of economic fluctuations.

[18] Samuelson, "Hansen as a Creative Economic Theorist," p. 25.

[19] Perhaps the work which best summarizes Hansen's attitude in this period is found in his essays in *Full Recovery or Stagnation?* (New York: W. W. Norton, 1938).

Interesting, but they were not convincing in 1936. Keynes's dry mathematical expositions, showing the need for added investment, did not adequately meet Hansen's demand that any government program be in harmony with private investment plans. Commenting on suggestions by Keynes that public works might effectively combat unemployment in 1933, Hansen was hardly taken with the idea.

> The justification of public works must always be something more than that they stimulate investment. . . . It is a mistake to suppose that it makes no difference whether the increase in the rate of investment is undertaken by the government in a program of public works or by private enterprise in an expansion of long range investment. Whenever the government emits a large issue of bonds it weakens the *confidence* in the capital market and therefore postpones, delays, and discourages private investment. . . . A public works policy is in danger of getting unwarranted support from a far too mechanistic interpretation of Keynes' equations. . . . Against implicit faith, derived from the fundamental equations, in the artificial stimulation of investment, we cannot warn too strongly.[20]

Hansen was not yet convinced by the theoretical arguments of Keynes. In fact, his own policy recommendations at the trough of the Depression in the United States followed precisely the neoclassical logic: he advocated wage cuts to restore full employment. It was not a recommendation which found favor in the bulk of the profession.[21] Yet his stand was consistent with a conviction that interference in the private markets was likely to do more harm than good in the long run. One Keynesian precept that Hansen never seemed to accept was the Britisher's dictum that "in the long run we are all dead."

His doubts were only slightly assuaged by the less technical presentation of the *General Theory*. In a review of that volume soon after it was published, Hansen still viewed Keynes's proposals as favoring "artificially contrived measures" of government investment.[22] He did concede, however, that the neoclassical policy recommendations seemed inadequate, and he noted with approval that Keynes "warns us, in a provocative manner, of the danger of reasoning based on assumptions which no longer fit the facts of economic life."[23]

The doubts Hansen expressed towards Keynesian prescriptions were changed in large part by the "facts of economic life" from 1936 to 1938. By 1940, his fear of intervention was pushed aside by the statistics of underemployment; he was criticizing the New Deal for its timidity in generating public works projects to promote expenditures of "a purely

---

[20] Alvin Hansen and Herbert Trout, "Annual Survey of Business Cycle Theory: Investment and Saving in Business Cycle Theory," *Econometrica* 1 (April 1933): 131–33. The comments were not directed at the *General Theory* but rather at Keynes's *Treatise on Money*, published in 1930.

[21] On the views of American economists in the early thirties, see J. R. Davis, "Chicago Economists, Deficit Budgets, and the Early 1930's," *American Economic Review* 58 (June 1968): 476–82.

[22] Alvin Hansen, "Mr. Keynes on Underemployment Equilibrium," *Journal of Political Economy* 44 (October 1936): 667–86. Quote on p. 682.

[23] Hansen, "Mr. Keynes on Underemployment Equilibrium," p. 682.

salvaging character."[24] His testimony before the Temporary National Economic Committee in 1939 was in a similar vein.[25] Say's Law was a myth in the context of twentieth-century America. Hansen was already reaching beyond Keynes towards an argument that government would have to intervene increasingly to avoid underemployment in the economy.

The path by which Hansen reached agreement with Keynes was influenced rather clearly by his previous background. Those influences were to carry him, and some of his students, well beyond the scope of the *General Theory*. By the time of World War II, Hansen had become profoundly pessimistic about the prospect of private investment opportunities continuing to enable full use of resources in the economy. The statistical evidence of the thirties was apparently overwhelming; the long-run prospect for the American economy was stagnation. Hansen's treatment of this question and his pursuit of problems in the postwar era greatly expanded the range of issues which the Keynesian framework had introduced. Before we consider this, however, we must pause to note Hansen's contribution to the theoretical development of the Keynesian system in the United States.

A Guide to Keynes

Alvin Hansen's acceptance of Keynes's view on government investment was, as we have stressed, a gradual transition. The evidence of the economic changes in the 1930's increasingly showed Hansen that the Keynesian framework was a more effective way of looking at the economic problems of a modern economy. But it was not just the abstract appeal of Keynes's ideas that led Hansen to take the lead in advocating the English economist's economic policies. As Paul Samuelson has pointed out, by the mid-1930's Hansen realized that

> . . . America, rather that Britain, was the natural place where the Keynesian model applied: the United States was a largely closed, continental economy with an undervalued dollar that gave ample scope for autonomous macroeconomic policies; Hansen's first Harvard years of the late 1930's . . . was the era par excellence when an approximation to Keynes's liquidity trap prevailed.[26]

Hansen also recognized that there were intellectual "traps" which might confound attempts to get academic support for economic policies based on Keynes's analysis. The *General Theory* raised as many issues as it had answered; so Hansen set out to examine those issues

---

[24] Hansen, *Fiscal Policy*, pp. 94–95. Chap. 18 of *Full Recovery or Stagnation?* shows an earlier (1937) emergence of this conviction that the New Deal was not moving fast enough to boost expenditures on public works.

[25] See U. S., Congress, Temporary National Economic Committee, *Investigation of Concentration of Economic Power*, 77th Cong., 1st sess., 1939, pp. 3495–520, 3538–59, 3837–59.

[26] Samuelson, "Hansen as a Creative Economic Theorist," p. 26.

more closely. He had a willing group of students at Harvard to assist him in his efforts at refining and clarifying Keynes's arguments. It was surely not a coincidence that a student from Hansen's seminar—Paul Samuelson—wrote the first truly Keynesian textbook in economics.[27]

Hansen himself took on a somewhat different task: explaining Keynes and integrating the Keynesian model of income determination with the older economic thinking. This led him to review very carefully the arguments of the *General Theory* in a book which he aptly titled *A Guide to Keynes*. Hansen's *Guide* went through the *General Theory* chapter by chapter and took up the issues which had developed from each. Most of his thoughts had been previously published; the *Guide* was primarily a teaching aid to understand Keynes. Its importance as an explanation which fostered understanding and acceptance of the Keynesian viewpoint was substantial. During the 1950's, more students studied the *General Theory* through Hansen's *Guide* than by reading the original, and even today *A Guide to Keynes* is a frequent companion to *The General Theory* on bookshelves.[28] Hansen's summary of Keynes is a convenient benchmark from which to observe the progress of the new economics. By 1953, the quantity theory, which had so thoroughly dominated economic thought up to the Depression, was no longer the only, or even the dominant, explanation of prices and incomes.[29]

Many of the arguments which attracted Hansen's attention in his effort to clarify Keynes seem trivial today. Arguments over definitions, heated exchanges involving the explanation of various equilibrium situations, and similar details were all part of the Keynesian revolution during the 1940's and early 1950's.[30]

There were more substantive issues as well. One of these involved the multiplier, which, as we have seen, was a crucial concept in the Keynesian approach to aggregate economics; it provided the analytical means of showing the effects of a change in aggregate demand. Hansen described Keynes's introduction of the concept as "an arithmetical multiplier which was tautological."[31] While it was not incorrect, such a view did little to illustrate the interaction of forces producing the new

---

[27] Paul A. Samuelson, *Economics* (New York: McGraw-Hill, 1948). See Chapter 9 for a discussion of the impact of this text and Samuelson's acknowledgement of a debt to Hansen.

[28] When the *General Theory* was first released in paperback in the United States, sales of Hansen's *Guide* increased appreciably.

[29] The quantity theory, as we shall see, was never quite extinct. In some areas it thrived and ultimately reemerged in the 1950's to challenge the now "orthodox" Keynesian paradigm. See the discussion in Chapter 13 on Henry Simons and Chapter 14 on Milton Friedman.

[30] Keynes introduced a new way of defining saving and investment, which caused considerable confusion. On the one hand, Keynes argued that intended saving (which depended on the level of income) need not always equal intended investment (which was largely "autonomous"). On the other hand, the total income saved must always be identical with the total income invested over any given period. This identity of saving and investment was confused by many as an equilibrium condition (that is, that intended saving must always be identical to intended investment). Hansen was one of the earliest to see the pitfalls in Keynes's definitions, and he carefully elaborated the difference between the accounting identity of saving and investment at the end of a period and the equilibrium condition that saving should equal investment ex ante.

[31] Hansen, *A Guide to Keynes*, p. 111. We discussed Keynes's treatment of the multiplier in Chapter 7.

level of income. Hansen developed a clearer explanation of how the multiplier worked, which did just that.

If the government increases investment in some period, income in that period obviously rises by the amount spent. What is less obvious is that, in succeeding periods, *consumption* must also rise from this added income. While this added income will gradually dwindle to zero, the *total income* resulting from the initial investment will be some multiple of the sum spent. In fact, the mathematical relation is given by the equation

$$k = I + MPC \ (I) + MPC(MPC(I)) + MPC \ (MPC^2(I)) + \ \ldots \quad (8.1)$$

$$= \frac{1}{1 - MPC}$$

which is precisely what Keynes's equation said in the *General Theory*.[32] Of course, if the government continues to spend funds equal to (I) each period, then income will eventually rise by $k(I)$ and remain at the higher level[33]

$$Y' = Y + \frac{1}{(1 - MPC)}(I) \qquad (8.2)$$

The multiplier is a cornerstone of the Keynesian analysis. Hansen's careful explanation of the way in which it operates was an important step towards greater understanding of the implications of Keynes.

To be able to use the multiplier as a tool of analysis, one must be able to estimate accurately the "leakages" from the flow of income in each period. In the simple case postulated by the *General Theory*, the only leakage was savings—given by the consumption function. But other leakages—such as taxes—might be far more complex; the estimation of a "tax multiplier" is complicated by the need to know exactly where the tax will generate a leakage.

Furthermore, the decision as to what is done with the savings is not irrelevant. Most economists would agree that a rise in expenditure might induce added investment as well as saving. Then, as the level of expenditure rose, still more investment would be forthcoming. This situation involves the *accelerator principle*. The interaction between the *accelerator* (expressing the effect of a changing rate of consumption on the level of investment) and the *multiplier* (expressing the effects of a change in investment on the level of income) is extremely

---

[32] The graphical presentation which Hansen used to explain the equation is illustrated in Figure 8.1. The initial investment (I) generates successive increments of added consumption ($C_1, C_2, \ldots$). When added together, the sum will be that of the *General Theory's* equation.

[33] Hansen's corresponding graphical treatment of the phenomenon is illustrated in Figure 8.2. Since the added investment continues, the increments of added consumption pyramid as each successive period elapses. The magnitude of the increase in income for succeeding periods will again work out to be $k(I)$.

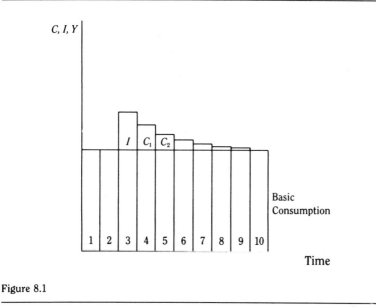

Figure 8.1

complex. While it was initially explored by Paul Samuelson in the academic journals, he credits Hansen with first developing the idea.[34]

We have already noted Hansen's blending of statistics and Keynesian analysis to make the arguments more persuasive. His caution regarding the complexity of the multiplier did not prevent him from insisting that it could provide a very useful approximation with which to evaluate policy alternatives. At one point, he felt that J. M. Clark's estimate that the leakages from income flows in the United States amounted to about one third was reasonably close.[35] He employed such rough estimates to point out the magnitudes of the government action which would have been required to avoid slumps such as those of 1929–31 and 1937–38.[36] The importance of such estimates is not so much their accuracy (or lack of it) as their role as an expository device to illustrate the merits of Keynes's approach. Hansen left it to others to develop the complex econometric models which show in detail the interactions of the multiplier-accelerator relationship; he merely pointed out the possibilities.

The Hicks-Hansen Synthesis

The *General Theory* had hardly appeared before economists were vigorously challenging some of Keynes's conclusions. Keynes had insisted

[34] Paul A. Samuelson, "Interactions Between the Multiplier Analysis and the Principle of Acceleration," in idem, *The Collected Scientific Papers of Paul A. Samuelson*, vol. 2, ed. Joseph E. Stiglitz (Cambridge, Mass.: M.I.T. Press, 1966), p. 1107. For Hansen's own thoughts on the accelerator, see Hansen, *Business Cycles and National Income*, Chapter 11.

[35] Hansen, *Fiscal Policy*, p. 282. He also cites work by Tinbergen and Kuznets.

[36] Hansen, *Fiscal Policy*, Chap. 4.

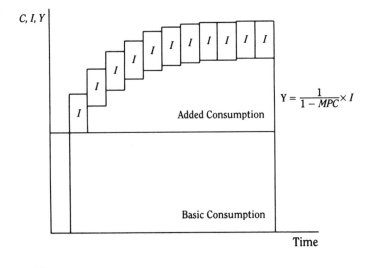

Figure 8.2

that the neoclassical theory of the interest rate was incomplete. His critics soon replied that his own explanation was itself incomplete. Hansen's statement of the debate provides an excellent synopsis of the protagonists as they argued the issue; and we thus quote him in some length:

> According to classical theory the [interest] rate is determined by the intersection of the investment-demand schedule and the saving schedule—schedules disclosing the relation of investment and saving to the rate of interest.
>
> No solution, however, is possible because the position of the saving schedule will vary with the level of real income. As income rises, the schedule will shift to the right. Thus we cannot know what the rate of interest will be unless we already know the income level. And we cannot know the income level without already knowing the rate of interest, since a lower interest rate will mean a larger volume of investment and so, via the multiplier, a higher level of real income. The classical analysis, therefore, offers no solution. . . . In the Keynesian case the money supply and the demand schedules cannot give the rate of interest unless we already know the income level; in the classical case the demand and supply schedules for saving offer no solution until the income is known. Keynes's criticism of the classical theory applies equally to his own theory.[37]

The impasse apparently created by these indeterminants is not, however, irreconcilable, for it involves no logical contradictions within the two economic models. An eclectic approach was soon taken by the

---

[37] Hansen, *A Guide to Keynes*, pp. 140, 141.

English economist J. R. Hicks, who showed that the Keynesian and neoclassical views could be examined in a single, consistent, economic model. Others hastened to elaborate on this point.[38]

In the United States, Hansen was a leading figure in the theoretical construction of this synthesis between the new economics and its predecessors. The "neoclassical synthesis" of Hansen argued that the level of savings might depend on *both* the interest rate *and* the level of income. Similarly, the money balances held by the public might vary not only with the rate of interest—Keynes's liquidity preference—but also with the level of income; a possibility not considered in the *General Theory*. Then the "indeterminacy" of both the new and traditional approaches disappears into a more general analytical framework. Hansen was a leading figure in developing such a general presentation in simple terms. It remains, nonetheless, a complex exercise for the nonspecialist, and we present it in an appendix for the interested reader.

Though much of the semantic debate over the construction of an internally consistent analytical framework has been removed through this eclectic approach to synthesis, basic differences between Keynes and his critics remain. Does a *liquidity trap* exist in the economy? Is the level of investment highly insensitive to the interest rate? These questions remain unanswered by the synthesized approach, and in fact are still the subject of some controversy.[39]

Hansen was a leading force in the theoretical developments in income and business cycle theory after World War II. Yet his main interest—and most important influence—has been the formulation of economic policy. Keynesian thought shook the foundations on which pre-Depression economic policy was constructed. The most obvious change which could be seen in the policy recommendations of economists was their loss of faith in monetary policy to correct cyclical disturbances. The experiences of the Depression had convinced the "new economists" that changes in the money supply had little or no effect on the level of demand.[40]

Although he conceded that monetary policy was important, Hansen concurred in the view that it was not nearly enough. The government,

---

[38] J. R. Hicks, "Mr. Keynes and the Classics: A Suggested Interpretation," *Econometrica* 5 (April 1937): 147–59. While Hicks was the earliest writer to propose a "synthesis" of the two approaches, he was by no means the only one to take an eclectic approach to the problem. Franco Modigliani discussed the two models in his "Liquidity Preference and the Theory of Interest and Money," *Econometrica* 12 (January 1944): 45–88. Don Patinkin started a whole new controversy with his statement of the neoclassical position in his "Price Flexibility and Full Employment," *American Economic Review* 38 (September 1948): 543–64. Nonetheless, it is Hicks's formulation of the synthesis which has been most often employed as an expository device comparing the two approaches. Hansen elaborated on Hicks's work in his *Monetary Theory and Fiscal Policy*. A somewhat different presentation of the "synthesis" was developed by A. P. Lerner in his *Economics of Employment* (New York: McGraw-Hill, 1951), pp. 117–21.

[39] See the chapters in this work on Paul Samuelson, Abba Lerner, and Milton Friedman for comments on the present state of the debate.

[40] Milton Friedman, as we shall see, insists that this view of money in the 1930's is incorrect. Nevertheless, he concedes that even his own mentor, Henry Simons, was deceived by the evidence. See Chapters 13 and 14.

he insisted, must be willing to make use of the accelerator-multiplier effect through *direct expenditures*. The system of *compensatory finance* which Hansen suggested was designed to provide for a long-run policy of economic stabilization.

One of the obvious steps in getting people to adopt his program of compensatory finance was to have the government establish a firm commitment to maintain economic stability. Hansen recognized this; and as one of his students noted, "More than any other single person, Hansen created in Washington and beyond the climate of opinion and understanding that led to the Employment Act of 1946."[41] A feature of the act, which Hansen particularly pressed for, was the creation of the Council of Economic Advisers, a group of professionals who would counsel the president on the appropriate economic policy.

There remained, of course, the task of convincing politicians to implement the "correct" policy. Two important prejudices had to be overcome to do this. The first was the time-honored dictum of the balanced government budget. Hansen was one of the most outspoken opponents of the balanced-budget view of government finance. His proposals called for a variable level of taxes and expenditures, depending on the needs of the economic system. But, his critics quickly pointed out, if the budget was not balanced, the deficit must be covered in some fashion. An obvious possibility was to create government debt.

This runs into the second prejudice: a national debt is very burdensome. Early in his fight for the new economics, Hansen insisted that internally held government debt—so long as it was in some "reasonable relation to income"—was *not* a burden on the economy. Payments for servicing the debt were, after all, paid to ourselves. The government could then finance projects with debt rather than taxes. In this case, aggregate demand could be sustained by the direct investment, while taxes need not rise. The overall effects of the expenditure would depend on who purchased the debt issued by the government. These effects might range from being highly "expansionary," if the bonds were taken by the central bank, to having very little net effect on total spending, if the bonds were purchased by individuals. In the first instance, the effect would be tantamount to printing money; total demand would rise by the amount of the government spending. In the second instance, the government spending might partially replace expenditures which the individuals would have made had they not bought the bonds; the rise in aggregate demand would be dampened. Debt financing was a critical part of Hansen's scheme.[42]

---

[41] Tobin, "Hansen and Public Policy," p. 34.

[42] His treatment of debt financing was challenged from both sides. A. P. Lerner, a leading Keynesian, insisted that there was no need to worry about debt financing at all—the internally held debt was irrelevant (see Chapter 10). Henry Simons, a neoclassical supporter, insisted creation of money was all that was required. He refused to say that the level of debt was irrelevant (see Chapter 13). In the intervening years, some economists have raised objections to Hansen's and Lerner's contention that there is no "burden" to government debt.

Hansen's concern with debt financing stems in part from his long-run view of the economic stabilization problem. He was not an advocate of "pump-priming" (the theory which argued that, once and for all, expenditures would generate a continuing stream of income). Such priming could not succeed in the face of leakages from the income stream. Hansen's multiplier analysis clearly showed that the effects of the priming would die out, unless there were periodic injections of new investment—and, in his view, this would have to come from the government. The long-range nature of such outlays made bonds a more appropriate means of financing than taxes. *Tax policy* was then a major weapon to meet cyclical changes in the level of aggregate demand. From his early Keynesian days, Hansen insisted that a compensatory tax policy was necessary.[43] Thus it is not surprising that Hansen vigorously supported such moves as the tax cut in 1964.

Hansen's compensatory finance reflects his deep conviction that the private sector could not—or would not—maintain a level of investment commensurate with a fully employed economy. To Hansen, the problem of the future on the eve of World War II was *stagnation*.

Maturity and Affluence: The Stagnation Thesis

In December 1938, Hansen delivered the presidential address to the American Economic Association at their annual meeting. He used the occasion to elaborate on a theme which had been gradually emerging in his writings over the past decade. His thoughts reflect very well the combinations of influences on his background.

> The business cycle was *par excellence* the problem of the nineteenth century. But the main problem of our times, and particularly in the United States, is the problem of full employment. . . . Not until the problem of full employment of our productive resources from the long-run standpoint was upon us, were we compelled to give serious consideration to those factors and forces in our economy which tend to make business recoveries weak and anemic and which tend to prolong and deepen the course of depressions. This is the essence of secular stagnation—sick recoveries which die in their infancy and depressions which feed on themselves and leave a hard and seemingly unmovable core of unemployment.[44]

Although the events of the Great Depression loomed large in his analysis, Hansen did not make his pessimistic prediction on the basis of the 1930's alone. He felt that earlier periods of stagnation—such as the 1890's—provided supporting evidence of the recurring difficulties of stagnation.[45]

---

[43] See in particular his comments on taxes in *Fiscal Policy*.

[44] Alvin Hansen, "Economic Progress and Declining Population Growth," *American Economic Review* 29 (March 1939): 4.

[45] See his comments in Chapter 1 of *Fiscal Policy*, pp. 13–19.

His approach to the question of long-run unemployment and "secular stagnation" was very much in keeping with what Hansen viewed as the classical treatment of the problem.

> . . . Fundamental to an understanding of this problem are changes in "external forces," if I may so describe them, which underlie economic progress—changes in the character of technological innovation, in the availability of new land, and in the growth of population.[46]

Thus, the "stagnation thesis" came to be identified with Alvin Hansen. The term *stagnation* is perhaps an inaccurate description for Hansen's views as they ultimately emerged, for it implies a certain inexorable tendency towards a stationary condition that is not, in fact, implied by Hansen's approach. As he viewed it, as an economy reached economic maturity, there would be a growing gap between the actual level of output and the potential level of output. Current output might be increasing, but there would be a tendency for it to fall further and further behind the path of potential output.

The stagnation thesis was never really spelled out in any of Hansen's writings. It represents a theme which runs through his investigations of conditions in the 1930's and his theoretical reasoning about the Keynesian system.[47] He began with the broad proposition that the principal variable assuring full employment is investment. He was not optimistic over the prospects for investment following the Depression; three factors would hinder expansion of opportunities:

1. Population expansion—a major impetus to investment in the past—had slowed markedly in the 1930's.
2. The opportunities afforded by the settlement and exploitation of new areas were gradually dying out without being replaced by new opportunities.
3. Technological change, which might counteract these tendencies, did not seem to be doing so. Hansen was very pessimistic about the appearance of new technologies, noting that such changes tended to come in "spurts." He did not see a new industry on the scale of automobiles or railroads arising to fill the needed investment outlets.

Hansen, in short, foresaw a declining demand for capital investment in the mature economy. This would be coupled, moreover, by the increase in the propensity to save. The result would be a persistent tendency for desired saving to exceed desired investment. The interest rate, more-

[46] Hansen, *Fiscal Policy*, p. 4.

[47] The AEA address is probably the best statement of the underlying forces behind stagnation, but it does not spell out the notion of a "gap" between actual and potential output very clearly. This appears in his testimony before the Temporary National Economic Committee and in his comments in Part IV of *Full Recovery or Stagnation?* His remarks in "Some Notes on Terborgh's 'The Bogey of Economic Maturity,'" *Review of Economics and Statistics* 28 (February 1946): 13–17, are addressed towards some difficulties in interpreting the concept of stagnation. A concise summary of Hansen's position relative to other theories of secular stagnation is given in Benjamin Higgins, "Concepts and Criteria of Secular Stagnation," in *Income, Employment, and Public Policy* (New York: W. W. Norton, 1948), pp. 82–107.

over, would not cure the excess supply of loanable funds. The *rate of profit*—which he considered the prime determinant of investment—would remain low due to the lack of investment opportunity. This explains the emergence of a gap between actual income and that income which could be potentially produced with the resources at hand.[48]

It was in the context of these gloomy predictions that Hansen formulated his *compensatory finance*. His program was intended to be a comprehensive set of government projects which would continuously fill the gap between potential and actual income. If one accepts the arguments of the stagnation thesis, the need for compensatory finance is strengthened. Not everyone was willing to do so; was it clear that stagnation was the main problem after 1945?

Stagnation and Economic Growth in the United States

The stagnation thesis was, on the one hand, a set of empirical observations concerning the outlook for investment opportunities, and, on the other, a framework for evaluating the performance of the economy. Much of the force of the argument came from statistical data extrapolated from the thirties. It is hardly surprising that people in 1940 took Hansen's pessimistic prediction of a growing gap between actual and potential output seriously. A decade of depression was clearly etched in their minds. The rapid economic growth following World War II for a time altered that perspective. Population growth turned sharply upward in the early 1940's, a development which removed one of the pillars of Hansen's statistical projections.[49] Nor does there appear to be much evidence that Hansen's fears regarding the capital-saving nature of invention have, in fact, materialized. One is tempted to conclude that, like Malthus's prognostications about population and a declining standard of living in the nineteenth century, Hansen's predictions underestimated the forces generating growth in the American economy of the twentieth century. However, such a claim would be premature, the stagnation thesis is *not* disproven by evidence of growth in actual income. Hansen himself may not have been as pessimistic on that score as some of his critics allege. As one of his defenders points out, "Hansen never believed that we had to stagnate: he believed that

---

[48] The clearest presentation of this argument by Hansen is in Chapter 19 of *Full Recovery or Stagnation?* It is interesting to note the extent to which he relies on Wicksell's analysis of interest and profits to explain the inability of the interest rate to stimulate investment.

[49] Paul Samuelson, who feels that Hansen has been misinterpreted on the issue of economic stagnation, insists that Hansen recognized this change at once and adjusted his expectations of economic growth accordingly. (Samuelson, "Hansen as a Creative Economic Theorist," p. 30.) However, the question of population changes remains a major concern of economic demographers up to the present. Following the baby boom of the 1940's and 1950's, there was again a sharp fall in the birth rate during the 1960's and 1970's. Current opinion remains divided as to whether there will be an upswing in population growth during the 1980's. The importance of the demographic variable in long-run growth trends is examined by Richard Easterlin, *Birth and Fortune* (New York; Basic Books, 1980).

any tendency toward ineffective demand could be offset by macroeconomic policy."[50]

The stagnation thesis, with its criteria of a hypothetical alternative is not susceptible to empirical verification, and casual empiricism will not provide an unambiguous answer. But the nagging question—whether the economy has, in fact, lived up to its potential growth path—persists, and difficulties of testing the theory do not remove the relevance of the question. The problem of economic growth in a mature society has become a prominent question in political discussions of economic policy for almost half a century. Even after the immediate experience of the Great Depression had receded, the need to maintain growth was accorded high priority. And failure to create an atmosphere of growth could be costly politically; in 1960, a young upstart named John F. Kennedy waged a successful campaign for the presidency stressing the lack of growth during the second Eisenhower administration. In the 1970's, the question of "stagflation"—an anemic rate of economic growth accompanied by rapid inflation and high unemployment—has become the dominant economic issue and one that undoubtedly contributed to President Jimmy Carter's defeat by Ronald Reagan in 1980. Whether Hansen's predictions were correct, his fears were well placed: that the American economy would not maintain the record of rapid economic growth that characterized our history before 1929.

Hansen was not one of the leaders in exploring the mathematical growth models which could be constructed from the Keynesian framework.[51] He did, however, become an early proponent of extending the Keynesian framework to deal with the issues posed by inadequate investment opportunities persisting over long periods of time, not just the business cycle. He was, in a sense, returning economics to the problems posed by the classical economists. Writers of the early period such as Adam Smith, David Ricardo, and John Stuart Mill were also concerned with the long-run prospects for growth. But, as we have seen, their acceptance of Say's Law obviated the need to measure performance other than the actual growth path.[52] In the classical system, the actual rate was the optimum rate, for the economy was always tending toward full employment.

The arguments of Keynes and the evidence supporting the stagnation thesis (in 1939) provided a basis for arguing that the government

---

[50] Samuelson, "Hansen as a Creative Economic Theorist," p. 30. Samuelson feels that "those who have not read Hansen carefully have often misinterpreted him. He was never pessimistic about the growth potential of the system. Hansen believed productivity trends were as good as ever, even better."

[51] Such models have become increasingly sophisticated in recent years. In the present volume, we have chosen to pass over the mathematical developments in growth theory. The basic contribution towards making the Keynesian system into a growth model was put forward by Roy Harrod and Evsey Domar in 1939. Their formulation of a supply function, based on the marginal propensity to invest, and a demand function involving the marginal propensity to save, set up the general identity which is present in most aggregate growth models.

[52] See Chapter 2.

should supplement private investment efforts to avoid having insufficient levels of aggregate demand. Yet even in 1938, as he discussed the problems of stagnation with his colleagues in the American Economic Association, Hansen was quite cautious in advocating large scale government investments. He warned that

> ... public spending is the easiest of all recovery methods, and therein lies its danger. If it is carried too far we neglect to attack those specific maladjustments without the removal of which we cannot attain a workable cost-price structure, and therefore we fail to achieve the otherwise available flow of private investment.[53]

The prosperity of the postwar years indicated that the pessimistic picture he painted in 1938 was not developing as predicted. In part, Hansen conceded that this reflected his error in accurately foreseeing trends in population and innovation. But the failure of the "gap" to appear in the statistics also reflected what he felt were some substantial changes in the economic system. Writing in 1957, he contended that

> The stagnation of the thirties forced us to undertake a remodeling of our economic system. We have equipped the economic machine with cushions which tend to stop the headlong crash into depressions. The consumption base has been broadened and made stronger. . . . The *extensive* forces having weakened, we have done a good deal to strengthen the forces making for *intensive* expansion.[54]

The combination of institutional change—including an expanded role for government—and appearance of new sectors of vigorous growth had apparently greatly *reduced* the problem of stagnation as Hansen had originally posed it. Yet, in 1960, Hansen stated the case for *added* government intervention far more vigorously than he had in the thirties.

> Our budgets, far from being too large, have been too small—too small in terms of needs, too small in terms of growth, and too small in terms of pushing the economy towards full employment and the most economical utilization of capacity.[55]

The threads of the stagnation thesis are still clearly visible, but one could hardly defend so strong an endorsement of added government action on the basis of the earlier model of secular stagnation; something new had been added.

Hansen and the Social Imbalance Hypothesis

Alvin Hansen had been one of the early economists to recognize the application of Keynesian analysis to the question of underemployment in the economy. From the late 1930's on, he had been hammering away

---

[53] Hansen, "Economic Progress and Declining Population Growth," p. 14.

[54] Hansen, *The American Economy,* p. 31.

[55] Hansen, *Economic Issues of the 1960's,* p. 67.

on the theme of government actions to ensure full employment in the United States. By the mid-1950's it appeared that this problem had been largely solved. Hansen turned to new areas of economics.[56]

Viewing the postwar changes in the economy, Hansen became convinced that the underlying basis for consumption in the United States had gradually shifted to the point where consumption was no longer generated by the "needs" of the individual; it was generated by the advertising of firms in the economy. Markets were "created" by the "distortion" of values in the society to promote the production of goods which were not really needed by the consumers. He sounds remarkably like Veblen when he insists that

> a not inconsiderable part of our productive resources is wasted on artificially created wants. Instead of the durable and quality products that are prized more and more as the years go by, we deliberately create things we soon tire of—things that an effervescent scheme of social values quickly renders obsolete. Never before has there been so great a waste of productive resources on things that have little or no inherent value.[57]

In addition to Veblen, it is clear that Hansen was influenced by his colleague, E. H. Chamberlin. To Hansen of the 1960's,

> . . . it is difficult to see how an economist who has been instructed in the theory of monopolistic competition can still adhere to the consumer sovereignty dogma. Nowadays consumers no longer act on their own free will. The demand curve is no longer the product of spontaneous wants. It is manufactured. . . . Consumer wants are no longer a matter of individual choice. They are mass-produced.[58]

In short, Hansen had concluded by 1960 that the cure for stagnation which had emerged was perhaps no better than the disease. In order to avoid the stagnation, the economy must "manufacture" wants to "create" the demand for the production of goods which have very little "inherent value." And so we arrive at his support of the "social imbalance hypothesis," which was independently developed by one of his colleagues, John Kenneth Galbraith. The necessary link between the stagnation view of the 1930's and Hansen's contemporary views is Chamberlin and monopolistic competition. The prospects for investment only expand due to the distortion of wants generated through market imperfections and advertising. Economists instructed in *The Theory of Monopolistic Competition* could easily be led to accept Hansen's basic premise that consumer sovereignty is dead. By insisting

---

[56] His change in emphasis is illustrated by a conversation related to us by Professor John Letiche. During a visit to Berkeley in the early fifties, Hansen inquired of Letiche what criticism he would make of his work. Letiche replied that it seemed as though Hansen was repeating himself in his works on employment theory. "You're right," Hansen replied, "and I intend to do something about it." He was just past 60 at the time that he started in this new direction.

[57] Hansen, *Economic Issues of the 1960's*, pp. 46–47.

[58] Hansen, *Economic Issues of the 1960's*, pp. 75–76. As we noted in Chapter 6, Chamberlin did not share this interpretation of his work.

that—due to the manipulation of demand—the composition of goods produced in an imperfect market represents misallocation, Hansen is able to come to the sweeping conclusion that

> ... an optimum rate of growth can not be reached without a change in the social values which permit a better use of our productive resources.[59]

And, indeed, this pattern of social values will, "if long pursued make us a second rate country."[60]

His comments on the "optimum rate of growth" again return us to the basic concepts behind the stagnation thesis, for Hansen's interpretation of the term stems from his view which holds that there is a significant deviation between the current level of production and the "optimal" level. The emphasis from monopolistic competition is that the *composition* of output, as well as its absolute level, must be considered in applying the criteria of "potential" performance.

Hansen's espousal of the social imbalance hypothesis in the 1960's is no more surprising than was his espousal of Keynes. Perhaps the outstanding feature of Hansen as an economist has been his pragmatism.

Alvin Hansen was 69 when he retired from Harvard in 1956. Born only four years after Keynes, his birth date would seem to place him in the same generation. Yet, intellectually we think of him as a major force in post-Keynesian economics, where his most influential work has appeared. And his imprint on the generation which followed was significant. Hansen is one of those scholars whose mark on economic thought appears through the students he taught as well as the books he wrote. A roll call of economists influenced by Hansen would include many of the most prominent men in the profession today. And they would represent many diverse areas of study. Two names will suffice to illustrate the diversity of interests which could be spurred on by Hansen's work. Paul Samuelson, perhaps the leading theorist of the new economics, and John Kenneth Galbraith, a modern critic of economic theory à la Thorstein Veblen, both give considerable credit to Hansen in shaping their present views.

Like Marshall, Hansen could inspire in his students intellectual curiosity, which is the aim of every teacher. For more than thirty years, Alvin Hansen sat at the apex of academic thought in the United States. In 1967, the American Economic Association awarded Hansen the Francis A. Walker Medal. The citation, read by his student James Tobin, neatly summarized Hansen's position in the development of economic thought in the United States. He was described as

> ... a gentle revolutionary who has lived to see his cause triumphant and his heresies orthodox, an untiring scholar whose example and

---

[59] Hansen, *Economic Issues of the 1960's*, p. 47.
[60] Hansen, *Economic Issues of the 1960's*, p. 47.

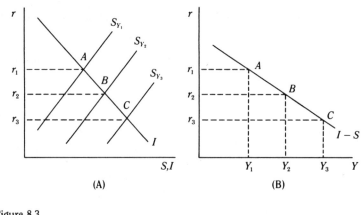

Figure 8.3

influence have fruitfully changed the directions of his science, a
political economist who has reformed policies and institutions in his
own country and elsewhere without any power save the force of his
ideas.[61]

Appendix: The Hicks-Hansen Synthesis

The demonstration through graphical analysis that the Keynesian and
neoclassical views of aggregate economic behavior could, in fact, be
shown within a single economic model is worth noting in some detail.
This appendix relies heavily on the reader's knowledge of the techniques of graphical analysis of equilibrium situations.

The *I-S* Curve

We begin with the behavior of saving and investment in the capital
market. Figure 8.3A shows the relation of investment and saving to the
interest rate. As the interest rate (r) falls, investment (I) will increase
while saving (S) decreases. Instead of a single saving curve, there is a
"family" of schedules; one for the relation of r and S at each level of
income (Y), (S_{Y1}, S_{Y2}, and so on).[62] At the points where desired saving
just equals the desired investment (A, B, C in Figure 8.3A), the market
will be in equilibrium. At combinations such as (r_1, Y_1), (r_2, Y_2) and (r_3,
Y_3,), there is no tendency for excess saving or investment to develop.
We can plot these points on another graph. (Fig. 8.3B) to derive what is
termed the "*I-S* Curve." The *I-S* curve shows all the possible combinations of interest rates and levels of income where the capital market is

---

61 Tobin, "Hansen and Fiscal Policy," p. 37.
62 The investment function could also be made responsive to income by showing a "family" of
    investment curves. The logic of the argument remains unchanged, although the solution is more
    complex. The reader should recall that the saving curve *implies* a consumption function. Thus
    Keynes's consumption function enters Figure 8.3 via the family of saving curves for each level of
    income.

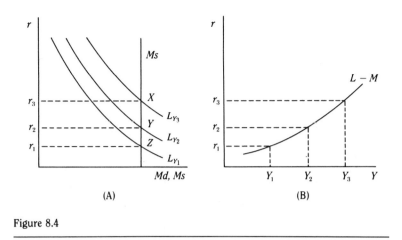

Figure 8.4

in equilibrium. At points off the *I-S* curve of Figure 8.3B, we will not have a situation where intended saving equals intended investment; there will be pressure on *r* and *Y* to move back to a combination on the *I-S* curve.

The *L-M* Curve

Using the same technique, we can derive a relationship which shows the demand for money balances (liquidity preference) at every level of income and interest rate. Figure 8.4A shows the typical Keynesian liquidity preference schedule. As with Figure 8.3, we show a "family" of liquidity preference curves (L_{Y1}, L_{Y2}, and so on); one for each level of income. The level of the money supply—determined by the monetary authorities—is fixed at the vertical line M_s. We can now determine the equilibrium points (*X, Y, Z* in Figure 8.4A), where the demand for money balances exactly equals the supply of money balances for every combination of interest rate and income. We now plot these points in Figure 8.4B to derive the *L-M* Curve. The *L-M* curve of Figure 8.4B shows those combinations of interest rate and income where the demand and supply for money is in equilibrium. The reader should note that the *L-M* curve will *shift*, if the money supply set by the authorities is changed. The effects of monetary policy as well as fiscal policy can thus be analyzed by this presentation.

Equilibrium of the *I-S* and *L-M* Curves

Neither the *I-S* nor the *L-M* curve alone can give the equilibrium interest rate or the level of income. For equilibrium in the economy to exist, *both* the capital markets and the money market must be in equilibrium. Combining the *I-S* curve and the *L-M* curve on a single graph will show that unique combination of interest rate and income which will produce such a result. This is shown in Figure 8.5. At any point other than *E*, there will be a tendency for change in one or both of

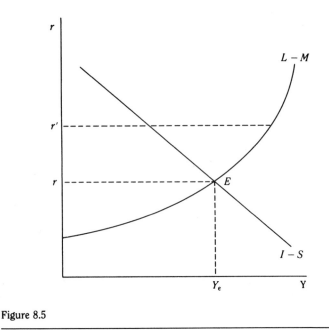

Figure 8.5

the markets. Suppose, for example, that the interest rate rose to r' with income still at Y_e. At r', people will wish to hold less money (Figure 8.4A); unless income *rises*, the demand for money balances will be less than the supply of money, creating a downward pressure on r. In the capital market, the increase to r' to the interest rate will cause a lower level of investment to be forthcoming, while the supply of saving (at Y_e) would increase. Unless income *falls*, the supply of saving will exceed the demand for investment, again creating a downward pressure on r. Clearly, unless the underlying curves change their position, only at E will there be no tendency for the level of income and the interest rate to change. The indeterminancy of the two approaches has been removed.

9

PAUL A. SAMUELSON

FROM ECONOMIC *WUNDERKIND*
TO POLICYMAKER

In the long run, the economic scholar works for the only coin worth
having—our own applause.

Paul A. Samuelson

In 1935, a brash young student from the University of Chicago appeared
at Harvard. It was, Paul Samuelson later recalled, a fortuitous choice,
since it put him

> . . . right in the forefront of the three great waves of modern
> economics: the Keynesian Revolution, . . . the monopolistic or imper-
> fect-competition revolution, and finally, the fruitful clarification of
> the analysis of economic reality resulting from the mathematical and
> econometric handling of the subject. . . .[1]

Samuelson's enthusiastic response to these revolutions in economic
thought eventually took him to Alvin Hansen's seminar on fiscal policy.
Two decades later, Paul Samuelson had replaced his mentor as the dean
of the new economics, a position he has held for an additional two
decades.

Samuelson's influence on the economics profession has been both
profound and ubiquitous. As he noted in his presidential address to the
American Economic Association in 1961,

---

[1] Paul A. Samuelson, "Economics in a Golden Age: A Personal Memoir," in idem, *The Collected Scientific Papers of Paul A. Samuelson*, vol. 4, ed. Hiroki Nagatani and Kate Crowley (Cambridge, Mass.: MIT Press, 1977), p. 890. Samuelson's articles have been collected and published in four volumes. Wherever possible, we shall cite page references from those volumes. Volumes 1 and 2 were published in 1966 and edited by Joseph Stiglitz; volume 3 was published in 1972 and edited by Robert Merton; and volume 4 was published in 1977 and edited by Hiroki Nagatani and Kate Crowley. As an indication of how prolific Paul Samuelson has been, we note that there are a total of 292 essays collected in the four volumes.

My own scholarship has covered a great variety of fields. And many of
them involve questions like welfare economics and factor-price
equalization; turnpike theorems and oscillating envelopes; nonsub-
stitutibility relations in Minowski-Ricardo-Leontief-Metzler matrices
of Mosak-Hicks type; or balanced budget multipliers under conditions of balance uncertainty in locally impacted topological spaces
and molar equivalences.[2]

He went on to say that, "my friends warn me that such topics are
suitable merely for captive audiences in search of a degree—and even
then only after dark."[3]

Accurate though it may be, such a description hardly seems to fit a
man whose comments can regularly be found in *Newsweek* and the *New
York Times*, and who authored a book which sold more than 10 million
copies. Paul Samuelson has chosen his words carefully for each audience, and more often than not the listeners or readers have been
captivated, not captive. His name is familiar throughout the world to
introductory students of economics, as well as to those in search of
higher degrees. Several generations of economists have been introduced to economics through Samuelson's textbook, which to date has
run through eleven editions.[4] Not since Alfred Marshall's *Principles*,
which went through eight editions at a time when two editions were
unusual, has a single book so dominated the teaching of economics.
The influence of Samuelson's text has been so great that when a group
of radical economists in the late 1970's put together a critique of
economics as it is taught today, they titled their two-volume effort *The
Anti-Samuelson*.[5] To assist his readers, the editor of *The Anti-
Samuelson* keyed the chapters of the critique to the chapters of the
then-current edition of Samuelson's text. Why did the critics decide to
key their effort to Samuelson's text? Because it allowed them to "focus
on the teaching of economics. The reason we selected S[amuelson]'s
book has to do with its 'originality' and 'popularity' in the U.S. and its
international use."[6]

The parallel between Alfred Marshall and Paul Samuelson could be
pushed beyond the fact that both were successful textbook writers.
Each sought to bring together diverse approaches to economics. Marshall tried to mesh the classical writing with the marginalist revolution
and in so doing created what today we call "neoclassical economics."
Samuelson was one of the first economists to put Hansen's synthesis of
Keynes and the "classics" in a context read by a wide audience. The

[2] Paul A. Samuelson, "Economists and the History of Ideas," *Collected Papers*, vol. 1, no. 113, p. 1499.

[3] Samuelson, "Economists and the History of Ideas," p. 1499.

[4] Paul A. Samuelson, *Economics* 11th ed. (New York: McGraw-Hill, 1980). The first edition appeared in 1948 and was soon the preeminent text in the field, a position it held for twenty years. Though no longer number one in sales, *Economics* has consistently ranked among the three best-selling texts for more than thirty years.

[5] Marc Linder, ed. *The Anti-Samuelson*, 2 vols. (New York: Urizen Books, 1977).

[6] Linder, p. x.

success of his textbook is shown not only by the 10 million copies sold but also by the imitation it has encouraged in competitors.

Samuelson's rise to the top of the economics profession was extraordinarily rapid. Born in 1915 in Gary, Indiana, he grew up in Chicago, where he attended high school and later entered the University of Chicago, where he received his B.A. in 1935. Over the next twenty-five years he won every major accolade which the economics profession could offer him. In 1947, at the age of thirty-two, he was awarded the first John Bates Clark Medal for the most distinguished achievement by an economist under the age of forty. In 1970, he became the first American to receive the Nobel Prize in Economics.[7]

When he left Harvard in 1941 as a young Ph.D., Samuelson was already a distinguished member of the profession. He had been elected to the Society of Junior Fellows, a position which elevated him into the upper strata of academic circles in Cambridge. "As a junior fellow," Samuelson recalled, "I was completely happy, turning out paper after paper."[8] He was quite successful in finding audiences for his efforts; eleven of his papers were published while he was still a graduate student at Harvard. These include some of his most significant contributions to economics. Three articles on consumer choice were later expanded into a new approach to that problem.[9] Two more dealt with the gains from international trade and laid the groundwork for pioneering analysis of factor returns and trade.[10] And, of course, it was while he was a graduate student in Hansen's seminar that he developed his contribution on the multiplier-accelerator principle.[11] Small wonder that he found it an exciting time to be an economist.

> To have been born as an economist before 1936 was a boon–yes. But not to have been born too long before!
> *Bliss was it in that dawn to be alive,*
> *But to be young was very heaven!*[12]

All this time, of course, Samuelson was also busily writing a thesis at Harvard. Finished in 1941, it won the David A. Wells Award as the outstanding economics dissertation at Harvard that year. In 1947, it

---

[7] Upon learning that he had been awarded the Nobel Prize, Samuelson's reaction suggested his own explanation of why he had risen to the top: "It's nice to have hard work recognized." (*Los Angeles Times*, 27 October 1970). On another occasion he conceded that "possibly I would have done well in any field of applied science or as a writer, but certainly the blend in economics of analytical hardness and humane relevance was tailor made for me or I for it." (Samuelson, "Economics in a Golden Age," p. 895.)

[8] Samuelson, "Economics in the Golden Age," p. 890.

[9] Samuelson, *Collected Papers*, vol. 1, no. 1, "A Note in the Pure Theory of Consumers' Behavior"; no. 2, "The Numerical Representation of Ordered Classifications and the Concept of Utility"; no. 3, "The Empirical Implications of Utility Analysis"; no. 4, "The End of Marginal Utility: A Note on Dr. Bernadelli's article"; pp. 1-37.

[10] Samuelson, *Collected Papers*, vol. 2, no. 60, "Welfare Economics and International Trade"; no. 61, "The Gains from International Trade"; pp. 775–91.

[11] Samuelson, *Collected Papers*, vol. 2, no. 82, "Interactions Between the Multiplier Analysis and the Principle of Acceleration"; no. 83, "A Synthesis of the Principle of Acceleration and the Multiplier"; pp. 1107–22. See the discussion of Chapter 8 above.

[12] Paul A. Samuelson, "The General Theory," *Collected Papers*, vol. 2, no. 114, p. 1517. (Here, of course, Samuelson is quoting Wordsworth's *The Prelude, XI*.)

was published as a book, *Foundations of Economic Analysis*.[13] *Foundations* was a seminal contribution to the area of mathematical economics. The impact of this work was specifically noted by the committee awarding Samuelson the Nobel Prize in 1970. In his Nobel Memorial Lecture accepting the award, Samuelson reflected on his early inquiries in economics.

> What is it that the scientist finds useful in being able to relate a positive description of behavior to the solution of a maximizing problem? That is what a good deal of my own early work was about. From the time of my first papers on "Revealed Preference" through the completion of *Foundations of Economic Analysis*, I found this a fascinating subject.[14]

Well before he finished his work at Harvard, it was clear that Samuelson was one of the brightest young economists in the United States. There seemed little question that he would be able to obtain an appointment at the school of his choice. Harvard was clearly his choice. However, precocity is not always regarded as a virtue in the academic establishment; Samuelson's youth, brash personality, and Jewish background all worked against him. Despite his glittering credentials, he was not offered a permanent position at Harvard; he was given only a post as instructor in the Department of Economics. When, a month later, the relatively unheralded department of economics at the Massachusetts Institute of Technology offered him a more promising position as an assistant professor, he took it. Harvard's reluctance to hire their prodigy proved a costly miscalculation; with characteristic audacity, Samuelson proceeded to build the department at MIT into one of the very best in the country, better, according to some, than Harvard itself.

The circumstances surrounding Samuelson's departure from Harvard have remained a matter of professional gossip for many years. Samuelson himself claims that the reports of his annoyance at being denied a position have been exaggerated. "I left Harvard in 1940," he insists, "for the same reason that James Tobin left it in 1950: I got a better offer."[15] There was not, he goes on to point out, any misunderstanding or broken promises between him and the department at Harvard, nor did he have regrets over his decision once he made it. As he summarized the situation years later,

> ... On a fine October day in 1940 an *enfant terrible emeritus* packed up his pencil and moved three miles down the Charles River, where he lived happily ever after.[16]

---

[13] Paul A. Samuelson, *Foundations of Economic Analysis* (Cambridge, Mass: Harvard University Press, 1947). Hereafter this work is cited as *Foundations*.

[14] Paul A. Samuelson, "Maximum Principles in Analytical Economics", *Collected Papers*, vol. 3, no. 130, p. 3.

[15] Samuelson, "Economics in a Golden Age," p. 891.

[16] Samuelson, "Economics in a Golden Age," p. 891. In his memoirs, John Kenneth Galbraith attributes the failure of Harvard to promote Paul Samuelson to the anti-semitism of the department chairman, Harold Hitchings Burbank. See John Kenneth Galbraith, *A Life in our Times*.

His colleagues at Harvard eventually did have second thoughts; over the years they made several attempts to lure Samuelson back—without success.[17] MIT proved a very fruitful place to "stay put." In an era when academic promotion was generally slow, Samuelson had become a full professor at the age of thirty-two.

Paul Samuelson has written in so many areas with great proficiency that it is impossible to do justice to his contributions in a single chapter of the present book. Much of his research has been in the realm of "pure theory," highly abstracted from the world of economic policy and difficult to simplify to the level of an elementary analysis for the nonspecialist. This is particularly true of his work in mathematical economics, where some of his earliest work had a major impact on the subsequent development of the field. "That is one of the mortal sins," Samuelson once admitted, "for which I shall have to do some explaining when I arrive at heaven's pearly gates."[18] Samuelson's *Foundations* carefully discussed the methodology of mathematical economics and then explored a variety of economic theorems using the techniques developed. His mathematics of income determination (already alluded to in our comments on Alvin Hansen's work) provided a substantial impetus to the exploration of properties of the Keynesian system. Subsequently, Samuelson developed mathematical models to pioneer work in the theory of government expenditures, and in the examination of what has come to be called the theory of "efficient markets."

His virtuosity as a mathematician notwithstanding, Samuelson's ability to develop straightforward explanations of economic phenomena (illustrated by the success of his introductory textbook in economics) has made him a leading voice in policy decisions for the past three decades. It is on his work and views which relate most directly to policy that our attention will be focused. But to do this, we must first note Samuelson's methodological views on the use of mathematics and economics.

Mathematics and the Foundations of Economic Analysis

Paul Samuelson was not the first economist to use mathematics as a means of explaining and exploring the economic problem. The marginal analysis of the late nineteenth century was based on an examination of incremental changes, which William Stanley Jevons expressed using calculus. Even earlier, Augustin Cournot had used mathematics to explore the equilibrium of the firm. Leon Walras, in his *Elements of Pure Economics*, used mathematics to explain equilibrium in all mar-

---

(Boston, Mass.: Houghton Mifflin, 1981), pp. 46–47. Of Burbank, Samuelson has written, "Burbank stood for everything in scholarly life for which I had utter contempt and abhorrence." (Samuelson, "Economics in a Golden Age," p. 897.)

[17] The reason he did not respond to these later overtures, Samuelson says, is that "after a cost-benefit analysis, I decided to stay put." Samuelson, "Economics in a Golden Age," p. 891.

[18] Paul A. Samuelson, "Liberalism at Bay," *Collected Papers*, vol. 4, no. 277, p. 868.

kets of the economy simultaneously.[19] Both Keynes and Marshall were well versed in the use of mathematics as a shorthand to express economic relations.

Samuelson sees mathematics as much more than a mere device to clarify verbal arguments. "With the assistance of mathematics," he observes, "I can see a property of the ninety-nine dimensional surfaces hidden from the naked eye."[20] Mathematics, in other words, can reveal aspects of economic theory which are not apparent from intuition alone. Most economic problems are concerned with the maximization or minimization of some variable (welfare, costs, profits, utility, and so on). If the basic behavior (such as a firm maximizing returns or a consumer maximizing satisfaction) is postulated as a mathematical problem, then one can derive important theorems by exploring the properties of its mathematical statement.

Such a view represents a distinct break with the neoclassical approach of Marshall, who regarded the role of mathematics in a secondary position. It was Marshall who warned the profession against putting literary propositions into mathematical form. In the opening pages of *Foundations*, Samuelson insists that this dictum should be "exactly reversed"; it is the effort of converting *essentially mathematical* propositions into *literary* form that is wasteful and "involves . . . mental gymnastics of a peculiarly depraved type."[21] Marshall's use of mathematics, Samuelson claims, was usually imprecise. Writing in 1967, Samuelson insisted that "the ambiguities of Alfred Marshall paralyzed the best brains in the Anglo-Saxon branch of our profession for three decades."[22] He does not agree with those who see Marshall's loose treatment of problems as an asset proving that "it's all in Marshall." Samuelson replies: "All the words of economics are in Webster's dictionary."[23]

Samuelson's break with the literary tradition of Marshall employed mathematical techniques which were quite sophisticated. (Or at least they were viewed as such by economists in 1947. It is perhaps an indication of the degree to which Samuelson's position has been accepted that today most graduate students would be expected to work

---

[19] Leon Walras, *Elements of Pure Economics*, trans. William Jaffe (Homewood, Ill.: Richard D. Irwin, 1954). This work was originally published in 1874. Samuelson feels that Walras and Cournot carried the development of mathematics in economic analysis to a highly sophisticated level by the beginning of the twentieth century. At that point, he claims, the study was interrupted by the "verbal" tradition of the English economists at Cambridge. An early statement of Samuelson's views on mathematical economics can be found in *Foundations*; a more recent statement appeared in his acceptance of the Nobel Prize ("Maximum Principles in Analytical Economics").

[20] Samuelson, "Maximum Principles in Analytical Economics," p. 3.

[21] Samuelson, *Foundations*, p. 6.

[22] Paul A. Samuelson, "The Monopolistic Competition Revolution," *Collected Papers*, vol. 3, no. 131, p. 22.

[23] Samuelson, "The Monopolistic Competition Revolution," p. 25. Samuelson hastens to add that not all economists agree with his rather harsh judgment of Marshall. However, he adds, ". . . it is significant that Marshall's remaining defenders . . . tend to be those satisfied with perfect competition as an approximation to reality." Idem, "The Monopolistic Competition Revolution," p. 26.

through the mathematical presentations of *Foundations*.) We shall not reproduce any specific proofs in detail here. The purpose in developing such rigorous mathematical proofs, many of which simply verified propositions of earlier marginal analysis, was to establish once and for all the validity of a set of *basic theorems in economics*. Samuelson felt that it was time for someone to do this, so that redundant literary proofs of these propositions would cease to appear in the literature.

Samuelson's presentation of a theorem was seldom confined to a simple statement of the proof; he wished to construct corollaries that would uncover and explore any additional inferences that might be reached from the initial hypothesis. It is important for these corollaries to be stated in a form which could yield *operational hypotheses*, or propositions which can be empirically verified in the real world. Thus, through the use of *comparative statics* (examining the change between an existing point of equilibrium and a new point of equilibrium), one can make inferences as to the direction of change, even though the equations may not yield the exact magnitude of that change. To be sure, in 1947 Samuelson was not overly sanguine about the prospects of such analysis yielding unambiguous results. Using a very simple Keynesian model of income determination, he found that the possible number of outcomes resulting from a major change in spending (investment, consumption, or government) was so great that, in the absence of empirical evidence on the values of parameters (such as the marginal propensity to consume), very little could be inferred regarding the most likely outcome.[24] However, three decades of development in computer technology, along with considerable refinement of empirical techniques, have reduced the limitations of this approach. In recent years, Samuelson has strengthened his beliefs in the efficacy of mathematical exposition as a means of resolving both empirical and doctrinal arguments.[25]

Revealed Preference and Indices of Welfare

One of the most original areas of Samuelson's *Foundations* was his treatment of consumer welfare. He began by arguing that a theory of demand based on the concept of marginal utility was fruitless, because it could never generate any hypotheses which were empirically observable. To overcome this shortcoming, Samuelson introduced the concept of *revealed preference*. Rather than postulating some unobservable field of "tastes" or "utilities," he based his analysis on the actual choice made by the consumer. Much of this work has remained outside the domain of the introductory textbook; yet it bears on a question that lies at the root of our economic analysis: the meaning and measurement of *economic welfare*.

---

[24] Samuelson, *Foundations*, p. 24.

[25] The most obvious example of this reaffirmation is the Nobel Prize speech which we cited above ("Maximum Principles in Analytical Economics").

Both economists and lay persons use measures of economic welfare all the time. "Personal income," "gross national product," "cost-of-living allowances," and similar concepts dealing with our welfare form the basis of many of our personal and collective decisions. All of these measures are what the economist-statisticians refer to as *index numbers*. They combine in a single composite index a number of individual measures. For the most part, these index numbers are the products of theories of statistics, not economics.

In recent years, the indexes used to measure the rate of change in prices—inflation—have become an important part of economic policy at all levels. Indices such as the cost-of-living index are constructed to measure the overall effect which changes in prices have produced on our individual welfare. Can such effects be exactly measured—even in theory? Using the logic behind revealed preference, Samuelson demonstrated that the answer is *no*. There will always be some bias which will make even the most ideal index number subject to some ambiguity.[26] The conclusion that price indices are inherently ambiguous leads to doubt concerning the other indexes of welfare we commonly use— particularly money income. Given changes in prices (or different prices in different locations), how can we compare incomes over time or between countries?[27] The shortcomings of the measures do not lead us to abandon them, but it is useful to demonstrate logically the extent to which they are constrained by theoretical limits irrespective of the problems of data.

Dynamic Aspects of Markets

The *comparative statics* approach to problems such as consumer welfare does not, of course, consider the *dynamic adjustments* involved in reaching the new equilibrium. This omission is significant, because the path by which a new equilibrium is reached may determine whether the system will ever get there. The situation may be one of unstable equilibrium, which will "explode" when jarred by a change. In such a case, the comparative statics analysis is inadequate.

Samuelson was, of course, aware of such problems. In the second part of *Foundations*, he turns to the dynamics of income determination in the context of the newly emerging Keynesian econometric models. It is in this area that he developed his own formulation of the multiplier-accelerator phenomenon with Alvin Hansen.[28] He credits Hansen with

---

[26] This proof is one of the most important demonstrations in *Foundations*. The interested reader should be able to follow the logical argument on pages 146–53; Samuelson then employs inequalities to demonstrate rigorously the impossibility of constructing an exact index of price change.

[27] Samuelson has touched upon this point in several of his papers. See particularly, idem, "Evaluation of Real Income", *Collected Papers*, vol. 2, no. 77, pp. 1044–72; and idem, "Analytical Notes on International Real-Income Measures," *Collected Papers*, vol. 4, no. 210, pp. 66–79.

[28] Samuelson, "Interactions Between the Multiplier Analysis and the Principle of Acceleration," and idem, "A Synthesis of the Principle of Acceleration and the Multiplier." It is in these articles, published in 1939, that Samuelson makes use of his invention of the so-called "Keynesian Cross," a

supplying the idea of the accelerator to him, claiming only to have extended Hansen's suggestion and to have "proceeded to analyze its algebraic structure."[29] This is hardly a trivial contribution; it illustrates Samuelson's approach to economic theory through mathematics. By setting up a Keynesian model of income determination involving second-order difference equations, Samuelson was able to explore the interactions of the multiplier-accelerator relationship. Hansen had contented himself with postulating some values for the propensities to consume and invest. His estimate of the marginal propensity to consume, for example, was based on a statement by another well-known economist J. M. Clark.[30] By establishing a more formal mathematical model, Samuelson was able to show the reaction of income to changes in investment with a variety of values for the parameters in the model. He discovered that Hansen's choice of 0.5 as a value for the marginal propensity to consume happened to produce a steady cyclical fluctuation. Other values would produce cycles which might explode into runaway growth (or collapse into ever-deepening depressions), while still others would produce a "dampened" cycle that would die out of its own accord.[31]

More recently, Samuelson has applied his talent for mathematical formulation of economic dynamics to the question of market adjustments, particularly the movement of prices in the capital markets. In 1965, he published an article entitled "Proof that Properly Anticipated Prices Fluctuate Randomly." The paper addressed the following enigma: "In competitive markets there is a buyer for every seller. If one could be sure that a price would rise, it would have already risen. . . . Is this a correct fact about well-organized . . . markets?" asks Samuelson, "or is it merely an interesting (refutable) hypothesis about actual markets that can somehow be put to empirical testing? . . . Or," he asks further, "is it a valid deduction . . . whose truth is as immutable as $2 + 2 = 4$? Does its truth follow from the very definition of 'free, competitive

---

diagram with a 45-degree line depicting the determination of national income in the Keynesian system. This device has become the standard approach when initiating beginning students to macroeconomics. Perhaps because of this invention, Samuelson has also been credited by some with coining the term *macroeconomics* in his textbook. This, he insists, is an error; the term *macroeconomics* did not appear in the first edition of his text. See Samuelson, "Liberalism at Bay," p. 867.

[29] Paul A. Samuelson, "Alvin Hansen and the Interactions Between the Multiplier and the Principle of Acceleration," *Collected Papers*, vol. 2, no. 84, p. 1123. For an excellent graphical representation of Samuelson's treatment of income determination, see Kenneth Boulding, "Samuelson's Foundations: The Role of Mathematics in Economics," *Journal of Political Economy*, June 1948, pp. 187–99.

[30] Such casual empiricism was typical of Hansen's approach, as we have noted. Commenting on the formulation of the multiplier-accelerator model, Samuelson credits Hansen's *Full Recovery or Stagnation?* (New York: W.W. Norton, 1938), as having a very "refreshing impact at the time." (Samuelson, "Alvin Hansen and the Interactions" p. 1123, n. 2).

[31] Samuelson did not push his investigation further. Later, another of Hansen's students, James Duesenbury, used a similar approach to the question of cyclical fluctuations by considering the interaction of fluctuations and economic growth with the parameters observed for the U.S. economy. See James Duesenbury, *Business Cycles and Economic Growth* (New York: McGraw-Hill, 1958).

markets'?"[32] In the proof that follows, Samuelson is able to deduce, from some very general assumptions about the properties of asset or commodity markets, that, in fact, markets are "efficient"; that is, they do adjust to expectations over time. As a consequence, any fluctuations in prices from one period to the next are *not* related to the previous period's prices. Movements of prices in markets for stocks or commodities are what the statisticians refer to as a "random walk."[33] Samuelson elaborated on his initial proof in several subsequent articles, where he applied the results more specifically to the question of asset pricing and portfolio selection.[34]

What implications does the "efficient markets" thesis (as it has come to be called) have for economic theory in a broader sense? Both in his initial 1965 proof and in subsequent comments on his work, Samuelson has been very cautious in drawing inferences from the fact that markets adjust to expectations. "One should not," he cautioned, "read too much into the established theorem. It does not prove that actual competitive markets work well."[35] Nor does it prove that a single buyer or investor who posesses better information will not be able to make a profit on that information. The point is that not everyone can have such "inside" information; if they did, the market would reflect the collective anticipations, and the price of the asset or commodity would adjust. Samuelson also went to some length to insist that his theorem did not imply that the price of an asset or commodity was a completely random event. "A determinate trend in the long-run normal price of bread," he pointed out, "is quite compatible with the fact that speculators will discount in advance all discernable events."[36] Efficient markets, in other words, still heed the law of supply and demand.

This theorem has a very practical implication for those seeking the best investment strategy for their assets. In his *Newsweek* column, Samuelson continually reminds his readers that it is unlikely that they can do better than the market average. His advice, therefore, is to "diversify broadly, hold down costly turnover, keep all fees (and book-keeping!) minimal."[37]

Though Samuelson confined his own applications of his theorem to the question of speculation and portfolio selection in the asset markets, others drew a much broader implication from the efficient markets

[32] Paul A. Samuelson, "Proof That Properly Anticipated Prices Fluctuate Randomly," *Collected Papers*, vol. 3, no. 198. p. 782.

[33] Stated more precisely, the argument implies that price changes over time (i.e., $X(t+1) - X(t)$ will exhibit no statistical correlation; they behave in a purely random fashion.

[34] The most significant of these were: "Rational Theory of Warrant Pricing," published in 1965 (*Collected Papers*, vol. 3, no. 199, pp. 791–817); and "Proof That Properly Discounted Values of Assets Vibrate Randomly," published in 1973 (*Collected Papers*, vol. 4, no. 241, pp. 465–70).

[35] Samuelson, "Proof That Properly Anticipated Prices Fluctuate Randomly," p. 789.

[36] Paul A. Samuelson, "Is the Real-World Price a Tale Told by the Idiot of Chance?," *Collected Papers*, vol. 4, p. 472.

[37] *Newsweek*, 6 March 1978, p. 88. Some months earlier Samuelson had explained to his *Newsweek* audience why, if markets were "efficient," individual investors would be unable to "beat the market." (*Newsweek*, 17 June 1977, p. 74.)

thesis. If, as Samuelson's proofs suggest, expectations of buyers and sellers are incorporated into market prices, then the intent of discretionary policymakers might also be discounted by the price mechanisms. In the late 1960's, an idea called "rational expectations" evolved among some macroeconomists. Based on the efficient market theorem, this approach insisted that economic policy would tend to be thwarted because people would anticipate the moves of the policymakers—and take steps to offset the intent of the policy.[38]

For his part, heeding his own warnings about the limits of his theorem, Samuelson is not willing to embrace the implications of the rational expectations approach. As we shall see below, Samuelson remained a strong advocate of discretionary economic policy long after the publication of his efficient markets paper in 1965.

Despite his influence in the development of mathematical models to explain the economic problem, Samuelson has remained largely apart from the growing trend to apply statistical tools to the analysis of the economy. "Econometrics"—the empirical application of economic theory through statistical inference—is an area in which Samuelson has not written. To be sure, he has been instrumental in helping to develop techniques such as linear programming and applying them to the theory of the firm.[39] Yet he clearly prefers to apply his mathematical analysis to investigations of pure economic theory; he has done very little applied work in econometrics.

Samuelson's reluctance to engage in empirical work may reflect more than his preference for theory. He has always been highly skeptical of the ability of econometric models to predict future economic events. The failure of many econometric models to forecast accurately events immediately after World War II illustrated the limited tools at hand. Samuelson's own experience as a prognosticator of events in 1944 did little to increase his confidence in the new techniques. In that year, he published a two-part article in the *New Republic* entitled "Unemployment Ahead."[40] The text was as pessimistic as its title implied; Samuelson forecast a serious slump in employment at the end of hostilities.

---

[38] We shall return to some of the implications of efficient markets and rational expectations in Chapter 14. Samuelson rejects the argument that, with rational expectations, people will be able to completely offset the effects of economic policy. See Samuelson's comments in "Reflections on the Merits and Demerits of Monetarism," *Collected Papers*, vol. 4, no. 264, pp. 773–75. An excellent summary of the rational expectations approach as it is applied to macro policy can be found in Samuelson's article "Rational Expectations—Fresh Ideas That Challenge Some Established Views of Policy Making," in Daniel Rosse, ed. *Readings on Inflation* (New York: Federal Reserve Bank of New York, 1979), pp. 200–12. See also the references to work in rational expectations cited in Chapter 14.

[39] A paper written by Samuelson in 1949 for the RAND Corporation, but not published until 1966, is acknowledged to be one of the clearest and most concise statements of the use of linear programming and maximization of profits by the firm. See Paul A. Samuelson, "Market Mechanisms and Maximization," *Collected Papers*, vol. 1, no. 33, pp. 425–92. Samuelson coauthored a text on linear programming with Robert Dorfman and Robert Solow: *Linear Programming and Economic Analysis* (New York: McGraw-Hill, 1958).

[40] Paul A. Samuelson, "Unemployment Ahead," *New Republic*, 11 September 1944, pp. 297–99, and 18 September 1944, pp. 333–35.

He was hardly alone in such a view. But he was wrong, and critics were able to jump on his boldness in publishing such a forecast as events unfolded. To those who saw Samuelson (with perhaps a touch of envy) as the young *wunderkind*, his error gave a feeling of smug satisfaction. Moreover, critics of his mathematical approach to economics were able to point out that one of the most brilliant expositors of that methodology had stumbled in predicting postwar economic adjustments. When *Foundations* appeared three years later, even a friendly reviewer such as Kenneth Boulding was unable to resist pointing out that, while Samuelson provided a "brilliant mathematical analysis" of Keynes,

> his skill in analyzing the variables of this system did not, however, enable him to avoid very substantial errors in forecasting when he tried to apply the system to problems of the transition after World War II.[41]

Samuelson did not quickly forget the experience. Ten years later, he still expressed skepticism about econometric estimates, and the problems which many forecasting models encountered in predicting inflation rates in the 1970's reinforced his reluctance to engage in prognostication of economic trends.[42]

The Theory of Public Expenditure

As the levels of government activity rapidly expanded in the 1950's, the issues surrounding social and private costs raised by A.C. Pigou returned to the forefront of economics. The existing economic theory of government expenditure was ill equipped to deal with the challenge posed by these problems. The vast bulk of attention in public finance had focused on taxation rather than on spending. Pigou's own treatment of externalities (such as his road congestion example, which we shall return to in Chapter 12) dealt with these phenomena largely in terms of taxes and subsides to equalize private and social costs.

Samuelson plunged into this vacuum in 1954 with a brief note entitled "The Pure Theory of Public Expenditure."[43] He sought to integrate the existing theory of taxation with the relatively unexplored question of allocating government expenditures. As he later noted, his effort was meant as "the culmination of a century of writing on public expenditures."[44] His own contribution was to develop a unified analysis

---

[41] Boulding, "Samuelson's Foundations," p. 189.

[42] In 1956, he expressed his doubts to a symposium on employment. See Paul A. Samuelson, "Economic Forecasting and National Policy," *Collected Papers*, vol. 2, no. 101, pp. 1331–35. For a more recent expression, see Paul A. Samuelson, "The Art and Science of Macromodels Over 50 Years," *Collected Papers*, vol. 4, no. 275, pp. 854–61.

[43] Paul A. Samuelson, "The Pure Theory of Public Expenditure," *Collected Papers*, vol. 2, no. 92, pp. 1223–25.

[44] Paul A. Samuelson, "Pure Theory of Public Expenditure and Taxation," *Collected Papers*, vol. 3, no. 172, p. 492. Samuelson specifically acknowledged the extensive work done by Knut Wicksell at the turn of the century as well as the more recent writings of Erik Lindahl and Richard Musgrave.

which demonstrated that a solution to the allocation of government spending did, in fact, exist. Unfortunately, the brevity and mathematical notation of the initial argument tended to obscure its contribution to the debate.[45]

Samuelson began his theory of public expenditure by making a fundamental distinction between two types of goods. At one extreme is the *private consumption good*, "which can be parcelled out among different individuals."[46] Consumption of these goods by someone will result in less being available for someone else. At the other extreme is the *public consumption good*, "which all enjoy in common in the sense that each individual's consumption of such a good leads to no subtraction from any other individual's consumption of that good."[47] An immediate problem arose from this dichotomy, for it was apparent that the vast majority of goods was not exclusively in either category. Eventually this led Samuelson to restate his definition of a public good simply as "one that enters two or more persons' utility."[48] Rather than the two polar cases, this leaves us with a "knife's edge of a private good case and with *all* of the rest of the world in the public good domain by virtue of involving some 'consumption externality.' "[49]

But why does the market fail to allocate properly the public goods? Samuelson's answer goes back to the *free rider problem* posed by Sidgwick and Pigou: ". . . with public goods the consumer has every reason not to provide us with revelatory demand functions."[50] Consumers hide their desire for these goods since they know that if someone else produces them, everyone will be able to consume them without charge. This *consumption externality* is the crux of Samuelson's formulation of the theory of public expenditure.[51] If consumers behave in

---

Musgrave's text, *The Theory of Public Finance* (New York: McGraw-Hill, 1958) was one of the first to bring together the elements of expenditure and taxation theory in a single treatment. Musgrave drew, of course, upon Samuelson's work on public goods.

[45] As critic Steven Enke put it: "Mathematical shorthand may permit a three-page article, but a few more words would have added many readers." Steven Enke, "More on the Misuses of Mathematics in Economics: A Rejoinder," *Review of Economics and Statistics*, May 1952, p. 132. Critics also complained that it was presumptuous of Samuelson to label his views as "the" theory of public expenditure. Samuelson responded to his critics by providing "A Diagrammatic Exposition of a Theory of Public Expenditure," *Collected Papers*, vol. 2, no. 93, pp. 1226–32.

[46] Samuelson, "The Pure Theory of Public Expenditure," p. 1223.

[47] Samuelson, "The Pure Theory of Public Expenditure," p. 1223. In the text Samuelson terms public goods "collective consumption goods."

[48] Samuelson, "Pure Theory of Public Expenditure and Taxation," p. 502.

[49] Samuelson, "Pure Theory of Public Expenditure and Taxation," p. 502. Italics in the original.

[50] Samuelson, "Pure Theory of Public Expenditure and Taxation," p. 497.

[51] It is interesting to note that Pigou preferred to treat market failure arising from each producer's decision matrix separately leading to suboptimal public goods *production*. Samuelson attacks the problem the other way around. He analyzes the consumer's decision matrix and shows that a suboptimal demand for public goods can be expected. Of course, the two approaches lead to the same result: market failure. Thorstein Veblen was also concerned with consumption externalities. But he approached them not from the point of view of consumers demanding inadequate amounts of public goods, but on the contrary, demanding the wrong goods of all kinds, both public and private. Thus, for example, Veblen would see no reason for public centers of higher learning to engage in any less wasteful activities than those of private institutions. Such an approach represents a far more general attack on the neoclassical model than that of either Samuelson or Pigou. A modern economist who more closely follows Veblen's ideas, John Kenneth Galbraith, is discussed in Chapter 11.

this fashion, is there any possible solution to the efficient allocation of public goods? Samuelson begins with an "individualistic approach" in which he attempts to determine the optimum distribution of goods— public and private. Such a situation would formally be stated as one where:

1. No additional gains can be realized from trading goods of any sort among people; and
2. No additional output can be realized through shifts of resources to other goods.[52]

The point of this initial argument was to show mathematically that there was an optimal solution—although it was not unique. A subsequent exposition of the issue by Samuelson serves to point out just how unlikely it is that an economy would ever, in fact, reach such a position.[53] The argument is as follows:

1. We first assume the existence of a "referee" or computer that is able to obtain the true preferences for all individuals. From these preferences, the referee-computer can construct "pseudo-demand functions" for all goods.[54]
2. The government now provides each consumer with a lump sum of income in addition to the consumer's income from ownership of inputs (wages, profits, rents, and so on).
3. Each person now engages in exchange of all goods—public and private—at some range of prices for private goods and "pseudo-tax" prices for consumption of public goods.
4. The referee-computer can now determine the optimal distribution and production of goods through appropriate juggling of the income subsidies and pseudo-tax prices of public goods. (The allocation of private goods is, of course, simultaneously determined by production and exchange of goods at the market prices set up under the third point above.)

Samuelson's construction of a "pseudo-market equilibrium" using an abstract mathematical model is another example of the way in which mathematics can be used to explore beyond the boundaries of intuition. Unfortunately, the outcome in this case is not very encouraging to those who seek answers to the issues surrounding government expenditure theory. For whatever its relevance to computer science, Samuelson's model has *no* relevance to market behavior. In fact, far from giving a solution to the question, it provides a "corrosive nihilism," which seems "needed to puncture the bubble of vague and wishful

---

[52] Stated in terms of the marginal analysis discussed in Chapter 5, these conditions state that the *marginal social value* of all goods was identical, and that the *marginal social cost* of production for all goods was identical.

[53] This section is based on the arguments in Samuelson's "Pure Theory of Public Expenditure and Taxation," especially the appendix of that paper. Essentially the same logical argument is in Samuelson's earlier writings. All the presentations are highly mathematical, and we shall eschew detailed discussion of the model here.

[54] The demand functions are termed *pseudo* since they could never be actually measured in the market due to the individual's incentive to hide a true perference for a public good.

thinking in these matters."[55] Having proven the market's inability to handle the presence of consumption externalities, Samuelson points out that theorists have provided very little additional insight into the questions of collective decisions which lie behind government expenditures.

This is not due to any lack of effort. Since the appearance of Samuelson's 1958 piece on public expenditures, the subject has been the focus of considerable debate among economists. Let us briefly look at some of the issues which have been raised in response to Samuelson's initial statement of the problem.

One of the most troubling points involved the nature of the consumption externality in public goods analysis. To a considerable extent, the problem of joint consumption could be curtailed by the use of exclusion devices which prevented nonpaying consumers from enjoying the public good. An example which has been used in the debate is television. Once broadcasted on a public channel, programs can be picked up by anyone with a TV set. Such programs are clearly public goods. However, by "scrambling" the TV signal, the reception can be limited to only those sets with "descramblers." Now the TV program is a private good. The size of the service may also limit a good's "publicness." Thus, for example, as one gets farther away from the originating TV signal, one's reception becomes less perfect, and eventually disappears.[56] The question of whether the good is a public good then turns upon the cost of excluding consumers. Where such costs are very high, as in national defense, the good will be classified as a public good; where such costs are quite low, as in the case of television, the good approaches a private good.[57] While he concedes that the presence of exclusion devices will limit the joint consumption of public goods, Samuelson insists that the use of such devices will not remove the inherent incentive on the part of consumers to hide their preference for the good. Even if exclusion devices allowed us to determine the "pseudo-prices" of his omniscient referee-computer, "it still pays that last man to dissemble and hide his true liking for the public good."[58]

The question of determining which goods shall be public leads to the broader issue of justifying government intervention in a market economy. An early criticism of Samuelson's public expenditure model was

---

[55] Samuelson, "Pure Theory of Expenditure and Taxation," p. 500.

[56] For more on the problem of exclusion, see Roland McKean, *Public Spending* (New York: McGraw-Hill, 1968), pp. 67–68. For Samuelson's comments on the TV case, see idem, "Public Goods and Subscription TV: Correction of the Record," *Collected Papers*, vol. 3, no. 173, pp. 518–20.

[57] The best discussion of this is in McKean, *Public Spending*. James Buchanan also presents a careful analysis of this issue in his book *The Demand and Supply of Public Goods* (New York: Rand-McNally, 1968), Chapters 5 and 6. Both of these authors stress the feasibility of excluding joint consumption of many goods. Samuelson is less certain of this; see his comments in Paul A. Samuelson, "Pitfalls in the Analysis of Public Goods," *Collected Papers*, vol. 3, no. 175, pp. 522–27. A highly technical presentation of the issue, which highlights Samuelson's contribution to the debate, is in Anthony Atkinson and Joseph Stiglitz, *Lectures on Political Economy* (New York: McGraw-Hill, 1980), Chapters 16 and 17. Stiglitz was one of Samuelson's most distinguished students from MIT.

[58] Samuelson, "Pure Theory of Public Expenditure and Taxation," p. 508.

that it failed to shed light on this important question. Samuelson's reply was that it was not intended to provide a criteria for government action; his public goods analysis was designed to deal with the issue of allocation of expenditures once the goods were determined. He did, however, elaborate on several criteria which he thought would justify government action:[59]

1. Paternalistic policies voted upon by the electorate which felt the market solution was not optimal.
2. Redistribution of income.
3. Regulation of industries which exhibit Marshallian "increasing returns."
4. A myriad of externality situations where public and private interests diverge.

This list helps illustrate the relation of public goods to the earlier framework of externalities. Samuelson's emphasis is on a *consumption externality* which arises from the government's offering of a good at no cost to the public. Clearly, the Pigouvian externalities are also likely to be present in many of these situations.[60] In fact, this has caused some confusion in the debate over the theory of expenditure, for *conditions of supply* in the production of public goods may be the factor which causes them to be produced by the government. Externalities of the Pigouvian type must be separated from the consumption externality arising in the case of public goods. Two situations of supply have received particular attention in the literature.

Almost every economist since Marshall has accepted the dictum that government regulation is required where *increasing returns* are present. Samuelson does not demur. A second aspect of supply is *joint production* of goods, a situation where more than one good or service is provided simultaneously. Here Samuelson concedes that the exclusion device is an appropriate means of achieving optimum conditions. In both cases, however, the consumption externality is a distinct problem apart from conditions of supply.[61]

Omniscient computers are useful devices of pure theory, and distinctions in classes of public goods may shed some light on the underlying issues of public expenditure. But where does this leave us? The theory of public goods does not provide ready answers even in a highly abstract environment; indeed, as we noted above, it emphasizes the *absence* of such ready answers. Here, as in the case of index numbers, Samuelson's

---

[59] Samuelson, "A Diagrammatic Exposition of a Theory of Public Expenditure," pp. 1231–32.

[60] One of the best treatments of externalities and public goods is that of McKean, *Public Spending*, Chapter 4. A more technical discussion of externalities and government can be found in Francis Bator, "The Anatomy of Market Failure," *Quarterly Journal of Economics*, August 1956, pp. 351–79. Bator distinguishes two additional externalities beyond the public goods case: technological relations which involve decreasing costs à la Marshall, and "ownership externalities" of the sort discussed by Frank Knight in the 1920s (See Chapter 12).

[61] On the questions surrounding supply, see the appendix to Samuelson, "Pure Theory of Public Expenditure and Taxation." Buchanan takes a somewhat critical position of Samuelson's analysis in his article "Which Goods Should Be Public," in idem, *The Demand and Supply of Public Goods*, pp. 171–90.

analysis points out the limits of our analytical abilities. So little is known of the manner in which government measures the welfare implications of their actions that economists can add very little for the moment. But at least Samuelson feels that his model has conclusively demonstrated that the "easy formulas of classical economics no longer light our way."[62]

Samuelson on the Importance of Money

While the issues surrounding public goods and the role of the government in producing goods and services in our economy remain largely unsettled, the responsibility of the government in maintaining aggregate stability is virtually unchallenged today. Indeed, maintaining economic stability has been the dominating issue of the post-Keynesian world. Though they agree on the objective, economists disagree on which policy will be most effective in maintaining economic stability.

To the neoclassicists of Marshall's time, the challenge of adjusting aggregate demand to maintain price stability and employment was met through the implementation of appropriate monetary policy. The central bank simply adjusted the availability of reserves for banks, and the economic system would respond to the greater or lesser availability of funds. This orthodoxy was still dominant at the time of the stock market crash—and subsequent collapse of the monetary system—in 1929–33, and it was this position which the early Keynesians attacked in the late 1930s. To the more extreme Keynesians, money did not matter at all! As we noted in our discussion of Alvin Hansen's policy recommendations, the new economics insisted that the link between changes in the stock of money and changes in effective aggregate demand was very weak. Monetary policy, they contended, had little or no impact on the level of economic activity.

This insistence that monetary policy was totally ineffective was gradually abandoned in the face of empirical evidence which showed rather clearly that money does matter. Experience in the postwar era has shown rather dramatically that changes in the money supply can have a very significant effect on aggregate demand, particularly in restraining an expansion in spending. One group of economists insists that money is the dominant variable in shaping aggregate demand. To these people, money alone matters.[63]

Eclectic as always, Samuelson rejects both extreme positions: "Personally, I prefer to stick to the middle-road of good, strong, value."[64] His

---

[62] Samuelson, "Aspects of Public Expenditure Theories," *Collected Papers*, vol. 2, no. 94, p. 1237.

[63] We shall explore this monetarist position in greater detail in Chapter 14 when we examine the views of Milton Friedman.

[64] Paul A. Samuelson, "Money, Interest Rates and Economic Activity: Their Interrelationship in a Market Economy," *Collected Papers*, vol. 3, no. 178, p. 569. The discussion of this section rests in large measure on his address to the American Bankers Association in April 1967. Several other sources for Samuelson's views on money include: his testimony before the Canadian Commission on Banking and Finance ("Reflections on Central Banking," *Collected Papers*, vol. 2, no. 104, pp. 1361–86); "The Merits and Demerits of Monetarism," vol. 4, pp. 765–79; and his testimony before

views on monetary policy clearly reflect the influence of Hansen's synthesis of Keynes and neoclassical thought. Samuelson was, of course, in a position to examine the merits of both views, having studied at Chicago prior to joining Hansen at Harvard.[65]

Samuelson advocates a mix of monetary and fiscal policy to maintain economic stability. As he once explained to Senator Edward Kennedy,

> I think God gave us two eyes, and with respect, I think he must have had a purpose in doing so. It is not necessary, as the monetarists say, to watch only one thing; namely the money supply. . . ."[66]

Though he accepts the role of money as very significant, Samuelson has reservations about relying extensively on monetary policy as a tool of stabilization. His reservations are representative of a sizable number of economists today, and it is worthwhile to examine them in some detail.

To begin with, Samuelson accepts the validity of what he terms a "depression-Keynes" model of the economy, where there is a liquidity trap that renders ineffective the adjustment of aggregate demand through changes in the money supply. Samuelson feels that, particularly in the short run, this model may be a reasonable approximation of the real world. In defense of the early Keynesian views on money, he points out that

> Most converts to Keynesianism became so during the slump years of the late 1930's. Then the deep-depression polar case did seem to be the realistic case. In 1938, the interest rate on Treasury Bills was often a fraction of a percent, and even a monetarist might despair of the potency of central bank monetary policy.[67]

More generally, Samuelson feels that monetary policy is asymmetrical in its impact on the economy. Monetary policy works primarily

> . . . *by lowering or raising the spectrum of interest rates*, thereby increasing or decreasing the flow of investment and durable-goods spending, which leads in turn to expansion or contraction in the aggregate of GNP flow.[68]

---

the House of Representatives, U.S. Congress, House, Committee on Banking, Housing and Urban Affairs, *Second Meeting on Conduct of Monetary Policy,* 94th Cong. 1st sess. 4 and 6 November 1975, pp. 49–75. The congressional testimony was one of the few times when Samuelson and his adversary Milton Freidman appeared on a panel together. In March 1980, Friedman and Samuelson presented their differing views on the same panel at Texas A & M University. See *Milton Friedman and Paul A. Samuelson Discuss the Economic Responsibility of Government* (College Station, Tex.: Center for Education and Research in Free Enterprise, 1980).

[65] As Samuelson has pointed out, he was a "classical" monetary theorist very briefly. To recall what that position involved, he has "merely . . . to lie down on the couch and recall in tranquility upon that inward eye which is the bliss of solitude, what it was that I believed between the ages of 17 and 22." Paul A. Samuelson, "What Classical and Neoclassical Monetary Theory Really Was," *Collected Papers,* vol. 3, no. 176, p. 529.

[66] U.S., Congress, Joint Economic Committee, *Midyear Review of the Economic Situation and Outlook,* 94th Cong. 1st sess. 23–25 and 29–30 July 1975, p. 91.

[67] Samuelson, "Reflections on the Merits and Demerits of Monetarism," p. 769. On the appropriateness of this model in the postwar era, Samuelson believes ". . . in the face of some doubters, that such a model has occasional empirical validity—certainly in the short run and possibly for a vexingly long time" (Samuelson, "Reflections on Central Banking," p. 1367).

[68] Samuelson, "Money, Interest Rates, and Economic Activity," p. 55. Italics in original.

Such an outcome, insists Samuelson, will be more effective both in restraining or expanding credit at times when real interest rates are high, and must be less effective when they are low.[69]

Finally, there are limits on the usefulness of monetary policy in pursuing a spectrum of policy goals. Institutional constraints, such as the Federal Reserve Board's commitment to maintain "orderly money markets," may inhibit the pursuit of a vigorous monetary policy.[70] Financial arrangements in the international market are another place where the objectives of domestic monetary policy may create problems for the objective of maintaining equilibrium in the balance of payments.[71]

As might be expected of a man who did much to develop the Hansen synthesis of neoclassical and Keynesian thought, Samuelson insists on a balance of monetary and fiscal policy. The possibility of effecting such a balance is greatly increased by the fact that government now accounts for almost one-third of total output. Even relatively small shifts of expenditures can have, through the leverage of the multiplier-accelerator, a substantial effect on aggregate demand. Through the 1950s and 1960s, economists felt that some of the countercyclical effects were automatic. Progressive taxes (particularly the personal income tax) meant that as income rose, tax revenues rose by a larger fraction. This should tend to dampen demand. If, as seems to be the case for the past two decades, the effect of larger tax revenues is to stimulate government expenditures, the dampening effect may be offset and perhaps even reversed.[72] While Samuelson favors such "automatic stabilizers," he does not feel that they can be counted on to ensure economic stability. To him, the essential difference between the new economics and its predecessors is the former's "activist attempts to stretch out the prosperity periods by explicit action."[73] In supporting

---

[69] This contention rests on the view that, when rates are high, borrowers will be "driven to the banks" as alternative sources of credit are eventually loaned out. Thus, the banking system's ability to lend funds carries greater leverage, since they are in this situation the principal source of credit. During periods of low interest rates, Samuelson argues that the leverage of the banks is reduced by the supply of credit from other intermediaries that can lend funds to prospective borrowers. See Samuelson, "Reflections on Central Banking," pp. 1366–67.

[70] An example of a market which can pose problems for the Fed in monetary policy would be the home mortgage market. In 1967 and again in the late 1970s, the central bank's objective of maintaining high interest rates created serious disruptions in the availability of funds for home loans—and threatened the stability of some of the financial intermediaries in those markets.

[71] For example, it may be an objective to stimulate domestic investment by keeping interest rates low. If, however, short-term interest rates fall, foreign capital will move away from American investments and seek higher returns elsewhere. The outflow of capital will create a deficit in the balance of payments, which might threaten the stability of the dollar. Samuelson has consistently argued that too much attention is currently paid to keeping the value of the dollar stable in the international marketplace.

[72] One of the effects of inflation has been to greatly increase the level of government spending as tax revenues increase due to the progressive nature of the income tax. In addition to the possible effects of taxes, transfer payments, such as unemployment insurance and social security payments, will provide a "floor" to aggregate expenditures in the event of a fall in demand. Here again, the effect can be destabilizing if cost-of-living allowances are routinely added to payments, thus increasing demand when stabilization policy calls for a curtailment of demand.

[73] Arthur Burns and Paul Samuelson, *Full Employment, Guideposts and Economics Stability* (Washington, D.C.: American Enterprise Institute for Public Policy Research, 1967), p. 96.

this view, one must be cognizant of the importance of assuring that the new economics is a two-way street. The policymaker must be willing to employ monetary-fiscal policy both to curtail and to stimulate demand. Unfortunately, achieving such symmetry in either fiscal or monetary policy is seldom easy in the political context of the United States. Academic acceptance of the postulates espoused by the new economics has not made congressmen any more eager to impose either higher taxes or lower levels of government services on their constituents.

Moreover, a new problem appeared in the late 1970s which further constrained the effectiveness of measures employing traditional monetary and fiscal policy: *inflation*. Inflation is an old phenomenon and one quite familiar to the neoclassical writers. They explained it using the quantity theory of money. Prices rose whenever there was an excess demand for goods. The remedy for such a problem was simple: reduce the stock of money relative to the level of income and aggregate demand would be diminished. Although it involved a different perspective, Keynesians took an equally straightforward view of the problem. Inflation occurred whenever the sum of consumption, investment, and government expenditures exceeded the full employment capacity of the economy to produce goods and services. The Keynesian prescription was also simple; employ fiscal policy to reduce aggregate demand.

Inflation and Unemployment: The Phillips Curve

Both of these explanations of inflation rely on an analysis where excess demand (or spending) bids up the general price level. Such a view has been challenged on the basis of empirical evidence since World War II, which indicates that inflation has been present during periods when considerable excess capacity remained in the system. This would not be consistent with a view that predicted rising prices as a consequence of full employment of all resources. Beginning in the early 1950s, economists began to develop different theories of inflation, which centered on the mechanism through which price increases are generated in our market economy.[74]

These new explanations were intended theoretically to explain a way in which inflation and unemployment could be present concurrently. In 1958, A. W. Phillips, a New Zealand economist working at the London School of Economics, attacked this problem empirically by presenting data on the relationship between wages and employment in the United Kingdom from 1862 to 1957. He developed a graphical

---

[74] We shall discuss one of these new approaches, Professor Lerner's "sellers' inflation," in the next chapter. An excellent review of the inflation literature up to 1960 is Franklyn Holtzman and Martin Bronfenbrenner, "Survey of Inflation Theory," *American Economic Review* 53 (September 1963): 593–661. Helmut Frisch provides an update to that survey in "Inflation Theory 1963–1975: A 'Second Generation' Survey," *Journal of Economic Literature* 15 (December 1974): 1284–1317. Samuelson has pointed out that the Keynesian "demand-pull" model is still occasionally appropriate. The inflation between 1965 and 1970 was, in his view, exactly of this sort. See his testimony in U.S., Congress, Joint Economic Committee, "1970 Midyear Review of the State of the Economy," 91st Cong., 2nd sess., 20–24 July 1970, p. 520.

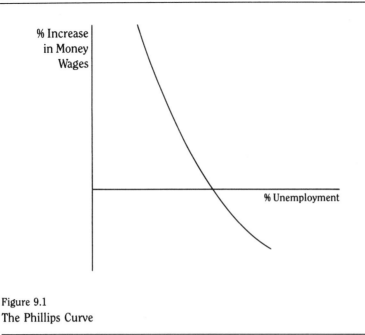

% Increase in Money Wages

% Unemployment

Figure 9.1
The Phillips Curve

presentation which has become known as the Phillips Curve.[75] A hypothetical Phillips Curve is shown in Figure 9.1. The vertical axis measures the *percent change in money wages*; the horizontal axis measures the *percent of the labor force unemployed*. Any point on the curve shows the level of unemployment which is associated with some level of increasing wages. It provides a measure, therefore, of the "trade-off" between employment and inflation. It is, we should immediately note, *not* a theory of inflation; rather it is an empirical relationship between the two variables plotted on the graph.

In 1960, Samuelson and Robert Solow brought the Phillips Curve to the United States in a paper read to the American Economic Association.[76] In generalizing Phillips's analysis, they presented a Phillips Curve showing the relation between increasing prices (inflation) and the unemployment rate.[77] Samuelson regards the Phillips Curve as "one of the most important concepts of our times."[78] It provides the policymaker with a "menu" of alternatives which monetary and fiscal

---

[75] A.W. Phillips, "The Relation Between Unemployment and the Rate of Change of Money Wage Rates in the United Kingdom, 1861–1957," *Economica* (1958), pp. 283–300.

[76] Paul Samuelson and Robert Solow, "Analytical Aspects of Anti-Inflation Policy," *Collected Papers*, vol. 2, no. 102, pp. 1336–53.

[77] Note that Samuelson and Solow have introduced an additional relationship by depicting the Phillips Curve as a relation between rising prices and unemployment. If wage increases are accompanied by increases in the productivity of labor, then the effect of some percentage increase in wages on prices is dependent upon the behavior of productivity and prices. The simplest case is to assume that only increases in wages which exceed the rise in productivity generate inflationary pressures.

[78] Burns and Samuelson, p. 54.

policy can achieve.[79] In the years since it was first introduced, the menu of the Phillips Curve came to dominate stabilization policy not only in the United States but elsewhere as well.

The Phillips Curve analysis implies that the policymaker must choose a combination of inflation and unemployment offered by the menu. To see the significance of this, let us imagine two situations depicted by the Phillips Curves of Figures 9.2. Figure 9.2A shows a Phillips Curve which would be present in the traditional demand-pull model. As long as aggregate demand is less than the full employment level (which is assumed to be about 5 percent), there is no pressure on prices. When unemployment is below 5 percent, increases in demand will quickly lessen unemployment, with little increase in the price level. Once we reach full employment, however, any increase in demand will generate a rapid rise in prices. The situation in Figure 9.2B is markedly different. Here it appears that inflationary pressures develop long before unemployment has fallen to 5 percent. If we seek to maintain a level of unemployment of 5 percent, prices will rise by 6 or 7 percent per year; keeping prices stable (that is, zero increase in prices) would result in 8 or 9 percent of the labor force being out of work.

Although the Phillips Curve analysis rests on the empirical finding of a relationship between wages and unemployment for Great Britain, verification that such a relationship exists in the United States remains imperfect at best. In their 1960 article, Samuelson and Solow only guessed that a curve such as that in Figure 9.2B typified the experience of the United States. Subsequent work has confirmed the rather obvious fact that we have an economy in which both inflation and unemployment can persist, but it has not uncovered a systematic relationship between the rate of inflation and the rate of unemployment. In fact, the only long-run relationship which has been found is that there is some "natural" rate of unemployment which is quite independent of the rate of inflation.[80] Samuelson does not dispute this result; however, he stresses that ". . . the measured Phillips Curves represent *short-term* relationships that will definitely shift in the long run."[81]

The Phillips Curve analysis suggests that to combat unemployment without inflation requires a movement of this short-run Phillips Curve.

---

[79] Robert Solow recalled the manner in which he and Samuelson discovered the importance of the Phillips Curve:

> I remember that Paul Samuelson asked me when we were looking at the diagrams for the first time, "Does that look like a reversible relationship to you?" What he meant was, "Do you really think the economy can move back and forth along a curve like that?" And I answered, "Yeah, I'm inclined to believe it," and Paul said, "Me too."

Daniel Bell, "Models and Reality in Economic Discourse," *The Public Interest*, Special Issue, 1980, p. 67.

[80] In other words, the long-run Phillips Curve is a vertical line at some level of unemployment. For a summary of the empirical debates surrounding the Phillips Curve, see Anthony Santomero and John Seater, "The Inflation-Unemployment Trade-off: A Critique of the Literature," *Journal of Economic Literature* 16 (June 1978): 499–544. Santomero and Seater conclude that "there appears to be no long-run trade-off between inflation and unemployment" (p. 514).

[81] Samuelson, *Economics*, p. 777.

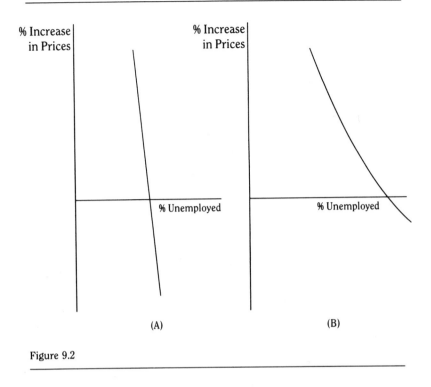

Figure 9.2

That is, you must transform a curve such as that in Figure 9.2B into one such as that of Figure 9.2A. This is a marked departure from the policies implied by the demand-pull analysis. How can this be accomplished? The answer is not a simple one, for the dilemma of concurrent inflation and unemployment is not likely, in Samuelson's view, to completely disappear.

"The art of economic policy," claims Samuelson, "is in the skillful compromise that the conflicting goals of price stability and high unemployment . . . necessitate."[82] He wastes few words in rejecting one of the most obvious solutions: wage-and-price controls. "The only good price-control program," claims Samuelson, "is a *repealed* price control program."[83] Referring to John Kenneth Galbraith's espousal of such controls, Samuelson remarked:

> He has simply not yet done his homework on how such measures work out in Scandinavia, Britain, and elsewhere. Anyone who has a notion that a few men in a Washington office can keep tabs on the prices and wages charged by the few hundred largest corporations and the unions they deal with should better occupy himself writing a bestseller about Utopia.[84]

---

[82] *Newsweek*, 17 May 1976, p. 82.

[83] *Newsweek*, 9 September 1975, p. 74. Italics in the original.

[84] Samuelson, "Liberalism At Bay," p. 876. We shall consider Galbraith's best-selling book on Utopia in Chapter 11.

While he opposes measures of this sort, Samuelson is less clear on what should be done to solve the Phillips Curve dilemma. He sees a very diverse set of forces at work behind the Phillips Curve, and they do not always push in the same direction.[85] Thus, for example, one obvious factor producing the Phillips Curve relationship is wage-and-price rigidities. To counter this problem, Samuelson argues for a vigorous policy of expansion. Over time, such a policy will produce a sustained demand which should cause the unemployment (even hard-core unemployment) to melt away like a block of ice. The Phillips Curve will be moved towards lower levels of unemployment and rates of inflation. On the other hand, an expansionist fiscal or monetary policy may encourage any expectations of increasing prices and thus feed the demands for higher wages and prices. Once people are caught up in such an inflationary psychology, it becomes difficult to stem a continued rise in prices. Unfortunately, in Samuelson's view, one of the only practical ways to break such a psychology is to slow down the economy.[86]

Samuelson's efforts to move the short-run Phillips Curve must eventually bring us to the issue of whether there is some "natural" rate of unemployment, that is, a long-run Phillips Curve which depicts a situation where changes in the rate of inflation have little or no effect on the level of unemployment. Samuelson is not prepared to accept such a position. He concedes that in the long run the trade-off between unemployment and inflation is more like the situation depicted in Figure 9.2A (twisted toward the vertical) than that of Figure 9.2B. Yet he denies that it will ever be completely vertical.[87] His skepticism rests in part on what people term a *money illusion*, which exists when people respond to the money values on income, prices, and so on, rather than to the real values.[88] During an inflation, money values rise more rapidly than real values. Demand will be stimulated by the apparent rise in income, thus spurring the employment of any remaining idle resources. The trade-off between increases in inflation and lower unemployment will not completely disappear.[89]

---

[85] In addition to his published remarks on the Phillips Curve, this section draws upon correspondence with Samuelson and the authors in 1969 when we prepared the first edition of this book. Among the best summaries of his views in print are his remarks in Burns and Samuelson, pp. 53–57, 64–66, and 124–29. He devoted considerable attention to the problem of an inflation-unemployment trade-off in the 1980 edition of Samuelson, *Economics*, pp. 775–80; and his various appearances before congressional committees over the past decade provide insights into his views on macroeconomic policy. See also his comments at the Texas A & M panel in 1980, (*Milton Friedman and Paul A. Samuelson Discuss the Economic Responsibility of Government*).

[86] As Samuelson rather reluctantly stated the case:
> I'm not the one to make the recommendation, but I think it might be argued that the optimal policy in a mixed economy like ours might be intermittent periods of letting a certain amount of slack develop, then going in strong.
Burns and Samuelson, p. 163.

[87] On Samuelson's views regarding the long-run Phillips Curve, see Burns and Samuelson, pp. 64–66, and Samuelson, *Economics*, 11th ed., pp. 777–78 (particularly note 7).

[88] Samuelson's belief that at least a slight money illusion persists over time is another part of his Keynesian heritage. Keynes made the money illusion an integral part of his *General Theory*.

[89] In the absence of a money illusion (or the ability of people to accurately anticipate inflation) increases in the price level would not affect decisions regarding employment, since the relative prices would remain unchanged, and the rise in the absolute price level would be anticipated. See the discussion in Chapter 14 for elaboration of this point.

The Politics of Macroeconomic Policy

One of the problems of an explanation as simple as the Phillips Curve is that excessive attention will be directed to the problems of employment and inflation. We may worry too much about the Phillips Curve trade-off. While admitting that unemployment and inflation are problems, Samuelson feels their effects may be exaggerated when weighing policy alternatives. "I would not . . . think it disastrous," he once told the Joint Economic Committee, "if we went from now until the end of the world at 6-percent inflation with everything adjusted to that."[90] At the same time, he notes that an increasing level of unemployment over the past few decades can be partially explained by structural changes in the economy, rather than as a trade-off with inflation. "There is," he points out, "a greater element of voluntary choice in today's joblessness than was true in the Depression. Our mixed economy has an elaborate set of welfare measures enabling people to receive some income despite their not finding jobs."[91]

Samuelson does not mean to suggest that unemployment or inflation are problems we can ignore. Rather, he is suggesting that the costs of these problems may not warrant excessive efforts which might curtail a third—and equally important—goal of macroeconomic policy: stimulating economic growth. Economic growth, he insists, is the most effective way to loosen the inflexibilities caused by the inflation-unemployment dilemma. Ever since he became an influential advisor to the government during the Kennedy years, Samuelson has consistently supported proposals which, if they erred, would do so in the direction of providing impetus to economic growth. In 1962, he vigorously supported the proposal for both a cut in taxes and an expansion of government spending. In 1964, the tax cut (amounting to about a 15 percent fall in income tax rates) became a reality. The proponents of the new economics had won a clear victory; one of the first acts of fiscal policy implemented on solely Keynesian grounds.[92] The tax cut had the desired effect; the economy did launch into a prolonged spurt of economic activity. In fact, within a few years the dominant issue of economic policy had become the need to restrain demand in the face of the expanding activity generated by the Vietnam War. By 1966, Samuelson was advocating a tax increase to stem inflationary pressures. Again,

---

[90] Paul A. Samuelson, "Testimony", U.S. Congress, Joint Economic Committee, 93rd Cong., 1st sess., 17-18 October 1973, p. 324. He hastens to add that should the rate of inflation rise to 8 or 9 percent, there would be cause for concern.

[91] *Newsweek*, 6 September 1976, p. 48. Samuelson also cited the increase in young people and women in the labor force as factors which would produce a higher level of unemployment in the society.

[92] Samuelson was one of many economists who supported the tax cut that year. For a more complete discussion of the politics of the tax cut, see E. Ray Canterbery, *Economics on a New Frontier* (Belmont, Calif.: Wadsworth Publishing Co., 1968), Chapter 18. Curiously, some liberal economists, such as John Kenneth Galbraith, opposed the tax cut because they feared that it might lead to a reduction of government spending at a time when they felt that the public sector was already too small. In the 1980s, conservative economists, known as "supply-siders," became the strongest advocates of tax cuts as a means of stimulating economic growth, not through an expansion of Keynesian aggregate demand, but through an increase in supply. See the discussion in Chapter 14.

the new economics triumphed; the passage of a surtax in 1968 was another example of compensatory fiscal policy.[93]

Though the tax changes of the 1960s proved that fiscal policy could have an impact on the economy, the experience also revealed some of the deficiencies of discretionary policy. Samuelson had wanted a tax cut as early as 1961; yet it did not materialize until 1964, and only then with some concessions to those demanding spending cuts which reduced its effects.[94] Similarly, though economists (including several in the Johnson administration) urged a tax increase as early as 1966, the action was not taken until 1968. In each case the delay meant that the appropriate policy was not implemented at the time it was needed. The timing of discretionary policy was hardly perfect.

More recently, Samuelson has been battling a new threat to discretionary fiscal policy: the effort to ratify a constitutional amendment which would force the federal government to operate with a balanced budget. Needless to say, Samuelson opposes such a change. "It is unwise," he warns, "to use the Constitution to freeze in for all time some particular economic formula."[95] All the more so, he added, when the formula is nothing more than a "passing fad."

Undaunted by the problems which compensatory fiscal policy has encountered, Samuelson continues to vocally support an activist economic policy and the need to promote economic growth. As the prolonged boom of the 1960s wound down into the recession of 1974–75, Samuelson again began agitating for a tax cut to provide economic stimulus to the economy. Optimistic that the election of a Democrat to the White House in 1976 would see a renewal of fiscal activism, he publicly counseled President-elect Jimmy Carter to cut taxes by $10-20 billion and to "expand the total fiscal spending stimulus in 1977."[96] A year and-a-half later he was still pressing the case, detailing a series of needed actions, including a $25 billion tax cut.[97] Samuelson is not haunted by fears of another great depression, nor does he expect inflation to get completely out of hand. "The asthma of stagflation rather than the galloping pneumonia of hyperinflation is what seems indicated by the history of the 1960s and 1970s," he observes.[98]

Samuelson continues to eschew the search for a simple answer to all this. Talking to one of the largest audiences in the profession—readers of his introductory textbook—he concludes the discussion of macroeconomic policy by saying:

---

[93] As we note in Chapter 14, not all economists concede that the surtax was successful in curtailing the inflationary process.

[94] Commenting on the delay and the subsequent course of events, Samuelson admitted that ". . . if I had the foresight in 1964 to have known what Viet Nam would do, then I might have had a different opinion on the tax cut" (Burns and Samuelson, p. 113).

[95] *Newsweek*, 9 April 1979, p. 79.

[96] *Newsweek*, 10 January 1977, p. 58.

[97] *Newsweek*, 8 May 1978, p. 78.

[98] *Newsweek*, 1 January 1979, p. 45.

The moral, I should think, is to persevere in trying to find structural reforms that will retain and augment humanitarianism—while at the same time hoping to encourage the system to behave more like the market-clearing mechanism that experience shows is conducive to both efficiency and stability.

The tasks of political economy are never done.[99]

Samuelson's opinions on macroeconomic policy reflect the pragmatism of a great many American economists—not the least of whom was his mentor, Alvin Hansen. They insist on judging any situation within its own particular environment; rejecting acceptance of some formula—simple or complex—which purports to guarantee stability of the economy. In Samuelson's case such pragmatism is reinforced by a healthy dose of skepticism regarding our ability to forecast the future with any great degree of accuracy. He appreciates the fact that economic relationships are seldom as simple as the diagrams or equations would lead us to believe. The fact that the present state of the art does not allow us to reach unambiguous or absolutely certain outcomes should not vitiate the vigorous exercise of discretionary policy. Nor, he hastens to add, should the fact that we have made mistakes in the past. Those who point to past errors as proof that discretionary policy does not work are incorrect. They are guilty, according to Samuelson, of two errors:

1.   They ignore the fact that there must have been some policy which would have improved the situation; and
2.   They assert that doing nothing (or following a fixed "rule") would always be a superior alternative to any policy alternative.

Samuelson insists that, at the very least, a policy of "leaning against the wind" will be a superior path to follow even if we make mistakes. "I much prefer a recession contrived by Fed Chairman Miller and Secretary of the Treasury Paul Volcker and President Carter," he explained, "rather than one created by blind nature. What man does man can undo; Acts of God and the King's enemies are harder to diagnose and reverse."[100]

Samuelson's position is that government has a clear responsibility to *actively* ensure that both economic stability and economic equity are provided. This, he believes, is not likely to be the automatic outcome of the market process. It is not that Samuelson is unappreciative of the arguments of Adam Smith and the older schools of economic thought; he simply feels that they must be considered in the context of their times, not in the twentieth century. In his words

---

[99]   Samuelson, *Economics*, p. 780.

[100]   *Newsweek*, 24 December 1979, p. 65. Samuelson's resistance to fixed rules is well documented in his writings and testimony. See, for example, his remarks when appearing with Milton Friedman before the House Committee on Banking, Housing, and Urban Affairs, *Second Meeting on Conduct of Monetary Policy*, pp. 49–75.

... Smith gave two resounding cheers for individualism; but for state interference of the pre-nineteenth century type, he could muster up only a bronx cheer.

And make no mistake about it: Smith was right. Most of the interventions into economic life by the State were then harmful both to prosperity and freedom. . . . In fact, much of what Smith said still needs to be said: good intentions by government are not enough; acts do have consequences that had better be taken into account if good is to follow.[101]

Scarcity of resources is a fact of life in every part of the world, past and present, rich and poor. The market, with its impersonal efficiency, can bring about a solution to the problem of allocating these scarce resources; and Samuelson, as we have seen, admires the fact that it can do this. Yet, in a sense, Samuelson argues, this efficient allocation is effected through a form of coercion: prices control the distribution of goods through a system of "rationing by the purse." "Economists defend such forms of rationing," Samuelson points out, "but they have to do so primarily in terms of its efficiency and fairness."[102] When the market solution is not efficient (as in the case of monopoly or externalities), or when observers feel the result is not "fair," the evil of market rationing is then, in Samuelson's words, "weighed pragmatically against its advantages, and modifications of its structure are introduced."[103]

When asked to weigh these problems "pragmatically" according to his own preferences, Samuelson sees many areas of useful government actions. He mentions projects in education, urban renewal, health and welfare, and resource development.[104] He does not see such programs as "interference"; they are public goods where government action is necessary to correct deficiencies in the private market. "My own concern," insists Samuelson, "is with improvements in living standards, not with expansion of bureaucrats' power."[105]

Samuelson's activism is not, moreover, confined to government expenditure programs. He has remained a staunch advocate of government action to assist women and minorities in the labor market. Commenting on the apparent swing to more conservative economic policies at the end of the 1970s, Samuelson insists that "there is still work for liberals to do—hard but rewarding work."[106] After all, he points out, the improvements which have been made in areas such as discrim-

---

[101] Paul A. Samuelson, "Modern Economic Realities and Individualism," *Collected Papers*, vol. 2, no. 106, p. 1409. Samuelson went on to add a few lines later that "Smith had a point, but he could not have earned a passing mark in a Ph.D. oral examination in explaining just what that point was."

[102] Samuelson, "Modern Economic Realities," p. 1415.

[103] Samuelson, "Modern Economic Realities," p. 1415.

[104] Samuelson, "Modern Economic Realities," pp. 1485–86. Compare Samuelson's list of areas where government programs would be beneficial with the even longer list by Milton Friedman of areas where less government activity would be beneficial. See Chapter 14.

[105] *Newsweek*, 26 June 1980, p. 64.

[106] *Newsweek*, 26 June 1980, p. 64.

ination and job opportunities "did not just happen out of the spontaneous workings of the laissez-faire marketplace. New laws and customs played an important role."[107]

It would not be unfair to say that Paul Samuelson mirrors the ideological views of many American economists today. He stops short of embracing the broad intervention of government advocated by Alvin Hansen in the 1930's or John Kenneth Galbraith in more recent times, just as he balks at the laissez-faire suggestions of Milton Friedman. As his analysis of public goods showed, Samuelson is not certain that we really have the theoretical tools to adequately deal with the complexities of collective choice. Scientist that he is, Samuelson vigorously pursues his own investigations to unravel some of the more perplexing economic riddles. But for now, he accepts the judgment of the electorate regarding the proper sphere of government action. He does so because he feels that democracy is not an evil. It is, as E.B. White insisted, "the recurrent suspicion that more than half the people will turn out to be right more than half the time."[108]

---

[107] *Newsweek*, 26 June 1980, p. 64.
[108] *Newsweek*, 25 October 1964, p. 132.

10

ABBA P. LERNER

THE ARTIST
AS ECONOMIST

The nearest thing to a systematic philosophy is my feeling that it is only a concern for improving the condition of man which justifies work in economics. This, in spite of the keen enjoyment I have always felt, and still do, in the mental exercise involved in the achievement of elegant proofs and diagrams. However I have always felt that this could have been obtained in a higher degree if I had gone in for mathematics or chess, which I refrained from doing for the very same reason, namely that I found economics about equally enjoyable and much more useful.

Abba P. Lerner

Although Keynes's *General Theory* is often thought of as revolutionizing popular attitudes towards the desirability of government intervention to stabilize the economy, the book itself is devoted almost entirely to pure theory. The reader of the *General Theory* will search in vain for the tools of fiscal policy that the beginning student is routinely taught in the macroeconomics portion of the course in principles of economics.[1] For the truth is that the systematic treatment of fiscal policy and the concepts associated wih it were not the work of Keynes but rather that of his brilliant disciples, principally in America. Thus, for example, it was Alvin Hansen and his student Paul Samuelson who first incorporated the idea of an accelerator into the Keynesian system. This device seemed to show that only ever-increasing government expenditures would be able to maintain full employment. Furthermore, it was Samuelson who worked out the arithmetic of the income-expenditure models and of the balanced budget multipliers.

[1] For more on this point, see Axel Leijonhufvud, *On Keynesian Economics and the Economics of Keynes* (New York: Oxford University Press, 1968), pp. 401–04.

And, as we saw in Chapter 9, he invented the "Keynesian Cross," or 45-degree-line diagram with which every new student is taught how fiscal policy, working through the multiplier, can close the "deflationary gap." Since in this diagram there is no mention of interest rates or money, it appears that fiscal policy is the Keynesian message for achieving full employment.

But perhaps the most important development in bringing about the revolution in economic policy associated with the new economics is the notion that government fiscal policy can be used to fine tune the economy in such a way that full employment without inflation is always possible.

The logic of this argument was worked out by one of Keynes's earliest converts, Abba Ptachya Lerner. To him is owed much of the credit for having secured the fetters of the new fiscal orthodoxy that had been welded by Keynes and put in place by Alvin Hansen. This work and his other ingenious contributions to economic theory, always written in the clearest of prose, have made Abba Lerner one of the most influential academic scribblers of our time.

Abba P. Lerner was born in Bessarabia, Russia, in 1903 and grew up in London. There he had a remarkably checkered career: Hebrew teacher, college drop-out, and a business failure. Having acceded to his friends' insistence that he really was a bright fellow who belonged in an academic environment, Lerner matriculated, at the age of twenty-six, as a student at the London School of Economics. When he found himself indifferent to the choice between economics and psychology, he settled the matter by a toss of a coin.

When Lerner first arrived on the scene at the London School in 1932, he was a socialist with Marxist leanings. But he had never accepted either dialectical materialism or the labor theory of value; both of which are cornerstones of the Marxist economics. Other influences on Lerner at the time included the writings of Thorstein Veblen and the single-tax argument of the American economist Henry George. To Lerner, Veblen was significant because he was "the only man who dared bring scientific method to social problems." His early infatuation with Marx and Veblen was disrupted at the London School of Economics (LSE) when he finally came to understand the implications of the neoclassical concept of marginal analysis. At first, Lerner did not see the importance of thinking in terms of marginal increments, and since it seemed to him that was the only thing he had learned by the end of his first year at LSE, he became quite depressed. But as he learned more economics with such teachers as John R. Hicks, Lionel Robbins, and F. A. Hayek, he went through what can best be described as a "conversion experience."[2] In his words:

---

[2] According to Lerner, it was Lionel Robbins who "is responsible for having made me into an economist." See A. P. Lerner, *Essays in Economic Analysis* (London: Macmillan & Co., 1953), p. v. (Hereafter cited as *Essays*.)

I became a rabid marginalist, fanatically enthusiastic about the principle that economic efficiency, which is, of course, socially desirable,
requires every price to be equal to the marginal cost (more strictly to
the value of the additional factors required to produce an additional
unit of the product where this is equal to the value of the alternative
products sacrificed).[3]

The collection of students and teachers at the London School at that
time included, in addition to Hicks, Hayek, and Robbins; R. G. D. Allen,
Ronald Coase, Nicholas Kaldor, Arnold Plant, and Paul Rosenstein-
Rodan. Seldom has such an impressive array of talent in economics
been assembled together. Lerner flourished in this stimulating environment. Within two years of entering the study of economics as an
undergraduate, he published his first paper, "The Diagrammatical
Representation of Cost Conditions in International Trade."[4] This article
was the first to make use of community indifference curves to illustrate
a two-country equilibrium of international trade. It was a virtuoso
performance, followed in two years by its sequel, "The Diagrammatical
Representation of Demand Conditions in International Trade."[5]

In between the publication of these two important papers, Lerner
read a paper entitled "Factor Prices and International Trade" before a
seminar at the London School. In this essay, Lerner showed that even
when factors are immobile, free trade will equalize their international
prices. After the seminar, the paper was placed in the files of Lionel
Robbins and was soon forgotten by everyone, including Lerner. In
1948, Paul Samuelson independently worked out the same proof, and it
was published in the *Economic Journal*.[6] When Lionel Robbins saw
Samuelson's article, he remembered Lerner's paper, exhumed it from
his files, and saw it eventually printed in *Economica* in 1952.[7]

On the occasion of Lerner's sixtieth birthday, Samuelson added a
"further amazing parallel." As he told it;

> When my 1948 *Economic Journal* paper appeared, Joan Robinson
> wrote to point out that if both goods have identical production
> functions, there will generally not be equalisation. This is a just
> observation, which points up the crucial need for factor intensity
> assumptions. Now recall that everyone had forgotten the existence of
> the 1933 Lerner paper, including Joan Robinson and its author. So
> you can imagine my surprise when, after Robbins sent me a copy of

---

[3] A. P. Lerner, "Marginal Cost Pricing in the 1930's," *American Economic Review* 67 (May 1977):
     236.
[4] A. P. Lerner, "The Diagrammatical Representation of Cost Conditions in International Trade,"
     Economica 1 (August 1932). Reprinted in *Essays*, pp. 85–100.
[5] A. P. Lerner, "The Diagrammatical Representation of Demand Conditions in International Trade,"
     Economica 3 (August 1934). Reprinted in *Essays*, pp. 67–100.
[6] Paul A. Samuelson, "International Trade and the Equalisation of Factor Prices," *Economic
     Journal* 58 (June 1948):164–84.
[7] A. P. Lerner, "Factor Prices and International Trade," *Economica* 21 (February 1952). Reprinted
     in *Essays*, pp. 67–100.

the paper, I found the footnote p. 73 of *Essays* where Lerner acknowledges this suggestion "by Mrs. J. Robinson of Cambridge." The French must have a saying for this sort of thing.[8]

While he was at the London School, Lerner helped found the *Review of Economic Studies* and was its managing editor from 1933 to 1937. All the while, he was turning out papers that were to become classics in their fields. In these papers, Lerner demonstrated his keen grasp of the elements of scientific prose and used his mastery of the tools of plane geometry to extend our understanding of economic theory. Lerner's name in economics soon became identified with lucidity of exposition. During this period at the London School, Lerner was a confirmed neoclassicist. His main efforts were devoted to extending the marginalism of Marshall, whom he greatly admired. Indeed, it was Marshall's *Principles* which had the greatest influence on young Lerner, especially during the third year of study for his bachelor's degree. The year consisted very largely of animated discussions among a group of students, concocting what seemed to them to be original ideas, and then finding out that these ideas could be found in Marshall's textbook.

During his last undergraduate year, Lerner attempted to teach the then-new ideas of E. H. Chamberlin and Joan Robinson to his fellow students. Like most cub instructors, Lerner was apprehensive over the prospect of giving his first lecture, so he wrote it out in full. As he began to read each sentence, he found himself thinking of alternative possibilities and coming up with novel ideas. To his surprise, the notes he had so carefully prepared for his first lecture lasted the whole semester. But Lerner has always felt that he learned more from his students than from his fellow economists. As he put it, "It was in the course of trying to simplify and clarify my ideas to what seemed like stupid students that most of my ideas got refined."[9]

Among the many significant contributions of this early period in Lerner's career was his rediscovery of the notion of "Pareto-optimality" and a clear statement of the reason why welfare is maximized when price equals marginal cost. In 1934, for the first time, Lerner made use of consumer indifference curves and production possibility curves to show the importance of the tangency point between them. This diagram remains standard equipment in the microeconomic sections of textbooks. Lerner then went on to show that an optimum is reached where no one can be made any better off without rendering someone else worse off. He also demonstrated that the loss involved in monopoly is the divergence between price and marginal cost, another exposition which remains standard fare in any textbook.[10]

---

[8]   Paul A. Samuelson, "A. P. Lerner at Sixty," *Review of Economic Studies* 31 (June 1964): 172.

[9]   Personal correspondence, 21 August 1967.

[10] A. P. Lerner, "The Concept of Monopoly and the Measurement of Monopoly Power," *Review of Economic Studies* (June 1934). Reprinted in *Essays*, pp. 3–37. In referring to this contribution by Lerner, Samuelson has said, "Today this may seem simple, but I can testify that no one at Chicago or Harvard could tell me in 1935 exactly why P = MC was a good thing, and I was a persistent Diogenes." Samuelson, "A. P. Lerner at Sixty," p. 173.

During this period, Lerner also refined Marshall's analysis of the elasticity of demand and showed how to derive it geometrically.[11] Other geometric exercises on the subjects of the elasticity of substitutions, spatial duopoly, and the theory of price-index numbers followed.[12]

In 1935, Lerner received a fellowship to spend a semester at Cambridge. There he met John Maynard Keynes and heard firsthand the new ideas on employment theory that Keynes was developing. A first draft of the *General Theory* had already been completed, and it was in the process of being criticized by Keynes's colleagues and students. Lerner joined the enterprise. Initially, he resisted mightily the new arguments. Eventually, however, Keynes and Robinson succeeded in changing the "Hayekian Saul into the Keynesian Paul."[13]

With this second conversion, Lerner turned his fine talent for clarifying exposition to the task of elucidating Keynes's new theory. In 1936, Lerner was invited by the International Labor Organization to summarize Keynes's new book in terms intelligible to the nonspecialist. Lerner wrote the article and showed it to Keynes, who gave it his blessing. The essay is noteworthy for the insight that it showed so early.[14] In particular, it once again demonstrated Lerner's uncanny ability to state the most difficult ideas in the clearest possible language, an ability that has survived throughout his career.

In 1939, Lerner moved to the United States where he began a peripatetic existence, moving from one university to another: Columbia, Virginia, Kansas City, Amherst, The New School for Social Research, Roosevelt, Johns Hopkins, Michigan State, California at Berkeley, Queens College in New York, and, finally, Florida State. During this time, he established his reputation as a brilliant theorist, publishing over 100 articles and nine books.

His lifestyle also helped establish a reputation as an eccentric. In appearance he is a cross between Woody Allen and Groucho Marx. With his bald pate surrounded by tufts of hair that jut out straight on the sides, Lerner gives the impression of a man with his finger perpetually stuck in an electric light socket. Indeed, he looks like nothing so much as the popular notion of the wild economist whispering absurd schemes into Franklin D. Roosevelt's ear. Long before it became customary to do so, Lerner had shunned neckties and wore open-toed sandals. He speaks with an inflection that combines an English accent with the

---

[11] Lerner suggested that elasticity should be measured as the relationship between *proportional* rather than *percentage* changes in price and quantity demanded. The usual formulation using percentages—the difference between two numbers divided by the first one mentioned—gives a different answer according to whether we are considering a price increase or decrease. This ambiguity is avoided if elasticity is measured as the difference between two numbers divided by either the smallest *or* the largest—providing you are consistent. See A. P. Lerner, "The Diagrammatical Representation of Elasticity of Demand," *Review of Economic Studies* (October 1933). Reprinted in *Essays*, pp. 137–46.

[12] All of these essays are reprinted in A. P. Lerner, *Essays*, pp. 147–212.

[13] The description is by Samuelson in "A. P. Lerner at Sixty," p. 176.

[14] A. P. Lerner, "The General Theory," *The International Labour Review* (1936). Reprinted in Seymour E. Harris, ed. *The New Economics* (London: Dennis Dobson, 1947), pp. 113–32.

singsong of a man reading from the Torah. There are few economists in the fold who can match Lerner for color, wit, or pure shock effect.

Lerner the artist usually left his imprint on the department he was inhabiting. Hanging from the ceiling of the department office would be a wire mobile of a cat or whale or some other creature whose graceful lines had captured Lerner's imagination and challenged his ingenuity. Lerner's wire sculpture has been exhibited at various meetings of the American Economic Association. In style, it is typically Lernerian: the distinguishing feature is its striving for simplicity of expression. This is a task that Lerner takes with the same seriousness that he does the elucidation of his most abstruse arguments on economic theory.[15]

Functional Finance

The most important contribution Lerner has made to the acceptance of Keynesian ideas and the establishment of a policy-structured new economics is his theory of functional finance. These ideas first appeared in 1941 in a relatively obscure journal published at the University of Kansas City, where Lerner was on the faculty.[16] In this article, Lerner fashioned an approach to Keynesian economics that clarified the policy tools needed to implement programs of full employment and put discussion of them on a fruitful basis. As with all of Lerner's work, the outstanding characteristic of his approach was its simplicity.

Lerner's point is that government financial activities should not be judged by the principles of "sound finance" (budget-balancing) but rather by considering the effects of each act and deciding whether these effects are desirable. Thus, for example, the effects of any tax payment are twofold: the government has more money, while the taxpayer has less. The fact that the government has more money is an unimportant effect, since the government can print money any time it wishes. But the effect on the taxpayer is important since the individual cannot legally resort to the printing press to obtain money. It follows, therefore, that the government should impose taxes only if there is a good reason for wanting the taxpayer to have less money. The government should tax only if it is desired to make taxpayers poorer. When would this be desirable? The most obvious case would be when the govern-

---

[15] "While many people make the regular remark that my sculpture must be a nice relaxation from my work, I have to say that it is not of that nature at all. It involves very strenuous concentration and is extremely similar to what I try to do in my economic theory, namely to get at the simplest possible presentation of an idea." Personal correspondence, August 21, 1967.

[16] The term "functional finance" was not used by Lerner in the article published in Kansas City's *University Review*. It first made its way into print in a 1943 article which appeared in *Social Research*. The ideas in the earlier article were virtually the same as those spelled out later. See A. P. Lerner, "The Economic Steering Wheel," *The University Review* (June 1941). This article subsequently became Chapter 1 of Lerner's *The Economics of Employment* (New York: McGraw-Hill, 1951). Also see A. P. Lerner, "Functional Finance and the Federal Debt," *Social Research* 10 (February 1943): 38–51. The fullest development of functional finance is to be found in A. P. Lerner, *The Economics of Control* (New York: Macmillan Co., 1944), Chapters 23–24.

ment wished to discourage spending; perhaps to combat inflation or because certain transactions are thought to be undesirable.[17]

If the government wishes people to have debt instead of cash, then it should borrow. If it wishes people to have more cash so as to encourage spending, then the government should cut taxes, buy goods, or repay debt, or any combination of the three. In this way, Lerner was able to reduce everything that the government can do through macroeconomic policy to one or more of six basic elements. The elements form three pairs of options, with one of each pair being the reverse of its partner:

1. Buying or selling goods;
2. Giving or taking money (that is, taxing or subsidizing activities);
3. Lending money to, or borrowing money from, the public.

Keynes had made the point that the level of employment depends upon the total level of spending in the economy—aggregate demand. But it was Abba Lerner who first showed how the level of spending might be regulated by policymakers to keep the total rate of spending from going too high or too low. If the rate of spending is insufficient to maintain full employment, then the government can buy goods and services. Selling goods that the government has acquired in the past has the opposite effect and is appropriate when the rate of total spending is so high as to be inflationary.

Government giving (or subsidizing) will increase the total rate of spending because it diminishes the price of subsidized commodities, or because it increases the money that the receivers of the subsidy can spend. A subsidy is, in essence, a negative tax, since taxing takes money out of the hands of individuals and reduces their ability to spend.

The function of *lending* is to make it easier for potential spenders to borrow for either consumption or investment. Of course, the government debt repayment has the same effect. The opposite effect is achieved by government *borrowing*, which makes it more difficult for others to obtain loans—thus lowering the total rate of spending.

These instruments thus provide the government with six ways to increase aggregate demand, and six ways to reduce it. This is true because, if the total rate of spending is deficient and there is unemployment, then the government can increase its *buying, giving*, or *lending*, and at the same time reduce its *selling, taxing*, or *borrowing*. And if the level of aggregate demand is too great, the process can be reversed.

---

[17] Of course, today it is recognized that this view is oversimplified. Since, as Samuelson points out, a major purpose of the fiscal system is to provide certain collective goods and services, decisions regarding the appropriate amount of such goods and services must be made on considerations which have nothing to do with inflation or employment. Much of modern public finance theory is concerned with the question of which goods should be provided collectively. Once this is decided, taxes might be the appropriate method for financing them. See Edgar K. Browning and Jacquelene M. Browning, *Public Finance and the Price System* (New York: Macmillan Co., 1979), pp. 21–52.

Lerner is careful to point out that functional finance is not a policy, since it does not tell us how to choose between this wealth of instruments. Moreover, it tells us nothing about the objectives of society other than that of avoiding depression and inflation.[18]

This set of analytical instruments was a tour de force, stripping economic policy to its barest elements. Of these ideas, Paul Samuelson was moved to remark that ". . . certainly no economist can be the same after reading Lerner's *Functional Finance.*"[19]

There is an important difference between Lerner's functional finance and Hansen's compensatory fiscal policy that has gone largely unnoticed. Indeed, the two conceptions are so hopelessly confused that it seems fruitful to spend some time noting the distinguishing characteristics of Lerner's approach.

Although functional finance is often referred to as fiscal policy, it might more accurately be interpreted as containing elements of both monetary and fiscal policy. Lerner puts his discussion mainly in terms of what happens to the money supply as a result of various government activities, both monetary and fiscal. In Lerner's schema, buying, giving, and lending are mainly effective because they increase the stock of money and, therefore, spending. Selling, taxing, and borrowing have a contractional effect on aggregate demand because they reduce the supply of cash in the hands of spenders. To clearly see the difference between Lerner's approach and that of Hansen, note the following statement of Hansen in regard to compensatory fiscal policy:

> It is amazing how many people, otherwise well-informed, have not yet learned that compensatory fiscal policy is not a one-way program. Properly managed, it is always on the job, prepared to fight *inflation*, no less than *deflation*. Responsible management of compensatory fiscal policy means the control of expenditures, taxes and borrowing so as to promote *stability*.[20]

So far the discussion sounds precisely like Lerner's functional finance. But in the next sentence Hansen presents what he considers the specific tools required to do the job. In so doing, the key difference between Hansen and Lerner on these issues is brought out: "To fight inflation, a budget surplus and debt reduction are in order."[21] Note that Hansen juxtaposed two basic elements of Lerner's functional finance that have, in fact, opposite effects. Lerner's analysis indicates that to fight infla-

---

[18] Lerner later attempted to show how functional finance can be applied to achieve various social objectives that have nothing to do with the problem of full employment. See A. P. Lerner, "An Integrated Full Employment Policy," in A. P. Lerner and Frank D. Graham, ed., *Planning and Paying for Full Employment* (Princeton, N.J.: Princeton University Press, 1946), pp. 163–220.

[19] Samuelson, "A. P. Lerner at Sixty," p. 177. Samuelson was so impressed by the originality of Lerner's conception that he once asked him why he did not call it "Lernerism." As Samuelson tells the story, "He answered, rather seriously, that some of his students at Kansas City had urged this, but he feared it might limit the popularity of the doctrines." Samuelson, "A. P. Lerner at Sixty," p. 177.

[20] Alvin Hansen, *Economic Policy and Full Employment* (New York: McGraw-Hill, 1947), p. 11. Italics in the original.

[21] Hansen, p. 11.

tion a budget surplus and a debt increase would be in order, not a debt reduction. Government borrowing has the effect of removing money from the economy, while debt reduction increases the money stock. In an inflation, therefore, the government should be increasing its borrowing, not reducing it. (Assuming, of course, that the proceeds of the borrowing are not spent.) Borrowing has the same effect as any open market sale of government securities and in itself is contractional. Debt reduction is, by itself, an open market purchase which is clearly expansionary.

That Hansen would suggest debt reduction as an anti-inflationary tool indicates that he sees the budget itself as the key to economic stability without regard to the supply of money. It is this emphasis on budgetary deficits and surpluses which characterizes compensatory fiscal policy and has led to a widespread belief that "money doesn't matter" to those Keynesians influenced by Hansen. Lerner is always careful to recognize the importance of what is happening to the money stock as governmental buying, selling, subsidizing, taxing, lending, and borrowing take place.

Lerner's Keynesianism is much truer to the intent of Keynes. For his interpretation of Keynes is essentially the view that to cure a depression, the quantity of money in real terms—that is, money relative to prices—must increase. To Lerner, the Keynesian approach differs from the neoclassical approach only in the way by which this ratio is increased. In Lerner's view, Keynes insisted that instead of trying to reduce the denominator P in the fraction M/P, we should increase M, the nominal quantity of money. Like Keynes, Lerner felt that there are tremendous difficulties in waiting for P to fall.[22]

To Lerner, it is wrong to interpret Keynes as having played down the importance of money. But readers of Hansen, one of Keynes's most influential disciples, can be forgiven this misinterpretation.[23] Lerner is also a disciple of Keynes in the sense that he believes, along with Hansen and Samuelson, that monetary policy is ineffective in a severe depression. He accepts the ideas of a liquidity trap and a highly inelastic investment demand schedule under such circumstances. As he puts it:

> In such cases monetary policy, with which the greater part of Keynesian analysis is concerned, does not work and something else is needed to cure the depression. This is where fiscal policy comes in. Fiscal policy can cure the depression by increasing expenditure and income *directly* instead of by way of an increase in the stock of money

---

[22] As we shall see in the chapter on Milton Friedman, the modern neoclassical economist is Keynesian in the sense that he prefers increases in the real quantity of money not by waiting for P to fall, but by having a rule that would increase the nominal quantity of money. The real issue between Lerner and his critics on this point is not over the economic analysis of the importance of money, but rather over the question of whether we should use discretionary policy rather than a policy based on rules. We have already alluded to this debate in our discussion of Samuelson in Chapter 9; see also the discussions in Chapters 13 and 14.

[23] On the argument that Keynes recognized the importance of money, see Leijonhufvud, pp. 401–16. The reasons why Hansen and his students played down the importance of money are discussed in Chapters 8 and 9.

in real terms. The government can increase its own expenditure or it can reduce taxes, leaving more money for the taxpayers to spend.[24]

Thus, it is Lerner's view that monetary policy is ineffective only in the very special case of a severe depression when there has been a collapse of confidence so that investment does not look profitable at any rate of interest, however low that may be, and the demand for cash to hold in idle balances is infinite.[25]

Because Lerner accepts the possibility of a highly inelastic investment demand schedule, he recognizes the importance of an unbalanced budget to fight depression. The point is that the government may find that increasing the money supply through the purchase of securities on the open market either to the public or to the commercial banks will only result in excess reserves or idle cash balances. On the other hand, if the government borrows money from the public and spends the proceeds, the money supply remains unchanged. But in addition to the same stock of money, the public now has a "near-money," a highly liquid asset that it did not possess before the selling of government bonds. Of course, the issuing of government securities might have some effect on interest rates, causing them to go higher since the government would now be competing with private enterprise for funds. However, assuming a highly inelastic investment demand schedule, this effect would not be very great. If the government then spends the funds it raised by borrowing on the purchase of goods and services, it will directly employ people who were formerly unemployed. Money would then flow from what were idle balances to active balances. In this case, with the same stock of money, velocity would be greater and income would rise. Or, to put it in more Keynesian terms, government investment would generate a multiplier effect (the magnitude of which would depend on the marginal propensity to consume), and income would rise by some multiple of the government investment. At higher incomes, the public would now wish to hold the same stock of money at the new higher interest rate. The net effect of such an operation, therefore, is to increase income and employment and the rate of interest, while leaving the money supply unchanged.

There are other effects which are also expansionary. The public now holds a greater supply of liquid assets than it held before and therefore is wealthier (as implied by the assumption that during the depression private enterprise would not be issuing bonds or other assets to the public which might have substituted for the government bonds). So we have the possibility of an unbalanced budget increasing society's wealth. The greater society's private wealth is in the form of government debt, and the greater its liquidity, the greater is the

---

[24] A. P. Lerner, "A Program for Monetary Stability," in *Proceedings*, Conference on Savings and Residential Financing, Chicago, Ill., 1962, pp. 37–38.

[25] As we noted in chapters 8 and 9, Lerner and others were influenced by their interpretation of the events of the Great Depression of the 1930's. In Chapter 14 we shall examine Milton Friedman's challenge to that view.

incentive to consume (or the less is the incentive to save out of current income). This means that the average propensity to consume will rise, generating a multiplier effect which further increases income. So long as there is any unemployment, the government can continue to engage in deficit finance by issuing bonds that would continue to increase private wealth and encourage further spending. Eventually, full employment would be reached. If full employment is maintained by the continuation of deficit financing, this keeps on increasing the size of the national debt. Because of the liquidity and wealth effects, this increases the total spending so that a smaller and smaller deficit is required to maintain full employment. Finally, a point is reached at which no more deficit financing is needed, and the budget can be balanced.

The effect on spending of a growing volume of outstanding government debt through liquidity and wealth effects is one of Lerner's most original contributions and has become known as the "Lerner effect." An important point to note about this tendency for the budget to eventually be balanced is that this is a result of applying the principles of functional finance; balancing the government budget is not itself a principle of functional finance.

Of course, Lerner recognized that full employment could be achieved by having the government simply print money to finance projects rather than by issuing debt. This could be done by borrowing from the central bank and spending the proceeds directly on some government project or distributing it to specific groups in society (the poor, the elderly, the young, etc.). But Lerner feels that "it is probably advisable . . . to allow debt and money to increase together in a certain balance, as long as one or the other has to increase."[26]

It is clear that if government projects were financed by printing money rather than by issuing interest-bearing debt, the liquidity effect identified by Lerner would be even stronger, since money is more liquid than government bonds and should stimulate even greater spending. But to Lerner the issuance of near-money, rather than money, would eventually produce full employment. In a sense, the "Lerner effect" is a quantity theory of near-money. As such, it has a distinctly Keynesian tone.[27]

---

[26] Lerner, "Functional Finance and the Federal Debt," p. 48.

[27] Note that one's belief in the efficacy of the Lerner effect rests on the following assumptions. (1) Private enterprise would not have been issuing assets in the absence of the new government securities (which is possible in a serious depression). (2) The loss in capital value of previously issued assets as a consequence of the rise in the interest rate must not offset the wealth effect of the increase in government debt. (We are indebted to Roland McKean for this observation.) However, it seems likely that the wealth and liquidity effects of ever-increasing government debt would eventually swamp the capital loss effect. This is so because the rise in interest rates when the debt is issued (assuming no liquidity trap) would be a once-and-for-all occurrence with new debts being issued at the same rate in subsequent periods. (We are indebted to Pat Culbertson and Joseph Camp for pointing this out to us). (3) It is assumed that the tax liabilities inherent in debt issue are not discounted by individuals who will eventually pay these taxes. Since Lerner assumes that interest payments can be paid for by issuing more debt, this is not a problem in his analysis.

The Burden of Public Debt

In order to support his argument for functional finance, Lerner recognized that he would have to overcome long-standing objections to the existence of a large amount of government debt and unbalanced budgets. The prejudice against unbalanced budgets is an old one, cutting across all lines of the political spectrum. For example, both incumbent President Hoover and Franklin D. Roosevelt campaigned on a promise to balance the budget in 1932.[28] Lerner recognized that he would have to show that government debt was not a burden on the nation if functional finance were ever to become an instrument for achieving full employment and price level stability. Lerner's clearest views on this were presented in 1948 and were quickly incorporated into the Keynesian-oriented textbooks of the time. The argument was lucid and persuasive and can be easily compressed.[29]

The declaration that public debt puts an unfair burden on our children, who are therefore made to pay for our profligacy, is a result of reasoning from false analogy. Since the internally held debt is one that the citizens of the country owe, through the government, to the holders of the government bonds (who happen to be the people in the country), we as a nation owe the national debt to ourselves. Thus, there is no analogy between the national debt and private debt. The payment of private debt implies consuming and enjoying less than one would otherwise be able to do. But if the national debt is repaid, some money is taken from some of the inhabitants of the country and is given to others. The nation as a whole does not have to consume any less than before. The converse is also true. When a personal debt is incurred, the funds enable the borrower to consume more than he earns himself. But this is not true for the national debt, since the lenders are also inhabitants of the country, and the borrowing involves only a transfer among consumers and investors within the country. Clearly, the issuance of government debt securities does not enable the country to consume more than it produces. Since a nation does not have to loosen its belt when debt is issued, it does not have to tighten it again when the national debt is being repaid.

It is a simple step from this reasoning to Lerner's contention that the national debt cannot be a burden on future generations. If the debt should be repaid by taxpayers in the future, the bondholders, who are members of that generation, would be receiving the repayment. Our grandchildren *qua* taxpayers are worse off since they must consume

---

[28] However, as Herbert Stein points out, Roosevelt's budget balancing proclivity was not so strong that he was willing to sacrifice much for it. See Herbert Stein, *The Fiscal Revolution in America* (Chicago: University of Chicago Press, 1969), p. 43.

[29] A. P. Lerner, "The Burden of the National Debt," in Lloyd A. Metzler et al., eds., *Income, Employment, and Public Policy: Essays in Honor of Alvin H. Hansen* (New York: W. W. Norton, 1948), pp. 255–75. Excerpts from Lerner's essay, as well as from other articles and books on the question of the burden of public debt, have been collected in James M. Ferguson, ed., *Public Debt and Future Generations* (Chapel Hill: University of North Carolina Press, 1964). For an opposing view to Lerner's, see James M. Buchanan, *Public Principles of Public Debt* (Homewood, Ill.: Richard D. Irwin, Inc., 1958).

less, but our grandchildren *qua* bondholders are better off because they can consume more. The two effects precisely cancel. Lerner's conclusion is that the burden of public debt rests squarely on the generation alive at the time the debt is issued. By parting with money, the bond purchasers are giving the government claims on real resources which would have been used to satisfy the desires of private individuals. Thus, resources are transferred from the private to the public sector. The burden of debt is measured by the loss of satisfaction incurred at the time the resources are shifted to the government. Since a project that uses up resources needs them immediately, the burden cannot be postponed or shifted.

Lerner on Sellers' Inflation

In the latter part of the 1950's, Lerner changed his mind about the ability of functional finance to provide simultaneously full employment and price level stability. He delivered a paper to the Johns Hopkins Political Economy Seminar in late 1957 in which he discussed the problem of the coexistence of inflation with depression, or unemployment. In this paper, he developed a third alternative to both the neoclassical or Keynesian approaches to inflation.

To the quantity theorist, the price level rises because the money supply is too great. A reduction in the supply of money will, other things being equal, reduce the price level. If the price level falls so low that it increases the real wage above the full employment level, money wages will fall and restore equilibrium at full employment. The result would simply be a lower price level and a lower money wage; the *real* wage rate and the level of employment remain the same. So the cure for inflation was a reduction in the rate of increase of the money supply, with full employment being guaranteed by price-and-wage flexibility.

To Keynes, classical and neoclassical economics "came into its own" in a period of inflation. Although increases in employment and output would be accompanied by rising prices as monetary and fiscal policy was used to bring the economy out of a depression, true inflation could not set in until relatively full employment was reached. After full employment, any increase in aggregate demand would lead to rising prices because the demand for real output would outstrip the ability of the producers to satisfy it. The Keynesian prescription for eliminating inflation would not have disturbed a quantity theorist: monetary and fiscal policy should be used to choke off the excessive demand. Neither Keynes nor the neoclassical economists discussed the possibility of inflation at a time when significant unemployment persisted in the labor market.

After 1955, however, economists witnessed an upward creep of prices despite the unprepossessing phenomenon of unemployment. Such a situation did not rest well on the foundation of either neoclassical or Keynesian theory. Both recognized inflation only occurring as a result of excessive demand, which is termed "demand-pull inflation." In the 1950's, a whole spate of literature issued forth in an attempt to explain the evidence of a coexistence of inflation with unemployment. The first attempts stressed the mechanics of what became known as "cost-push inflation"; that is, increases in the price level resulting from strong unions administering wage increases without consideration given to demand. Emphasis shifted from the *demand side* to the *supply side* of the inflation process. But this explanation seemed rather unsatisfactory since it stressed only the unilateral actions of trade union leaders and typically neglected the question of profits and the monetary and fiscal policies of the government.

In his paper to the Johns Hopkins Political Economy Club, in testimony before the Joint Economic Committee of Congress, and in a number of further papers, Lerner urged the more precise idea that inflation can only be understood as a result of increased wages and profit margins that are made in anticipation of being validated by permissive monetary and fiscal policy. This type of inflation, stressing both the demand-pull and cost-push aspect of the problem, was designated "sellers' inflation" by Lerner.[30] This discussion provided a theoretical rationalization for the Phillips Curve analysis, which Paul Samuelson and Robert Solow introduced to the United States in 1960.

Lerner's argument was essentially that monopolies, trade unions, government controls, and other institutions can circumvent the market in the determination of wages and prices. These institutions not only prevent wages and prices from falling in the event of unemployment but can make wages and prices rise even in the face of deficient demand. Any attempt to cure inflation by contractional monetary and fiscal measures simply increases the unemployment. The attempt to cure the unemployment by expansive monetary and fiscal policy aggravates the inflation. So, as the Phillips Curve showed, there is some amount of unemployment that is necessary to maintain price level stability. Lerner developed his sellers' inflation to explain this. In order to make Lerner's analysis clear, it will be helpful to utilize the same diagram that we introduced in Chapter 7 to discuss Keynes's notion of unemployment equilibrium.

In Figure 10.1, we depict the Keynesian labor supply curve, S, which is a function of the money wage rate; and the value of the marginal product curve VMP_0, intersecting the labor supply curve at N_1 with unemployment in the amount N_1N_2. With a money wage of W_0 and demand curve VMP_0, there is equilibrium unemployment in the amount N_1N_2. In order to eliminate this unemployment, the Keynesian prescription would be to increase aggregate demand through appropri-

---

[30] A. P. Lerner, "Inflationary Depression and the Regulation of Administered Prices," in U.S., Congress, Joint Economic Committee Compendium of Papers, *The Relationship of Prices to Economic Stability and Growth*, 1958, pp. 257–68. See also idem, "On Generalizing the General Theory," *American Economic Review* 50 (March 1960): 121–43; idem, "Sellers' Inflation and Administered Depression: An Analysis and a Suggestion for Dealing with Inflationary Depression," in U. S., Senate, Subcommittee on Antitrust and Monopoly of the Committee on the Judiciary, *Administered Prices: A Compendium on Public Policy*, 1963; and idem, *Everybody's Business* (East Lansing: Michigan State University Press, 1961), Chapter 11, pp. 81–92.

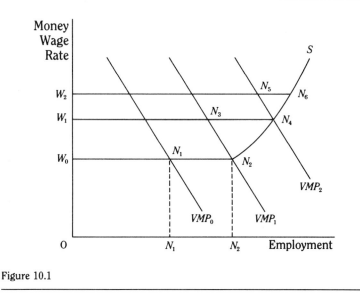

Figure 10.1

ate expansionary monetary and fiscal policies under the rules of functional finance.

As aggregate demand increases, however, prices begin to rise (under
the Keynesian assumption of increasing marginal costs) and the value
of the marginal product rises. This is represented by a movement to the
right of the *VMP* curve, which is associated with a fall in the real wage,
since the money wage remains constant. The ideal situation would be
for functional finance to be employed until the new *VMP* curve cuts the
labor supply function at N_2, so that full employment is reached. In this
case, we would have full employment and stable prices. If inflation set
in, the tools of functional finance would simply be put into reverse gear.

But in this Keynesian world—in which full employment is guaranteed by proper use of functional finance *and* in which there are strong
labor unions and business monopolies—it is impossible to have full
employment with price stability. This is so because these groups may
attempt to use their market power to obtain more than 100 percent of
the available product by raising their prices and wages. Profit-push as
well as wage-push can occur in the absence of full employment.
Assume, for example, that strong labor unions demand higher wages as
the slack in the labor force is removed. These wage increases might not
be very fiercely resisted so long as producers are confident that price
increases will be validated by an expansion of demand fueled by permissive monetary and fiscal policies. So the money wage rate moves up to
W_1 even before the *VMP* curve cuts the labor supply curve at N_2. At this
new wage rate, there may be no increase in employment (in the extreme
case), or the effect could be split between increases in employment and
increases in wage rates. With wage rate W_1 and demand curve VMP_1,
there is unemployment N_3N_4. If the government decides to use Lerner's
functional finance to cure the unemployment, the *VMP* curve shifts to

the right in an effort to cut the labor supply function at N_4. But once again there is a round of wage increases, and a new money wage of W_2 results, associated with unemployment $N_5 N_6$. Any attempt to increase aggregate demand to N_6 will continue the inflationary depression process.

On the other hand, if the government tries to stop inflation through functional finance, it would reduce spending in order to shift the *VMP* curve to the left, creating greater slack in the labor force. Although this helps eliminate inflation, it does so at the cost of a loss in real output. Nevertheless, as people become increasingly restless over inflation, the government comes under political pressure to reduce the rate of increase in the price level by engineering a recession. The outcome of this process has come to be called "stagflation."

Such an administered recession has great costs. In 1978, Lerner estimated that the United States economy was losing $50-100 billion of potential output because of the excessive unemployment resulting from government efforts to check inflation by reducing aggregate demand. To entirely eliminate the inflation through restrictive monetary and fiscal policy would, by Lerner's calculations, require 20-30 percent unemployment.[31]

Lerner then attempted to answer the question of what we can do to avoid this unhappy choice between depression and inflation. The cure for stagflation was his next order of business.

The Market Anti-Inflation Plan

The possibility of stagflation and the necessity of a "reserve army of unemployed" to maintain price stability was discussed as early as 1951 by Lerner in his book *The Economics of Employment*. He argued that the downward inflexibility of money wages would mean that wages would rise in some parts of the economy whenever there are scarcities of labor, but would not fall elsewhere. If the increase in the general level of wages was greater than the overall increase in productivity, there would have to be an increase in the price level. That could start an inflationary price spiral that could not be cured with the tools of functional finance without causing unacceptable levels of unemployment. In his 1951 volume, Lerner proposed a plan that he had developed in the late 1940's for a seminar at New York's New School for Social Research. He suggested a mechanism which would allow wages to rise according to increases in productivity. In industries where labor was scarce, the increase in wages could be greater than the overall increase in productivity. In industries where labor was overabundant, the increase in wages would be less than the overall increase in productivity. In that way, the average rate of wage increases would be held to

---

[31] This estimate was made in a letter to Senator William Proxmire, May 10, 1978. It is reprinted in David Colander, ed., *Solutions to Inflation* (New York: Harcourt Brace Jovanovich, 1979), pp. 193–97.

the estimated average rate of increase in output per laborer. A variant of this plan appeared in his book *Flation*, published in 1972.[32]

Lerner was not satisfied with these proposals. They did not, he realized, permit enough flexibility for the market mechanism to bring about the required degree of efficiency in the economy. This led him to put forward an alternative plan in 1978, which he called the Wage Increase Permit Plan (WIPP). In essence, WIPP involved a voucher system whereby marketable permits would be issued to firms in a limited number. These vouchers permitted a specified rate of money wage increase during a certain period of time. Firms wishing to grant wage increases beyond their initial allotment would be free to purchase vouchers from others who thereby gave up their right to increase wages. In this manner, wage increases could be kept within limits that might control inflation.[33]

It should be noted that these early plans stressed the importance of downward wage rigidities in explaining the spiraling nature of inflation. It was therefore natural to attack the problem at its source and try to control wage increases in order to mitigate the price level increases. But Lerner came to recognize that sellers' inflation, which stressed the attempts of all sellers to buy more than 100 percent of the output of the economy, could not justify attacking the problem by penalizing wage increases alone. Indeed, any attempt to solve the inflation problem by restricting wage increases would meet with justifiable antagonism on the part of workers and labor union leaders. In that event, it would be unlikely that Lerner's WIPP plan—or any plan based only on the penalization of wage increases to stop inflation—could be implemented in a democracy. Unfortunately, attempts to control prices in general were even worse. Lerner, like Paul Samuelson but unlike John Kenneth Galbraith, insisted that inflexible controls on wages and profits to stop inflation would lead to waste since relative prices could not adjust to bring about the optimal degree of efficiency in the utilization of scarce resources. Moreover, rigid controls would also lead to shortages and black markets in areas where quantities demanded exceeded quantities supplied.

What was needed was a plan to stop inflation that avoided the rigidities of controls while at the same time did not appear to be placing the burden for that beneficial result upon labor alone. In that way the plan could be made politically acceptable. In 1979, Lerner abandoned WIPP and put forward a more sophisticated program, which he called the Market Anti-Inflation Plan (MAP). This idea, which he developed in collaboration with David C. Colander, is highly ingenious and very subtle in its operation.[34]

---

[32] A. P. Lerner, *Flation* (New York: Quadrangle Books, 1972). A slightly revised version was brought out in paperback in 1973 by Penguin Books.

[33] A. P. Lerner, "A Wage-Increase Permit Plan to Stop Inflation," *Brookings Papers on Economic Activity* 2 (Washington D.C.: The Brookings Institution, 1978): 491–505.

[34] A. P. Lerner and D. C. Colander, *MAP: A Market Anti-Inflation Plan* (New York: Harcourt Brace Jovanovich, 1980).

In order to understand the Market Anti-Inflation Plan, it will be helpful to review one of Keynes's most deceptively simple insights: one person's expenditure is another person's income. Everytime someone spends a dollar, someone else ultimately gets that dollar in the form of either wages, salaries, interest, rent, or profits. Indeed, every price can be broken down into these component parts, which are called "factor incomes" by the economist. This means that the sum total of all incomes in the economy is exactly equal to the total value of all goods and services sold. That is the fundamental proposition and lesson of the system of national income developed from Keynes's insights in the *General Theory*. Perhaps it can be best understood when we look at the process by which everyone receives income in the economy. At each stage of the productive process (say, from growing wheat on a farm to turning the wheat into flour and turning the flour into bread), workers, employers, landlords, and lenders of money are receiving income. The amount of income received at each stage of the productive process is called the *value-added* at that stage. When we sum the value-added at each stage, we get the total value of all incomes earned in the production of the commodity from the earliest to the last stage of production. The total value-added must add up to the final retail price of the product. This is another way of saying that for each commodity, the income received in producing it must equal the price at which it is sold.[35]

The national income of an economy is nothing more, and nothing less, than all of the value-added in the economy at all stages of production for all goods and services sold in the market. Not understanding the value-added concept has led some noneconomists to believe that it is possible to have a depression because income generated in the process of production will be less than the total value of final output.[36] If this were the case, people would be unable to buy all of the products produced at profitable prices. This, however, is a fallacy.

However, a slight change in perspective will change what is a fallacy about the possibility of unemployment supposedly resulting from a flaw in the national income-accounting mechanism, into a truth about the possibility of generating inflation. If, in the process of production, income is generated at a greater rate of increase than the increase in total real output, then the average level of prices must rise. In other words, if the flow of value-added should rise faster than the ability of the economy to produce real goods, then the average price of goods and services will rise. That is what is meant by inflation; indeed, it *is* inflation.

It occurred to Lerner that inflation could be stopped if the value-

---

[35] Note that this relationship is an *accounting identity*, which will always hold because the proceeds from the sale must be distributed in some form of payment, and hence be counted as value-added (and income) at some stage of production.

[36] A tragic instance is provided by the bizarre case of poet Ezra Pound. See William Breit and Kenneth G. Elzinga, "Ezra Pound and the GNP," *Southern Economic Journal* 46 (January 1980); 904–12.

added could be kept equal to the increase in output per unit of input (i.e., productivity). At the same time, Lerner wanted to avoid the greatest defect of price controls: the inability of relative prices and wages to adjust to changes in tastes, techniques, and availabilities. What Lerner wanted was a true "incomes policy" rather than controls; that is, a policy that worked *with* the market rather than *against* it. Furthermore, he wanted a plan that would minimize the social and political frictions that arise when only one element of value-added (for example, wages) is controlled.[37]

To do this, Lerner suggested that the Federal Reserve System be authorized to set up a credit office which would issue to each firm in the economy a basic MAP credit equal to its dollar value-added in the previous year. In addition, each firm would be given "free" credit equal to the estimated national average growth of net output per unit of input. This would keep national average increase in value-added equal to the increase in productivity. In addition, firms would be required to keep their value-added and their MAP credit equal to each other by buying or selling credit, or by increasing or decreasing their value-added (accomplished by increasing or decreasing their prices). The Federal Reserve System's MAP credit office would maintain a market in MAP credit with the responsibility of buying and selling the credit on the open market and adjusting the price of MAP credit to keep quantity demanded equal to quantity supplied.

Since every firm is granted an amount of "extra" MAP credit equal to the national *average* increase in the value of output per unit of input, there will be some firms which are above average in their net output per unit of input, and others below that average. But the *total* amount of MAP credit is equal to that average. Therefore, the increase in value-added (and hence the increase in profits, interest, salaries, rents, and wages) cannot be more than the increase in real output for the economy as a whole. Firms which, because of a more than average scarcity of their product, may want to raise their prices may do so only if they can buy MAP credit from other firms which have a less than average scarcity for their product. Thus, the price of MAP credit is determined by supply-and-demand forces, and is always adjusted by the market so that it is equal to the inflationary pressure. The greater the expected rate of inflation, the more firms will be willing to pay for additional credit to enable them to charge higher prices; at the same time, the less eager will be the suppliers of MAP credit to sell. The price of MAP credit will be relatively high, discouraging firms from raising their prices, which would force them to purchase additional credit. In fact, firms would be encouraged to lower their prices (and value-added) in order to sell their

---

[37] This, as we noted, was a defect in Lerner's own earlier plans. For more on "incomes policies," see Henry Wallich and Sidney Weintraub, "Tax Based Incomes Policies," *Southern Economic Journal* 5 (June 1971): 1–17. There is a large literature on this subject, much of it represented by essays in Colander, *Solutions to Inflation*.

extra high-priced MAP credit. In this way, the supply of MAP credit becomes equal to demand.

Notice that relative prices still adjust to scarcities (as they are intended to), and yet the average price remains unchanged. The price which a firm must pay in the market for its MAP credit is part of its costs of production. This payment will reduce the amount the firm has for increases in wages, salaries, interest, rent, and profits. But which of these factor incomes will be affected more adversely than the others will be determined by bargaining and negotiation in the marketplace. The MAP credit affects *all* factor incomes, not just wages. The value-added is reduced by the price of the MAP credit for the firm which is demanding credit and is increased in precisely the same amount by the firms supplying credit. The total value-added in the economy cannot rise or fall by more than the total allotment of MAP credit disbursed by the Federal Reserve System. Value-added is simply shifted between firms in order to bring about relative price adjustments in accordance with factor and product scarcities.

Lerner's cure for stagflation is thus based on his insight that firms and workers do not take into account the inflationary impacts of their wage and price decisions. This is reminiscent of Pigou's argument that firms do not take into account the environmental and health impacts of their production decisions. Just as taxes and subsidies must be used to make marginal social and marginal private costs and benefits equal in order to attack the problem of polluted rivers and air, so too individuals and firms must be made to take the inflation "externality" into account in the making of their wage-and-price decisions. In proposing his MAP, Lerner is simply extending Marshallian and Pigovian tax and subsidy schemes from the micro to the macro area. What MAP does is to translate "the *social harm* from the inflationary element in price and wage increases into a *private cost* that the firm will try to avoid, and to do this through the market mechanism so as to avoid all administrative control or regulation of wages and prices."[38]

MAP would eliminate sellers' inflation. But Lerner takes care to stress that it must be combined with his functional finance tools in order to work properly. It is an addition to functional finance, not a substitute for it. This is true because excessive aggregate demand can still cause demand-pull inflation even in the absence of seller's inflation. Once MAP eliminates sellers' inflation, functional finance can be used to achieve full employment without inflation.

Of course, the MAP scheme has potential defects. Questions have been raised about the costs associated with the bureaucracy needed to administer and monitor the program. Lerner does not deny that problems may arise. But he insists that the alternatives are even more costly and less effective. Monetary and fiscal restraint alone will lead to stagflation and a politically unacceptable level of unemployment. Such a program would be abandoned after taking its toll in unemployment

---

[38] Lerner and Colander, p. 3.

but before it could prove effective in curing inflation. Wage-and-price controls will then be imposed; lead to inefficiencies and inequities, shortages, and black markets; and ultimately be abandoned after inflicting painful costs on society. Eventually, some kind of incomes policy similar to MAP must be accepted. Since it will come sooner or later, why not now? Lerner drives home his point with a parable.

> The local, noble tyrant of a Russian village gave a man who had displeased him a choice of three punishments—eat a dish of stinking fish, receive 40 lashes, or pay the enormous fine of 1,000 rubles. Initially, the man chose the fish. But after eating half of the dish, he could not keep any more down, so he chose the 40 lashes. But after 30 lashes, he could bear no more so he finally agreed to pay the 1,000 rubles.[39]

Abba Lerner's Legacy

Since this chapter is concerned with the contributions of Abba Lerner to the new economics, we will not discuss his many pivotal ideas unrelated to his attack on neoclassical economic policy. His writings have covered a catholic range of issues from the question of the rational calculation of prices in the absence of a price system,[40] to the prevention of nuclear annihilation by applying the principles of economic reasoning to foreign policy.[41]

In his attack on both Marxist planners and extreme laissez-faire free enterprisers, Lerner attempted to show that a decentralized system of bureaucratic firms could be compelled to follow rules that would produce an optimum in accordance with Paretian efficiency. Lerner advocated the use of market socialism in which the rule of setting price equal to marginal cost would be followed in every nook and cranny of the economy.

Abba Lerner's contributions to the new economics have been enormously significant. By helping to make Keynes intelligible to the rest of the economics profession and by his contribution of functional finance, he seemed to have provided the "tool box" which administrators could use to achieve full employment and price level stability. Furthermore, his sellers' inflation theory helped explain the new inflation of the 1970's and provided a rationale for the development of a sensible incomes policy.

Lerner has never been one to underestimate the power of academic economists to change the world. He has stated the importance of his own contributions to economic literacy in the following passage:

---

[39] Lerner and Colander p. 119

[40] A. P. Lerner, "Economic Theory and Socialist Economy," *Review of Economic Studies*, (October 1934): 51–61; idem, "Statistics and Dynamics in Socialist Economics," *Economic Journal* 47 (June 1937): 253–70; and idem, *The Economics of Control*.

[41] A. P. Lerner, "Nuclear Symmetry as a Framework for Coexistence," *Social Research* 31 (Summer 1964): 141–54.

When I say that we may be witnessing in our lifetime the failure of the free world to withstand the totalitarian onslaught, it is not my language but the objective situation that is melodramatic. We may fail because we are unprepared to make the effort needed and because we are using the superstition of the primacy of the balanced budget to excuse the failure to make the effort. Economic knowledge, by re-exploding this reincarnation of an old fallacy, and by showing how the authorities can avoid sellers' inflation, can set us free to apply our vast resources for the defense of the free world and the economic development of the poor world in our fight with the totalitarian world. This is the task and this is the case for political economy.[42]

A true student of Keynes, Lerner has never disparaged the power of ideas "for good or evil."

---

[42] Lerner, *Everybody's Business*, p. 134.

11

JOHN KENNETH GALBRAITH

ECONOMIST AS SOCIAL CRITIC

I believe that a good phrase is better than a Great Truth—which is usually buncombe.

H.L. Mencken

Despite the increasing interest which the subject of economics has generated in recent decades, few, if any, of the really important tracts in economic thought are ever read by a wide audience. Keynes's *General Theory* or Samuelson's *Foundations of Economic Analysis* are rarely found on household bookshelves; few laymen have ever heard of E.H. Chamberlin, A.C. Pigou, Alvin Hansen, Abba Lerner, or Alfred Marshall. Indeed, of the men considered thus far in the present volume, only Thorstein Veblen achieved a very wide audience for his views on the subject of economics, and he was depressed that his work was considered so "popular." To be sure, Nobel laureates such as Paul Samuelson and Milton Friedman reached large audiences through their columns in *Newsweek* and periodic pieces in the popular press. Yet the collective audience of all the economists in this book could probably be matched by that of a single man: John Kenneth Galbraith.[1]

Long before it became fashionable to invite economists as guests on TV talk shows, Galbraith had succeeded in brightening the "dismal science" enough to spark the interest of the average reader. A sort of unofficial recognition of Galbraith's unique status as a celebrity within the profession came in June 1968, when *Playboy* Magazine published an extensive interview with him. By the 1970's, his name had become familiar enough to warrant two biographies of his life and works, and he

---

[1] The closest challenger would unquestionably be Milton Friedman, whose book and TV series, *Free to Choose*, captured large audiences in the late 1970's—twenty years after Galbraith's first best seller.

was frequently featured as a personality by the news media.[2] In 1973, Galbraith was invited by the British Broadcasting Corporation to organize a television series on "some unspecified aspect of the history of economic or social ideas." He accepted the challenge and, in 1976, hosted a twelve-part series entitled "The Age of Uncertainty" that was aired on the Public Broadcasting System throughout the United States. The essays by Galbraith which formed the basis for each episode were published as a book the following year.[3]

At a time when the economics profession turned increasingly towards greater division of labor within the various fields of economics, Galbraith was remarkably successful in swimming against the tide. Eschewing the gains from specialization in a narrow field, he chose to include as the scope for his analysis the entire range of economic and social problems confronting society. His approach has always been disarmingly simple. As he explained in *Playboy* in 1968: "All I've done is sought to write economics, however difficult, in clear English."[4] It was in this spirit that he teamed with French journalist Nicole Salinger for a series of interviews, discussions which produced, in Galbraith's judgment, "a well-considered line of questioning in which any literate person might have participated."[5] Always cognizant of the controversies among economists, Galbraith and Salinger cautiously titled their book *Almost Everyone's Guide to Economics*.[6] The book was an instant success. Parts of it were reprinted in *Consumer Reports*, and Consumer Union printed a special edition for marketing to its members.

Although his range of interests harkens back to the views which Adam Smith, David Ricardo, and John Stuart Mill had of the domain of political economy, Galbraith has rarely been in agreement with the political philosophy of the classical economists. For more than two decades he has represented, for many, the epitome of the twentieth-century liberal.[7] At every turn he assails the social and economic values of modern society and the institutions and beliefs which reinforce them. He argues for change, and he is quite willing to entrust to the

---

[2] Myron E. Sharpe, *John Kenneth Galbraith and the Lower Economics* (White Plains, N.Y.: International Arts and Sciences Press, 1973); and John S. Gambs, *John Kenneth Galbraith* (Boston: Twayne Publishers, 1975).

[3] John Kenneth Galbraith, *The Age of Uncertainty: A History of Economic Ideas and Their Consequences* (Boston: Houghton Mifflin, 1977).

[4] *Playboy* Magazine 5, no. 6 (June 1968): 138.

[5] John Kenneth Galbraith and Nicole Salinger, *Almost Everyone's Guide to Economics* (Mount Vernon, N.Y.: Consumers Union, 1978).

[6] In the preface to the book, the authors admit that the thought crossed their minds to title the work, *The Intelligent Frenchwoman's Guide to Economics and Economists* in recognition of Nicole Salinger's effort to provide guidance through the world of economics and economists.

[7] Galbraith is well aware of his liberal stature. Queried in 1968 as to whom he might nominate as the "head" of the Establishment, he answered that "some people believe that I am studying hard for the job." *Playboy*, p. 78. Paul Samuelson put the same point in a broader perspective when he commented: "Followers of Milton Friedman think he is the new Keynes. Galbraith, I suspect, thinks that it is *he* who is the real Napoleon." Paul A. Samuelson, "Liberalism at Bay," in idem, *The Collected Scientific Papers of Paul A. Samuelson*, vol. 4, ed. Hiroki Nagatani and Kate Crowley (Cambridge, Mass.: MIT Press, 1977) p. 874.

state the task of accomplishing that change. To those who warn that government intervention impairs economic freedom, Galbraith replies:

> The instinct which warns of danger in this association of economic and public power is sound. . . . But conservatives have looked in the wrong direction for the danger. . . . The danger to liberty lies in the subordination of belief to the needs of the industrial system.[8]

To those who argue against government intervention on the grounds of its inherent inefficiencies, Galbraith pragmatically replies:

> I agree that the Federal Government is a highly imperfect instrument. I think we should, on occasion, remind ourselves, however, that it is still, in its own league, the best government there is.[9]

Winston Churchill might have been proud of that sentiment, but Adam Smith or Alfred Marshall would surely have cringed at the thought that it came from a political economist.

During the past three decades, John Kenneth Galbraith has emerged as one of the leading social critics in American life. He may never win a Nobel Prize in Economics, and his name is not likely to be permanently placed alongside those credited with pioneering new and pathbreaking analytical contributions to the science of economics. Nevertheless, he may well be the most widely read economist of this or any other time. The two works which first elaborated his critique of American capitalism—*The Affluent Society* and *The New Industrial State*—remained on the best seller list for prolonged periods following their publication. His subsequent tracts on economic subjects, *Economics and the Public Purpose* (1973), *Money: Whence It Came, Where It Went* (1975), and *Almost Everyone's Guide to Economics* (1978), have been well received by the public and can be found on most booksellers' shelves.

Unlike Veblen, Galbraith was not at all upset by this turn of events. He has always sought a large audience, and he has not confined his literary efforts to economics. His published books deal with history (*The Age of Uncertainty*), politics (*The Liberal Hour*), personal memoirs (*The Scotch, Ambassador's Journal, A Life in Our Times*), and polemical arguments on foreign affairs (*How To Get Out of Viet Nam*), as well as a novel (*The Triumph*).

His success in disseminating economic doctrine to such a large group of readers has not been a source of unmitigated joy among economists generally. For, of all the targets he chooses to attack, Galbraith reserves some of his most blistering comments for what he calls the "conventional wisdom" governing economic thought. Not since Veblen's attacks a half century earlier, has economics been subjected to such a withering fire. At least some of his colleagues have been listening, for in addition to the popular recognition accorded his work,

---

[8] John Kenneth Galbraith, *The New Industrial State* (Boston: Houghton Mifflin, 1967), pp. 412–13.
[9] John Kenneth Galbraith, "Testimony" in U.S., Congress, House, Committee on Government Operations, 94th Cong., 1st sess., 17 and 23 September 1975, p. 25.

Galbraith has garnered his share of professional awards. In 1972, the American Economic Association elected him president of their august body, an honor that did not dull the critic's knife. In his presidential address, Galbraith pointed out that "for a new and notably articulate generation of economists a reference to neoclassical economics has become markedly perjorative."[10] Rather than dwelling on the failures of neoclassical economics in his talk, however, Galbraith went on "to urge the means by which we economists can reassociate ourselves with reality."[11] Most of those in the audience were already familiar with Galbraith's view of reality, since he had been expounding it for more than a decade.[12]

Unlike Paul Samuelson, Galbraith has always relished political involvement. As early as 1952, he was a leading figure in the Democratic Party as an advisor to Adlai Stevenson. As chairman of the Americans for Democratic Action in 1968, he vigorously supported Eugene McCarthy, thus exacerbating a bitter split in that organization. Galbraith remained undaunted; he had been a leading spokesman against the Vietnam involvement since the early period of the Kennedy administration. He had been fairly close to President Kennedy, an association which dated back to Galbraith's tutoring at Winthrop House when the future president was at Harvard. The two men corresponded frequently while Galbraith was ambassador to India in the early 1960's, and the economist is credited with playing a major role in convincing Kennedy of the efficacy of the new economics.[13] He brought Paul Samuelson and the president-elect together in 1960, and advised Kennedy to name the MIT professor as chairman of the Council of Economic Advisers. (The advice was followed, but Samuelson refused the offer.) After the unsuccessful Democratic campaigns of 1968 and 1972, Galbraith became less active in party affairs, although he remains an outspoken commentator and critic on political and economic events, directing his remarks at Democrats and Republicans alike. In the 1970's, Galbraith became associated with the economic policies of Canadian Prime Minister Pierre Trudeau.[14]

As a leading spokesman for the liberal element in American politics, Galbraith has offered considerable amounts of advice over the past thirty years. It may be, as he notes, that people are prone to mistake the

---

[10] John Kenneth Galbraith, "Power and the Useful Economist," *American Economic Review* 63 (March 1973): 1.

[11] Galbraith, "Power and the Useful Economist," p. 2.

[12] This, Galbraith hastened to add, should have reassured his listeners, since "to speak well of one's own published and unpublished writing, whatever one's other aberrations, is strongly in our professional tradition." (Galbraith, "Power and the Useful Economist, p. 2.)

[13] Galbraith cites Kennedy's espousal of the new economics in policy as the single most impressive accomplishment of the president's tenure in office. *Playboy*, p. 70. For reminiscences of his years as ambassador to India and of his relationship to John F. Kennedy, see John Kenneth Galbraith, *Ambassador's Journal* (Boston: Houghton Mifflin, 1969).

[14] In 1976, Trudeau commented that "I'm not as wise and as experienced as Galbraith, but there's no doubt that his thinking has permeated my thought and that of a lot of other people." *Washington Post*, 3 June 1976, p. A21.

quantity of advice *offered* for that which was actually *taken*. Nevertheless, it can hardly be said that his voice has been ignored. Apart from his personal influence on government officials, his books have occasionally caused official reaction as well. The appearance of *The New Industrial State* prompted the Senate Subcommittee on Monopoly to hold hearings and gather testimony on the implications of the Galbraithian system for government antitrust policy. He has been a frequent vistor to that, and other congressional committees, over the course of three decades. Galbraith has never been flustered by such attention, even though his comments have, on occasion, caused a commotion on Capitol Hill. In 1954, he appeared before the Senate Subcommittee on Banking and Finance to testify about the stock market. Drawing heavily from his forthcoming book *The Great Crash*, Galbraith told the senators that the 1929 experience could be repeated. While he was speaking, the New York stock market experienced a sharp decline in prices. There were some who went so far as to draw a causal connection.[15]

Galbraith began his career as an observer of social life in the Scotch community along the northern edge of Lake Erie, where he was born.[16] He worked his way through Ontario Agricultural College and eventually earned a doctorate in agricultural economics from the University of California at Berkeley in 1936. The young Galbraith was already showing himself to be a very heterodox economist; while at Berkeley, he not only steeped himself in the reigning orthodoxy but read extensively from the writings of Veblen and Marx as well. The following year, he went to Harvard as an instructor, then traveled to Cambridge, England, for a year as a social science research fellow. He did not meet Keynes then, although the ideas in the *General Theory* were quickly accepted by the youthful American scholar. Galbraith returned to the United States and taught at several schools prior to his appointment as deputy director of the Office of Price Administration in 1941. He later became director of the United States Strategic Bombing Survey, and head of the Office of Economic Security Policy in the State Department. President Truman awarded him the Medal of Freedom for his work in these capacities. Before returning to Harvard on a permanent basis in 1949, Galbraith paused briefly to serve as an editor of *Fortune*.[17] Soon thereafter, he became the Paul Warburg Professor of Economics at Harvard, a post he held until his retirement in 1976.

---

[15] In fact, Senator Homer Capehart of Indiana was sufficiently upset over Galbraith's statements (and a few others that the economist had made at one time or another) to suggest that Galbraith should be called before another senate subcommittee to account for his views. Nothing came of it, although Galbraith and Capehart exchanged statements in the press. Galbraith's principal regret over the incident was that it failed to stimulate sales of the forthcoming book. See his account of the incident in John Kenneth Galbraith, *The Great Crash* (Boston: Houghton Mifflin, 1961), pp. xii-xix.

[16] For a highly entertaining look at his childhood society, see John Kenneth Galbraith, *The Scotch* (Boston: Houghton Mifflin, 1964).

[17] According to a report in *Time* Magazine, Galbraith credits Henry Luce with teaching him how to write while an editor with *Fortune*. *Time*, 16 February 1968, p. 28. In his memoirs, *A Life in Our Times* (Boston: Houghton Mifflin, 1981) Galbraith devotes a chapter to his experiences at Fortune, and stresses his debt to Luce.

The "Conventional Wisdom" and the Power of Ideas

Our concern is primarily with Galbraith's economics, and his basic contributions here are spelled out in three major works: *The Affluent Society* (1958), *The New Industrial State* (1967), and *Economics and the Public Purpose* (1973). The three books form the basis for what has come to be called the "Galbraithian System," an approach to economics that is markedly different from that espoused by either mainstream or radical economists.

As we have seen in earlier chapters, neoclassical economists assumed that people are "rational" and therefore that they will always make rational decisions. While he does not completely reject this possibility, Galbraith is openly skeptical (as Veblen was) that such a proposition is a useful description of behavior in the marketplace. To Galbraith, *ideas* are important, so important that they dominate the actions of groups or individuals in our society. If ideas were always the product of careful reasoning, this might not pose a problem. But they are not. Ideas are accepted by people not because they are logical but because they are *familiar*. Familiarity, Galbraith argues,

> . . . may breed contempt in some areas of human behavior, but in the field of social ideas it is the touchstone of acceptability.
>
> Because familiarity is such an important test of acceptability, the acceptable ideas have great stability. They are highly predictable. It will be convenient to have a name for the ideas which are esteemed at any time for their acceptability and it should be a term that emphasizes this predictability. I shall refer to these ideas henceforth as the conventional wisdom.[18]

The notion that there exists a conventional wisdom appears again and again in Galbraith's work. Initially, he employed it as a device to characterize the body of economic thought which dominated professional economists in the 1950's and 1960's—the neoclassical paradigm. But ideas are not limited to economics and economists; they influence all facets of what we loosely refer to as economic behavior. A decade after he coined the phrase in reference to economic theory, Galbraith wrote of "accepted beliefs" and a "convenient social virtue," terms which described accepted social norms that governed behavior in the society.[19]

The importance of the conventional wisdom lies in its power over people's actions. Accepted behavior of consumers, producers, or any other group is defined by the conventional wisdom, and that inhibits any tendency towards unacceptable behavior—in particular, behavior which might result in significant change. "Ideas," Galbraith insists,

---

[18] Galbraith, *The Affluent Society*, p. 9.

[19] The most extensive discussion of this is in Galbraith, *Economics and the Public Purpose* (1973), Chapter 22. More recently Galbraith has employed a similar concept to describe what he terms the "accommodation" of poverty in societies where a majority of the people are poor. See John Kenneth Galbraith, *The Nature of Mass Poverty* (Cambridge, Mass.: Harvard University Press, 1979), especially Chapters 4 and 5.

"are inherently conservative."[20] He therefore attacks economic theories not only because they fail to provide answers to the economic problems they examine, but also because these incorrect economic theories reinforce the inherently conservative tendency of the conventional wisdom to resist changes in behavior, specifically changes in economic policy. Galbraith leaves little doubt as to the importance of this problem:

> The emancipation of belief is the most formidable of the tasks of reform and the one on which all else depends. It is formidable because power that is based on belief is uniquely authoritarian; when fully effective, it excludes by its nature the thought that would weaken its grasp.[21]

This perhaps explains the avidity with which Galbraith attacks contemporary economic theory. It is, he feels, imperative that the now widely held ideas on how our economic system works be replaced by new approaches to the problems of a changing economy and society. Like Veblen, he attacks the foundations of *all* the accepted paradigms of modern economics.

The Conventional Wisdom in Economics Today

Like Keynes, Galbraith faced the problem of identifying those economic propositions which were widely held by everyone. Keynes chose the work of A.C. Pigou as representative of the classical economic thinking that he was attacking; critics quickly accused him of setting up a "straw man." Avoiding Keynes's difficulty of choosing a single work, Galbraith based his characterization of modern economics on a source few would challenge as a measure of consensus within the profession: Paul Samuelson's textbook.[22]

To Galbraith, the accepted explanation of consumer choice remains essentially that of Alfred Marshall and the neoclassical economists. On the supply side, Galbraith notes the alterations introduced by the introduction of monopolistic competition, but he points out that the basic tenets of the theory of the firm remain firmly rooted in a notion of competitive firms regulated by the "invisible hand" of the marketplace. In macroeconomics, Galbraith concedes that the conventional wisdom has been altered over the past few decades with the Keynesian attack. But the overthrow was incomplete. As Galbraith notes,

> . . . it's always important to see first what Keynes did not do. He did not attack the notion of the motivating power of self-interest. And he

---

[20] Galbraith, *The Affluent Society*, p. 20.

[21] Galbraith, *Economics and the Public Purpose*, p. 223.

[22] Galbraith's views on contemporary economic thinking are scattered ubiquitously throughout his writings. The summary which follows is, of course, our own interpretation. It rests primarily on Galbraith's early remarks in *The Affluent Society* (particularly Chapters 3–5), together with his later (and more specific) exposition of the neoclassical model in *Economics and the Public Purpose* (particularly Chapters 2 and 3).

didn't attack the benign regulatory role of competition and the market.[23]

Because Galbraith focuses his attack on the foundations of contemporary economic theory, the fact that his description of the superstructure might be regarded by some as incomplete makes little difference. He does seem to be focusing his attack on three points, which are widely accepted by mainstream economists.

Galbraith's first objection, which was the major point raised in *The Affluent Society*, challenges the assertion that consumers' tastes or preferences are derived outside the economic system and thus must be taken for granted by the economist. In the modern industrial economy, claims Galbraith, wants are a result of the economic process itself; they are not independent of the system.

The second objection, which occupied Galbraith's attention in *The New Industrial State*, concerns the assumption of profit maximization on the part of the producers in our economy. Galbraith argues that large corporations, which dominate over one-half of the production of goods and services in the United States today, are run by an elaborate planning process which subordinates the profit imperative and insulates the firm from market pressures.

The third, and perhaps most crucial, objection which Galbraith raises is that contemporary theory ignores the role of *power* in the economy. In the introduction to his book *Economics and the Public Purpose*, Galbraith wrote: "On no conclusion is this book more clear: Left to themselves, economic forces do not work out for the best except perhaps for the powerful."[24] The failure of contemporary economics to deal with the issue of power was also the major theme of his presidential address to the American Economic Association in December 1973.[25]

As is often the case with criticism on a broad scale, Galbraith has collected a large number of ideas and welded them together into a set of propositions regarding the analysis of the modern economy. His general approach to the entire setting of the economic problem is highly reminiscent of Thorstein Veblen, particularly his attack on the theory of demand and his view of technology in the modern world. Although he makes relatively little mention of Veblen in his major works, the ideas of Galbraith's predecessor clearly influenced his thoughts.[26] The two men center their attacks on the assumptions behind the elegant

---

[23] Galbraith and Salinger, p. 18.

[24] Galbraith, *Economics and the Public Purpose*, p. xiii.

[25] Galbraith, "Power and the Useful Economist."

[26] See the comments in Galbraith, *The Affluent Society*, pp. 54–55. In personal correspondence with the authors (June 12, 1967), Galbraith commented on the fact that Veblen's work influenced his own thought. In his interviews with Nicole Salinger, he also mentioned Veblen's influence. See Galbraith and Salinger, pp. 23–24. For the fullest statement he has made to date on Veblen, see John Kenneth Galbraith, "Who Was Thorstein Veblen?" in idem, *Annals of an Abiding Liberal* (Boston: Houghton Mifflin, 1979), pp. 123–47. This book contains many of Galbraith's writings during the 1970's, including scraps of autobiography and portraits of literary and political figures. Veblen's influence on Galbraith is also explicitly acknowledged in Galbraith, *A Life in Our Times*, pp. 29–31.

logic of economic theory. They reject the notion of consumer rationality by questioning the values which are produced in an industrial society, and they argue for a revision of these values.

Galbraith's literary skill is sufficiently refreshing in a profession such as economics that one ought not complain.[27] Nevertheless, his style at times makes it difficult to distill the basic elements of his attack into propositions which can be carefully evaluated. As we have already noted, his system involves three basic arguments: one on the irrelevancy of consumer demand, one on the distortions of production in the "industrial system," and one on the problem of power in the economic system.

We begin with the attack on the theory of demand.

The Affluent Society

It is an indisputable fact that the United States has become a much more affluent society than it was in Adam Smith's day. Scarcity of resources may still govern the allocative mechanism, but such grim specters as the "necessities of life" and the "subsistence level of wages" which dominated nineteenth-century tracts on political economy no longer haunt the industrial society as we near the close of the twentieth century. The subject matter of economics has been made correspondingly less depressing as the success of the processes of production finally removed the constraints which had so long held outputs to such meager levels. The problem, according to Galbraith, is that the conventional wisdom has not kept pace; it continues to act as though we are analyzing an economy of nineteenth-century poverty rather than twentieth-century affluence.[28]

There are, as we have seen, two basic propositions underlying the theory of demand: (1) the law of diminishing marginal utility and (2) the notion that there exists a world of consumers—individuals, households, and the like—that make decisions based on a rational set of tastes which are determined outside of the economic system. Both of these assertions, claims Galbraith, seem untenable in the modern industrial state.

In the neoclassical analysis of the consumer, the concept of diminishing marginal utility implied that as the stock of a good increased, the additional satisfaction to the purchaser from successive units would decline. Galbraith wonders why, with rising income, this would not also be true for all goods taken as a group.

---

[27] People have complained, of course. To such claims that he "popularizes" economics with his best-selling books, Galbraith replies (*Playboy*, p. 138.):
> Economics, like all sciences, has its crotchets, its petty jealousies, and its minor feuds. I have no doubt that a certain number of people have said from time to time, "Galbraith is unfair by not making use of the normal tendencies to obscurity; he's as guilty as a doctor who writes his prescriptions in clear English instead of illegible Latin." But these are the attitudes of inconsequential people, and I've always successfully ignored them.

[28] Moreover, according to Galbraith, the conventional wisdom is equally ineffective in analyzing twentieth-century poverty in what is termed the Third World. See his remarks in *The Nature of Mass Poverty*.

> With increasing per capita real income, men are able to satisfy additional wants. These are of a lower order of urgency. This being so, the production that provides the goods that satisfy these less urgent wants must also be of a smaller (and declining) importance.[29]

He is aware, of course, that the earlier theorists attempted to come to grips with this problem. For it is the utility of each good which declines as the stock of that good increases. This is the crucial relationship which explains the decline in satisfaction from each good and the corresponding lessening in the desire to pay. Since purchases of separate goods are made over time, not all at once, the level of wants will be sustained. Moreover, the range of new goods confronting consumers will ensure that they will not experience declining levels of satisfaction as they collect more and more goods. Galbraith demurs, insisting that ". . . presumably, the more important things come first."[30]

Neoclassical—and modern—theories of consumer choice do not deny the possibility of such a phenomenon. Indeed, this very point caused difficulties in Marshall's analysis of utility and demand. Did the marginal utility of money (that is, income) fall as the level of income rose? As Galbraith rather contemptuously points out, the economist bounded by the notion of diminishing marginal utility can have "nothing to say" on this point.[31] To Galbraith, this neutrality, forced by the logic underlying the theory of demand, flies in the face of common sense.

> Beyond a certain point the possession and consumption of goods becomes burdensome unless the tasks associated therewith can be delegated. . . . Otherwise the limits on consumption are severe.[32]

The Dependence Effect

Since marginal utility is a very convenient tool to explain the allocation of expenditures, there is little incentive for economists to explore the issue further. Galbraith suggests that if they did, they might find out that

> . . . there is a flaw in the case. If an individual's wants are to be urgent, they must be original with himself. They cannot be urgent if they must be contrived for him. And above all, they must not be contrived by the process of production by which they are satisfied. For this means that the whole case for urgency of production falls to the ground. One cannot defend production as satisfying wants if that production creates the wants.[33]

---

[29] Galbraith, *The Affluent Society*, p. 145.

[30] Galbraith, *The Affluent Society*, p. 148.

[31] Galbraith, *The Affluent Society*, p. 150.

[32] Galbraith, *Economics and the Public Purpose*, pp. 29–30.

[33] Galbraith, *The Affluent Society*, pp. 152–53.

This brings us to one of the cornerstones of the Galbraithian system: the assertion that "contrived wants" (which are clearly less urgent than "original wants") cannot provide a basis for evaluating the need for production. The defense of production is weakened still further when the wants are contrived by the production process itself. It is a point sufficiently important that it is worthwhile to quote Galbraith at greater length on the matter.

> As a society becomes increasingly affluent, wants are increasingly created by the process by which they are satisfied. . . . Wants thus come to depend on output. In technical terms, it can no longer be assumed than welfare is greater at an all-round higher level of production than at a lower one. It may be the same. The higher level of production has, merely, a higher level of want creation necessitating a higher level of want satisfaction. There will be frequent occasion to refer to the way wants depend on the process by which they are satisfied. It will be convenient to call it the Dependence Effect.[34]

This dependence effect is one of the most controversial aspects of Galbriath's analysis, and both he and his critics agree that it is crucial to his later conclusions.

The dependence effect has been met with some skepticism by economists. Is it in fact the case, as Galbraith argues, that the level of welfare may remain constant as production increases because wants increase proportionately?[35] The conclusion is hardly obvious, since the line between those wants based on necessity and those which are contrived by production is not distinct. The most vehement of Galbraith's critics would agree with Professor Hayek that the notion of the dependence effect is a non sequitur since virtually *all* wants are acquired.[36] Others might content themselves with simply pointing out that the application of the dependence effect will necessarily require some implicit set of values by which we rank the urgency of wants expressed by consumers. As with Veblen, this involves a value judgment of considerable importance. Unfortunately, it is a subjective issue, which lies at the center of the Galbraithian view of the economic system. The reader can judge the merits of the dependence effect as an analytical tool. One should note, however, the implications which acceptance of this phenomenon can have for economic analysis.

Once the dependence effect is granted, we can easily dispose of the notion of consumer sovereignty. The consumer cannot be viewed as sovereign if he is continually manipulated by producers into accepting new and artificial wants which suit the aims of those producers. The

---

[34] Galbraith, *The Affluent Society*, p. 158.

[35] It is common today to point out that the *costs* of economic growth may be substantial, perhaps substantial enough to outweigh the benefits. That is not the issue here. The dependence effect suggests that the gains from growth might be zero even in the absence of any costs.

[36] F. A. Hayek, "The Non Sequitur of the 'Dependence Effect,' " *Southern Economic Journal*, April 1964, pp. 346–48. Reprinted in Edmund Phelps, ed., *Private Wants and Public Needs* (New York: W.W. Norton, 1965), pp. 38–39. Hayek contends that, aside from "food, shelter and sex," every want is culturally determined.

whole idea of a rational consumer loses its meaning, and only social nostalgia leads us to insist that the market is a reasonable allocator of scarce resources according to the social need.

The greatest impact of the dependence effect is as a basis for the argument of social imbalance. The operation of a dependence effect generates a very sizable bias in demand by consumers towards the production of private goods (even those associated with relatively low levels of urgency) at the expense of the more urgently needed public goods. The result is an imbalance in the collective choice of goods. By eliminating the need to worry about the urgency of private production, the extension of government goods and services can be justified by insisting that private production has been overvalued by consumers (due to the influence of producers) while public goods are undervalued.[37]

In fact, *any* intervention which is deemed necessary by the public interest can be at least partially defended through the logic of the dependence effect. In his typically sardonic vein, Galbraith acknowledges that

> It is easy to see why the conventional wisdom resists so stoutly such a change. It is far, far better to have a firm anchor in nonsense than to put out on the troubled seas of thought.[38]

Twenty-five years after that was written, there remain those who are still not anxious to weigh anchor and put to sea. Galbraith has hardly been daunted by such skeptics, for the dependence effect was only the introduction to his attack on modern economics. It is time to turn to his second avenue of assault: the theory of the firm.

The Industrial System

> The modern economy can only be understood as a bimodal structure. On the one hand, and occupying half the private sector, are a very small number of very large firms. Fewer than 2,000 of these giants now produce approximately half of all private product.
>
> On the other side, occupying the other half of the economy are some 10 to 12 million small firms, the number depending on what is called a firm.[39]

The means by which the United States has gained its affluence—the creation of an industrial system—has fundamentally altered our social system. For the past 200 years, what is commonly termed the "industrial revolution" has been the dominating force for change in the Western world. At the center of those changes, in Galbraith's view, is

---

[37] The picture as we leave it here is incomplete. We shall return to the issues of social imbalance and the role of the state.

[38] Galbraith, *The Affluent Society*, p. 160.

[39] John Kenneth Galbraith, "Testimony" in U.S., Congress, House, Subcommittee on Antitrust, Consumers, and Employment of the Committee on Small Business, 95th Cong., 2nd sess., 17 and 18 May 1978, p. 32.

what he terms the *industrial system*, the 2,000 "giants" which control half of our economic activity. According to Galbraith,

> To understand it is to understand that part which is most subject to change and which, accordingly, is most changing our lives. . . . To understand the rest of the economy is to understand only that part which is diminishing in relative extent and which is least subject to change.[40]

To analyze the industrial system, Galbraith has developed a series of hypotheses, which we shall summarize in three basic propositions:[41]

1. The technological revolution in the past century has generated a pervasive force leading to ever-increasing size of industrial enterprise. The complexities of modern technology require a group of skilled engineer-managers to run these giant firms. Because this group does not own any part of the company, they will not necessarily be governed by the traditional assumption that managers will maximize profits.
2. Size greatly increases the cost of failure. Large firms will seek to minimize this risk by controlling markets through planning. This results in a determination of price and output which is not dependent upon supply and demand.
3. The concentration of economic power in the hands of those who control the industrial system necessitates major changes in the institutional arrangements of our economy, particularly in the relationship of government and the industrial system.

Large Firms and the Technostructure

The emergence of large firms in the United States has been a statistical fact for the past 100 years. A variety of factors has been named as causes for this tendency towards large enterprise. Among the more common are: economies of large-scale production; protection against risk; advantages in the capital market; and, perhaps most compelling of all, the monopoly profits possible from domination of a market. All of these possibilities create a situation where, in Galbraith's view, there may be *no* upper limit on the size of the firm.

> No one fifty years ago would have imagined that corporations could be as big as they are now. And by dividing the corporation up into separate units for administration, it does seem possible that the inefficiencies of large scale can be avoided.[42]

To understand the behavior of these giant firms, one must examine the role of modern technology. Technology exerts a continuous and perva-

---

[40] Galbraith, *The New Industrial State*, p. 10.

[41] The most careful discussion of the industrial system can be found in Galbraith, *The New Industrial State* and *Economics and the Public Purpose*. For a less formal outline of the industrial system as seen through Galbraith's eyes, see *Almost Everyone's Guide to Economics*, particularly Chapters 3–5 and 10.

[42] Galbraith and Salinger, p. 54.

sive pressure forcing ". . . the division and subdivision of any task into its component parts." It provides the necessary element which enables us to apply knowledge to the development of better means of production. The result has been to alter greatly the structure of the firm. The impact of technology can be seen in a variety of areas: capital needs are greatly enlarged by the scale of enterprise necessitated by modern techniques. Organization within the firm becomes more and more geared to the decentralized decision-making required by an increasing division of labor within the management of the firm. Most important of all, there will develop a greatly enlarged pressure for comprehensive planning within the firm to cover the entire range of the production process, from inputs to the sale of the output.[43]

In the face of these changes, the decision apparatus of the firm has undergone a considerable transformation. The entrepreneur, whom neoclassical economic theory pictures as controlling the capital and organizing the other factors of production, is no longer a captain of industry, barking out commands to his subordinates. Group decision-making replaces the single entrepreneur. The owner-managers of the enterprise ostensibly continue to run the firm, but in fact they depend on others to actually run it. As Galbraith puts it,

> . . . The directors of the modern large corporation are treated with ceremony and respect and allowed to ratify decisions that have already been taken.[44]

Galbraith's description of the group which makes the decisions for the directors to ratify is worth careful notice.

> This . . . group is very large; it extends from the most senior officials of the corporation to where it meets, at the outer perimeter, the white- and blue-collar workers whose function is to conform more or less mechanically to instruction or routine. It embraces all who bring specialized knowledge, talent, or experience to group decision-making. This, not the narrow management group, is the guiding intelligence—the brain—of the enterprise. There is no name for all who participate in group decision-making or the organization which they form. I propose to call this organization the Technostructure.[45]

Here again, the Galbraithian system seems very much like the world of price engineers described by Thorstein Veblen.[46] And, like Veblen, Galbraith insists that the division of labor within the technostructure introduces a complication into the accepted explanation of the firm's

[43] This summary draws heavily on the comments in Galbraith, *The New Industrial State*, pp. 12–21. Galbraith's emphasis on technology as the driving force behind the industrial system is another aspect of his work which makes him so closely associated with Veblen, who similarly emphasized the importance of industrial technology on the evolution of the modern business enterprise.

[44] Galbraith and Salinger, p. 57.

[45] Galbraith, *The New Industrial State*, p. 74.

[46] See the discussion of Chapter 4 above. While he admires Veblen, Galbraith insists that the similarity is only superficial. See Galbraith's remarks in idem, "A Review of a Review," *Public Interest*, Fall 1967, pp. 109–18.

behavior. The standard theory of the firm insists that whoever is in control of the firm must be motivated by a desire to maximize profits. How can we be sure that the division between ownership (the stockholders as represented by their managers) and the control (by the technostructure) will not produce a different set of goals for the corporation? The drive for personal gain—when properly restrained by Adam Smith's invisible hand—is a necessary assumption for the proposition that firms in the economy will operate efficiently. For it is this pressure to maximize profits that leads the entrepreneur to seek the most efficient mix of resources in producing his output. A demonstration that such incentives do not exert a strong influence would seriously undermine the conventional wisdom.

This, insists Galbraith, is precisely the problem which emerges with the technostructure operating the firm. They will be motivated to increase their own utility, whether or not their actions result in higher profits for the owners. Galbraith is hardly the first to present this case for the divorce of ownership and control in the modern corporation. Indeed, he quite pointedly cites a number of studies by scholars which reinforce the charge that large corporations today do not seek to maximize profits when setting their prices and outputs.[47]

If the profit motive is not the driving force behind the firm's behavior, then what is? Galbraith responds in two parts. First, he argues that the most plausible set of goals for an individual member of the technostructure will be identification with a successful organization. This being so, the second step is to construct a set of goals which the technostructure will see as creating a successful firm. Galbraith draws up the following goals, listed in descending order of importance:

1. The primary aim must be *survival*. To ensure this, the technostructure will act to maintain some minimum level of earnings. Such behavior will guarantee the position of the technostructure in the firm, and it will also reduce the possibility of outside interference.

2. Given some level of minimum earnings, the technostructure will act to *maximize the rate of growth of the corporation*. This is more than a matter of prestige. A major problem confronting the large firm is its dependence on capital to finance large investments necessary in modern markets. Ideally, this capital will be supplied by earnings retained in the firm. The higher the rate of growth, the less will be any need for outside interference. Here again, the technostructure is acutely aware of the threat from outside interference.

3. In the event that both of these goals are met, a set of subsidiary goals may then exert an influence on decisions. Technical vir-

---

[47] The most notable references cited include: Adolph Berle and Gardiner Means, *The Modern Corporation and Private Property* (New York: Macmillan Co., 1934); Robert A. Gordon, *Business Leadership in the Large Corporation* (Washington, D.C.: Brookings Institution, 1952); and Earl Cheit, *The Business Establishment* (New York: John Wiley, 1964).

tuosity is the most prominent of these; support of education is another.

And so we have Galbraith's view of the industrial system. Huge firms, run by a technostructure which is only marginally affected by the drive for profit maximization, dominate the markets for goods and services. It remains only to see how these firms will behave differently from those described in the traditional theory of Alfred Marshall and his followers.

Planning and the Revised Sequence of Pricing

The conventional wisdom argues that the firm's price and output are determined through a process of equilibrium dictated by market pressures. Generally, the situation would be such that the firm—however great its monopoly control over supply might be—must still accept the constraint imposed by the limited demand for its product(s). In other words, the firm faces a trade-off between higher revenues possible from higher prices and the downward influence on revenues from any decline in sales as a consequence of higher prices. Galbraith postulates a revision of that process. Rather than the *firm adjusting to the market demand*, he maintains that the *market will adjust to the supply of the firm*. The key to this lies in the size of the firm and its use of planning to implement the dependence effect.

The greatest threat to the stability of the firm is uncertainty. Thus, the technostructure will attempt to minimize risk. The greatest risk is from market uncertainty. With large capital investments at stake, it is imperative that unexpected shifts in prices be prevented or effectively hedged against. In short, the strategy of the technostructure will be that of *risk avoidance*. Galbraith is quite emphatic on this point.

> In specific terms this means that prices must, if possible, be under control; that decisive costs must also be under control or so managed that the adverse movements can be offset by the controlled prices; that the effort must be made to ensure that the consumer responds favorably to the product; that if the state is the customer, it will remain committed to the product or its development. . . . In other words, the firm is required . . . to control or seek to control the social environment in which it functions. . . . It must plan not only its own operations; it must also, to the extent possible, plan the behavior of people and the state as these affect it. This is not a matter of ambition but of necessity.[48]

The immediate problem is control of the consumer. The large corporation cannot be so docile as to take consumer tastes as given; it must act to create those wants which are necessary for the sale of its output. This is the logic of the dependence effect on a micro scale. In terms of E.H. Chamberlin's analysis, Galbraith is suggesting that the firm incurs

---

[48] Galbraith, *Economics and the Public Purpose*, pp. 39–40.

"selling costs." The firm is aided in this effort by two factors, both of which we have already encountered.

The first is the dependence effect itself. Within rather broad limits, the firm is able to take advantage of the increasing affluence of the modern economy.

> The further a man is removed from physical need the more open he is to persuasion—or management—as to what he buys. This is, perhaps, the most important consequence for the economics of increasing affluence.[49]

The firm employs modern technology—particularly the mass media— to shape its demand curve in accordance with its planned production.

There is a second, subtler effect which also assists the firm in its attempt to continually expand production. That is what Galbraith calls the *convenient social virtue*. As people become more affluent, a new problem will arise: they will seek either to avoid work altogether or, at the very least, to avoid those tasks which are undesirable. Either would have unfortunate consequences for the consumer-oriented industrial system. The convenient social virtue "ascribes merit to any pattern of behavior, however uncomfortable or unnatural for the individual involved."[50] How does this help firms increase consumption? By enforcing a social role for women which, in Galbraith's terms, reduces them to a class of "crypto-servants" whose principal role is

> . . . to select, transport, prepare, repair, maintain, clean, service, store, protect and otherwise perform the tasks that are associated with the consumption of goods in the modern economy. . . .
>
> In few other areas has the economic system been so successful in establishing values and molding resulting behavior. . . . It is women in their crypto-servant role of administrators who make an indefinitely increasing consumption possible. As matters now stand (and for so long as they so stand), it is their supreme contribution to the modern economy.[51]

Because of these factors, the firm is not bound by the constraint of the marketplace. The industrial system, through management of consumer demand to its own interests, operates under what Galbraith terms a "revised sequence" of pricing.

The management of consumer demand in the interests of producers is only the most obvious result of the changes which accompanied the rise of an industrial system. There are others. In its quest to reduce uncertainty, the technostructure finds itself involved in many areas of

---

[49] Galbraith, *The New Industrial State*, p. 210. Galbraith refers at this point to his previous work, particularly *The Affluent Society* and *American Capitalism: The Concept of Countervailing Power* (Boston: Houghton Mifflin, 1951), for a more detailed discussion. That he has not backed away from the argument in subsequent years is evidenced by his comment to Nicole Salinger that the large corporation "must extend planning to the consumer and ensure that the consumer will want what it has produced." See Galbraith and Salinger, p. 149.

[50] Galbraith, *Economics and the Public Purpose*, p. 30.

[51] Galbraith, *Economics and the Public Purpose*, pp. 33, 37.

economic policy. As an illustration of the manner in which the interests of the industrial system permeate the rest of the economy, we shall briefly touch on five such areas singled out by Galbraith himself.[52]

1. *The Control of Aggregate Demand*. The firm can control its own demand, but it cannot do so for the system as a whole. Yet economic stability is an "organic requirement" for the industrial system. Small fluctuations in aggregate demand could impose heavy losses by presenting the firm with unexpected shifts in market prices or the availability of capital. As a result, Galbraith argues, leaders of the industrial system came to embrace the tenets of Keynesian doctrine as being in their own interest. The widely acknowledged hostility of the business community toward deficit finance should not be misconstrued as a rejection of the need to maintain full employment through a planned fiscal policy. "Though devout free-enterprisers suppress the thought," argues Galbraith, "all modern industrial economies are extensively planned. They must be."[53] Of course, the economic policies must produce results. Businessmen's confidence in the efficacy of deficit finance as a tool of economic stabilization waned in the face of mounting inflationary pressures in the late 1960's and through the 1970's.

2. *Employment and Labor*. While labor clearly gains from the reduction of toil brought about by the efficiency of production, certain conflicts are likely to develop between labor and the industrial system. The technostructure will have a strong bias toward's replacing labor with capital. This is due to the greater certainty which the purchase of capital equipment affords. The firm has its own resources with which to plan investment; it has no such guarantee of available labor force in the factor market. Moreover, although it favors high levels of employment in the aggregate (to maintain demand for its products), a problem develops with regard to the demand for labor within the industrial system. Technology requires an ever-rising level of skills. The result is a decline in the importance of blue collar workers within the industrial system. There will be a large (and growing) pool of labor which is rejected by the system and will never be employed. These people are, in effect, shuttled off to the "other" part of the economy, typically experiencing lower rates of pay and longer hours of work. Here again the impact of the convenient social virtue works to the advantage of the industrial system. The stigma attached to being unemployed discourages outright idleness; yet the virtues of being self-employed (or, in the case of women, employed by the house-

---

[52] The points are drawn from *The New Industrial State*, Chapters 20–25. Discussion on most of these points can also be found in Galbraith's subsequent writings.

[53] Galbraith and Salinger, p. 7. Galbraith insists that most of the resistance to Keynesian policies of finance come from businessmen *outside* the industrial system. Aggregate economic stability is less of a requirement for these firms. If so, this is an ironic twist, for most economists would argue that small businesses are much less able to withstand the effect of a recession.

hold) are extolled, and consequently the need to expand industrial employment is eased.

3. *Unions and the Industrial System.* Producers are not the only powerful organizations which operate in the industrial system. Over the past half-century, labor unions have also managed to gain considerable economic power. What about the relations between unions and the large firms? Galbraith concedes that no clear pattern can be predicted. He points out that, contrary to the usual notion of management-labor conflict of interests, the technostructure is not inimically opposed to unions. Unions serve to regulate the supply of labor, thereby reducing the uncertainty of supply in the labor market. Large, industry-wide unions ensure a uniform pricing of labor throughout the industry. Nor are wage demands necessarily a threat to the firm's position. So long as the firm is able to generate some improvement in productivity through technological change, the revised sequence of pricing will enable the firm to grant regular wage increases. In fact, Galbraith is rather skeptical about the advantages of increasing the influence of workers on management. Questioned about European proposals to put workers on the board of directors of companies, he replied,

> It's called codetermination, and I'm not wildly enthusiastic about it. . . . I've always believed more is to be gained from direct trade union bargaining—a rather traditional American view.[54]

4. *Education and the Industrial System.* The demands for increasing skills to cope with changing technology means that the industrial system strongly supports education. Thus, the rise of industry coincides with the emergence of a new and powerful group in society: "the educational and scientific estate." As the importance of technology and science in production increases, the power of this group grows commensurately. For the technostructure depends on this group to provide the skilled manpower required by the industrial system. Historically, the intellectuals have remained aloof and often rather hostile to the aims of industry. But, with the decline in the acquisitive monetary goals of the technostructure, much of the friction between these two groups vanishes. Education finds a powerful ally in the industrial system. And, notwithstanding an occasional reservation over the goals of the industrial system, the educational and scientific estate acts to reinforce the aims of the technostructure. In economics, this is particularly true. The conventional wisdom, as Galbraith has lamented all these years, has consistently supported the policies of stabilization and a "mixed economy," which have proven to conducive to the health of the industrial system.

---

[54] Galbraith and Salinger, p. 59. Galbraith himself has subscribed to this view for many years. One of his earliest works, *American Capitalism,* stressed the benefits of having labor unions and large firms balance each others' economic power in the marketplace.

5. *Technology, National Security, and the Industrial System.* The dominance of technological pressures in the large firm generates a significant demand for investment in basic research. Continued expansion of technological progress depends on a steady flow of new ideas. But investment in this area is far too risky for the firm—even a very large firm—to support alone. The government must fill the void. And it does. A substantial share of basic research both in private industry and in the educational system is supported by government funds. Unfortunately, a major impetus for this funding stems from the Cold War. With its steady demand for newer and more sophisticated weapons, the arms race provides an ideal rationale for developing new technology in the name of national security. Such projects are seldom questioned. Galbraith stops short of arguing that the industrial system inherently supports war; rather, he suggests, the reliance on defense expenditures to finance technological research arose as a matter of convenience, not design. Any program which provides funds for basic research, such as NASA's space projects, would serve equally well. But such projects, though they seem plentiful to one who stops to review our national needs, have not been forthcoming. We depend on the Cold War to generate our high-powered technology.

Galbraith objects not so much to the fact that government sponsors defense research as to the method by which it is done. "I have always thought," he has said, "that there was a powerful case for nationalizing our big weapons firms. They get their business from the government, operate on and with capital extensively provided by the government. Only their profits are in the private sector."[55]

Galbraith has cleverly tied the diverse interests of various groups to those of the industrial system. Labor is rewarded for its cooperation by reaping the gains of rising productivity. The educational and scientific estate is content to reinforce the aims of a system in which its role is becoming increasingly important. Even those who do not benefit from the system tolerate it, thanks to the power of belief. The conventional wisdom provides an intellectual defense of the system, and the convenient social virtues condemn those who argue against the established way of doing things.

Inflation and the Industrial System

As has been noted in the chapters on Samuelson and Lerner, control of inflation through conventional monetary-fiscal policy tools may involve an expensive trade-off between inflation and unemployment. The menu offered by the Phillips Curve is the best that we can achieve short of changing the structural relationships in the market. Throughout the 1960's, this unpalatable choice made economists uncomfortable; by the mid-1970's, their inability to offer a better solution to the problems of

---

[55] Galbraith and Salinger, p. 63.

inflation and unemployment had become something of a professional embarrassment.

Galbraith watched this embarrassment with at least a touch of amusement. In 1977, he explained to Nicole Salinger:

> With fiscal policy or monetary policy or both we curb inflation by creating a recession and unemployment. And . . . it takes a good deal of unemployment to prevent inflation. Whoever arranged matters in this way is open to criticism.[56]

Galbraith does not pretend that the problem of inflation is a simple one; nor does he suggest that there is a single, simple remedy. As to the causes, he argues that there are a number of forces which create

> . . . a persistent and continuing pressure on markets. So one has the combination in the modern economy of a cost push driving up prices, and the demand pull growing out of both public and private demands that are pushing up prices.[57]

While he concedes there are many causes of inflation, Galbraith rather clearly identifies as a major villian the industrial system, with its planning and revised sequence of pricing. "Inflation," he notes, "is a process which reflects, in part, the power of the firm." Moreover, he argues, the technostructure of the industrial system can "live in reasonable comfort with both inflation and the orthodox efforts to control it that presumed the continued preeminence of the market."[58] Galbraith is particularly critical of the use of monetary policy to fight inflation, since "the effect of this restraint will always be highly unequal."[59] While the small firm which depends on the capital market are greatly affected by tight money, large corporations, with their access to internal funds, feel very little effect. Fiscal policy also has very unequal effects; it is the expenditure programs favoring the poor which are the first victims of the drive to cut back government as a cure for inflation.

Galbraith does not deny the necessity of keeping government spending within limits, and he certainly does not favor a monetary policy which unnecessarily fans the flames of inflation. However, he sees little reason to rely on either of these alternatives as the main weapon. As he told a group of congressmen in 1979,

> I have long felt, and it is . . . one of the . . . most badly kept secrets of my economic agitation, that in a modern society there is no alternative to firm, forthright, mandatory controls on those instruments of direct power, the large corporations, and the companion capacity of trade unions that are dealing with them, wage and price controls.[60]

---

[56] Galbraith and Salinger, p. 97.

[57] John Kenneth Galbraith, "Testimony" in U.S., Congress, House, Subcommittee of the Committee on Government Operations, 96th Cong., 1st sess., 3–18 May 1979, p. 555.

[58] Galbraith, *The New Industrial State*, p. 191.

[59] Galbraith and Salinger, p. 85. Galbraith's views on inflation are scattered over a wide area, but the message is invariably the same. His most systematic treatment of the problem as it relates to the industrial system can be found in *Economics and the Public Purpose*, particularly Chapters 18–20. We have also drawn heavily from his testimony before congressional committees.

[60] Galbraith, "Testimony" in U.S., Congress, Subcommittee on Government Operations, p. 555.

Orthodox economists—even those of very liberal persuasion—tend to shrink from such drastic measures as wage-and-price controls because of the disruption they cause in the marketplace. But in the Galbraithian analysis, no such reservations are needed. "One should never be under the impression," Galbraith insists, "that wage-and-price controls are interfering with free markets. One is interfering with prices that are already fixed by corporate power. . . ."[61] Nor is Galbraith impressed with the arguments that wage-price controls are unworkable. To begin with, he notes that

> Any logical system of direct controls would be confined to those prices and incomes where there is substantial power—it is only needed where restraint, operating through the market, does not serve, which is to say where corporate, union and other organized power is great.[62]

If the wages and prices of these powerful economic groups can be controlled, the marketplace will effectively deal with the millions of other producers. Placing wage-and-price controls on these firms, Galbraith insists, is quite feasible today. Here he draws upon his experience as the deputy director of the Office of Price Administration during World War II. Contrary to popular belief, he insists, "to control the prices of the economy, 1,000 or 2,000 large corporations, the 200 or 300 major trade union contracts, is not administratively a difficult task."[63] Galbraith is particularly annoyed by the suggestion that past history of price controls shows that they are unsuccessful.

> We have all been subject to some extraordinary brainwashing on this past history, and the American people will remember the history much more accurately than a University of Chicago professor. . . .[64]

In fact, Galbraith insists, controls on the industrial system would almost certainly be both easier to administer and more equitable than the widely suggested plan of "indexing" wages and prices to the rate of inflation. "I have never been very happy about indexing," he told Nicole Salinger.

> It involves some technical problems. Also some inequities . . . I would make economists earn their living—produce proper remedies and not evade the problems.[65]

Galbraith has a further objective in advocating controls on wages and prices: reducing the gross inequality of income present in our system. What he ultimately seeks is "a new social contract, what in France has

---

[61] Galbraith, "Testimony" in U.S., Congress, Subcommittee on Government Operations, p. 555.

[62] Galbraith, "Testimony" in U.S., Congress, Subcommittee on Antitrust, Consumers and Employ-ment, p. 35. Galbraith submitted a paper on inflation to the subcommittee which outlined in considerable detail both his objections to the policy then (1978) being pursued by the Carter administration, and also outlined his own proposals.

[63] Galbraith, "Testimony" in U.S., Congress, Subcommittee on Government Operations, p. 559.

[64] Galbraith, "Testimony" in U.S., Congress, Subcommittee on Government Operations, p. 559.

[65] Galbraith and Salinger, p. 104.

been called a new moral contract, incomes policy, wage and price policy, controls." Galbraith calls it a Comprehensive Incomes and Prices Policy—a CIPP.[66] This CIPP involves a combination of controls, taxes, and government spending aimed at reducing the effects of inequality of wealth and economic power. It is, of course, a far more comprehensive set of controls than he advocates simply to stem inflation. In effect, what Galbraith proposes in his CIPP is that the current system of planning within the industrial system—which is guided by the private interests of the large firms—be replaced with comprehensive *social* planning guided by broader goals of the society.[67] Why are these extensive controls necessary? Because, in Galbraith's view, the gross inequality in income and power represents a fundamental problem in our society. The failure of the conventional wisdom to deal with the relations of power is one of its gravest shortcomings.

The State and the Industrial System

This brings us to the role of the state. The need for the state to become intimately involved with the operation of the industrial system is obvious enough from the analysis presented above. Not surprisingly, Galbraith sees control of the state falling into the hands of those groups which will support the industrial system.

And so we have the *industrial state*. It is dominated by the interests and goals of the powerful firms comprising the industrial system. Other groups, despite their potential power, allowed this sector to gradually replace the social objectives of society with those of the technostructure and the industrial system. Therein lies the threat to our society in the mind of Galbraith. For these goals are essentially *economic* objectives: increasing levels of production, income, and employment. Such goals are not, Galbraith points out, "the best proponents of the public, aesthetic, and intellectual priorities on which the quality and safety of life increasingly depend."[68] What will result is a rather pronounced bias against expenditures on important social investment. An imbalance will develop between public needs and those of the industrial system. This is a familiar argument to the reader of this book. Alvin Hansen reached much the same conclusion reasoning from the Keynesian and Chamberlinian economic models. Paul Samuelson approached the same problem through his discussion of public goods and the theory of public expenditures—and found that the public sector was likely to be too small.

---

[66] Galbraith and Salinger, p. 109. Chapter 8 of this book represents a very complete statement of Galbraith's views on the subject of income inequality.

[67] It is not clear to what extent Galbraith would expand his CIPP into the "market sector" outside of the industrial system. As we noted above, he defends his more modest proposals for wage-price controls on the grounds of simplicity as well as equity. The CIPP appears to be several orders of magnitude more complex; a point which Galbraith concedes, although he does not elaborate on the subject.

[68] Galbraith, *The New Industrial State*, p. 384.

But Galbraith arrived at this conclusion from a very different direction than the other two. He chose to attack the basic premises upon which economic theory was constructed. Moreover, his broader view of the problem allowed him to push on to the issue of social imbalance with a more general exposition than either Hansen or Samuelson. In Galbraith's system, there is no choice between public or private goods, since the state is essentially an arm of the industrial system itself. So long as the values and beliefs of consumers (and voters) remain unchanged, the system will fail to meet the needs of society. That is why, to Galbraith, the "emancipation of belief" is the essential first step to introducing meaningful economic change into the system.

Galbraith identifies four "specific instruments" which perpetuate the conventional wisdom and reinforce the convenient social virtue, and which must be nullified if we are to accomplish this emancipation of ideas.[69]

1. The conventional wisdom in economics must be redirected towards a better understanding of the industrial system. At the moment, says Galbraith, "it is designed, however innocently, to keep the individual from seeing how he is governed, to accommodate his views in the planning system."[70]

2. The educational system, which presently tends to serve the ends of the industrial system, must "see that education is not social conditioning. This means the elimination of all distinction between useful and unuseful fields of learning, all suggestion that there is an economic standard of social achievement."[71]

3. Something must be done to counter the present reaction to overt persuasion. "The emancipation of belief," Galbraith notes, "requires presumption against all persuasion by the planning system."[72]

4. The "manufacture of public policy" must be curtailed. Crucial to this is the breaking up of what Galbraith characterizes as the "symbiotic" relationship of the industrial system and the government, which includes the legislatures, the executive, and (most important of all) the bureaucracy. "It is important to recognize," Galbraith urges, "that as authority on public policy serves the planning system, so also does authority on public morality."[73]

The emphasis on "belief" as a cornerstone of his economic analysis is a feature of the Galbraithian system which breaks sharply with the neoclassical approach to economics. Where most economists have assiduously avoided mention (much less analysis) of people's beliefs, Galbraith has placed them at the center of his explanation of how our

[69] The organization of this section is taken from the discussion in Galbraith, *Economics and the Public Purpose*, pp. 227–29. The points raised are, of course, also discussed elsewhere in Galbraith's writings.

[70] Galbraith, *Economics and the Public Purpose*, p. 227.

[71] Galbraith, *Economics and the Public Purpose*, p. 227.

[72] Galbraith, *Economics and the Public Purpose*, p. 227.

[73] Galbraith, *Economics and the Public Purpose*, p. 228.

modern economic system works. Far from accepting the institutional arrangements as given, he insists on a revision of our system which will allow us to deal with the problems of an affluent society. In pursuing his inquiry, he openly states his position: it is time that we reassess our values to recognize that "what counts is not the quantity of our goods but the quality of life."[74]

The Affluent Industrial State v. The Conventional Wisdom

John Kenneth Galbraith is unquestionably one of the most literate of the present generation of economists. No other leading member of the profession can claim to be a fellow—in literature—of the National Institute of Arts and Letters. His work has drawn a large audience on its literary merit alone. However, popularity with the reading public is not always associated with popularity among one's academic peers.

We have alluded in several places to the parallels between Galbraith and Thorstein Veblen. Veblen's attacks on the neoclassical system failed to have any appreciable impact when they appeared. Most economists agreed with Frank Knight, who insisted that Veblen's observations were simply not relevant to the structure of economic theory. And the theory remained unshaken. There are economists—particularly those who trace their intellectual heritage back to Frank Knight—who level the same charge against Galbraith. But if there are similarities, there are also differences in the two careers. Veblen wrote in a period when the progressive movement had yet to make any appreciable headway against the orthodoxy of nineteenth-century liberalism and laissez-faire economics. His was a voice in the wilderness. That can hardly be said of Galbraith. Writing in a period when people both inside and outside the academic establishment are questioning the existing ortho-doxy, Galbraith has certainly not been ignored by economists. As early as 1968, he commented that

> I've never been disposed to sacrifice truth to modesty. I think that there are certain ideas from my own books that slightly modify the way people think about economic life.[75]

The fact remains, however, that much of Galbraith's work has not been well received by a substantial number of academic economists. His sneering attitude towards the conventional wisdom has contributed a degree of irritation in the cries of his critics, but the vigor with which his work has been criticized involves more than professional jealousy. Galbraith has, according to his critics, glossed over the difficult points in his analysis in order to reach sweeping conclusions which cannot stand up under close scrutiny. Without presenting a detailed critique of the Galbraithian system, we shall look at some of the more frequently lodged complaints made by the critics.

---

[74] Galbraith, *The New Industrial State*, p. 80.
[75] *Playboy*, p. 78.

Of all the areas of economics that he has criticized, it is Galbraith's analysis of what he terms the industrial system which has drawn the most detailed response.[76]

Economists readily concede the presence of large firms. Less obvious is the extent to which there exists some "system" of 1,000 or 2,000 firms, with General Motors as a stereotype. In his most recent writing and testimony, Galbraith has argued that the largest 2,000 firms, which account for half the total output in our society, represent a workable definition of the "industrial system." Within this system, he argues, the market has very little effect. Critics object that his definition of the system is far too encompassing and that markets exert an important influence on even the largest firms of the system. Even in markets which are characterized by only a few firms (what the conventional wisdom calls *oligopoly*), rival firms are able to exert strong market pressures on their competitors. The Galbraithian analysis is, to most economists, incomplete. It fails to take account of the interaction between firms in determining a *general equilibrium* in the economy as a whole. What of the interdependence between oligopolistic firms, which was so prominent in the monopolistic models of E.H. Chamberlin? Nowhere does Galbraith really come to grips with such interdependence. "The truly giant corporations," he insists, "are independent republics of their own management."[77] Galbraithian oligopolists apparently act on the assumption that they can safely ignore any reactions by other firms to their plans. Such a situation seems to most economists rather rare—much too rare to include the largest 2,000 firms as examples.

Critics single out two respects in which Galbraith fails to take account of the larger market pressures in his treatment of the individual firm. First is the firm's ability to shape demand to suit its particular marketing needs. Notwithstanding the marvels of modern marketing techniques, Galbraith's assertion that the firm can shape consumer demand to its own purposes seems to be stretching a point. Even if one were willing to concede that the dependence effect is a useful description of consumption behavior in the aggregate, it is still not necessarily true that the demand for products of a single firm can be expanded indefinitely in response to the powers of persuasion. In making this point, early critics noted the spectacular failure of the Ford Motor Company to sell its new car, the Edsel, in the late 1950's. More

---

[76] Both Galbraith and his critics have been busily writing for a quarter of a century now. Each time one of Galbraith's major works appeared, so did a spate of critical (and a few favorable) reviews. For the reader interested in concise summaries of the objections lodged by adherents of the conventional wisdom, we recommend two reviews, which appeared shortly after publication of *The New Industrial State*: Robert Solow, "Son of Affluence," *Public Interest*, Fall 1967, pp. 100–08; and Scott Gordon, "The Close of the Galbraithian System," *The Journal of Political Economy* 77, pt. 1 (July-August 1969): 635–44. Galbraith chose to reply to each of these reviews. See John Kenneth Galbraith, "Review of a Review," *Public Interest*, Fall 1967, pp. 109–18; also idem, "Reply," *Journal of Political Economy* 77 (July-August 1969). The tone of these exchanges between Galbraith and his critics reveals the schism between Galbraith's views on the subject and those of orthodox economists.

[77] Galbraith and Salinger, p. 57.

recently, one might ask why the Lockheed Corporation or the Chrysler Corporation were unable to sell their products.[78] Much more evidence needs to be presented before we can conclude that the firm's control over demand is sufficiently great that it can evade market uncertainties altogether.[79] As one critic (Scott Gordon) put it, Galbraith's analysis fails to perceive the distinction between planning in a market-oriented firm and planning in a nonmarket situation. Planning under conditions of market constraint does not remove those constraints.

The second respect in which Galbraith fails to consider a more general market setting is his analysis of the allocation of capital in the industrial system. Galbraith insists that the firm can ignore the capital market because it generates sufficient internal funds for its planned investment needs. But life is seldom that simple. Galbraith himself is fond of ridiculing the inaccuracy of economic projections. What if the internal flow of savings is insufficient for all contingencies? Will the firm always eschew borrowing in the market? Or suppose there are ample funds for the planned projects? Does the firm accumulate liquid balances regardless of the rate offered in the money market? Surely a point is reached where the firm will enter the capital market as either a borrower or lender, and even the best of planners cannot be certain when this will occur. Like other "independent republics," industrial firms will become aware of the limitations imposed by the cost of money in the capital markets, and they will be forced to make plans for their capital needs with this in mind.

Proponents of the conventional wisdom have centered their objections on the inadequacies of the Galbraithian analysis of the industrial system. They reject both his theory of a "dependence effect" and his notion of a "revised sequence of pricing." In neither case, they claim, does Galbraith's analysis add insight to the problem. Those critics who feel that Galbraith's analysis of the industrial system is seriously flawed are then rather skeptical of the further ramifications of the Galbraithian analysis. They concede Galbraith's point about the threat of economic power (just as they concede that there are large firms in the economy). However, they do not accept his analysis of the state as a tool of the industrial system.

There is one group which is quite willing to accept Galbraith's contention that the state is captured in the grip of the industrial system: the Marxist or "radical" political economists. Galbraith is, however, reluctant to accept their support. Marx, he insists, is as obsolete as Marshall.

---

[78] Galbraith cleverly anticipated the example of the Edsel by pointing it out as the exception that proved the rule. We comment on his reaction to some of the more recent corporate difficulties below.

[79] In fact, as Roland McKean has pointed out to us, if the firm can completely control demand for its existing products, why undertake the risk of a new product (like the Edsel) at all? Galbraith's analysis of the technostructure suggests that they would hardly be eager to undertake the costs and risks associated with the introduction of new product lines. Yet, as we observe in the United States, the industrial system is very busy doing precisely that.

His ideas are, of course, as indelibly a part of our life and times as those of Adam Smith. . . . But the development of the capitalist firm . . . has not been as Marx foresaw. It has taken power from the capitalist and given it to its own bureaucracy, to what I have called the technostructure. Partly in consequence, there has been much less sharp confrontation with the workers than Marx thought would occur.[80]

Galbraith: Reformer or Revolutionary?

For the most part, Galbraith dismisses his critics' objections as being beside the point. Nevertheless, he did articulate the details of his system more fully in *Economics and the Public Purpose*, partly in response to complaints that his earlier books had failed to spell out the details of his economic model. And in recent years he seems inclined to give market influences more weight than he did in his early writings. Though he still insists that the operation of the industrial system dominates the economy, Galbraith readily concedes that "there is no reason to believe that the small-scale sector of the economy will disappear."[81] Indeed, Galbraith identifies a number of activities in the market sector of the economy which are expanding: agriculture; service enterprises; and "design, music and other artistic enterprises." Galbraith agrees with his critics that, in this sector of the economy, market forces work quite well in allocating resources.

Even in the industrial system, Galbraith seems willing to concede that market pressures have an effect. In 1971, he was one of many economists who opposed any financial aid to the troubled Lockheed Corporation. He opposed it for several reasons, one of which is particularly intriguing.

> I would hold to the general theory that if a firm gets into financial difficulty, goes through receivership, one of the great benefits is from changing the management, and that the penalty that a bad management faces is that with receivership it will get thrown out.[82]

Invoking such dire threats of financial failure as a corrective measure sounds more like Milton Friedman than John Kenneth Galbraith. Notwithstanding the role of planning in the industrial system, the bottom line remains financial solvency. And that, as officials at Penn Central, Lockheed, Chrysler, and other corporate giants know all to well, ultimately rests on the behavior of market forces.

"Personal bias makes me a reformer rather than a revolutionary," Galbraith claimed in 1978.[83] Perhaps so. Nonetheless, when *The Affluent Society* appeared in 1958, it presented ideas which constituted

---

[80] Galbraith and Salinger, p. 22.

[81] Galbraith, "Testimony" in U.S. Congress, Subcommittee on Antitrust, Consumers and Employment, p. 32.

[82] John Kenneth Galbraith, "Testimony" U.S., Congress, Senate, Committee on Banking, Housing, and Urban Affairs, 92nd Cong., 1st sess., pt. 2, 7–9 June 1971, p. 863.

[83] Galbraith and Salinger, p. 20.

a very radical departure from the conventional wisdom—radical enough that some viewed them as revolutionary. But times change. Ten years later, when he published *The New Industrial State*, he was regarded as a liberal but hardly a radical economist. By the end of the 1970's, Galbraith had himself become part of the conventional wisdom he so often ridiculed.

It was the conventional wisdom, more than Galbraith, which had changed. The issues which he raised—problems of consumer manipulation, corporate power, economic stability—emerged as the issues of the 1960's and 1970's. Whether they agreed with Galbraith's analysis, economists were forced to acknowledge that the issues he raised were pertinent. And throughout the 1960's and 1970's, the conventional wisdom was under attack from both those who were more conservative than Galbraith and those who were far more radical. Rather to his surprise, Galbraith found his ideas to be "middle of the road" in the heated debates of radicals and the proponents of the post-Keynesian synthesis.

Galbraith succeeded in maintaining his own course through these debates. In 1958, before it was fashionable to do so, he had insisted that the problem of allocation was no longer the central issue in our economic system because "one of the marks of an affluent society is the opportunity for the existence of a considerable margin for error on such matters."[84] The important issues are the *normative implications* of the economic processes in our society. In the conclusion of *The Affluent Society*, Galbraith stated rather clearly the agenda he proposed for his subsequent work.

> To have failed to have solved the problem of producing goods would
> have been to continue man in his oldest and most grievous misfor-
> tune. But to fail to see that we have solved it and to fail to proceed
> thence to the next task, would be fully as tragic.[85]

That task, in Galbraith's eyes, includes the development of a more complete understanding of industrial society. His response to his critics has tended to take the form of shaking his head and lamenting the fact that they continue to cling to an approach to economics which is geared to the last quarter of the nineteenth century. It is not so much that he feels they are wrong; he considers their criticisms irrelevant.

What continues to separate Galbraith from his critics is not only the alleged reluctance of economists to confront issues; the problem is, as Robert Solow pointed out in his review of *The New Industrial State*, that economists are determined "little thinkers," whereas Galbraith is a determined "big thinker."[86] A biographer of Galbraith makes the same

---

[84] Galbraith, *The Affluent Society*, p. 321.

[85] Galbraith, *The Affluent Society*, p. 356.

[86] Solow, p. 100. Solow illustrated his point with an analogy to the household where the wife makes the unimportant decisions, such as what job they should take, where they should live, how to bring up the children, while the husband makes the important decisions on what to do about the Middle East, the United States policy on China, and the like.

point when he comments that he "agrees with Galbraith about every-thing in general and nothing in particular."[87]

Undaunted by his detractors, Galbraith continues on in his role as all-purpose critic. Even if his writings are viewed by subsequent schol-ars of the intellectual debates of our time as mere curiosities, he can rest assured that he has caused at least some discomfort among the self-satisfied, the self-righteous, and the rich. "Nothing gives me more pleasure than to look over something I've written and say, 'I don't think David Rockefeller will like that,' " Galbraith once said. "Sadness comes only when I realize that David probably won't bother to read it."[88]

Galbraith has only one other regret: having lived through the excite-ment of seeing the new economics emerge triumphant in the Keyne-sian revolution, he is no longer young enough to be fully involved in the changes that lie ahead. His thoughts on those changes reveal the vision, the energy, and the character of John Kenneth Galbraith, economist, reformer, and social critic.

> The design of a system that reconciles the various claimants on income and devises a workable—and equitable—alternative to the market will be greatly exciting. The battles will be wonderful, the distress of the comfortable extreme. It will be good for political economists; even those who are most contented with their compu-ters, their models of competitive market behavior and their loving wives may be stirred to thought.[89]

---

[87]   Sharpe, p. xii.

[88]   Galbraith and Salinger, p. 24.

[89]   Galbraith and Salinger, p. 153–54.

Part Four

THE NEW
NEOCLASSICISM

Chapter 12

FRANK H. KNIGHT

PHILOSOPHER OF
THE COUNTERREVOLUTION
IN ECONOMICS

> So far as I can make out, I believe in only one thing: liberty. But I
> do not believe in even liberty enough to want to force it upon
> anyone. That is, I am nothing of the reformer, however much I
> may rant against this or that curse or malaise. In the ranting there
> is usually far more delight than indignation.
>
> *H. L. Mencken*

In 1924, four years after A. C. Pigou fired his lethal salvo at the policy
prescriptions of neoclassicism, an economist at the University of Iowa
published a rather technical paper in the prestigious *Quarterly Journal
of Economics*. The author, Frank Hyneman Knight, already had some
slight reputation in economics. Eight years earlier he had submitted a
dissertation to the faculty of Cornell University, which was accorded a
second prize in a competition sponsored by Hart, Schaffner and Marx.[1]
The dissertation was published under the title of *Risk, Uncertainty and
Profit*.[2] It won for its young author a considerable amount of fame as a
skillful analyst of one of the more difficult, unsettled questions in
economic theory, namely, the nature and determination of profits in
the competitive economy. In his 1924 article, Knight believed he had
detected a major fallacy in the Pigovian argument for taxing increas-
ing-cost industries and subsidizing decreasing-cost industries.

---

[1] The name of the winner of the first prize in this contest seems to have been lost in the mists of
antiquity.

[2] Frank H. Knight, *Risk, Uncertainty and Profit* (New York: Hart, Schaffner and Marx, 1921).

Pigou on Market Failure

The reader will recall that Pigou had contended that the laissez-faire market mechanism necessarily failed to achieve efficient resource allocation. One example was that of road congestion, and it will be instructive to review his reasoning at this point.

Pigou attempted to demonstrate that profit-maximizing entrepreneurs will invest excessively in industries of increasing cost and underinvest in industries of constant or decreasing cost. His concrete example was that of two roads connecting two cities. The first road is wide enough to easily accommodate all the traffic that cares to use it, but is badly surfaced and graded (the decreasing cost industry). The second highway is well graded and superior in every way except that it is quite narrow and limited in capacity (the increasing cost industry). Pigou demonstrated that if operators of road vehicles were free to choose either of the two routes, they would tend to distribute themselves in such a way that the average cost of transportation would be the same for each unit of traffic on both roads. But, as we know, it is the equating of marginal costs that guarantees efficiency.

As more vehicles use the better but narrower road, traffic congestion would develop to the point where it would become equally advantageous or profitable to use the poorly graded but wider route. But in equilibrium, where marginal private costs are equal, there are too many vehicles on the well-surfaced road and too few on the wider road. The reason for this surprising result lies in the Pigovian distinction between private costs and social costs. Each individual road user would select the highway that is *privately* most beneficial to him, but would have no reason to calculate the costs of the congestion he imposes on others using the same routes. The congestion resulting from the addition of any particular vehicle to the traffic on the good road would affect in the same way the cost of all the vehicles using that road. Thus, the addition to total costs from adding one more automobile to the narrow road (the marginal social cost) is necessarily greater than the additional cost borne by that car alone (the marginal private cost). The latter cost would be the *average* cost of all vehicles using the road up to that point. But the true marginal cost for all vehicles as a result of adding the additional vehicle would be higher than the average cost for all vehicles. In equilibrium, the average costs on the two roads would be equal, but it is clear that the marginal costs would differ. For if we could transfer a vehicle to the broad road, after this equilibrium is reached, the decrease in costs to those units remaining on the good road would be a pure gain to *all* traffic. The traffic that had been rerouted would incur no loss since the marginal private costs on both roads are the same in equilibrium. Any individual unit of traffic has an incentive to use the narrow road, as long as there is a difference in costs to him of using the two roads; but because of the externality of congestion, the advantage is reduced to zero for all the vehicles together. So Pigou was able to conclude that individual freedom results in misallocation of resources between increasing and decreasing cost industries.

Table 12.1
Cost Schedules for Alternative Units of Traffic

Vehicles	Total (Private) Cost I	Marginal (Private) Cost II	Total (Social) Cost III	Marginal (Social) Cost IV	Average (Social) Cost V
1	5	5	5	5	5
2	15	10	20	15	10
3	35	20	60	40	20
4	75	40	160	100	40
5	175	100	500	340	100

Some simple numbers will help enlighten us at this point. The figures in Table 12.1 show the various cost schedules for alternative units of traffic on the narrow road.

The marginal private cost to the first vehicle using the narrow road is $5, to the second $10, to the third $20, to the fourth $40, and so on. The rapidly increasing cost is due, of course, to the increased congestion. Vehicles will enter the flow of traffic on this road up to the point where the marginal private cost on the narrow road is exactly equal to the marginal private cost of using the bad road. But the crucial point to note is that the individual, in making this private adjustment, does not calculate the costs he imposes on all other vehicles using the road. These costs can be seen in a glance at columns III and IV. In column III, we have calculated the *total* social costs of using the good road. It is computed by multiplying the number of vehicles on the road by the marginal private cost of each vehicle. Column IV shows the marginal social cost, which is simply the addition to total social cost of adding another vehicle to the road. Note that this cost is greater than the marginal private cost at some point. (In our example, that point is reached after more than one vehicle enters the traffic flow.) But this column reflects the true marginal costs when all costs, including that caused by the traffic congestion, are taken into account. It is important to note, further, that the average social cost (column V) is the total social cost divided by the number of units of traffic. This is precisely equal to the marginal private cost for each vehicle. Thus, the individual who is free to choose, in equating his marginal private cost on the good road with that on the bad road to reach equilibrium, is actually equating the *average* social costs with each other. The marginal social costs are above the average, as we can see when we compare columns IV and V. But efficient allocation requires, as we have noted before, that marginal costs be equated. Hence, an inefficient allocation of resources occurs under a laissez-faire scheme of production.

From this subtle reasoning, Pigou contended that government interference is justified. The proper prescription, of course, as with most of Pigou's welfare-increasing recommendations, was to levy a tax on each vehicle using the narrow road. The owner of the vehicle would now take this tax into his calculations when trying to determine which route was most advantageous to him. The flow of traffic would then be reduced to the point where the marginal cost on the narrow road, taking all social costs into account, would be equal to the marginal cost on the broad road. The tax would simply be the difference between the average cost and marginal cost of an additional unit of traffic on the well-surfaced road. Since the total amount of tax proceeds is precisely equal to the total costs of congestion, no individual vehicle would incur higher costs than if no tax had been imposed. Hence, welfare is increased by the tax policy.

Knight's Response to Pigou

Knight's devastating critique of this Pigovian argument caused Pigou to drop his road example from subsequent editions of his *Economics of Welfare*. But it is doubtful whether Pigou understood the full implications of Knight's argument. For encompassed in its relatively few pages is an approach to economic problems that ran counter to the antineoclassical trend of economic thought. Those who accepted Knight's message and followed through on his reasoning became counterrevolutionaries who were to form a major part of a school of thought that, for descriptive convenience, we call the "new neoclassicism."

For Knight's article, in effect, rehabilitated the neoclassical view that under competitive conditions, efficient allocation of resources would prevail. The results that Pigou discovered were only valid if private property rights were not clearly established. This can be demonstrated if we assume private ownership of Pigou's good but narrow road. Assuming competitive conditions, so that the traffic could use the wide, unsurfaced road for free, how would the profit-maximizing entrepreneur set his toll for use of the narrow road? He could always charge a price which was precisely equal to the difference between the value to the vehicle owner of using the narrow road and the wide road. But this difference is exactly equal to the difference between the marginal cost and the average cost of an additional vehicle using the good road.[3] This, in effect, means that private owners of the road would be induced to charge a toll which would be exactly equal to the ideal tax that Pigou recommended. So traffic will flow to the superior road, up to the point where the marginal cost to the vehicle (which now includes the vehicles' toll) is equal to the marginal cost to him of using the alternative road. At that point, the vehicle owner would be indifferent in choosing between the two roads. In Knight's words, "The toll or rent will be so

---

[3]   The reader familiar with the history of economic thought will perhaps have noted that Knight is applying Ricardo's differential rent theory to the problem of optimal pricing in the case of two roads of differing productivity. The analogy between Ricardo's land of differing fertility and Pigou's roads of differing productivity should be evident. The difference between the value of the product on the good road and the bad road is Ricardo's definition of "rent."

adjusted that *added* product of the last truck which uses the narrow road is just equal to what it could produce on the broad road. No truck will pay a higher charge, and it is not in the interest of the owner of the road to accept a lower fee. And this adjustment is exactly that which maximizes the total product of both roads."[4] The full implications of this technicality in economic theory are far-reaching. The market failure which Pigou and his disciples thought they had demonstrated was precisely the opposite of market failure. It was the failure of government to establish property rights in scarce resources that caused the congestion. To Knight, the market order is efficient if property rights are clearly identified. One of the basic functions of government—the identification of property rights—has not been carried out. After all, the establishment and enforcement of property rights had always been accepted as a function of government by both classical and neoclassical economists. Now Knight showed that a failure of government to carry out its clearly delegated function had misled Pigou and other economists to call for government intervention into the economy.

The keen insight revealed by Knight in this article was to form the basis for much research into the study of property rights and externality problems at the hands of his disciples. In particular, the labors of Armen A. Alchian, James M. Buchanan, and Ronald Coase were to be an intensive tilling of the ground broken by Knight in this pioneering essay.[5]

The Philosophy of Skepticism

That Frank Knight should have paved the way for the counterrevolution of the new neoclassicism is perhaps not surprising. Born in McLean County, Illinois, in 1885, and brought up in the religious orthodoxy of prairie evangelism, he studied at Milligan College in Tennessee and the University of Tennessee. Eventually he moved to Cornell and studied economics under Allyn Young, the same man who so influenced E. H. Chamberlin. But in every sense Knight was a product of the Midwest, and in the words of one of his students, "it is difficult to imagine that he could have emerged from the more sophisticated culture of the eastern seaboard."[6] After receiving his Ph.D. in 1916, he taught at the University of Chicago from 1917 to 1919, then

---

[4] Frank H. Knight, "Some Fallacies in the Interpretation of Social Cost," *Quarterly Journal of Economics* 38 (May 1924): 582–606. Reprinted in Frank H. Knight, *The Ethics of Competition and Other Essays* (New York: Harper and Row, 1935), pp. 221–22.

[5] Armen A. Alchian, "Pricing and Society," Occasional Paper, no. 17 (London: Institute of Economic Affairs, 1967); James M. Buchanan, "Congestion on the Common: A Case for Government Intervention," *Il Politico* 33, no. 4 (1968): 776–86; Ronald Coase, "The Problem of Social Cost," *The Journal of Law and Economics,* October 1960, pp. 1–44. Reprinted in Breit and Hochman, *Readings in Microeconomics* (New York: Holt, Rinehart and Winston, 1968), pp. 423–56.

[6] James M. Buchanan, "Frank H. Knight," *International Encyclopedia of Social Sciences,* ed. D. L. Sills (New York: Macmillan Co. and The Free Press, 1968), p. 424.

moved to the University of Iowa. But it was after he joined the faculty at Chicago in 1927 that Knight began to have his greatest impact on students. He retired in 1955 and died in 1972.[7]

Knight was to students of economics at Chicago in the 1930's what Alvin Hansen was to their counterparts at Harvard, namely, the father image and social philosopher, whose seminars and classrooms were attended with reverence and who awakened within some of the best young minds of a generation the excitement of the intellectual quest. He was a critic of orthodoxy, including what he considered the new dogma of the new economics. As Buchanan put it, "His reaction against religious orthodoxy was perhaps an essential ingredient in his intellectual development: having rejected it, the less rigid dogma encountered in the world of scholarship became easy prey to the midwestern skeptic." Skepticism is perhaps the best single-word summary of his philosophic approach. For Knight was in the tradition of the classical liberals of the late eighteenth century. Like David Hume, he rejected the view that the solution of social problems is to be found by the direct approach to them. And like Adam Smith, he had little hope that social reformers or "do-gooders" would solve problems, and he thus was willing to allow the market to solve them.

His presidential address to the American Economic Association in 1950 contains the best succinct statement of Knight's philosophical view of social reform, a view that is dominant in the thinking of those who followed Knight's lead and whom we regard as members of the new neoclassicism.

> Time was no doubt when society needed to be awakened to the possibility of remedying evils, and stirred to action, mostly negative action, establishing freedom, but some positive action too. Now, we have found not only that mere individual freedom is not enough, but that its excess can have disastrous consequences. And a reaction has set in, so that people have too much faith in positive action, of the nature of passing laws and employing policemen, and the opposite warning is needed. At least so I hold; perhaps it is a prejudice—how can one tell?—I mistrust reformers. When a man or group asks for power to do good, my impulse is to say,"Oh, yeah, who ever wanted power for any other reason? And what have they done when they got it?" So, I instinctively want to cancel the last three words, leaving simply "I want power;" that is easy to believe. And, a further confession: I am reluctant to believe in doing good with power anyhow. With

---

[7] Papers delivered at a memorial service held in Knight's memory by a colleague in philosophy, a colleague in economics, and a former student were printed in the *Journal of Political Economy*. They contain some delightful reminiscences and valuable insights into his personality. See Warner Wick, "Frank Knight, Philosopher at Large"; T. W. Schultz, "Frank Knight as Colleague"; and George J. Stigler, "Frank Knight as Teacher," *Journal of Political Economy* 81 (May/June 1973): 513–20. Also see Scott Gordon, "Frank Knight and the Tradition of Liberalism"; and Arthur H. Leigh, "Frank Knight as Economic Theorist," *Journal of Political Economy* 82 (May/June 1974); 571–86.

William James, I incline to the side of "the slow and silent forces,"
slow as though in all conscience they are—and though time is
fleeting.[8]

It is asserted that to understand Frank Knight completely, one had to
have been a student in his courses. Otherwise, his writings remain
somewhat obscure. A rather bombastic personality, he approached life
similarly to David Hume and, perhaps surprisingly, H. L. Mencken.
Although he had the healthy skepticism of both, and the bombast of
Mencken, his writing style fell woefully short of the latter's lucidity.
Perhaps the best place to get the flavor of the man is in his last work,
Intelligence and Democratic Action,[9] since these essays were delivered
orally at the University of Virginia and edited from tapes made during
his lectures.

Some of Knight's contributions have become so central to the core of
economics that they are standard fare, included in the beginning texts.
For example, he was the first economist to spell out, in a clear and
unequivocal form, the functions of an economic system, into which the
beginning student usually is initiated on the very first day of class.
Another device adopted by textbook writers is Knight's concept of the
wheel of wealth or circular flow model of the economy. Moreover, he
must be credited with having spelled out the most complete formulation of the assumptions of the perfectly competitive model.[10]

But it was not Knight's shaping of the teaching of economics with
which we are concerned, but rather with his shaping of economic
policy. Here the impact is not direct; rather it was to be felt through his
social philosophy as depicted in the typically Knightian prose noted
above.

Knight's Rehabilitation of Economic Man

One of Knight's most important contributions to the revival of neoclassicism was his original and refreshing approach to the concept of
economic man. Knight's objection to Veblen and his followers was not
that the economic man of neoclassical thought was in any way realistic.
Indeed, Knight repeatedly emphasized that economic man was not the
actual man of the world. The criticisms of Veblen and his disciples were
really wide of the mark. To Knight, the "man" of economic theory must
be an unrealistic replica of his actual counterpart in order to abstract
from reality and build a rigorous and useful science of economics.

---

[8] Frank H. Knight "The Role of Principles in Economics and Politics," *American Economic Review*
41 (March 1951): 29.

[9] Frank H. Knight, *Intelligence and Democratic Action* (Cambridge, Mass.: Harvard University
Press, 1960).

[10] Frank H. Knight, "The Ethics of Competition," *Quarterly Journal of Economics* 37 (August 1923):
579–624. Reprinted in Knight, *Ethics of Competition,* pp. 41–75. See George J. Stigler, "Perfect
Competition, Historically Contemplated," *Journal of Political Economy* 45 (February 1957): 1–17.

Knight pointed out that man is indeed multidimensional as Veblen argued: he has a physical, biological, and social dimension. But the economist makes use of one aspect of man's social dimension: his actions which are deliberately purposive, in which he consciously uses means to attain his ends in some predefined manner. Economic theory takes it that man maximizes his ends in his role as consumer (utility maximizer) and producer (profit maximizer). Consumers and producers are seen in a constant process of maximizing the attainment of their ends. This view of man is analogous to that of the frictionless machine or the perfect vacuum of physics and is just as essential to the analysis. But, avers Knight, once such an assumption is made, economic theory loses its behavioral content, since the rational calculator is truly predetermined. He has no real choice. For this reason Knight has always cautioned against the overzealous application of economic theory to noneconomic problems.

> It is . . . one of the errors, not to say vices, of an age in which the progress of natural science and the triumphs of its application to life have engrossed men's attention, to look upon life too exclusively under this aspect of scientific rationality. It is requisite to a proper orientation to economic science itself as well as necessary to a sound philosophy of life, to see clearly that life must be more than economics, or rational conduct, or the intelligent manipulation of materials and use of power in achieving results. . . . Living intelligently includes more than intelligent use of means in realizing ends; it is fully as important to select the ends intelligently, for intelligent action directed toward wrong ends only makes evil greater and more certain.[11]

Knight's restatement of economic man became the basis of the methodological approach of his followers who accepted his view that the assumptions of economics cannot be "realistic", just as the assumptions of the natural sciences are abstractions from reality. But they often paid little heed to his caveat that theories constructed on the basis of the rationally calculating man must not be pushed too far into other social sciences, since the noneconomic behavior of man may be better analyzed using assumptions more directly relevant to those fields. For economic theory is simply a representation of idealized behavior and can have relevance for real-world behavior, only to the degree that man in fact acts in conformity with these assumptions. Economic theory is a logical system for analysis and understanding—but not for prediction. For this reason, Knight rejects the view that economic theory can "be operational in the modern methodological sense."[12]

---

[11] Frank H. Knight, "Social Economic Organization," *Readings in Microeconomics*, p. 4. Reprinted from Frank H. Knight, *The Economic Organization* (New York: Harper and Row, 1933; reprinted 1951), pp. 3–30.

[12] See Buchanan, "Frank H. Knight," p. 426. See also Frank H. Knight, "Social Science," *On the History and Method of Economics* (Chicago: University of Chicago Press, 1956), pp. 121–34.

In sum, then, Knight accepts the view that economic theory must proceed on the basis of unrealistic assumptions, but must not be used to exceed the "common sense" limits of applicability. It is the clarification of the nature and significance of economic man that Knight considers his major contribution to economic methodology.

Knight's Response to Veblen

Having rehabilitated economic man by pointing out his usefulness as well as limitations in social science, Knight took up the question of the Veblenian dichotomy between industrial and pecuniary employments. He notes that the simplest view of Veblen's antithesis is that industrial or technological values are those of which he disapproves. But Knight argued that all such distinctions ultimately resolve into value judgments, and at that point, argument must cease. When Veblen sarcastically described the conspicuous consumption of the business culture, he meant to disapprove of consumption devoted to keeping up appearances. But all consumption above the level of brute material existence smacks of such emulative behavior. And it is doubtful if Veblen would want to abolish such gratifications. Hence, Veblen's attack on the consumer sovereignty criterion of welfare in essence comes down to disapproving of "improper" consumption, which, as Knight points out, is consumption "of which he (Veblen) disapproves. If he (Veblen) has an objective test for distinguishing between valid and false aesthetic values . . . he does the world grievous wrong in withholding it from publication."[13] Knight also pointed out that in a democracy it is extremely difficult to apply the distinction between Veblen's "real value and trumpery." These remarks by Knight have been repeated in one form or another by almost all critics of those who followed Veblen in attempting to castigate consumer sovereignty. And to the diehard advocate of free enterprise and political democracy, they have never been successfully answered.

Risk and Consumer Sovereignty

Any summary statement of Frank Knight's influence on economic thought and policy would be inexcusably incomplete if no mention were made of his key ideas in his first book, *Risk, Uncertainty and Profit*. For this book contains his chief contribution to the body of contemporary economic thought—Knight's theory of the nature and role of profits in the competitive model. Here Knight adumbrated a

---

[13] Frank H. Knight, "Review of the Place of Science in Modern Civilization," *Journal of Political Economy* 28 (June 1920): 520. Notwithstanding his reservations about Veblen's dichotomy, Knight was appreciative of some aspects of Veblen's economics, and he was one of those who insisted that the American Economic Association select him as president in 1925. J. Dorfman, "The Source and Impact of Veblen's Thought," in Douglas Dowd, ed., *Thorstein Veblen: A Critical Reappraisal* (Ithaca, N.Y.: Cornell University Press, 1958).

sketch of a theory of the firm which has been accepted by his students, and which contains their answer to the Veblen-Galbraith notion of the manipulation of consumer preferences by corporations. The basic contribution is Knight's distinction between risk and uncertainty. The perfectly competitive model assumed perfect knowledge on the part of consumers and producers. But, under such an assumption, profit would be nonexistent. If every entrepreneur had complete knowledge of future demand and cost conditions, each would immediately move into areas of highest return, and profit would disappear. And there would exist no residual income after all costs of production, including the wages of management, were paid.

But Knight insists that a slight relaxation of the extreme assumptions of perfect competition would permit an explanation of the existence of profit. By eliminating the assumption of perfect knowledge, the element of "uncertainty" becomes a part of the economic game. And it is from this uncertainty that profit arises. The real world can be characterized by a probability calculus, by which we can infer from events what the future will be like with certain degrees of confidence. The degree of confidence with which we predict a future event is a measure of how likely it is that this past event will recur. If this can be done with complete accuracy, then there is no uncertainty. Uncertainty exists only when we cannot accurately determine the probability of an event. This is a concept to be contrasted with "risk." The latter exists if we can attach some accurate probability distribution to its occurrence. Thus, risk is a measurable uncertainty and can be insured against. In Knight's words:

> The practical difference between the two categories, risk and uncertainty, is that in the former the distribution of the outcome in a group of instances is known (either through calculation *a priori* or from statistics or past experience), while in the case of uncertainty this is not true, the reason being in general that it is impossible to form a group of instances, because the situation dealt with is in a high degree unique.[14]

In order to clarify Knight's meaning, an example will perhaps prove instructive. Let us assume the existence of an individual who prefers to bear risk and decides to enter the women's fashion industry. By one who prefers risk, we mean that he is willing to take the consequences of a decision involving an uncertain outcome. Since the occurrence is uncertain, others with similar willingness to bear risks may not have the same belief regarding the outcome of the individual's prediction. Indeed, since the outcome is uncertain, many possible eventualities would in fact be predicted.

Let us further assume that the uncertain event involves the question of hemlines. Specifically, how many inches above the knee will women

---

[14] Knight, *Risk, Uncertainty and Profit*, p. 233.

prefer their hemlines next season? Since the women's fashion industry is highly competitive and women's future fashions are difficult to predict with accuracy, there many different guesses can be expected regarding women's preferences next year. But the prediction regarding future tastes must be made today since the productive process is time-consuming and an order with a manufacturer must be made at least a season in advance. While our risk-bearing entrepreneur makes the prediction that the fashion to be preferred next season is a hemline four inches above the knee, it can be expected that other risk takers predict varying degrees of hemline lengths. But if our individual is right and his prediction is borne out, his inventories will be in great demand in comparison with those of other fashion entrepreneurs. After paying his contractual obligations—wages, rent, and interest—he will have a residual. Now what is the nature of this residual? It is a return that he gets on the basis of no advance contract, but is the difference between his total contractuable costs and his total revenues.[15] It is this difference that Knight calls *profit*.

Note that our individual has this return because the predictions of his competitors proved incorrect regarding consumer preferences. Had they all made the same prediction as had our successful entrepreneur (that is, had no uncertainty existed), there would be no profit. In our example, however, in which at least one entrepreneur turned out to be a correct predictor, those who predicted wrongly have negative profits, also arising from uncertainty. Profit is thus a return—both positive and negative—for bearing uncertainty.[16]

Thus, as we have seen, the entrepreneur such as our individual above must determine both the quality and quantity of his final output. But the decision in regard to these matters is made on the basis of imperfect knowledge regarding consumers' tastes, incomes, and alternatives. This knowledge is imperfect because the productive process is time-consuming, and the longer the period of time involved, the greater the amount of uncertainty. The consumer cannot help him out, since he does not himself know precisely his future tastes. He does not know what he will want nor how badly he will want it. Furthermore, the consumer is not willing to bear the uncertainty and cost of predicting his own tastes. This problem of prediction is left to the producer. Thus, consumers willingly allow the manufacturer to bear the uncertainty of

---

[15]   The reason it is the difference between the total *contractuable* costs and total revenues is because the entrepreneur could have hired himself out to a competitor for some contracted salary. This is a cost in the sense that it is an opportunity foregone at the time of decision making, and it must be added to his wages, rent, and interest actually contracted to get the total costs in the economist's sense.

[16]   It should be noted that if our entrepreneur were able to repeat his feat of accurate prediction season after season, it would become evident to his competitors that he had a unique skill to forecast accurately. Under these conditions, he would doubtlessly find that he could contract his talent out for a salary equal to some average of his previous profits. If he is offered a contract that he can accept at any time, but refuses the offer, he no longer receives Knightian profits (except for the amount that he receives over and above the amount for which he could sell his services). Uncertainty for him no longer exists and what previously was calculated as profit—for which he is now able to contract—would be a rent.

future demand. The entrepreneur is the uncertainty bearer because he is a decision maker in a situation where the outcome is unknown and unpredictable.

It is here that Knight anticipates the answer to Galbraith's main attack on consumer sovereignty, the answer to Galbraith's contention that consumer demand is manipulated by producers in the sense that wants are "created," which producers then proceed to satisfy. Knight's analysis in *Risk, Uncertainty and Profit* casts a different light on the problem. For the producer is the uncertainty bearer—the decision maker—and this role is assigned to him by the uncertainty averting consumer. The consumer merely maintains a veto power if the resulting product fails to meet his preferences at the time.

In sum, through his writings and, probably more important, through his teaching, Frank Knight contributed to the contemporary revival of interest in neoclassical economics. In attempting to answer some of the main critics of neoclassicism, specifically Veblen and Pigou, he was led to restate in solid analytical form the basic premises of that model and indicate its vitality for dealing with significant issues. In his magnum opus, *Risk, Uncertainty and Profit*, he completed the neoclassical system by examining the nature of profit and the role of the entrepreneur in economic life. This reexamination of the neoclassical economics contains an alternative interpretation to that of Veblen and Galbraith of the activities of producers in influencing consumer tastes. More important, his social philosophy was attractive enough to some of the brightest young people studying economics at Chicago in the thirties and forties, that they made it their own. But it should be noted that Knight's counterrevolutionary influence was in the realm of philosophy and microeconomics. It was left to one of his colleagues at Chicago, Henry Simons, to question the validity of the macroeconomics of the Keynes-Hansen variety and, thus, help to complete the building of the new neoclassicism.

13

HENRY C. SIMONS

RADICAL PROPONENT
OF LAISSEZ-FAIRE

> Torturing straw men and raping straw women is eloquently sanc-
> tioned by your favorite oracle, precedent . . . (But) your audience
> may be credited with suspecting . . . that the blood-assay of straw is
> like that of turnips.
>
> *Letter from Henry C. Simons to Harold Groves, October 26,1943*

At the time of his death in April 1946, John Maynard Keynes was
unquestionably the best known economist in the world. Not surprisingly, his death merited front page attention in the United States. In a
lengthy obituary, the *New York Times* praised Keynes's substantial
contributions to economic thought and policy.[1] Two months later, the
death of another economist received far less attention; buried far inside
the June 20, 1946 issue of the *Times* was a story noting the death of
"Henry Simons, forty-six, associate professor of Law and Economics at
the University of Chicago." After commenting on the immediate circumstances of his death—an apparent overdose of sleeping tablets—
the *Times* provided the following summary of Simons's career:

> Born on October 19, 1899 in Virden, Illinois, Professor Simons was
> educated at the University of Michigan. He became an instructor and
> member of the faculty at the University of Iowa, remaining there until
> 1927 when he received his appointment at the University of Chicago.[2]

---

[1] *New York Times*, 22 April 1946, p. 1. Ironically, the same issue of the *Times* provided evidence that
at least one major group still was reluctant to accept the arguments of the *General Theory*. In a
two-column item above the report of Keynes's death was a story beginning:

> Endorsing the principle that a balanced budget is essential to national solvency, 26
> Republican and Democratic governors issued statements yesterday criticizing deficit
> spending and continued borrowing as an "unsound fiscal practice" and calling on Con-
> gress to provide a balanced budget beginning July 1.

[2] *New York Times*, 20 June 1946.

The *Times*, and the rest of the public, may be excused for paying so little heed to the passing of a relatively unheralded academic. Henry Calvert Simons wrote no major opus in economics to compare with Keynes's *General Theory*, nor was he a prolific writer in the style of Keynes or Alvin Hansen. His work was cut short by his early death; virtually all his important contributions to economics appeared in the short span of years between the onslaught of the Depression and the end of World War II. They have been collected into a single 300-page volume appropriately titled, *Economic Policy for a Free Society*.[3]

His obscurity as a public figure belied the influence which Henry Simons exerted on the shaping of economic thought in the turbulent years of the Roosevelt era. While the students at Cambridge—and increasingly elsewhere in the United States—were pondering the advantages of the Keynesian Doctrine, a generation of students at the University of Chicago listened to Simons's articulate defense of the laissez-faire philosophy and neoclassical economic theory. Not surprisingly, Simons was a great admirer of another influential teacher at the University of Chicago—Frank Knight. They had been on the faculty at the University of Iowa, and when Knight moved to Chicago in 1927, Simons came with him. Their interests complemented each other well: Simons concerned himself with policy; Knight with theoretical issues. A social philosophy which insisted that the preservation of individual freedom was a goal far more important than the achievement of narrow economic objectives made each of them less interested in the technical details of economic logic than in the broader implications of economic reasoning for the free market society. Each was branded a "conservative" (and in Simons case, a "radical conservative") as a result of their reluctance to favor government over private actions in a market economy. Such views ran counter to the prevailing atmosphere in Washington. Doubtlessly this reluctance to support the New Deal stemmed in large part from their midwestern mistrust of bureaucratic power; neither Simons nor Knight could see substantial gains from placing power in the hands of the few—whether it be government or any other group.

Simons v. Keynes and Hansen

Curiously, Simons also had a great deal in common with the leader of the new economics—John Maynard Keynes. Each was primarily concerned with issues of policy. Both recognized the catastrophic dimensions of the Depression, and sought ways to effect recovery. Moreover, their economic analysis of the collapse was strikingly similar. Keynes

---

[3]   Henry C. Simons, *Economic Policy for a Free Society* (Chicago: University of Chicago Press, 1948). Hereafter cited as *Economic Policy*. Although we shall indicate the particular article concerned, the page references in this chapter will refer to this book except where noted. Two other books by Simons involved taxation. Henry C. Simons, *Personal Income Taxation* (Chicago: University of Chicago Press, 1938), and idem, *Federal Tax Reform* (Chicago: University of Chicago Press, 1950). The latter was published posthumously. Neither of these works had the impact of the essays in *Economic Policy for a Free Society*.

placed considerable blame on the uncertainty of investment markets; Simons concurred. The sudden shift in liquidity, which Keynes explained through his "liquidity preference" schedule, is reflected by Simons's emphasis on what he viewed as the "perverse" behavior of velocity.[4] But there the similarities ended, for when they turned to the question of appropriate policies to combat the Depression, the two economists drew very different conclusions from their common empirical judgments. Keynes's outlook was on the short run; one of his more celebrated comments pointed out that "in the long run we are all dead." Accordingly, his proposals centered on programs to effect immediate recovery—stimulation of investment by direct government spending. Simons thought that this emphasis on the short view was dangerous; he felt the government intervention suggested by Keynes would result in an encroachment of freedom, which far outweighted its monetary benefits. He was highly skeptical of the implications of the Keynesian assault on economic orthodoxy.

> Not content to point out the shortcomings of traditional views, Mr. Keynes proceeds to espouse the cause of an army of cranks and heretics simply on the grounds that their schemes or ideas would incidently have involved or suggested mitigation of the deflationary tendencies in the economy. . . . Attempting mischievious and salutory irritation of his peers . . . he may only succeed in becoming the academic idol of our worst cranks and charlatans—not to mention the possibilities of the book as the economic bible of a fascist movement.[5]

Keynes, of course, was himself aware of the appeal of his policy recommendations to totalitarian regimes. Writing a preface for the German edition of the *General Theory*, he commented:

> The theory of aggregate production, which is the point of this following book, nevertheless can be much easier adapted to the conditions of a totalitarian state (*eines totalitarishen staates*) than the theory of production and distribution of a given product put forth under conditions of free competition and a large degree of laissez-faire.[6]

Simons would certainly concur. He was firmly convinced that the proposals which in fact emerged from the implications of the *General Theory* would undermine the essential prerequisites of a free market. This made him an implacable foe of the new economics; he became a

---

[4] Simons, of course, wrote within the framework of the quantity theory. Thus, the increase in liquidity of Keynes is a sharp fall in velocity to Simons. For an interesting interpretation of Keynes and Simons in the 1930's, see the remarks of one of Simons's more illustrious students: Milton Friedman. Milton Friedman, "The Monetary Theory and Policy of Henry Simons," *Journal of Law and Economics* 10 (October 1967): 1–13. As it happens, Friedman later gathered substantial evidence which tended to refute Simons's interpretation of the demand for money during the depression.

[5] Henry C. Simons, "Keynes' Comments on Money," *Christian Century*, 22 July 1936, pp. 1016–17.

[6] John Maynard Keynes, *The General Theory of Employment Interest and Money*, German Edition (Berlin and Munich: Duncker and Humblot, 1936), pp. 39–41.

virulent critic of the various schemes for postwar economic programs. His style at times produced caustic remarks on the implications of government intervention. Commenting on one such proposal by Lord Beveridge in Great Britain (from what he admitted was an "unsympathetic view"), Simons noted:

> So a sporting old Englishman urges England to take over the German Game, not diffidently as in the thirties but zealously, and to show the world how it should be played. England's commercial power is to be mobilized and concentrated, to improve her terms of trade, to recruit satellites for a tight sterling bloc, and to insulate herself and them from unstable, unplanned, economies, that is, from the United States.[7]

His salvos at the interventionist government policies were generally made from afar, for Simons's intense distaste for bureaucratic affairs made him assiduously avoid appearances in Washington. Yet his attacks were not unnoticed by those he singled out for comment. And his favorite target was the leading academic Keynesian—Alvin Hansen. Simons appreciated the appeal of Hansen's writing. Reviewing *Fiscal Policy and Business Cycles*,[8] he commended the book's "clarity of statement and excellence of style." But he went on to say that

> I come to bury Hansen—albeit respectfully and despairingly. Praise he will receive elsewhere, for learning and assiduous inquiry which merit all praise and because he accepts and applauds the powerful political trends of the day. . . . So, as an unreconstructed, old fashioned liberal, I must counterattack as best I can, hoping thereby to diminish slightly that impetus which the book must give to trends of thought and action which to me seem wholly dangerous.[9]

Simons made no apologies for his "old fashioned liberalism." He insisted that philosophical beliefs are necessarily the foundations of any economist's policy conclusions. He scoffed at those who tried to practice economics as a "science" devoid of any set of values.

> It has become conventional among students of fiscal policy . . . to dissemble any underlying social philosophy and to maintain a pretense of rigorous, objective analysis untinctured by mere ethical considerations. The emptiness of this pretense among economists is notorious. . . . Having been told that sentiments are contraband in the realm of science, they religiously eschew a few proscribed phrases, clutter up title pages and introductory chapters with pious references to the science of public finance and then write monumental discourses on their own prejudices and preconceptions.[10]

---

[7]   Simons, *Economic Policy*, p. 278.

[8]   Alvin Hansen, *Fiscal Policy and Business Cycles* (New York: W. W. Norton, 1941).

[9]   Simons, *Economic Policy*, p. 185.

[10] Simons, *Personal Income Taxation*, pp. 1–2.

The opening paragraph of his "Positive Program for Laissez Faire"[11] provides a typical example of his own frankness regarding underlying philosophies.

> This is frankly a propagandist tract—a defense of the thesis that traditional liberalism offers, at once, the best escape from the moral confusion of current (1934) political and economic thought and the best basis or rationale for a program of economic reconstruction.[12]

His defenses of this position—and his "counterattacks" against Keynesians such as Hansen—provide some of the most articulate statements of the laissez-faire position to be found anywhere in the literature of economics. Defenses of laissez-faire were hardly uncommon in the 1930's; what singles out Simons was his insistence on recognizing the *positive* actions which were required of a government to maintain a free market. His overriding concern was with policy, and his approach to the issues was invariably that of a "radical." He did not propose new monetary policies; he insisted on a thorough reform of the *entire financial system*. His aim was not to regulate private monopoly, but to *eliminate its sources*. It is in connection with these radical proposals that Simons is best known.

Simons seldom dwelled on the intricacies of economic theory—more often than not such points were relegated to lengthy footnotes. Using the neoclassical approach to allocation and money as the foundation, Simons tried to explore the institutional arrangements which would best suit the operation of a free market in the modern world. His academic post reflected this interest in institutional arrangements; he was the first of several eminent economists to become a member of the law faculty at the University of Chicago.[13] The relevance of law to economics was apparent in Simons's approach to the "economic problem." A market can only operate effectively in the context of a stable environment. It is the responsibility of the government to seek actively to create such an environment. In what is perhaps his most significant economic essay, Simons stated this responsibility very clearly.

> The liberal creed demands the organization of our economic life largely through individual participation in a game *with definite rules*. It calls upon that state to provide a stable framework of rules within which enterprise and competition may effectively control and direct the production and distribution of goods. The essential conception is that of a genuine division of labor between competitive (market) and political controls—a division of labor within which competition has a major, or at least proximately primary, place.[14]

---

[11] Henry C. Simons, "A Positive Program for Laissez Faire," in idem, *Economic Policy*, pp. 40–77.

[12] Simons, *Economic Policy*, p. 40.

[13] He held a joint appointment from 1937 on. The continuing contact between the two disciplines ultimately produced the *Journal of Law and Economics* in 1957. One of Simons's students, Aaron Director, was the journal's initial editor.

[14] Simons, *Economic Policy*, p. 160.

The need for establishing some rational set of rules to constrain the arbitrary authority of government is a dominating theme throughout all of Simons's writing. He did not favor the establishment of a status quo; nor did he advocate a government policy involving a complete absence of intervention. He called for a positive program of government action which would emphasize that delicate division of labor between government and the free market. In Simons's view, this division of labor had seldom been optimal in the past. Government had intervened in many areas where it should have remained aloof; but more important, it had ignored several fundamental areas where forceful control was essential to the operation of the market system. In his discussion of positive action by the state, Simons spelled out five broad areas of concern:[15]

1. Elimination of all forms of private monopoly.
2. Reform of the monetary system and the establishment of "rules of the game" for monetary authorities to follow.
3. Reform of the tax system.
4. Removal of all tariff levies.
5. An effort to limit the "squandering of our resources" on merchandising and advertising practices.

Simons took great care to point out that the suggestions are presented in order of their importance as he viewed it. In particular, he noted the overriding importance of the first proposal, since

> The case for a liberal-conservative policy must stand or fall on the first proposal, abolition of private monopoly; for it is the *sine qua non* of any such policy.[16]

While elimination of monopoly power is the cornerstone of Simons's approach to economic policy, it has been his views on monetary policy which received the widest audience. His ideas in the area show the rationale behind the establishment of "rules" to curb the exercise of arbitrary "authority" in the economic system. Accordingly, we shall take up the issues of his monetary reform before tackling the broader aspects of his program for laissez-faire.[17]

Rules v. Authorities

The most hotly debated issue at the time Simons wrote was, of course, government policy toward economic stability. He felt that the elimination of monopoly power—and thus greater price flexibility—would

---

[15] This list was paraphrased from the proposals in "A Positive Program for Laissez Faire" in Simons, *Economic Policy*, pp. 40-77.

[16] Simons, *Economic Policy*, p. 57.

[17] Two of Simons's articles contain the basic logic of his policy proposals on monetary policy: Henry C. Simons, "Rules vs. Authorities in Monetary Policy," *Journal of Political Economy* 44 (February 1936): 1–30, reprinted in *Economic Policy*, pp. 160–83; and idem, "Hansen on Fiscal Policy," *Journal of Political Economy* 50 (April 1942): 161–96, reprinted in *Economic Policy*, pp. 184–219. The latter is his scathing review of Hansen, *Fiscal Policy and Business Cycles*.

lessen the impact of economic cycles. Yet—quite apart from his own pessimism as to the possibility of actually reducing monopoly—Simons contended that this would not be sufficient to guarantee stability.

> The major responsibility for the severity of industrial fluctuations . . . falls directly upon the state. Tolerable functioning of a free-enterprise system presupposes effective performance of a fundamental function of government, namely, regulation of the circulating medium (money).[18]

The details of Simons's monetary policy are not always explicit in his writings. His basic framework of analysis was that of the neoclassical quantity theory.[19] Yet he was moving toward a more sophisticated treatment of the argument than appeared in the literature up to that time. He certainly agreed with the neoclassicists that the stock of money was an important element in the level of what he termed "aggregate turnover" (that is, Keynes's aggregate demand). Simons's emphasis on the aggregate turnover led him to concentrate his analysis on the behavior of *velocity*—people's behavior in desiring and spending money. Velocity, he felt, was subject to sudden and very wide fluctuations in the short run. His interest in velocity stemmed from his puzzlement over the lethargic condition of the economy following the Great Crash.

> What we need now to understand and explain is why our economy of the thirties, though flooded with money, failed to revive adequately or to function effectively.[20]

In his work on monetary reform, Simons appears to be moving towards a formulation of the quantity equation of exchange, which would envision the term *velocity* as some sort of behavioral variable depending on a large number of possible influences.[21] The variable to which he particularly addressed himself in the context of the 1930's was the influence of institutional arrangements. He insisted that the climate of uncertainty generated by the periodic collapse of financial markets led people to react sharply in their attitudes on holding money.

Simons was appalled by the "preposterous" rules under which the medium of exchange was controlled in the United States. A reluctance on the part of the federal government to provide a circulating media had resulted in this fuction being "usurped" by the private sector—that is, the commercial banks. The "money" of the United States economy was for the most part a huge mass of short-term debt held in the form of demand deposits. Simons described the evolution of the "money" industry with characteristic candor.

---

[18] Simons, *Economic Policy*, p. 54.

[19] See our discussion of the quantity theory of money in Chapter 2.

[20] Simons, *Economic Policy*, p. 186.

[21] For the more sophisticated version of the quantity equation, see Chapter 14. It is interesting to note that the leading proponent of the "modern" theory describes Simons's views on monetary theory as "highly sophisticated." (Friedman, "The Monetary Theory and Policy of Henry Simons.")

> During the past century or more, a thriving economy, denied adequate proper media for liquid reserves, created and encouraged private agencies to provide what government itself blindly failed to provide. Thus, we evolved a fantastic financial structure and collections of enterprises for money-bootlegging, whose sanctimonious respectability and marble solidity only concealed a mass of current obligations and a shoestring of equity that would have been scandalous in any other type of business.[22]

He conceded that the arrangement had thus far been able to satisfy the secular demand for money in the system, but it did so at enormous cost, for it exposed the economy to frequent "precipitous, catastrophic deflations."

The core of the problem is the *fractional reserve banking*, which allows the commercial banks to hold liabilities in the form of demand deposits up to some multiple of the "reserves" available in the bank. Simons was convinced that such an arrangement could *never* be truly secure from potential liquidity crises.

> No real stability of production and employment is possible when short term lenders are continuously in a position to demand conversion of their investments, amounting in the aggregate to a large multiple of the total available circulating media, into such media.[23]

He preferred an economy where all debt would be of a very long maturity—preferably "consols" issued in perpetuity. Recognizing the impossibility of achieving such a situation, Simons contented himself with a proposal which was less ambitious but still highly radical: all commercial banks would be required to hold reserves behind 100 percent of the demand deposits in hand. This would remove much of the inherent instability of a fractional reserve system; the presence of a myriad of "near monies" created by financial institutions would be removed.[24]

An interesting postscript to the arguments put forward by Simons in his plan for monetary reform involves a subsequent debate among monetary economists in the early fifties, surrounding the proliferation of highly liquid assets issued by "non-bank financial intermediaries." These institutions—savings banks, insurance companies and the like—may affect velocity by their creation of liquid debt. This, in turn, could

---

[22] Simons, *Economic Policy*, p. 198.

[23] Simons, *Economic Policy*, p. 166.

[24] Simons's plan for banking reform is summarized in his "A Positive Program for Laissez Faire," and spelled out in more detail in several mimeographed essays circulated at the University of Chicago. It proposed to set up two groups of financial institutions. The first would serve merely as warehouses for money, deriving income from the charges for deposits held. These deposits would be covered by 100 percent reserves. The second group would perform the lending function of commercial banks. They would obtain their capital through security issues and be in effect "investment trusts." Naturally, Simons recognized that restrictions on debt issue of other financial institutions might be necessary. Simons would regulate these functions through the terms of corporate charter.

affect the efficacy of monetary policy in meeting a situation. Apart from this controversy, the issues raised by Simons in his banking scheme have been largely ignored in the postwar literature.[25]

The aspect of Simons's monetary proposals which does appear in contemporary policy discussion is his insistence that monetary authorities should be curbed in their freedom to exercise discretionary power.

> ... first that monetary authorities must be bound by simple, definite rules (a price index) and, second, *that their only real powers should be those of conducting operations in the public debt.*[26]

This recommendation was in no way dependent upon acceptance of his banking reforms.[27] Restriction of the discretionary power of the monetary authority follows directly from his insistence that the government must establish some consistent and stable framework within which the market can operate. Monetary policy is not the domain of the central bank, for it depends essentially on the levels of expenditure and taxation, not the bank rate. Hence his insistence that the central bank be confined in its operation to debt management.

Simons was not really concerned over the nature of the rule which should be adopted; what was essential was the agreement that *some* rule must be followed. In his writing, Simons toyed with two possible alternatives and was unable to really decide which of the following rules was better:

1. Fix the money supply and maintain it at that level.
2. Establish a price index and instruct the central bank to maintain that index at a given level.

He recommended the second rule (constant prices) for the time in which he was writing; but he clearly preferred a situation where the first (fixed money supply) could be introduced. The impracticality of the fixed-money rule was a result of the erratic (and sudden) shifts in velocity. Since he insisted that this stemmed in part from the instability of a fractional reserve banking system, adoption of this rule must await banking reform. Simons was also cognizant of the problems of a fixed supply of money with a rigid price structure. Here his monetary proposals dovetail into his general advice to remove monopoly. With more flexible prices, the establishment of a fixed money stock becomes feasible.

The price level guideline would, he thought, serve as a suitable substitute. Here again, he was aware of the practical problem such a proposal would encounter. For the monetary authorities to carry out such a rule,

---

[25] Economists such as Milton Friedman, however, continue to support quietly 100 percent reserve banking. See his comments in "The Monetary Theory and Policy of Henry Simons."

[26] Simons, *Economic Policy*, p. 205. (Italics in original.)

[27] See, for example, his comment in reviewing Hansen's book where he notes that some would regard his monetary scheme as that of a "crank." He proceeds to present the rules versus authority argument independently of monetary reform. Simons, *Economic Policy*, pp. 184–219.

> . . . it must be accepted by the whole community, and obeyed by the
> legislatures, as the guiding principle of sound government finance—
> as the basic criterion of sound fiscal policy.[28]

Thus far our discussion of Simons's proposals has centered on his
radical proposals for long-run reform. What of his suggestions for
immediate response to the Depression? Clearly, Simons felt his long
run objectives would be a necessary part of any recovery. Yet he did
comment on the appropriate fiscal-monetary policy for the early thirties. His prescription was simple and to the point: the money supply
should be increased through government deficits. He was very clear in
this proposal that the money financing the deficit must be *printed*, not
borrowed.[29] The danger of borrowing on the part of the government was
not an economic one—it stemmed from Simons's basic distrust of
bureaucratic power. Assaulting (once again) the proposals of his adversary Hansen, Simons wrote:

> Vulgar prejudice will support Hansen's implication that borrowing is
> less dangerous than issue. I am firmly convinced of the opposite.
> Injection of money, within limits, is like putting fuel in the furnace;
> borrowing, like accumulating dynamite in the basement, with the
> explosion risk growing as the pile accumulates.[30]

Advocating a government deficit through the use of a printing press in
the basement of the treasury is—as Simons himself noted—a rather
Keynesian approach to the problem of unemployment. It illustrates
again the willingness of Simons to approve government intervention to
correct imbalance *as long as a set of rules limits the arbitrary use of
authority*. His attacks on Keynes's proposals reflect the fact that they
did not, in his judgment, properly consider the need for constraint of
government power.[31] It is his "political credo" which leads him to reject
much of the policy proposed in the thirties.

A Positive Program for Laissez-Faire

"The great enemy of democracy is monopoly, in all its forms," Simons
wrote, and he went on to define monopoly broadly as "any organization
and concentration of power within functional classes." His writing
emphasized the need to remove the *sources* of such concentrations of
economic power. He found two major flaws in the existing system:
inadequate control of the privilege of incorporation, and the inability to
check the rising power of labor unions.

The corporation, as a means to organize and finance production
efficiently, is a useful device. Simons did not deny this. However, it

---

28 Simons, *Economic Policy*, p. 176.

29 Note the relationship between this proposal and Lerner's functional finance.

30 Simons, *Economic Policy*, p. 196.

31 See in particular his review of the *General Theory*. Simons, "Keynes' Comments on Money." He
sharply criticizes Keynes's failure to discuss the monetary institutions behind the problem of
liquidity.

could also serve as a vehicle to obtain massive monopoly power in the market. Thus, the right to incorporation must be carefully regulated by the government. The responsibility for this supervision had been largely abdicated in the nineteenth century. State governments passed lenient incorporation laws without any effective control of the use of that privilege. Simons favored a *federal incorporation law* to charter all corporations from the federal government. This would allow checks on monopoly power to be built into the incorporation charter. Size of the firm, assets held by the firm, and similar variables could be controlled by the terms of the charter rather than regulation. Simons recognized the old Marshallian concern with increasing returns industries.[32] Such cases, he argued, should be operated by the government as a public monopoly.

In spite of his adamant demands to eliminate monopoly, Simons was somewhat ambivalent towards the antitrust policy of the government. To the extent that its enforcement successfully undermined monopoly power, he was on the side of the "trust-busters." But he could never shake an inherent mistrust of bureaucracy. His restrained applause for the exploits of Thurman W. Arnold reflects his rather jaundiced view of the Justice Department in Washington.

> Carrying the ball for free trade, he runs toward and behind his own goal line whenever he imagines an opponent in the offing; but he never gets downed behind his goal and somehow keeps on the offensive throughout. In the end he is headed squarely in the right direction and, unlike his opponents, exhausted merely from watching his frightened rushes, is fresh and fit at the end as at the start.[33]

Simons always preferred to see halfbacks on his team head straight down field.[34]

The presence of substantial monopoly in the industrial economy was readily admitted by Simons. But he became increasingly convinced that *labor monopoly*, not *enterprise monopoly*, was the true threat to the free market system.[35] His opposition to union monopoly was based on the fundamental nature of a politically organized monopoly. While admitting that "it was shameful to have permitted the growth of vast corporate empires," enterprise monopoly is still only a "skin disease" whose cure is "easy to correct if we will."[36] Labor "syndicalism," on the

---

[32] We noted in Chapter 2 that $P = MC$ is the efficiency point. However, in the case of a decreasing cost industry, the marginal cost curve is below the average cost curve. Marginal cost pricing thus would not permit the firm to cover average costs. This firm is called a *technical monopoly*.

[33] Simons, *Economic Policy*, pp. 93–94.

[34] And, of course, Arnold was a member of the New Deal team. Roosevelt's program—especially legislation such as the National Recovery Act—made Simons uneasy for this clearly created substantially *more* monopoly power.

[35] The most complete treatment of his views on labor is his essay, "Some Reflections on Syndicalism," *Journal of Political Economy* 52 (March 1944): 1–25 and reprinted in *Economic Policy*, pp. 121–59.

[36] It should be added that Simons was extremely pessimistic that such a "will" would in fact prevail in the United States.

other hand, is "a different kind of animal." Here the source of monopoly power lies in coercion. Once established, Simons saw no ready check to such power. Certainly, he argued, there is no reason to expect the labor leaders to constrain themselves. Echoing Frank Knight's dictum against power he wrote: "Monopoly power must be abused. It has no use save abuse." He noted with alarm the apparent harmony of interests between the union and the industrial monopolist in attaining profits.

Such views on monopoly are, of course, wholly consistent with the neoclassical beliefs. Here Simons ran into the problem facing Chamberlin—and others—who observed a marked divergence between theoretical models and the structure of firms in the real world. Chamberlin sought to change the theory; Simons to bring reality closer to the postulates of the competitive model. He saw very clearly the dilemma of trying to argue on the one hand that the theoretical analysis is essentially correct (as he thought it was) while also maintaining that unrealistic assumptions approximated the real world (which he admitted they did not). Monopoly *did* exist in substantial amounts, and one result was to produce inflexible prices. Rigid prices undermined the degree to which Say's Law would produce full employment of all resources. Simons's antimonopoly position was therefore a crucial aspect of his aggregate policy. Writing in the mid-1940's, Simons was discussing the problem which the modern decision maker sees in the Phillips Curve.[37] Simons abhorred forms of price regulation such as those embodied in "incomes policies" or "wage-price guidelines." His solution to the dilemma of the Phillips Curve would be to "shift" the curve by eliminating rigid prices. His shift would be accomplished by eliminating private monopoly.

Like many radicals, Simons recognized his prescriptions might be bitter medicine for the society to swallow. As he pointed out with regard to his views on labor syndicalism,

> Questioning the virtues of the organized labor movement is like attacking religion, monogamy, motherhood, or the home. Among the modern intelligentsia any doubts about collective bargaining admit of explanation only in terms of insanity, knavery, or subservience to "the interests."[38]

Simons was deeply pessimistic regarding the outcome of a struggle between labor and capital. Writing in 1944, he commented:

> It is easy to argue that the whole problem is so hard and ominous politically that no effort should be made to solve or even to see it—that the real choice lies between a certain, gradual death of economic democracy and an operation . . . which would cure if successful but is almost certain to kill. I am no forecaster and am not in direct communication with the Almighty. Consequently, I can only

---

[37] On the issues surrounding the Phillips Curve, see Chapters 9, 10, and 14.

[38] Simons, *Economic Policy*, p. 121.

maintain that it is immoral to take such absolute dilemmas seriously. Democracy would have been dead a thousand times if it paid much attention to historical extrapolations. . . .[39]

Yet his writings at times belie his own concern over precisely this dilemma. Beneath his attacks on the policies of the Depression and war years lay a gloomy prognostication of the future of the Western world. As a biographer put it shortly after his death,

> Simons died before the outlines of the peace were clearly defined. Perhaps for his own state of mind, never too peaceful, it was just as well.[40]

Henry Simons is best known today for his outspoken views of government economic policy. This is not surprising; Simons took a dogmatic stand at a time when the traditional functions of government were being seriously challenged. His proposals also dealt with taxes, tariffs, and merchandising. On each subject, he carefully thought through proposals consistent with his "old-fashioned liberal" position.

On the subject of taxes—which was his academic specialty—Simons insisted that government levies be *direct* and *simple*. Apart from the obvious need for sufficient revenue, the basic aim of tax policy should be to: (a) ensure that the true cost of government is levied equitably on the citizens; and (b) that a more equitable distribution of income and wealth be obtained through taxation. Looking back on his myriad of specific proposals, one is struck by their appropriateness today as the government reviews the entangled tax structure of the postwar era. For example, Simons espoused the following proposals:[41]

1. The basic source of revenues should derive from a personal income tax.
2. The tax should be levied on *all income*, regardless of source—capital gains, dividends, gifts, and wages would be treated alike.[42]
3. The revenues from this tax should be shared with the state governments.
4. "Averaging" of incomes should be allowed where an individual's income fluctuates markedly from year to year.
5. Those with incomes below some minimum level should have no tax imposed at all.

Note that much of the foundation for these proposals lies with Simons's philosophical background rather than a detailed analysis of the taxes.

---

[39] Simons, *Economic Policy*, p. 157.

[40] John Davenport, "The Testament of Henry Simons," in *Economics and the Study of Law*, Reprint and Pamphlet Series No. 4 (Chicago: University of Chicago Press, 1946); reprinted from *The University of Chicago Law Review* 14 (December 1946).

[41] Most specific proposals were incorporated in his monograph, *Federal Tax Reform*. His support for the personal income tax is justified in Simons, *Personal Income Taxation*.

[42] Simons favored a very simple definition of income: it would be the algebraic sum of (1) consumption during the period and (2) the change in the value of assets held. His discussion of income is found in Chapters 2 and 3 of idem, *Personal Income Taxation*. His policy aim was to remove the differential treatment given incomes from different sources.

They are careful extensions of his belief that government should adhere as much as possible to simple "rules of the game."

In all the arguments listed, Simons appears as the advocate of what today is described as the "conservative" position in modern economics. One would hardly expect to find him expressing a sentiment in accordance with the views of, for example, John Kenneth Galbraith. Yet consider the following remark in the light of our discussion of Galbraith.

> It is a commonplace that our vaunted efficiency in production is dissipated extravagantly in the wastes of merchandising. . . . Profits may be obtained either by producing what consumers want or by making consumers want what one is actually producing. The possibility of profitability utilizing resources to manipulate demand is, perhaps, the greatest source of diseconomy under the existing system. If present tendencies continue, we may soon reach a situation where most of our resources are utilized in persuading people to buy one thing rather than another, and only a minor fraction is actually employed in creating things to be bought.[43]

This is surely a statement of the *dependence effect* worthy of Galbraith himself. In fact, Simons's economic analysis closely paralleled the conclusions of Chamberlin. He foresaw a situation where most advertising expenditures would tend "only to counteract the expenditures of competitors." In the end, "all of them may wind up with about the same volume of business as if none had advertised at all." This is much the same result as Chamberlin's "monopolistic competition."

Just as he tended to accept Keynes's diagnosis of the illness and reject the cure, so it is doubtful that Simons would today be alongside his arch-foe Alvin Hansen in espousing the social imbalance hypothesis. Distortions from advertising are the least important aspect of Simons's program; he felt it was only a special case of the monopoly question. What he would say today is, of course, impossible to predict, for he said very little about the issue before his death.[44] His followers have, in general, not echoed sentiments favoring the Galbraithian quote above. But then, it was never the particular policy that Simons propounded which made him important to current thought. His legacy—like that of Knight—is written in the political philosophy which he so ably expounded in defense of his economic policy statements. Milton Friedman has summarized the impact of Simons very well.

> No man can say precisely whence his beliefs and values came—but there is no doubt that mine would be different than they are if I had not had the good fortune to be exposed to Henry Simons. If . . . I express much disagreement with him, that, too, bespeaks his influence. He taught us that an objective, critical examination of a man's ideas is a truer tribute than slavish repetition of his formulas.[45]

---

[43] Simons, *Economic Policy*, p. 71.

[44] Simons's views on advertising are very briefly put forward at two points in idem, *Economic Policy*, pp. 71–73, 85–86.

[45] Friedman, "The Monetary Theory and Policy of Henry Simons," p. 1.

14

MILTON FRIEDMAN

CLASSICAL LIBERAL
AS ECONOMIC SCIENTIST

Little man whip a big man every time if the little man's in the right and keeps a'comin'.

Motto of the Texas Rangers

The intellectual revolutions that we have been describing in this volume were spawned from what their architects took to be empirical evidence. Pigou, Veblen, and Chamberlin were convinced from their observations that the assumptions of neoclassical economics were unrealistic; thus, they attempted to develop new and more relevant theories for their own time.

But it should be clear that no single event in the history of the United States had more sweeping impact on economic thought than the Great Depression. Through the commentaries of Keynes, Hansen, and Lerner, academic thinking on economic matters underwent an upheaval, whose suddenness can be compared to no prior change in the development of the discipline. These men cast into doubt the central core of the monetary and employment theories of neoclassicism: the quantity theory of money and Say's Law. In retrospect, the success of these men is perhaps not surprising. The seeming inability of the Federal Reserve System to bring respite from the economic collapse of the 1930's threw into disrepute long-accepted propositions about the role of monetary factors in economic change which the quantity theory had propounded. Idle land and capital, coupled with the destitution of more than twelve million unemployed people, seemed to belie the logical beauty of Say's Law.

The new economics of Keynes provided a diagnosis and a remedy. The problem was to increase the flow of aggregate demand, mainly investment, which (through the Keynesian multipler, aided, perhaps, by a Hansen-Samuelson accelerator effect) would lead to a magnified increase in the flow of income. The quantity theorists' belief that the level of money income and the price level were largely determined by the stock of money was held to be true, if at all, only in periods of full employment. Alvin Hansen's confident prediction that the great issue of the future was to be secular stagnation led him and his influential students to advocate easy monetary policy, but only as a means of keeping interest rates down. The point was to avoid interfering with the increasing government investment that alone could offset the slide into economic maturity. In addition, Abba Lerner's functional finance provided the set of instruments needed for government to do the fine-tuning that would restore the economy to full employment. Almost all agreed that the stock of money was the inert companion of the real economic force of increasing investment.

At Chicago, Henry Simons demurred. Though he attacked with vitriolic fervor the notions of Keynes—and especially Keynes à la Hansen—his words did little to stem the tide in the late 1930's and early 1940's. It remained for one of Simons's students to contribute the analytical depth, scientific precision, and empirical arguments that alone could effectively challenge the Keynesian orthodoxy of the new economics.

This student was Milton Friedman, the son of Jewish immigrants from Ruthenia (at that time part of the Austro-Hungarian Empire). From such inauspicious beginnings, Friedman was to eventually help set the agenda for the major economic debates of the post-World War II era. The movement away from the monetary implications of neoclassical economics was to be brought to a standstill by the empirical research and theoretical arguments of this brilliant economist. No one testifying before congressional committees investigating economic affairs was listened to with more respect. Accounts of his performances before sessions of the Joint Economic Committee and the Committee on Banking and Currency make fascinating reading in the art of persuasion that would have been relished by Keynes himself.

Friedman's testimony at such proceedings have the aspect of a classroom seminar, with the senators and congressmen his attentive students. After one particularly difficult session in which Friedman explained his new version of the quantity theory of money through a series of equations in the clearest possible terms to the hushed assembly of senators and congressmen, the following colloquy took place:

> The Chairman: Mr. Friedman, the Federal Reserve Board loves to brief Senators and Congressmen on economic affairs in order to diminish our economic ignorance, and so does the Council of Economic Advisers.
> I wonder if we could arrange a seminar in which you could brief these gentlemen on these equations. I will be glad to invite them and have you brief them on these equations, if you would be willing to come and, of course, we will pay you an honorarium for it.

I think an advanced course for the Federal Reserve and possibly
even the Council of Economic Advisers would be very good.
Could you possibly do that?

Mr. Friedman: A professor is always willing to profess.[1]

The reply was typical and apt. For Friedman has "professed" and made
his influence felt not only in testimony before Congress but also
through his articles and books; his classroom lectures; his column in
Newsweek; and most recently, in his television series, "Free to
Choose," which was broadcast on virtually every Public Broadcasting
System station in the United States. Indeed, Friedman's most powerful
means of persuasion has been the force of his personality that has
allowed his heretical and radical ideas in defense of market capitalism
to capture the imagination of scores of economists and legislators.

A short, balding man with a large intellectual head, a round face, a
smiling expression, and eyes that gleam brightly from behind broad
spectacles, Friedman charms his supporters and dismays his detractors
with his buzz-saw debating technique, which, when combined with a
cherubic appearance, is devastating. Leo Rosten has taken Milton
Friedman as the prototype for his character, Fenwick, and painted an
accurate portrait of Friedman in action.

> . . . He listens carefully to anything you tell him, and *promptly* wants
> to know where and how you found out whatever it is you told
> him—and how you know it is so. Worse, he separates inferences from
> proof. Fenwick enjoys following every little chug in your train of
> thought—indeed, he gets right on the train with you. And you have
> barely begun to move before Fenwick excitedly demonstrates that: (a)
> you have taken the wrong train; or (b) it doesn't stop where you want
> to go; or (c) the tracks don't lead from your premise to your preferred
> conclusion; or (d) that train will land you where you don't want to go
> and didn't even know you were going.[2]

It is this talent for argumentative discourse combined with his capacity
to do solid research and master the deepest intricacies of economic

---

[1] U.S., Congress, Joint Economic Committee, *Employment, Growth and Price Levels*, 86th Cong.,
    1st sess., 25 May 1959, p. 634. The inquisitor was Senator Paul Douglas of Illinois, who was himself
    a highly respected economist.

[2] Leo Rosten, "An Infuriating Man," in idem, "The World of Leo Rosten," *Look* 15 (November 1966):
    14. Friedman also inspired the creation of another fictitious character, Professor Henry Spearman,
    the economist-sleuth in the mystery novel *Murder at the Margin*. As one writer described this
    work,

> The novel tells of a short, balding, articulate, brilliant professor of economics (an apt
> description of Friedman) who solves a murder through the use of Chicago-style eco-
> nomics. As the fictitious Professor Spearman puts it: "I am interested only in economic
> laws, laws that cannot be broken." Though the murder violated man-made law, the
> murderer slipped up because the economic law remained intact.

    E. Ray Canterbery, *The Making of Economics*, 2nd ed., (Belmont, Calif.: Wadsworth Publishing
    Co., 1980), p. 165. The mystery novel was penned by Marshall Jevons, the joint pseudonym for two
    academic scribblers not covered in this volume. Marshall Jevons, *Murder at the Margin* (Glen
    Ridge, N.J.: Thomas Horton and Daughters, 1978).

theory that have made Friedman the most prominent new neoclassicist. Today, he challenges Keynes as the twentieth century's most influential economist.

Friedman was born in Brooklyn, New York, in 1912. His father was a dealer in wholesale dry goods, and his mother worked as a seamstress in a New York sweatshop and later managed a retail dry goods store. Milton's father died when his son was fifteen, and the family was left with little money. Friedman received a partial scholarship to attend Rutgers University, and he supplemented his income by working as a waiter in a nearby restaurant and clerking in a department store. He graduated in 1932 with a double major in economics and mathematics. At Rutgers, he came under the influence of Arthur F. Burns, who was to instill in Friedman an appreciation for the importance of empirical inquiry that has persisted throughout his career. Upon graduation, Friedman had offers of scholarships from Brown University (in mathematics) and the University of Chicago (in economics). Burns and another instructor whom he admired, Homer Jones, together persuaded Friedman to pursue his studies in economics at Chicago, which had one of the outstanding economics departments in the country.

Friedman's choice of economics was also influenced by the events of the Great Depression, which made the understanding of economics seem vital. While at Chicago, he took courses with Frank Knight, Henry Simons, Jacob Viner, and Henry Schultz. From Simons and Knight, he developed his philosophy of classical liberalism and a deep skepticism about the appropriateness of most government intervention. From Viner, he developed a feel for the vitality and importance of economic theory.[3] From Arthur Burns, Friedman had already developed his keen appreciation for his standards of objectivity and thoroughness. From Schultz and later from Harold Hotelling at Columbia University, he received a thorough training and developed an abiding interest in mathematical economics and statistics. The distinctiveness of his scientific work is his blending of these three strands of analysis.

During his first year of graduate work, he met fellow student Rose Director. Her brother, Aaron Director, was on the University of Chicago faculty and was to become an influential economist in later years through his work combining the study of law with economics at the University of Chicago, pioneering the present field of "law and economics." Rose married Milton while still in graduate school, and she came to play an important part in his life, eventually collaborating on two of his most popular books.

After receiving his M.A. in 1933, Friedman entered Columbia University, where, in addition to taking work under Harold Hotelling, he

---

[3] "Without question, one of the greatest intellectual experiences of my life was the first-quarter course in economic theory with Jacob Viner. This opened my eyes to a world I had not realized existed. I was made aware of both the beauty and the power of formal economic theory." Personal correspondence with Milton Friedman, 22 June 1967.

enrolled for classes under Wesley C. Mitchell (one of Thorstein Veblen's most distinguished students). Mitchell taught the history of economic thought and business cycles. The Great Depression had given the latter subject a special sense of urgency, and Mitchell was, by wide agreement, the leading authority in the world on that topic. An institutionalist, Mitchell stressed the importance of good data and their proper interpretation. Friedman's training at both Chicago and Columbia was important in shaping the young scholar. Chicago gave to Friedman the powerful theoretical structure of neoclassical price theory and monetary theory with which to analyze the economic system. Columbia gave him the institutional arrangements and facts to fit into that structure.

In the fall of 1934, Friedman returned to Chicago for further study, but financial pressures forced him in 1935 to join the National Resources Committee, part of Roosevelt's New Deal, for a short stint in Washington. In 1937, he accepted a post at the National Bureau of Economic Research in New York City. The National Bureau had been founded by Wesley Mitchell and was in the process of gathering and interpreting data on the American economy. Friedman's assignment was to rework a version of an earlier manuscript on income from professional practice that had been completed by Simon Kuznets. Friedman's contribution to this project was so large that it was to result in a doctoral dissertation ultimately accepted for the Ph.D. by Columbia University in 1946.[4] The study was a pioneering effort in a field that later evolved under the rubric "human capital," an approach that was to have impact on the future study of "labor economics." Another prescient feature of the study was the distinction Friedman made between the concepts of "permanent" and "transitory" income, a distinction which was to play an important role in Friedman's later work on the consumption function.

After leaving the National Bureau, Friedman joined the faculty of the University of Wisconsin at Madison, but a rather ugly episode, involving departmental politics and overtones of anti-Semitism, led Friedman to refuse any permanent appointment. Friedman left Wisconsin and returned to Washington, where he worked for the Division of Research of the United States Treasury. He became a leading spokesman for the withholding tax and clashed frequently with Senator Robert Taft on this issue, despite the enormous respect he held for the Ohio senator.

After World War II, Friedman spent one year at the University of Minnesota before joining the faculty at the University of Chicago in 1946. There he finally found a permanent home, settling into the serious business of economic theory and controversy. His work brought him early recognition. In 1951, he received the John Bates Clark Medal, becoming the third recipient of that award, after Paul Samuelson and Kenneth Boulding. In 1967, Friedman was elected

---

[4] An expanded version was published with Simon Kuznets as *Income from Independent Professional Practice* (New York: National Bureau of Economic Research, 1945).

president of the American Economic Association, and, in 1976, he was awarded what many consider the ultimate accolade: the Nobel Prize in Economics.[5] He retired from the Chicago faculty in 1977, moving to California where he joined the Hoover Institution at Stanford University as a senior research fellow. He continues to play the key part that he began so early in his career in attempting to turn the tide against the new economics.[6]

Milton Friedman's attack on the new economics was many-pronged. First, he painstakingly reconstructed and tested the quantity theory of money. Second, he reemphasized the power of monetary policy. Third, he questioned the Lerner view of the flexibility and potency of fiscal policy and the Lerner-Samuelson belief in the trade-offs between inflation and employment. Fourth, he argued that the orthodox interpretation of the Great Depression was incorrect and constructed his own formula for preventing such catastrophes in the future. Fifth, he challenged the logic of the methodological approaches of Veblen, Chamberlin, and Galbraith. Finally, Friedman restated the classical liberal philosophy in terms pertinent to his own time.

The Quantity Theory of Money

The quantity theory of money is a venerable doctrine, which, as we saw in Chapter 2, goes back in the history of economic thought at least to David Hume and reached its fullest flower in Cambridge at the hands of Alfred Marshall and A.C. Pigou. The theory was presented in most textbooks in a highly rigid and extreme form. Without qualification, it was asserted that a change in the stock of money would produce a proportionate change in prices and money income. In this naive version, where the relation of money and prices was considered so precise, extravagant expectations were created about the possibility of using monetary policy to produce prolonged periods of uninterrupted economic stability and progress. The Keynesians, in using this naive version, argued that changes in velocity were, in fact, so unstable as to make the effects of changes in the quantity of money equally unpredictable.

Friedman developed a much subtler and more sophisticated statement of the quantity theory of money, and refining and giving precision to the Henry Simons version that had been part of the "oral tradition" at Chicago.[7] In this version, velocity is regarded as a variable which is a

---

[5]   Characteristically, Friedman did not consider the Nobel Prize "the pinnacle of my career." The verdict of his peers was more important to him than the opinion of seven people in Stockholm. *Washington Post*, 15 October 1976, p. A1.

[6]   Much of the material on Friedman's career came from the authors' personal correspondence with him. We are also indebted to a series of articles by Rose Friedman, which appeared as a special serialization in *The Oriental Economist* during 1976 under the title "Milton Friedman: Husband and Colleague."

[7]   Friedman's is not the only interpretation of that tradition. For a contrary view, see Don Patinkin, "The Chicago Tradition, the Quantity Theory, and Friedman," *Journal of Money, Credit and Banking* 1 (February 1969): 46–67.

stable function of several other variables. In order to analyze velocity, it is necessary to look at the factors influencing the demand for money. The quantity theory attempts to answer the question: What determines the demand for money? That is, what determines velocity? Friedman's answer is that the demand for money is determined by the following factors: the rate of interest on bonds, the rate of return on stocks, the rate of change of the price level, and how much income is received from the ownership of property that people have. In short, the demand for money is determined by the cost of holding money, which in turn is dependent on the rate of return that can be earned by holding alternative assets. The higher the interest rate on bonds, or yields on equities, and the greater the anticipated rise in the price level, the *greater* will be the incentive to *not* hold idle cash balances.[8]

But the important question is, how stable is the velocity of money? To the Keynesian economist, it is highly variable and unpredictably so. As we saw in Chapter 7, Keynes devised his liquidity preference schedule to show that increases in the quantity of money would be accompanied by a fall in the rate of interest which would lead to an increase in the quantity of money demanded. What is worse, in an extreme situation, there might be a liquidity trap, in which case changes in the stock of money would have no effect on income at all since it could not affect interest rates and, therefore, stimulate investment and income. As we saw in Chapters 9 and 10, both Paul Samuelson and Abba Lerner accepted this as a distinct possibility.

Friedman postulated that the demand for money is a stable function of a limited number of variables that can be reliably specified. A sharp rise in velocity does not, therefore, discredit this version of the quantity theory. Suppose, for example, that such a rise occurs during hyperinflation. In this situation, the cost of holding money would be increasing rapidly, and, therefore, the demand for money would be predicted to decline. The importance of Friedman's formulation is that it sharply limits the number of explicitly specified variables to which the demand for money is related. In short, Friedman hypothesized that there would be a predictable response to the few variables he specifies.

To test this hypothesis, Friedman's students in his famous Money and Banking Workshop at the University of Chicago examined the stability of the demand for money during various episodes in the United States and foreign countries. The chief result of the studies indicated that interest rates do indeed affect the demand for money, as the Friedman and Keynesian versions of the quantity theory predict; but the effect is not very great in magnitude. Furthermore, the rate of

---

[8] Note the relationship between the Friedman and Keynesian formulations. In both, the demand for money is a function of the interest rate. See Milton Friedman, "Money: Quantity Theory," in *International Encyclopedia of the Social Sciences* (New York: Macmillan Co. and the Free Press, 1968), p. 439. Note also that the relationship between changes in the demand for money and changes in the velocity of circulation is *inverse*. The reason is obvious enough: if the demand for money increases, then people will hold more cash, thus slowing the rate at which money circulates in the economy. The reverse is also true.

change in prices has a clear-cut and dramatic effect only during periods of extreme inflations and deflations.

The most significant finding was that velocity is a stable function of long-run income, or what Friedman calls *permanent income*.[9] Since money is a luxury good, the demand for which rises as income rises, one would expect velocity to decline over time as long-run income rises. The policy implication is that the monetary authority, if it wishes to maintain price level stability, must increase the stock of money to offset this decline in velocity.

But the main conclusion that Friedman and his students reached was that the quantity theory of money is an extremely useful tool for analyzing changes in prices and money income. In Friedman's words:

> ... There is perhaps no other empirical relation in economics that has been observed to recur so uniformly under so wide a variety of circumstances as the relation between substantial changes over short periods in the stock of money and in prices; the one is invariably linked with the other and is in the same direction; this uniformity is, I suspect, of the same order as many of the uniformities that form the basis of the physical sciences."[10]

This restatement of the quantity theory went a long way towards rehabilitating the doctrine and putting it back into place as one of the key tools in the economist's kit.

Friedman, however, was not satisfied with this demonstration of the resiliency of the neoclassical monetary theory. He recognized that, in order to effect a successful counterrevolution, it would be necessary to show that the quantity theory was a more powerful instrument of analysis than was the Keynesian alternative. To put this more directly, it was necessary to demonstrate that the demand for money was not only a stable function but was *more* stable than the consumption function and autonomous investment. This was his next order of business.

The Power of Money

In 1963, Friedman presented his findings in one of the most controversial and provocative papers he has ever written. For the first time, someone had attempted directly to test the predictive power of the Keynesian, as opposed to the quantity, theory of money. His conclusion

---

[9]   See Milton Friedman, *A Theory of the Consumption Function* (Princeton: Princeton University Press, 1957), pp. 7–37.

[10]   Milton Friedman, "The Quantity Theory of Money—A Restatement," in idem, ed., *Studies in the Quantity Theory of Money* (Chicago: University of Chicago Press, 1956), pp. 20–21. Adherents of Friedman's restated quantity theory of money and of the importance of monetary, as opposed to fiscal, action in economic stabilization policy have come to be labeled "monetarists." It is a term Friedman considers "unlovely," but no other single term has achieved such currency in referring to Friedmanesque monetary views. The term itself seems to have been coined by Karl Brunner in the late 1960's but did not come into widespread use until the early 1970's. See Karl Brunner, "The Role of Monetary Policy," *Review of the Federal Reserve Bank of St. Louis*, July 1968, pp. 9–29.

was that, contrary to the claims made by the new economics, monetary velocity is stabler than the investment multiplier.

In order to test the hypothesis, Friedman and his student David Meiselman compared a very simple model of the Keynesian and quantity theories, and attempted to discover if there is a better correlation between money and consumption than between Keynesian "investment and consumption."[11] The result indicated that money is a more successful predictor of income than autonomous expenditures (which, for purposes of this study, Friedman defined as the sum of net private investment expenditures plus the government deficit). The results held for year-to-year and quarter-to-quarter changes. What is more, autonomous expenditures seemed to have no explanatory power. Hence, "the critical variable for monetary policy is the stock of money, not interest rates or investment expenditures."[12]

Of course, this finding did not go unchallenged. Other economists, using definitions of autonomous expenditures different from that used by Friedman and Meiselman, concluded that both money and autonomous expenditures are powerful.[13] This interchange with his critics at least proved an important Friedman point. One of the central concepts of the Keynesian income-expenditure approach, autonomous expenditures, is not a clear-cut operational concept. Furthermore, it showed that the Keynesian revolution had by no means produced "a carefully formulated, logically coherent theory of income determination. . . ."[14] Regardless of the definition chosen for "autonomous investment," money turned out to be important in the determination of income, a result which suggested that monetary policy would be effective.

What is more, Friedman's findings have held up astonishingly well over time. In a study conducted by the Federal Reserve Bank of St. Louis, Leonall C. Andersen and Jerry L. Jordan estimated the response of total spending in the economy to changes in various measures of monetary and fiscal actions. They tested the Keynesian proposition that the response of economic activity is more sensitive to fiscal actions than to monetary actions. Their conclusion was that the evidence was not consistent with this proposition. There was, according to Andersen and Jordan, no measurable net influence from fiscal actions during the first quarter of 1952 through the second quarter of 1968. Furthermore, the

---

[11] Consumption was used as a proxy variable for income. Since autonomous expenditures were part of income, correlating them with income would introduce a bias since it would in effect be correlating income with a part of itself.

[12] Milton Friedman and David Meiselman, "The Relative Stability of Monetary Velocity and the Investment Multiplier in the United States, 1897–1958," in The Commission on Money and Credit, *Stabilization Policies* (Englewood Cliffs, N.J.: Prentice Hall, 1963), p. 166.

[13] See, for example, Albert Ando and Franco Modigliani, "The Relative Stability of the Monetary Velocity and the Investment Multiplier," *American Economic Review* 55 (September 1965): 693–728; see also Michael DePrano and Thomas Mayer, "Tests of the Relative Importance of Autonomous Expenditures and Money," *American Economic Review* 55 (September 1965): 729–52.

[14] Milton Friedman and David Meiselman, "Reply to Ando and Modigliani and DePrano and Mayer," *American Economic Review* 55 (September 1965): 753–85.

response of economic activity to monetary actions compared to fiscal actions is greater, more predictable, and faster.[15]

Friedman's theories have been supported by other evidence as well. Those economists who relied on fiscal policy as a major determinant of aggregate demand predicted a marked slowdown in economic activity beginning in late 1968 and extending into 1969. Their predictions were based on the ten percent surtax on individual income taxes that went into effect in July 1968. Friedman and his followers were skeptical that the surcharge would have any effect on slowing down the economy. They based their skepticism on the fact that the money supply was growing roughly at a ten percent annual rate at that time.

In November 1968, Friedman debated these issues with Walter Heller, (who had served as chairman of the Council of Economic Advisers under Presidents Kennedy and Johnson), at the Trinity Place campus of New York University's School of Business. In the course of the discussion, Friedman explained his reason for believing that the surtax would not work.

As he pointed out, it certainly would seem obvious on the face of it, that an increase in taxes would have contractional effects. The disposable income of the taxpayers would be reduced, and through the Keynesian multiplier, income should decline. The trouble with this naive Keynesian view was that it told only half the story. For, if the federal government continued to spend the same amount of money after it imposed the surtax, that must reduce the amount it had to borrow. This must mean that the people who would have loaned the government the funds with which to finance the deficit now had more money on hand. They could use these funds to lend to others or to pay their taxes or for any number of other purposes. But the result should, predicted Friedman, be a fall in the interest rate, which in turn would induce people to borrow the funds that would have been lent to the government before the imposition of the new tax. An increase in private investment, expenditures on consumer durables, and so forth, would all take place. When both sides of the story were told, the two sides offset each other, leaving fiscal policy measures with little or no effect. And that was precisely Friedman's prediction regarding the impact of the tax surcharge.[16]

The tax surcharge episode turned out to provide a controlled experiment of the sort seldom encountered in the social sciences. If you looked at the high-employment budget[17] alone during this period, you

---

[15] Leonall C. Andersen and Jerry L. Jordan, "Monetary and Fiscal Actions: A Test of Their Relative Importance in Economic Stabilization," *Federal Reserve Bank of St. Louis Review* 11 (November 1968): 11–23.

[16] See Milton Friedman, "Has Fiscal Policy Been Oversold?," *Monetary vs. Fiscal Policy, A Dialogue Between Milton Friedman and Walter W. Heller* (New York: W.W. Norton, 1969).

[17] The high-employment budget is a measure of the size of the surplus or deficit which would occur in the federal government budget if the economy were at full or high employment. The actual amount of tax collection is dependent upon the level of economic activity, once the government has set the tax and expenditure rates. In a paper before the Econometric Society in September, 1947,

would forecast, if you were Keynesian, a sharp slowdown in economic activity. If you looked at monetary policy alone, as Friedman would suggest, you would predict no slowdown in the early part of 1969. As it turned out, notwithstanding a tremendous stimulus to restraint in the federal budget, the slowdown predicted by advocates of the new economics did not occur. The money supply continued to expand and so, too, did economic activity. This was completely consistent with Friedman's assertion that the "state of the budget itself has no significant effect on the course of nominal income, on inflation, on deflation or cyclical fluctuations."[18]

This conclusion would not have surprised a quantity theorist as much as a Keynesian. For to the quantity theorist, "money burns a hole in your pocket." That is, an increase in cash relative to other assets, will *always* cause a spillout that has effects in every nook and cranny of the economic system. No sector is safe from its impact. Thus, even if business investment is completely unresponsive to a fall in interest rates (in Hansen's sense), the increased money supply will still have its income-generating effects. To a quantity theorist, the channels through which monetary policy works are quite different from those envisioned by a Keynesian. Friedman takes pains to indicate precisely what those channels are. The following scenario might be likely. If, through open-market purchases of government securities, the monetary authority increases the stock of money, the stock of cash is now high relative to other assets. Money holders may well attempt to purchase common stock to achieve a desired relationship between money and these assets. This causes the price of stock to rise and yields to fall. As this occurs, the relative prices of other assets will make them more attractive to purchase, and so some of the cash spills over into these relatively tempting areas. The chain may be from government securities to stock market equities to houses, durable goods of various kinds, or even consumer goods. But note that the increased money supply spreads out into both investment and consumption goods and services. For as the price of, say, houses rises relative to the renting of apartments, the demand for and the production of dwelling units for rent increases. But this in turn increases the price of such services relative to other assets, undoing the initial effects on divergencies in relative prices. So the train may be traced from relatively low-yielding assets into the purchase of a wide spectrum of assets acting ultimately on services and the income stream.

Notwithstanding Friedman's belief in the potency of monetary weapons, he later felt it necessary to enter a caveat against the use of monetary policy to fine-tune the economy or to apply Lerner's tools of

---

Friedman was one of the first to suggest that we examine fiscal policy in terms of the high-employment budget. The suggestion was later taken up by the Council of Economic Advisers under Walter Heller. See Milton Friedman, "A Monetary and Fiscal Framework for Economic Stability," *American Economic Review* 38 (June 1948).

[18] Friedman, "Has Fiscal Policy Been Oversold?," p. 51.

functional finance. To Friedman, the proven effectiveness of monetary policy might lead policymakers to believe that they could use this device to make minute adjustments in the economy, and so always maintain price level stability and full employment simply by manipulating the stock of money.

Friedman v. Lerner on Functional Finance

Early in his career, Friedman had warned against Lerner's functional finance principles, which came to dominate the thinking of Keynesian-oriented policymakers. In a review article of Lerner's *Economics of Control* published in 1947, Friedman referred to Lerner's functional finance as a "brilliant exercise in logic," and went on to say that

> It strips governmental fiscal instruments to their essential: taxing and spending, borrowing and lending, and buying and selling; and throws into sharp relief the function of each. In the process it throws into discard conventional patterns of expression, verbal cliches which at times embody valid implications of more subtle reasoning but which, taken by themselves, muddle analysis of the effect of governmental actions. Reading Lerner's discussion of functional finance is almost sure to induce a much-required reorganization of the mental filing-case that one has been using to classify the factors involved in governmental fiscal operations.[19]

Although Friedman admired Lerner's dialectical skills, he expressed the opinion that the problem of maintaining economic stability is far more complex than Lerner's rules implied. The work of Arthur Burns and Wesley Mitchell on business cycles had impressed upon Friedman the unevenness and variable timing of economic activities. Economists not only find it extremely difficult to predict the course of business but even to identify the current situation. Of course, to Lerner, this difficulty would be irrelevant. The errors in forecasting are unimportant in his scheme of things because the government can always reverse itself by changing policy. But to Friedman, this facile optimism regarding the power of government to fine-tune conflicts with the fact that

> . . . Neither government action nor the effect of that action is instantaneous. There is likely to be a lag between the need for action and government recognition of this need; a further lag between recognition of the need for action and the taking of action; and still a further lag between the action and its effects.[20]

To Friedman, the time lags are a substantial proportion of the duration of cyclical activity. Since we do not have the ability to forecast correctly both the direction and the magnitude of the necessary policy, gov-

---

[19] Milton Friedman, "Lerner on the Economics of Control," *Journal of Political Economy* 55 (October 1947); reprinted in Milton Friedman, *Essays in Positive Economics* (Chicago: University of Chicago Press, 1953), p. 313.

[20] Friedman, *Positive Economics*, p. 315.

ernmental attempts to use Lerner's functional finance prescriptions, far from stabilizing the economy, might very well exacerbate the fluctuations. "By the time an error is recognized and corrective action taken," Friedman points out, "the damage may be done and corrective action may itself turn into a further error."[21]

The Great Contraction

One of the most significant parts of Friedman's attack on the new economics consisted of a reexamination of the conventional interpretation of the Great Depression. As was pointed out at the beginning of this chapter, the period of the 1930's was the great watershed in the history of the private market economy, for that catastrophe caused a searching reexamination of the precepts of laissez-faire economic philosophy. No other series of events in America has led to such a dramatic shift in opinion regarding the role of the state in economic life. What is more, this change was recognized early.

In a paper presented to the American Economic Association in 1946, Clarence E. Ayres, one of America's leading adherents of Veblenian economics, commented on the suddenness with which economic ideas changed in the thirties, the extraordinary rapidity with which they gained adherents, and the amazing response which was extended to Keynes's ideas. In this sense, he referred to the Keynesian revolution as being "comparable to the Darwinian revolution or even perhaps the Copernican revolution."[22] The events of that time led to a scrutinizing reappraisal of the roles that should be assigned to the state in economic life. As Victor Abramson pointed out, "There can be no doubt that the Great Depression has had the pervasive result of stimulating an awareness of the importance of the positive contribution that government can make to the maximization of social product."[23]

Thus, it was widely agreed that the Depression was evidence that the private market economy is inherently unstable and that only a vigorously interventionist government can offset or prevent such episodes. Furthermore, as we have seen, monetary policy fell into disrepute because it was believed to have failed to bring about recovery. Even Henry Simons shared Keynes's view as to the causes of the Great Depression. His interpretation of the evidence led him to place greatest reliance on fiscal powers as the key weapon of economic policy.[24]

---

[21] Friedman, *Positive Economics*, p. 316. Friedman's analysis of the problem of the destabilizing effects of countercyclical actions in the absence of accurate economic forecasting techniques is contained in "The Effects of a Full-Employment Policy on Economic Stability: A Formal Analysis," in idem, *Positive Economics*, pp. 117–32. A fuller statement of his "lags" hypothesis can be found in idem, "A Monetary and Fiscal Framework for Economic Stability."

[22] Clarence E. Ayres, "The Impact of the Great Depression on Economic Thinking," *American Economic Review* 36 (May 1946): p. 112.

[23] Victor Abramson, "Discussion," *American Economic Review* 36 (May 1946): 146.

[24] See Milton Friedman, "The Monetary Theory and Policy of Henry Simons," *Journal of Law and Economics* 10 (October 1967): 1–3.

Friedman's thoroughgoing study of the events of 1929-39 reached almost precisely the opposite conclusion. His examination led him to conclude that the 1929-33 debacle was an unnecessary episode and that the Federal Reserve System bears the main responsibility for the Great Depression. The sharp and unprecedented decline in the stock of money was a consequence of the monetary authority's failure to provide the liquidity that would have enabled the banks which were failing (and, therefore, destroying demand and time deposits) to meet their obligations. Furthermore, far from monetary policy having failed during the contraction, the period "is in fact a tragic testimonial to the importance of monetary forces."[25] At the time, this was an astounding conclusion. Friedman's claim, if correct, suggested that the belief held by many intellectuals and others who influence popular thought that government intervention, planning and control is necessary to maintain a stable economic environment may have been formed on a misconception of the facts. If the Great Depression is responsible in large part for shaping not only the intellectual community's attitude toward economic policy but also its philosophy of government, then Friedman's research might have shattering consequences. For it indicates that economic instability, far from resulting from unfettered free enterprise, has largely been born of inappropriate government intervention. Indeed, as Friedman put it, "Perhaps the most remarkable feature of the record is the adaptability and flexibility that the private economy has so frequently shown under such extreme provocation."[26]

The book in which Friedman presented the results of his research into America's economic history is a massive and scholarly work, written in collaboration with Anna J. Schwartz and entitled *A Monetary History of the United States, 1867-1960*. This is the book which Friedman considers his most important work.[27] Certainly, it is a body of research which has sparked a very spirited debate in the years since its appearance. Whether or not he finally won the debate, Friedman redirected attention, by his pioneering study of monetary forces, to a question which had, up to that point, been largely taken for granted by the Keynesian interpretations of the Great Depression.

Friedman set out to examine the historical experience which he considered so important in supplementing the theoretical work on the direction of influence between monetary change and business condi-

---

[25] Milton Friedman and Anna J. Schwartz, *A Monetary History of the United States, 1867–1960* (Princeton: Princeton University Press, 1963), p. 300.

[26] Milton Friedman, *A Program for Monetary Stability* (New York: Fordham University Press, 1959), p. 9.

[27] In personal correspondence, Friedman said that the work that he thinks "most deserves to be remembered, yet which has not been much noted, are the final pages of my *Price Theory* dealing with capital theory. It has always been my intention to write a little book based on those pages, but whether I shall ever get around to doing so or not, I do not know." (Personal correspondence, 22 June 1967). Since these pages are highly technical contributions to the most abstruse of all subjects in economics and have little direct influence on economic policy, we shall not attempt a summary of Friedman's presentation in these pages. The interested reader should consult Milton Friedman, *Price Theory* (Chicago: Aldine Publishing Co., 1976), pp. 283–322.

tions. From the point of view of the Keynesian revolution, the most significant period covered by *A Monetary History* were the years 1929 to 1933.[28]

The popular view which emerged from examinations of the events following 1929 was that "money does not matter."[29] This is not, Friedman insists, what a careful analysis of this period reveals. Instead, Friedman and Schwartz interpret the events of these four years as strongly implying that money is crucial. They assert that monetary policy, far from failing during the contraction, was never really tried.

Friedman and Schwartz note that there might have been a business recession from 1929 to 1930 as a consequence of the Federal Reserve System's undue concern with stock market levels. Monetary policy was unusually tight. From 1927 to 1929, a period of business expansion, prices were stable while the stock of money declined. From 1929 to 1930, there was a 3 percent fall in the stock of money, more than it had fallen in all except the most severe depression periods. But the stock market crash, which some economists take to have triggered the Great Depression, would probably have led to a rather ordinary recession.[30] There were no bank failures on any substantial scale, nor any sign of weakening of public confidence. Prior to the Federal Deposit Insurance Corporation, the best sign of the public's attitude towards the banking system was the ratio of deposits to currency. This ratio remained relatively high during this period. Until September 1930, there was no evidence of a banking crisis or a liquidity decline.

It is during this period from 1930 to 1933 that Friedman and Schwartz feel the monetary authorities bear chief responsibility for the economic performance of the American economy. A concatenation of bank failures spread across the country, culminating in the failure of the Bank of the United States in New York on December 11, 1930. Although an ordinary commercial bank, this bank was widely believed by people abroad and immigrants in the United States to be a government bank. The failure of this bank precipitated an enormous liquidity crisis. The character of the contraction changed after the failure of this large bank, which had held roughly $200 million of deposits. There was a marked fall in the ratio of deposits to currency. As depositors started to withdraw deposits, a string of bank failures followed like a line of toppling dominoes.

What role did the Federal Reserve play during this period? Friedman and Schwartz insist that the Federal Reserve behaved impassively and inactively! They found no evidence that the Federal Reserve engaged in

---

[28] The chapters of *A Monetary History* covering the period 1929–33 have been published separately as Milton Friedman and Anna J. Schwartz, *The Great Contraction 1929–33* (Princeton: Princeton University Press, 1965).

[29] Or, at least, that monetary policy could not stimulate economic recovery. A popular analogy of the 1950's was to say that monetary policy was "like pushing on a string"; that is, you could pull on it to check business expansion, but you could not push on it to stimulate recovery.

[30] For example, see John Kenneth Galbraith, *The Great Crash 1929* (Boston: Houghton Mifflin, 1955).

open-market operations or tried in any significant way to provide banks with liquidity. This is a surprising conclusion, since the system was established as "a lender of last resort" largely to provide just such liquidity during the kind of crisis that occurred during this period. Notwithstanding the pleas of George Harrison, the governor of the Federal Reserve Bank of New York, that the system engage in open-market operations to purchase securities (and thus place cash in the hands of the public and the banks), the Federal Reserve System did nothing while scores of banks failed.

The next important date in the Friedman-Schwartz chronology of events is September 1931. In that month, Great Britain went off the gold standard. This led to an external drain of gold from the United States. In response to that drain, the Federal Reserve System *raised* discount rates. Indeed, within two weeks, the system raised discount rates more than it had ever done before. The discount rate in New York went from 2½ percent on October 9 to 3½ percent on October 16. The increased rates did end the gold drain within two weeks. At the same time, however, there was a spectacular rise in bank failures. In October 1931, 522 commercial banks closed their doors and in the next three months, 875 did the same. During this period (August 1931 to January 1932), the money stock fell 12 percent.

At only one time in the period, Friedman and Schwartz point out, were expansionary open-market operations of any significance attempted by the monetary authorities. After the second of the three banking crises, there was growing support in Congress for more government spending and monetary expansion. These views were attacked in the business and financial communities as "greenbackism" and "inflationary." Nevertheless, congressional pressure resulted in the Federal Reserve beginning large-scale open-market purchases in April 1932. By August, the Federal Reserve had raised its security holdings by an amount of roughly $1 billion. Bank failures subsided and interest rates fell; soon all economic indicators began to rise. The recovery was only temporary, however; in late 1932, the Federal Reserve once again lapsed into passivity and the money stock ceased to grow and began falling in January 1933. Overall, the money stock had declined by over one-third by early 1933.[31]

Friedman and Schwartz believe that if vigorous open-market operations had been employed in 1930, the banking crisis could have been avoided and the depression would not have been so deep. Moreover, if Benjamin Strong, the influential governor of the New York Reserve Bank and a staunch advocate of open-market operations, had not died

---

[31] These figures should have come as a revelation to established Keynesians in the early 1960's. As late as 1958, R. F. Harrod, Keynes's biographer and one of his leading disciples wrote:

> In the thirties, after the Wall Street crash, there were terrific non-monetary forces making for depression. The central banks, both in Britain and the United States, did all they could to counteract them.... With this end in view, they maintained a credit policy of ultra-ease.

Roy Harrod, *Policy Against Inflation* (London: Macmillan and Co., 1958), p. 63. We note below some of the Keynesian counterarguments against the Friedman-Schwartz arguments.

in 1928, there might have been large-scale open-market purchases by the Federal Reserve System early in the contraction. Had such purchases been made, say Friedman and Schwartz, the financial collapse and the depression which ensued might have been avoided.

The publication of *A Monetary History of the United States* created shock waves throughout the economics profession. For, as we have noted, Friedman and Schwartz were arguing that the interpretation of the great contraction based on Keynesian analysis was incorrect. Monetary policy *did* matter; the 1930's were, in fact, dramatic proof of just that fact. That was a very bold claim, and reviewers quickly voiced their skepticism. "My overall reaction to Friedman and Schwartz's *History* is mixed," wrote Robert Clower in 1964. "Viewed as an intellectual accomplishment, the book has qualities of greatness. . . . Still, the thread of money has strands which even Friedman and Schwartz have no hope of unravelling."[32] Keynesian macroeconomists continued to attack. In 1976, MIT economic historian Peter Temin published the most comprehensive attack on Friedman-Schwartz, a book entitled *Did Monetary Forces Cause the Great Depression?*[33]

Temin employed econometric tests to distinguish between two competing "hypotheses" about the Great Depression. Proponents of what he called the *spending hypothesis* claim that the Depression resulted from a fall in aggregate demand. Temin traces the roots of this hypothesis back to the early attempts of Alvin Hansen to explain the Depression.[34] The other view is what Temin calls the *money hypothesis*, which he identifies with Friedman and Schwartz. Though Temin musters a considerable array of data and arguments to show that the money hypothesis is not supported by the evidence, his arguments boil down to two crucial points:

1. According to Temin, the *real* stock of money *increased* between 1929 and 1931. "If the real supply of money did not fall," insists Temin, "it follows that it could not have caused the level of real income to fall by means of this relation."[35]
2. Temin insists that, if the money hypothesis is correct, short-term interest rates should have *risen* sharply in response to the alleged decline in the money supply.[36] But, insists Temin, short-term rates *did not* rise; in fact, they *fell* between 1929 and 1931. Temin's data are not consistent with the Friedman-Schwartz model.

---

[32] Robert Clower, "Monetary History and Positive Economics," *Journal of Economic History* 24 (September 1964): p. 379.

[33] Peter Temin, *Did Monetary Forces Cause the Great Depression?* (New York: W.W. Norton, 1976).

[34] Temin, pp. 31–3. The econometric models employed by Temin and others who have examined this problem were developed by one of Paul Samuelson's most brilliant students, Lawrence Klein. Klein was awarded the Nobel Prize in Economics in 1980.

[35] Temin, p. 170.

[36] Temin, pp. 99–102. The argument is rather involved. The most obvious relation Temin points to as an explanation is the *IS–LM* analysis developed by Hansen and Hicks. If the supply of money falls, the *LM* curve will shift upwards. This will produce a movement along the *IS* curve so that the new equilibrium interest rate should be higher as a consequence of the fall in the supply of money.

Proponents of the spending thesis could take little solace from Temin's econometric results. For, while he insisted that the money hypothesis was not supported by the data, Temin was unable to support the spending hypothesis either.[37] Apparently, neither explanation is complete enough to be a wholly satisfactory explanation of the historical record. By ignoring monetary factors altogether, the Keynesian explanations are unable to account for the events connected with the collapse of the financial sector, a point which Friedman and Schwartz emphasize in their criticisms of the accepted interpretation. Friedman and Schwartz stress the importance of money, but they cannot explain why the monetary authorities were so inept. Ultimately, they must fall back on what historians call a "great man" theory of the depression: had Benjamin Strong lived, the debacle *might* have been averted.[38]

The criticisms of Friedman and Schwartz, while they may leave the causes of the Great Depression in some doubt, have not diminished Friedman's accomplishment in revitalizing interest in the effectiveness of monetary policy. His empirical arguments forced economists to take a closer look at the accepted wisdom—and the closer look had caused the profession to once again incorporate monetary factors in their macroeconomic models.

Friedman's study of the Great Depression had another consequence on his own thinking. He was impressed with the extent to which one man, Benjamin Strong, might have been so important in preventing a depression. Economic stability, it would seem, depends on fate, luck, and happenstance. Nor was this the only time that successful economic policy in a financial crisis had depended upon the leadership of one or more outstanding individuals willing to assume that leadership and responsibility. To Friedman, such a situation cried out for alternative arrangements: a system not resting on the capriciousness of nature or the whim of gods. Friedman's most developed and far-reaching scheme for monetary reform as an alternative to this perilous situation had been presented in one of his earlier books, *A Program for Monetary Stability*. We now turn to this analysis.

Toward Monetary Reform

To Friedman, a stable monetary framework is essential for effective operation of a private market economy. In such an economy, the

---

[37] Temin's test of the spending thesis found that the Depression stemmed from a very large fall in consumption in 1930. He could not, however, explain the source of this decline with his Keynesian consumption function. As he rather ruefully noted, "It is somewhat unsatisfactory to say that the Depression was started by an unexplained event. . . ." Temin, p. 83. Thomas Mayer has challenged Temin's interpretation in his article, "Consumption in the Great Depression," *Journal of Political Economy* 86 (February 1978): 139–45.

[38] Ironically, one of the leading proponents of the new economics tends to agree with Friedman and Schwartz that the leadership of the Federal Reserve was crippled by Strong's death and the resentment of other banks to New York's dominance. (See Galbraith, *The Great Crash 1929*.) For an account of the great contraction which stresses the institutional weaknesses of the American economy at that time, see Roger L. Ransom, *Coping With Capitalism: The Economic Transformation of the American Economy: 1776–1980* (New York: Prentice–Hall, 1981), Chapter 5.

central tasks for the monetary authorities are to: (1) set an external limit to the amount of money, and (2) prevent counterfeiting. If these tasks are carried out properly, a stable monetary framework will result.

Friedman claims that economic cycles in the United States have been produced or intensified by government intervention or uncertainty. Until the most recent experience, major inflations in United States history have all been associated with war and were produced by the printing press or its equivalent. The Federal Reserve System was established with the specific responsibility of stabilizing monetary conditions and ostensibly was armed with adequate power to prevent great instability. However, Friedman charges that, in the half-century following the creation of the system in 1914, we have experienced more instability in the stock of money and in general economic conditions than in the half-century prior to 1914. Friedman traces through the evidence of various inflations and contractions to support this contention and concludes that government intervention in monetary matters has proven to be a "... potent source of instability."[39] His interpretation of the historical record is that "... the central problem is not to construct a highly sensitive instrument that can continuously offset instability introduced by other factors, but rather to prevent monetary arrangements from themselves becoming a primary source of instability."[40] In other words, unlike Abba Lerner, Friedman does not think that the nation needs a skilled monetary driver of the economic vehicle always turning the wheel to adjust to the unexpected turns in the road, but rather a way to keep a backseat monetary passenger from occasionally leaning over the seat and jerking the steering wheel, threatening to send the car off the road.[41]

Friedman argues that open-market operations alone are sufficient to carry out monetary policy. At the same time, he convincingly argues that two other monetary tools, discount rate and reserve requirements, are defective tools for affecting the quantity of "high-powered money," and, thus, for altering the stock of money in circulation.[42] Both, he thinks, are blunt instruments and yield unpredictable results.

Friedman's views on monetary policy were enormously influenced by Henry Simons's rules v. authorities argument. As was noted in the last chapter, Simons favored price level stability as the general goal of monetary policy. However, Friedman thinks there are many problems that would arise with this as a general goal, since changes in the level of

---

[39] Friedman, *A Program for Monetary Stability*, p. 23.

[40] Friedman, *A Program for Monetary Stability*, p. 23.

[41] Obviously, Lerner did not agree. See Abba P. Lerner, "Milton Friedman's *A Program for Monetary Stability:* A Review," *American Statistical Association Journal*, March 1962, pp. 211–20. As we noted in Chapter 9, Paul Samuelson has also taken sharp exception to Friedman's proposals dealing with monetary policy. See the discussion in *Milton Friedman and Paul A. Samuelson Discuss the Economic Responsibility for Government* (College Station, Tex.: Center for Education and Research in Free Enterprise, 1980).

[42] "High-powered money" is the amount of currency outside of the Treasury and Federal Reserve available for use by the public, plus all deposits at the Federal Reserve banks. The quantity of money that can be created by private banks is directly proportional to the amount of high-powered money.

prices and changes in the money supply are uncertain at best in the short run. Besides, the Federal Reserve System does not control the price level, it controls the stock of money. Since monetary changes have their effect only after a lag and that lag is long and variable, Friedman thinks it would be better to have a "rule" connected more directly with something the Federal Reserve System can control: the stock of money.[43]

Friedman's rule is that the stock of money be increased at a fixed rate year-in and year-out without any variation in the rate of increase to meet cyclical fluctuations. Friedman insists that, according to his definition of the money supply (currency outside commercial banks plus demand deposits), empirical evidence for the ninety years following the Civil War indicates that an annual growth rate in the money stock of about five percent per year would be most desirable.[44] The research findings of Friedman and his co-workers had demonstrated the power of money to influence economic activity. But this demonstration had perhaps proved too convincing. The change in opinion from reliance on fiscal policy through the use of Lerner's functional finance tools and Hansen's compensatory fiscal policy to a thoroughgoing reliance on a fine-tuning approach to monetary policy suggested

---

[43] The notion that monetary actions affect economic conditions only after a lag that is long and variable is one of Friedman's more controversial conclusions that has led to much debate and empirical testing. Friedman's fixed-rule policy proposal rests in part on his observations regarding this lag in effect of monetary policy. To Friedman, this position is supported by his conception of the channels through which monetary policy works, and extensive historical studies. He also buttresses his argument with observations about the sheer inertia of the government decision-making process and the "political costs of implicitly or explicitly admitting error by reversing course rapidly." See Milton Friedman, "The Lag in Effect of Monetary Policy," *Journal of Political Economy* 69 (October 1961): 447–66; J.M. Culbertson, "Friedman on the Lag in Effect of Monetary Policy," *Journal of Political Economy* 68 (December 1960): 617–21; and Milton Friedman, "The Lag in Effect of Monetary Policy: Reply," *Journal of Political Economy* 69 (October 1961): 467–77. Support for Friedman's lag hypothesis is also found in the accuracy of Friedman's predictions. For example, in October 1979, Friedman noted that the Federal Reserve System had sharply reduced the rate of growth in the money supply and predicted that a recession would hit in April 1980, based on his empirical estimate of a six-month lag between the taking of action and their effects on economic activity. As *Business Week* reported, "Friedman's forecast was right on the money." See *Business Week*, 12 May 1980, p. 16. Friedman has received much praise in the press for his pinpoint accuracy in prediction.

[44] Friedman's initial choice of a growth rate was based on his findings for *A Monetary History of The United States*. He has since modified his views somewhat. In his paper "The Optimum Quantity of Money," he suggested that a 2 percent rate of increase might prove better than the 5 percent rule. While admitting in "a final schizophrenic note" that his new view contradicted his earlier position, Friedman insisted that in any event either ". . . a 5 percent or a 2 percent rule would be far superior to the monetary policy we have actually followed. . . . I shall continue to support the 5 percent rule as an intermediate objective greatly superior to present practice." See Milton Friedman, "The Optimum Quantity of Money," in idem, *The Optimum Quantity of Money, and Other Essays* (Chicago: Aldine Publishing Co., 1969), p. 48.

Friedman's change of mind was doubtlessly a result of long and hard reflection on the logical properties of a new analysis that was worked out after he had become the persuasive champion of the 5 percent rule. In testimony before the Committee on Banking and Currency of the House of Representatives in 1964, after Friedman had strongly supported his 5 percent rule of monetary increase, Representative Reuss of Wisconsin suggested that should he be proven wrong, Friedman would be "the first man to come in here and confess error and say change the law tomorrow." Friedman replied, "It is a natural human quality of every one of us that the hardest thing in the world to do . . . is to admit error." U.S., Congress, House, Subcommittee on Domestic Finance, Committee on Banking and Currency, *The Federal Reserve System after Fifty Years*, 88th Cong., 2nd sess., 1961, p. 1143. It would appear that Friedman's change of opinion must not have come easily.

that the pendulum may have swung too far back to the pre-Depression period of thinking. Friedman devoted his presidential address at the annual meetings of the American Economic Association in 1967 to the question of the limits of monetary policy.[45]

Inflation and Interest Rates

Perhaps the most important conclusion reached in this address was Friedman's statement that monetary policy cannot peg interest rates or the rate of unemployment for more than limited periods. In the typical Keynesian-oriented textbook approach, an increase in the stock of money, given the negatively sloping liquidity preference schedule, would mean that at the current rate of interest there is an excess supply of money. People can be induced to hold this larger quantity of money only at lower interest rates. But in their attempts to get out of money and into bonds, the prices of securities rise and the yields fall.

Friedman agrees with this analysis only to a point. For he adds that this initial drop in interest rates is only the beginning of the process. As he demonstrated in his restatement of the quantity theory of money and in his explanation of the channels through which monetary policy works, the increasing rate of monetary expansion will have effects not only on investment markets (resulting from the initial fall in interest rates) but on all spending, thereby raising income. But the rising income raises the liquidity preference schedule and the price level. These effects reverse the downward pressure on interest rates, eventually returning them to their initial level. Furthermore, if the public comes to expect that a higher rate of monetary growth will correspond with an increasing price level, borrowers will be willing to pay and lenders will insist upon higher interest rates. So Friedman sees four effects of an increasing rate of growth in the money stock:

---

[45] Milton Friedman, "The Role of Monetary Policy," *American Economic Review* 58 (March 1968): 1–17.

The questions of functional finance and fine-tuning of the economy were still very much in Friedman's mind at the time he delivered his presidential address. Gerald R. Rosen interviewed Friedman in his Washington hotel suite just before he presented his address. At one point, Rosen asked Friedman how he would evaluate the new economics' accomplishments between 1961 and 1967. Friedman replied:

It's very hard to say that the New Economics has accomplished very much of anything, except getting a great deal of publicity. I have always been amused by the fact that the New Economists emphasize fine-tuning—or changing direction of the economy within a short span of time. But if you look at what actually happened, it certainly did not occur over a short span of time. The 1964 tax cut was said to be an absolute necessity in 1962. It was stressed again in 1963, and it was finally enacted in 1964.

So the fine-tuning took two years. Once again, if you take the present 1967 surtax proposal, it was first made a year ago and said to be absolutely essential then. The proposal was later, in effect, retracted and then reinstated. If a surtax is enacted, it will certainly not be before sometime in 1968. So it would seem clear that whatever the New Economics has accomplished, it is not on the side of fine-tuning through the tax route.

In this interview, Friedman repeated one of his favorite propositions, "The best is often the enemy of the good," to point out that the use of both monetary and fiscal policy according to the well-intentioned precepts of functional finance has made the economy more erratic rather than smoother. See "Has the New Economics Failed? An Interview with Milton Friedman," *Dun's Review* 91 (February 1968): 38–39, 93–96.

1. *A Liquidity Effect*: This is the initial impact of a falling rate of interest, described above.
2. *An Income Effect*: As the increasing stock of money increases income, the demand for money increases leading to a shift upwards in the liquidity preference schedule. This will tend to send the interest rate back to its initial level.
3. *A Price Effect*: The increased spending resulting from the increased money supply will raise the price level, thus reducing the real quantity of money—and also raising interest rates back to their initial level.
4. *A Price Expectations Effect*: Since, as a result of the inflation, the borrower expects to pay off his loans in dollars of reduced purchasing power, he is willing to pay more for the use of money. And since the lender has the same expectation with regard to the rising price level, he will insist on a higher price for the use of his money. This causes interest rates to rise above their original level.

Paradoxically and contrary to the Keynesian teaching, Friedman concluded that

> . . . Low interest rates are a sign that monetary policy *has been tight*—in the sense that the stock of money has grown slowly; high interest rates are a sign that monetary policy *has been easy*—in the sense that the stock of money has grown rapidly. . . . These considerations . . . explain why interest rates are such a misleading indicator of whether monetary policy is "tight" or "easy." For that, it is far better to look at the rate of change of the quantity of money.[46]

This analysis of the relation between inflation and interest rates seems to square with the situation in the United States during the 1960's and 1970's, when the increasing stock of money was accompanied by rising prices and interest rates. During those decades, the United States economy experienced one of its severest inflations and, at the same time, record-high interest rates. Furthermore, it squares with the evidence in countries that have had the most persistent inflations, such as Brazil, Chile, and Argentina, where interest rates are highest.[47]

Inflation and the "Trade-off":
The Accelerationist Hypothesis

Friedman's view of inflation leads him to deny the importance of Lerner's and Samuelson's emphasis on the trade-offs between inflation and employment. In regard to Lerner's notion of sellers' inflation, Friedman argues that the empirical evidence simply does not support

---

[46] Friedman, "The Role of Monetary Policy," p. 7. See also Milton Friedman, "Factors Affecting the Level of Interest Rates," *Proceedings of the 1968 Conference on Savings and Residential Financing* (Chicago: United Saving and Loan League, 1968), pp. 10–17.

[47] An excellent discussion of the issues surrounding the Friedman v. Keynes view of the relation between interest rates and the price level can be found in "A Classical Look at 'Real Cost' of Money," *Business Week*, 28 June 1969, pp. 130–31.

the theory. In the postwar period, for example, prices in the more competitive sectors of the economy rose more rapidly than did prices in the monopolistic sectors. As an example, Friedman notes that the wages of domestic servants rose more rapidly than did the wages of steelworkers.

Nevertheless, for the 1933-37 period, Friedman admits the existence of a sellers' inflation. He attributes this rise in the price level to a very large rise in the stock of money resulting from a gold influx, in combination with a period of growing strength of unions and the price regulations associated with Roosevelt's attempt to stabilize prices in the early years of the New Deal. Friedman's main objection to Lerner's thesis is that Lerner identifies "stickiness" in prices with "administered prices." Administered prices are a reflection of monopoly power on the part of a buyer or a seller. Friedman feels that stickiness in prices occurs when people become adjusted to rising prices and therefore routinely renegotiate contracts based on their anticipation of future inflation. In such a situation, there may still be a tendency for prices and wages to rise even after the monetary basis for inflation has been eliminated. In short, the Phillips Curve becomes vertical.[48]

Because of Friedman's views on people's ability to adjust to inflation so that price increases become fully anticipated, he rejects the Samuelson-Lerner view that there is, in the long run, a trade-off between inflation and the level of unemployment. It is true, Friedman argues, that an increase in the rate of inflation can have the *temporary* effect of reducing unemployment; but as people come to anticipate inflation, they start adjusting their contracts, interest rates rise, and the initial benefit proves ephemeral. In order to stimulate employment, it becomes necessary to inflate at a still faster rate. As Friedman put it, "I would be inclined to say that if a 2 percent rate of inflation is consistent with any given level of employment from the long-run point of view, then a zero percent rate of inflation is also consistent."[49]

This viewpoint is called the *accelerationist hypothesis* because it predicts that any attempt to reduce the level of unemployment below the point where the Phillips Curve cuts the horizontal axis must lead to

---

[48] Lerner eventually came to accept this view of inflationary expectations and devised his Market Anti-Inflation Plan as an adjunct to his functional finance to cure it. See the discussion in Chapter 10.

[49] Milton Friedman, *Proceedings of a Symposium on Money, Interest Rates and Economic Activity* (Washington, D.C.: American Bankers Association, 1967), p. 121. See also, idem, "The Role of Monetary Policy," pp. 7–11; and especially idem, *Unemployment Versus Inflation? An Evaluation of the Phillips Curve* (London: Institute of Economic Affairs, 1975). This lecture, delivered in September 1974, contains the fullest exposition of Friedman's views on this topic. His Nobel lecture was also devoted to a discussion of these issues. See Milton Friedman, "Inflation and Unemployment," *Journal of Political Economy* 85 (June 1977): 451–72.

As we saw in Chapter 9, Paul Samuelson does not completely accept Friedman's analysis of this problem. Samuelson remains skeptical of the view that there is never any money illusion. Although he believes that the long-run Phillips Curve is twisted toward the vertical, he does not believe that people make the necessary adjustments to make it completely vertical. In his Nobel Prize address, Friedman argued that there is reason to believe that the long-run Phillips Curve is *positively* sloped.

an accelerated inflation. It is also termed the *natural rate hypothesis* because Friedman emphasized what he called a "natural rate of unemployment" (a phrase borrowed from Wicksell who referred to the "natural rate of interest"). In Friedman's use of the term, he does not refer to some minimum level of unemployment below which the economy cannot be pushed. He means that there is a level of unemployment consistent with real conditions in the labor market. That is, he agreed with Keynes that there is always some frictional and transitional unemployment in the economy. The level depends upon such factors as the amount of information regarding the availability of workers and jobs; the number of workers in transition between jobs; workers in the process of retraining for new skills; the composition of the labor force in terms of age and sex; and the extent of unemployment insurance relief, which might reduce the pressure to search for new jobs when unemployment occurs.

Friedman makes the point that any attempt to reduce unemployment below its "natural rate" through monetary and fiscal policy would only lead to accelerated inflation. This result, as we have seen, follows because people will shift their anticipations. Current inflation must always be ahead of anticipated inflation in order to keep unemployment below the natural rate. An important implication of Friedman's analysis was that expectations and their formulation must be given high priority in macroeconomic analysis. A significant offshoot of Friedman's approach, and of his monetarism generally, was the development of a new approach to macroeconomics during the 1970's: "rational expectations."

The Rational Expectations Hypothesis

Both Lerner and Friedman insist that peoples' expectations with regard to price movements play a crucial role in encouraging inflationary tendencies in the economy. Until the mid-1970's, the dominant hypothesis in macroeconomics concerning the formation of expectations was called the *adaptive expectations hypothesis*. This theory said that people form and revise their expectations about inflation on the basis of the difference between the current rate of inflation and the anticipated rate. If the current rate is 15 percent but the anticipated rate was 10 percent, the anticipated rate will be revised upward by some fraction of the difference between 15 and 10. The anticipated rate is formed as a weighted average of past rates of inflation. Those rates of inflation farther back in time are given less weight than the more recent rates.

The adaptive expectations hypothesis was severely shaken by the development of the *rational expectations hypothesis*, which emerged in the 1970's. The seminal paper on the new hypothesis was by John F. Muth in 1961.[50] The notion did not have great impact until Robert

---

[50] John F. Muth, "Rational Expectations and the Theory of Price Movements," *Econometrica* 29 (July 1961): 315–35.

Lucas of the University of Chicago and Thomas Sargent of the University of Minnesota applied the idea to the theory of macroeconomic policy, where it has been shown to have startling implications.[51] In essence, the argument is that the adaptive expectations hypothesis cannot be taken seriously as a description of the way in which people form their anticipations. People are not going to base their expectations solely on the past history of prices as that approach assumes. Rather, on the average, they are going to form their anticipations on the basis of a scheme that is consistent with the way inflation is really being generated. Muth argued that people expect what economic theory predicts. Sometimes they will form anticipations on the basis of adaptive expectations; at other times they will not. But they will be right in the long run.

What does this arcane-sounding hypothesis have to do with the question of economic policymaking? What are its implications? As Franco Modigliani put it in his presidential address to the American Economic Association in 1976, "The death blow to the already battered Keynesian position was to come . . . by incorporating into Friedman's model the so-called rational expectations hypothesis."[52] The rational expectations idea was implicit in much of what Friedman wrote about inflation during the 1960's and most especially in his presidential address. But nowhere did he make an explicit statement of this insight. Only after Robert Lucas applied Muth's idea to stabilization policy did the rational expectations "revolution" occur.

The rational expectations extension of Friedman's model leads to the conclusion that no systematic economic policy can be devised that will be successful in influencing the level of real output. Moreover, as Friedman had long argued, a stable set of predictable rules should be devised in place of government policy designed to manipulate the economy. This follows from the simple idea, expressed so well by Abraham Lincoln, that "you can't fool all of the people all of the time." Keynesian economics was based on the premise that you could do so. As we saw in the chapter on Keynes, he assumed that workers were perpetually subject to a "money illusion." They bargained for and responded to changes in money wages, not real wages. Monetary and fiscal policies were effective because they caused the price level to rise and brought about a fall in the real wage rate. Firms would have increased profits, since the rise in prices was greater than the rise in the cost of labor. This would induce employers to offer more employment. Workers, believing that their real wage had not fallen and, in some instances, that it had risen, would accept the offer of employment. In

[51] Robert E. Lucas, Jr., "Expectations and the Neutrality of Money," *Journal of Economic Theory* 4 (April 1972): 102–24; Thomas J. Sargent, "Rational Expectations, the Real Rate of Interest and the Natural Rate of Unemployment," *Brookings Papers on Economic Activity* 2 (1973): 429–72.

[52] Franco Modigliani, "The Monetarist Controversy, or Should We Forsake Stabilization Policies?," *American Economic Review* 67 (March 1977): 1–19. It might be noted in passing that Modigliani was himself an important contributor to the formulation of the synthesis which produced the Keynesian orthodoxy of the postwar era.

effect, workers were fooled into accepting wages with less purchasing power.

What the rational expectations hypothesis predicts is that if the Keynes-Lerner-Samuelson approach of fine-tuning is followed every time there is a recession, workers will learn to anticipate the policy actions of government and their effects. When they do so, they will demand even higher money wages to maintain their purchasing power. The result will be inflation without any increase in employment. So if the results of policy are anticipated, the policy can have no effect other than on the rate of inflation. Only by surprising people can governmental policy affect real output and employment. The Keynesian notion of involuntary unemployment thus works both ways: just as workers have no expedient for influencing the real wage by taking a money wage cut, workers likewise cannot influence the amount of employment by taking money wage increases. Workers would remain unemployed even in the face of expansionary monetary and fiscal policy designed to provide employment. Increasing aggregate demand in a systematic way to increase employment will be thwarted if workers anticipate the policy.

What are the implications of this policy for the efficacy of deficit financing? When first attempted, a tax cut combined with deficit financing might have a salutary effect. The increasing government bonds might make people feel richer, as the Lerner effect argued, and induce them to spend more on consumption. But if the expanded debt is serviced, taxes must rise to pay for it. If not, the price level rises and the economy experiences the implicit tax of inflation. The public learns this lesson. Any deficit signals higher taxes—explicit or implicit—for the future. The expectations of future repayment will destroy a large part of the original stimulus provided by the wealth effect of the necessary debt. The more often it is tried, the more likely the public will learn to anticipate the result and real increase in national income will not occur. Only by acting in an unpredictable way—that is, only by "fooling" the public—can government affect the course of real economic events. The upshot is that government cannot use fine-tuning to stabilize the economy. On the contrary, the use of monetary and fiscal policy to counteract increases in employment will only lead to uneven inflation around a rising trend. Thus, the rational expectations theory gives added support to Friedman's arguments for a fixed monetary rule in order to reduce erratic and unpredictable monetary movements, which act like a series of random shocks to the economy.[53]

[53] This explanation of the rational expectations hypothesis is highly simplified. A good summary of the literature on this topic is found in Brian Kantor, "Rational Expectations and Economic Thought," *Journal of Economic Literature* 17 (December 1979): 1422–41. A nontechnical but careful exposition is that of Bennett T. McCallum, "The Significance of Rational Expectations," *Challenge* (January/February 1980), pp. 37–43.

It should be noted that although the rational expectations hypothesis supports Friedman's most important policy proposals, he is by no means a totally enthusiastic supporter of this approach. He sees it as extremely important for the theory of stabilization policy, but he has warned that "some of the people working on rational expectations have a tendency to carry their splendid idea too far and convert it into something of a fad." (Milton Friedman, "How Stands the Theory and Practice of

In sum, the rational expectations approach was an offshoot of Friedman's monetarism. Its adherents simply replaced Friedman's belief in adaptive price level expectations, which lag behind the actual rate of inflation, with the view that individuals would not form their expectations in such a manner since they would be consistently wrong. Lucas, Sargent, and others substituted "rational" expectations for "adaptive" expectations and were thereby able to jettison even the notion of a short-run trade-off between inflation and unemployment.

A Walk on the "Supply-Side"

Friedman's imprint on the development of rational expectations represented an addition to the economist's "box of tools," as Joan Robinson called it, or to the "engine of analysis," to cite Alfred Marshall's phrase. But in the case of a second important development in the thinking of many economists in the 1970's, Friedman's influence is much harder to characterize, even though it was of paramount importance. Through his contributions to the intellectual and social tensions of his time, Friedman affected the conciousness of economists and politicians. Out of this changed ethos came what has come to be called *supply-side economics*.[54] Supply-siders have returned to concerns which were central to those of the earlier classical economists. As we have seen in Chapter 2, Adam Smith and his followers urged that economic welfare could only be augmented by the release of the powerful incentive of self-interest, a motivating force all too often stifled by the heavy hand of the state. By unleashing the desire of each man to better his condition, saving and investment would increase, the quantity of capital stock would grow, markets and physical output would expand, and thereby the per capita income of society would be maximized. Contemporary supply-side economists insist that the same logic holds today in combating the problems of inflation and unemployment. They argue that if individuals are left free to pursue their self-interest with the hope of being rewarded by the maximization of their income, then production and output will expand fast enough to reduce the rate of inflation and stimulate employment at the same time. In that way, the problem of stagflation will be solved.

Monetary Policy?," unpublished paper, 1978.) Paul Samuelson is even more critical than Friedman: "Most rational expectations claims—beyond 'there's no easy pickings'—at this stage still represent rhetoric." (Personal correspondence, 12 July 1979). Samuelson's wariness about this approach may not be surprising in light of his long-time advocacy of fine-tuning. Nevertheless, it should be noted that Samuelson himself presented the first coherent theorem on "efficient markets" in the 1960's, and efficient market theory is, in a sense, the micro side to macro's rational expectations. (See the discussion in Chapter 10.)

[54] The term was coined by Herbert Stein, who referred to "supply-side fiscalists" in a paper delivered at a conference at The Homestead in Hot Springs, Virginia, in 1976. The paper was published in 1978 after his phrase had been picked up by proponents of this idea in search of a convenient label for their way of thinking. Ironically, Stein is a leading critic of this approach. See Herbert Stein, "The Decline of the Budget-Balancing Doctrine or How the Good Guys Finally Lost," in James M. Buchanan and Richard E. Wagner, eds., *Fiscal Responsibility in Constitutional Democracy* (Leiden and Boston: Martinus Nijhoff, 1978), pp. 35–53.

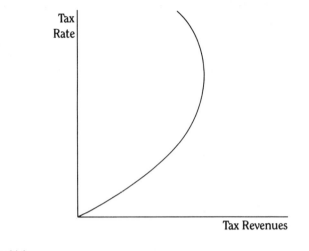

Figure 14.1

The fulcrum for the supply-side way of thinking was provided by a construct known as the Laffer Curve, named for its originator, Arthur B. Laffer. This curve first made its appearance at the Two Continents Restaurant in Washington, D.C., in 1974. Laffer, an economist at the University of Southern California, was dining with a number of journalists and public officials. He had been invited to explain his rather novel ideas on taxes and incentives, and in the course of the discussion drew his curve for the first time on a paper napkin. In appearance, the curve resembles a single McDonald's arch turned on its side.[55]

The Laffer Curve (Fig. 14.1) demonstrates the relationship between tax rates and government revenues. At zero tax rates, no government revenue is generated. As the tax rate goes up, revenues rise but not proportionately. This is because taxes have two effects: the first is to generate revenue; the second is to discourage work and investment, which thereby reduces money income and the taxes that such income would generate. As tax rates rise, people tend to avoid taxes by spending more time on untaxed (or lower-taxed) activities. This leads to choosing leisure over work and consumption in place of investment. It is Laffer's contention that at some point higher taxes actually *reduce* government revenue. The discouragement effects of the tax burden swamp the effect of the higher tax rates in bringing in more revenue from the surviving taxable activities. So the Laffer Curve turns backward towards zero. Laffer's implication is that it is possible to raise government revenues by cutting tax rates.

The Laffer Curve impressed representatives and senators. Congressman Jack Kemp from upstate New York found it a revelation: "It was

55 To John Kenneth Galbraith, the Laffer Curve has a different aspect, resembling ". . . a wishbone in shape as well as substance." (*Time*, 27 August 1979, p. 35). See Michael Kinsley, "Alms for the Rich," *New Republic*, August 1978, pp. 19–26.

like a light went off. I knew there had to be a better way, and that was it."
With Senate colleague William Roth of Delaware, Kemp sponsored the
Kemp-Roth tax bill, which was first placed before Congress in 1978.
Kemp characterized Laffer's theory as "an alternative to the Keynesians
and the Monetarists."[56] The idea also caught the imagination of Ronald
Reagan during his successful bid for the presidency in 1980. Reagan
supported the Kemp-Roth Bill as part of his economic program.

Keynesians and monetarists were not so impressed. To orthodox
Keynesians, Laffer's ideas are likely to be highly inflationary if the tax
cuts are enacted in a period of inflation. For a cut in taxes has the
immediate effect of increasing the budget deficit and that will, through
the multiplier effect, stimulate aggregate demand at a time when
inflationary pressure is already present. Monetarists, such as Friedman,
continue to see the control of the money supply by the Federal Reserve
as the key to eliminating stagflation. Although Friedman supports the
reduction in taxes that the supply-siders are urging, he does so mainly
because he believes that experience demonstrates that government
spending is highly correlated with tax receipts. If tax revenues are
reduced, government spending will tend to be less. He does not believe
that the increases in productivity likely to occur as a result of the
increased incentives associated with lower tax rates will do a great deal
to eliminate inflation unless inflationary rates are already relatively
low.

Nevertheless, it is clear that the intellectual ethos out of which the
supply-side arguments have emerged is to some extent a result of
Friedman's influence. Supply-siders tend to believe that efforts to
control the money supply are doomed to failure so long as the Federal
Reserve finds it difficult even to define what the money supply is.
Supply-siders also tend to favor a return to the gold standard, a proposal
Friedman rejects. But their emphasis on a reduction in the size of the
government sector, the freeing up of incentives to increase productivity
and growth in the private sector, and their belief in the validity of Say's
Law place the supply-siders much closer to the new neoclassicism than
to the new economics. The malaise with activist economics, out of
which their proposals developed, is in large measure a reflection of
Friedman's influence.[57]

The Methodology of Positive Economics

To understand Friedman's contribution to economics, it is important
that his philosophical ideas be separated from his scientific work. As we
have seen, the major body of his work has been strictly scientific and

---

[56] See David Blum, "The Laffer Curve: A Social History," *The New Republic*, 19 August 1978, pp.
24–25.

[57] The *locus classicus* for the discussion of supply-side economics is Jude Wanniski, *The Way the
World Works* (New York: Simon and Schuster, 1978). Aside from Arthur Laffer, leading supply-side
proponents include Robert Mundell of Columbia University and Paul Craig Roberts, who was
appointed by President Reagan to be assistant secretary of the Treasury. See "A Guide to Understanding the Supply-Siders," *Business Week*, 22 December 1980, pp. 76–78.

dictated by his characteristic approach. This approach stems from his methodological insistence on the extreme importance of separating out the knowledge of *what is* from judgments about *what ought to be*. This philosophy shaped the character of Friedman's "positive economics." In addition, Friedman views economic theory as a kit of tools which is instructive in dealing with almost every problem. He agrees with Abba Lerner that it is most definitely not a work of art to be developed for its own sake.

A distinctive feature of Friedman's philosophy is his belief that most of the differences of opinion about policy derive from differences about what is, rather than differences in values of what ought to be.[58] This means that most differences of opinion are not over goals or values but are disagreements over predictions of the effects of various policies. The disagreements can, in principle, be resolved by empirical evidence. It is for this reason that Friedman stresses that hypotheses be formulated as statements that can be tested. For only in this way can disagreements be resolved. This implies, of course, an entirely sanguine view of human nature, since it is based on an assumption that human beings are reasonable and ultimately committed to rational discourse. Friedman's strong commitment to this position is reflected in his important essay "The Methodology of Positive Economics."[59] The distinction between positive and normative economics was first developed by the father of John Maynard Keynes, John Neville Keynes. The elder Keynes distinguished between "a *positive science* . . . a body of systematized knowledge concerning what is; and a *normative* or *regulative* science . . . a body of systematized knowledge discussing criteria of what ought to be. . . .[60]

To Friedman, this is a fundamentally useful distinction since normative policy conclusions necessarily rest on a prediction derived from positive economics about the consequences of alternative policies. So normative economics cannot be independent of positive economics. Friedman believes that a large proportion of economists would agree on policy conclusions if they agreed on the implications of alternative policies. It is therefore the progress of positive economics that is crucial to the resolution of normative differences. If reasonable men in a given cultural context agree on goals, they need only discover the course of action that will enable them to realize these goals. If differences over fundamental values are so profound as to be irreconcilable, then these are "differences about which men can ultimately only fight."[61]

This is a major reason why the free market is so crucial. Friedman's view that differences in values are differences over which men must

[58] See Milton Friedman, "Why Economists Disagree," in idem, *Dollars and Deficits* (Englewood Cliffs, N. J.: Prentice Hall, 1968), pp. 1–16, especially pp. 6–10.   —

[59] Milton Friedman, "The Methodology of Positive Economics," in idem, *Positive Economics*, pp. 3–43.

[60] John Neville Keynes, *The Scope and Method of Political Economy* (London: Macmillan and Co., 1891), p. 34.

[61] Friedman, *Positive Economics*, p. 5.

ultimately fight focuses his attention on the market mechanism as a device for reconciling value differences. For exchange to occur, it is clear that values must differ. Individual parties engaging in exchange must have different tastes. This means that all will benefit from exchange. As Friedman notes, "the essence of exchange is the reconciliation of divergent values; of achievement of unanimity without conformity."[62] Individuals will continue to exchange until, at the margin, each attaches the same relative value to a little more of the commodities in question. So, through the free exchange of commodities, they are brought into agreement. And throughout the marketplace, all participants will come to have common values at the margin. Friedman argues that, for a society to be stable, there must be a common set of values that must be unthinkingly accepted by most of the people most of the time. One of Friedman's most original contributions is his argument that this set of commonly shared values can be developed and changed and accepted by the free market. This view of the market as a reconciler of divergent values is part and parcel of his classical liberal philosophy.

Friedman as a Marshallian

It is Friedman's insistence on the importance of the predictive power or implications of a theory that allows him to demur sharply from the strictures of Veblen and Chamberlin, and so to attack two other harbingers of the new economics. He explicitly refers to Veblen's criticisms regarding the "unrealism" of economics because it assumes a rational economic man. To Friedman, such criticism is entirely wide of the mark. The issue is not the realism of the assumptions but the ability of a theory to yield predictions for a wide range of phenomena. To Friedman (as to Alfred Marshall), economic theory is an engine of analysis and economists should not seek a "photographic reproduction" of the world.

In regard to Chamberlin's monopolistic competition revolution, Friedman accepted the usefulness of Alfred Marshall's grouping of firms into "industries" in which similarities among firms were more important than the differences arising from each firm's production of a single "product", that is, goods that were perfect substitutes to perchasers. In the case of a monopolist, the firm *is* the industry. Obviously, the assumption of a perfectly elastic demand curve for all firms in an industry is an abstraction. For some purposes, the industry can be considered perfectly competitive; for other problems, it might be appropriate to treat the firms as if they had some monopolistic power. But, to Friedman, Marshall did not assume perfect competition in a descriptive sense. It was only a useful simplification for problems "in

---

[62] Milton Friedman, "Value Judgments in Economics" in Sidney Hook, ed., *Human Values and Economic Policy* (New York: New York University Press, 1967), pp. 85–93.

which a group of firms is affected by a common stimulus, and in which the firms can be treated *as if* they were perfect competitors."[63]

Chamberlin's attempt to build a more general theory was, in Friedman's view, a failure, except insofar as he refined Marshall's monopoly analysis and enriched the economics vocabulary. The point at issue is Chamberlin's treatment of product differentiation, which, as we noted in Chapter 6, was the distinguishing feature of his theory. How can firms producing similar but different products be grouped together in the same industry? If products are differentiated, doesn't this mean that each firm *is* the industry? Thus, "the theory of monopolistic competition offers no tools for the analysis of an industry and so no stopping place between the firm at one extreme and general equilibrium at the other."[64] So Friedman was able to dismiss much of Veblen and Chamberlin on the grounds that their criticisms of neoclassical economics were in large measure directed at the unreality of neoclassical theory. Since the test of a theory is its ability to yield accurate predictions, not the realism of its assumptions, much of the Veblen and Chamberlin analysis has been construed by Friedman and his disciples as largely irrelevant.[65]

Capitalism and Freedom

In the field of social philosophy, Friedman has restated the case for classical liberalism. In developing this philosophy, he was influenced by his teachers Frank Knight and Henry Simons. To Friedman, the liberalism of the eighteenth and nineteenth centuries stressed the

> doctrines relating to a "free man" which are diametrically opposed to the modern day concept which stresses "welfare" and equality over freedom. Freedom is the highest value and is the opposite of coercion. It implies the right to make and act on one's own decisions.[66]

---

[63] Friedman, *Positive Economics*, pp. 37–38.

[64] Friedman, *Positive Economics*, pp. 37–38.

[65] Friedman's pragmatic approach to methodology was doubtlessly influenced by his acquaintance with the writings of Charles Sanders Peirce, the founder of American pragmatism. Ironically, Peirce had been a teacher of Veblen at Johns Hopkins and might have had much to do with Veblen's appreciation of social Darwinism. See Philip Wiener, *Evolution and the Founders of Pragmatism* (Cambridge, Mass.: Harvard University Press, 1949), pp. 70–96.

The ideas of Peirce which seem to have had the most impact on Friedman are contained in Peirce's collection of philosophical essays, Charles S. Peirce, *Chance, Love and Logic* (New York: Harcourt Brace, 1923). In this work, Peirce argues that to be useful, theories must be simpler than the complex facts they seek to explain. It is convenient to employ a principle of certainty where the facts would justify only some degree of probability. Friedman's methodological prescription that a theory's usefulness is its test by implication, is essentially the Peircian criterion of meaning. According to Peirce, an idea is clear if we understand its conceivable effects or the logical consequences necessitated by adopting it as a premise for resolving a problem. Just as the meaning of an idea is found *not* by intuition but by working out its implications, so the usefulness of a theory is found not by considering its assumptions but by examining its implications.

[66] Milton Friedman, *Capitalism and Freedom* (Chicago: University of Chicago Press, 1962), p. 39. As an example of Friedman's point, note the definition of freedom in John Stuart Mill's *On Liberty*: "The only freedom which deserves the name is that of pursuing our own good in our own way, so long as we do not attempt to deprive others of theirs, or impede their efforts to obtain it." John

In society, the basic problem of social organization is the coordination of the economic activities of large numbers of people. This coordination can be carried out in two ways: through voluntary means such as a market, or through central control of political coercion. The classical liberal does not view these two choices indifferently. Economic freedom is an important part of overall freedom and an "indispensible means toward the achievement of political freedom."[67] For only if one's livelihood is independent of government control can one express his true opinions.

Friedman's views on the proper role of government are little different from those of Adam Smith:

1. To provide a framework for law and order by protecting individuals from external enemies (national defense) and from coercion by their fellow citizens.
2. To promote economic freedom by providing, interpreting, and enforcing the "rules of the game." In effect, this means enforcement of voluntary contracts, the definition and enforcement of property rights, and the provision of a stable monetary framework.
3. Although coercive, government action may be justified in the case of Pigovian externalities (or market failure) and where there are technical monopolies.
4. The government may be coercive on paternalistic grounds by supplementing private charity and the family in order to protect children and the insane.

Friedman is not insensitive to the problem of poverty in our contemporary society. In *Capitalism and Freedom*, he advocated that a subsidy be paid to individuals whose income fell below some socially acceptable level of poverty.[68] The proposal, which Friedman labeled a "negative income tax," would set a limit beneath which no family income could fall. It would allow us to eliminate all other social welfare schemes, such as social security, farm price supports, unemployment compensation, public housing, and the whole rag-bag of welfare programs that, according to Friedman, have not only failed to help the poor but have also impoverished them further.

So as to minimize the adverse effects of such a plan on work incentives, Friedman's proposal involved a sliding-scale feature. Assume, for example, that we agree that the poverty line is $3,000 and that the rate of subsidy should be 50 percent. In that case, someone earning no income at all would receive $3,000 and pay no taxes. If, however, the person earned $1,000 as income, he would be "taxed" at some rate of 50

Stuart Mill, *On Liberty* in *The Utilitarians* (Garden City, N. Y.; Dolphin Books, Doubleday, 1961), p. 487.

To Friedman, the goal of liberalism is "to preserve the maximum degree of freedom for each individual separately that is compatible with one man's freedom not interferring with other men's freedom. (Friedman, *Capitalism and Freedom*, p. 39)

[67] Friedman, *Capitalism and Freedom*, p. 12.

[68] Friedman, *Capitalism and Freedom*, pp. 191–95.

percent on the earned income. In this case, he would owe $500 in taxes. Put another way, his subsidy would be reduced from $3,000 (at zero income) to $2,500 (at an income of $1,000). The *net* income would therefore be $3,500 after earning income. Friedman argues that this provides for incentives to earn income, since the individual would always get some increase in income from a dollar earned.[69]

Friedman does not advocate the negative income tax in order to redistribute income. He advocates it because he believes that an over-whelming majority of the upper-income groups would be willing to impose taxes on themselves for this purpose. His argument really rests on his belief that charity is a collective good involving Pigovian exter-nality problems. If people want to eliminate dire distress and poverty, they can optimally do so only through collective action.[70] However, Friedman warns that any government action beyond promoting free-dom and providing the rules creates a dangerous externality. This is true because every act of government intervention limits the realm of individual freedom directly and threatens the preservation of freedom.

This means that government intervention has neighborhood effects of its own, which should be weighed against those it is designed to remove. But how large a weight the classical liberal attaches to the negative effects of additional government intervention depends on the scope of existing government control. "This is an important reason why many earlier liberals, such as Henry Simons, writing at a time when government was small by today's standards, were willing to have gov-ernment undertake activities that today's liberals would not accept now that government has become so overgrown."[71]

Thus, for example, where Simons would advocate government own-ership in the case of technical monopolies (monopolies that arise because it is efficient to have a single enterprise), Friedman would elect to keep a private monopoly. He would do so not only because the powers of government have grown so large in recent times, but because technological changes are so rapid that what is a technical monopoly today might not be one tomorrow. If government ownership or regula-tion is chosen, there is, in Friedman's view, little chance that future technological considerations will lead to a removal of government from this sphere.

Friedman argues that democracy is the appropriate form of govern-ment to foster political freedom. But the necessary prerequisite to democracy is a free market, that is, a capitalistic, free enterprise system. This is so because in order for a political decision to be freely

---

[69] This is an important feature of the negative income scheme. Many programs impose what amounts to a 100 percent tax on recipients by completely withdrawing support when the applicant reaches some poverty line. For a careful exposition of how the negative income tax proposal might be implemented, see Edgar K. Browning and Jacquelene M. Browning, *Public Finance and the Price System* (New York: Macmillan Co., 1979), pp. 21–52.

[70] Friedman, *Proceedings of Conference on Savings and Residential Financing*, p. 54.

[71] Friedman, *Capitalism and Freedom*, p. 32.

made, the act must be severed from connection with one's livelihood. If the government is the sole employer and the only source from which the requisite instruments of effective political advocacy can be had, then the individual hostile to the existing government—but dependent upon it for his livelihood—would have to hope that the government is indeed self-denying. Government would not only have to be imagined to continue employing this advocate of its destruction but would also have to be willing to supply the paper, presses, and halls for the dissenter to propagandize for its overthrow. Thus, the political advocate in the socialistic state would have to raise funds. But those with the most funds are likely to be those in the greatest positions of power in the government with the most to lose in the event of a political overthrow.

According to Friedman, only a capitalistic system separates economic and political power, allowing one to offset the other. It was not by chance that capitalism and democracy grew up together in a limited corner of the world.

> Historical evidence speaks with a single voice on the relation between political freedom and a free market. I know of no example in time or place of a society that has been marked by a large measure of political freedom and that has not also used something comparable to a free market to organize the bulk of economic activity.
>
> Because we live in a largely free society, we tend to forget how limited is the span of time and the part of the globe for which there has ever been anything like political freedom: the typical state of mankind is tyranny, servitude, and misery.[72]

It can be seen that Friedman has restated for his time the relevance of the classical liberal philosophy of Adam Smith and John Stuart Mill. On this basis, he has developed policy proposals that would return our economy to a largely laissez-faire system. But the classical liberal is not an anarchist. For a government which maintained law and order, protected property rights, defined and adjudicated the rules of the economic game, enforced contracts, promoted competition, provided a stable monetary framework, dissolved monopolies, overcame the important Pigovian externalities, and protected the insane and children would have many notable functions. But not nearly so many as the government now takes on. In *Capitalism and Freedom*, Friedman lists fourteen activities of government that he feels violate classical liberal principles. All of these activities, though well intentioned, do not produce the results intended. Indeed, in most cases they produce the opposite result. Among the government activities listed are tariffs and quotas in foreign trade, and interferences with international payments;

---

[72] Friedman, *Capitalism and Freedom*, p. 9. For a dissenting view of Friedman's position that capitalism is a necessary, albeit insufficient, condition for political freedom, seen through the lens of a political scientist, see C. B. MacPherson, "Elegant Tombstones: A Note on Friedman's Freedom," *Canadian Journal of Political Science* 1 (March 1968): 95–106.

fixing of prices and wages; control of entry into occupations through licensure; regulation of output; conscription of young people into the armed forces; and compulsory social security system.

We do not have space to develop in detail Friedman's specific proposals for removing government from these activities in which it is now engaged. But because our society has come to take so many of these functions for granted, Friedman's advocacy of alternative arrangements seems shocking to many.[73]

The Achievement of Milton Friedman

When the Nobel committee honored Milton Friedman in 1976, he was lauded for his "independence and brilliance," and the citation said: "It is very rare for an economist to wield such influence, directly or indirectly, not only on the direction of scientific research but also on actual practice." By this time, Friedman had emerged from the category of cult hero to the status of international celebrity, rivaling John Kenneth Galbraith's public fame. *The Wall Street Journal* called him "one of the busiest men in the world." With that pronouncement, even casual television viewers would have agreed. Friedman has increasingly been invited to make appearances on television talk shows, and, in 1980, viewers could watch him on public television in ten one-hour programs in which the economist traveled the globe talking about the causes of the Great Depression, inflation, problems of the welfare state, consumer protection, international trade, and other issues. Over an eighteen-month period Friedman filmed the program, appearing before cameras in Hong Kong, in a small community in India, in London, in front of Thomas Jefferson's Monticello in Virginia, and in a sweatshop in New York's Chinatown. The program was called "Free to Choose" and it served as a counter to Galbraith's program, "The Age of Uncertainty," aired a few years earlier. The book which Milton and Rose Friedman wrote to accompany the program became an unexpected bestseller, appearing on the *New York Times* non-fiction list in first place for many weeks.[74] In Great Britain, where the show appeared, one of its biggest fans was Prime Minister Margaret Thatcher. As a result of her interest in Friedman's ideas, he became a prominent figure on the British political scene. He defended his ideas in public and consulted

---

[73] The reader interested in pursuing Friedman's arguments on these issues should consult idem, "The Case for Flexible Exchange Rates," *Positive Economics*, pp. 157–203; Milton Friedman and Robert V. Roosa, *The Balance of Payments: Free versus Fixed Exchange Rates*, Rational Debate Seminars, (Washington, D.C.: American Enterprise Institute for Public Policy Research, 1967).

Most of Friedman's specific policy proposals can be found in his *Newsweek* columns. Many of these have been collected into one volume and published under idem, *An Economist's Protest: Columns in Political Economy*, 2nd ed., (Glen Ridge, N.J.: Thomas Horton and Daughters, 1975). Recently, Friedman has supported the notion of a constitutional amendment to limit the increase in government spending to the percentage increase in gross national product, with an escape hatch in times of recession and a more severe limitation in times of inflation. See the article by William Safire, "Friedman's Amendment," *New York Times*, 5 February 1979, p. A19.

[74] Milton and Rose Friedman, *Free to Choose: A Personal Statement* (New York: Harcourt Brace Jovanovich, 1980).

privately with Mrs. Thatcher and her chancellor of the exchequer. Advising politicians was not new to Friedman. He had served as an unofficial advisor to Barry Goldwater in 1964, to Richard Nixon in 1968, and to Ronald Reagan in 1980. In 1977, he consulted with the government of Prime Minister Menachem Begin in Israel.[75]

Friedman's willingness to "profess" to any nation that wanted his advice got him into difficulties. At the end of March 1975, Friedman served a six-day stint in Chile as the guest of a private foundation. He attended meetings, researched economic data in government offices, and made speeches. Subsequently, he wrote a paper giving his views on the inflation that afflicted the country. As might be expected, he suggested cutting government spending, limiting the printing of money, and letting free-market forces establish prices and exchange rates. His paper was sent to a member of General Augusto Pinochet's junta. Pinochet was the successor to Salvador Allende, the Marxist who was killed in the October 1973 coup. Adherents of the left argued that Friedman's "advice" to the Pinochet government led to policies that allegedly brought distress to the people of Chile. Demonstrators tried to disrupt almost all of Friedman's public appearances, including the ceremony in Stockholm when he accepted the Nobel Prize. Friedman was distressed by these actions, but he feels vindicated by the dramatic results the implementation of his policies achieved. Chile reduced its inflation rate from roughly 350 percent per year in 1975 to 38 percent in 1979; unemployment at the same time dropped from 19 percent to 12 percent. Friedman believes that the reconstruction of the Chilean economy will be regarded as one of the economic "miracles" of the 20th century.[76]

Friedman's remarkable success in putting across his once unpopular ideas, in seeing what he alone had for so long advocated become respectable economic opinion, is a tribute to his intellect, his courage, his scholarship, and his indefatigable energy. With the exception of Keynes, no economist of his time can match his power of persuasion in the black art of debate.[77] What Mencken once said of Nietzsche can appropriately be said as well of Friedman: "When he took to the floor to argue it was time to send for ambulances." In 1978, Canadian economist James W. Dean interviewed fifteen prominent economists at the

---

[75] See "The World Tests Friedman's Theories," *Newsweek*, 1 November 1979, pp. 73–75; "Israel Turns to Milton Friedman," *New York Times*, 26 June 1977; "Margaret & Milton Ltd.," *Washington Post*, 31 March 1980, p. A23.

[76] See "Monetarism, Chilean Style," *Business Week*, 26 November 1979, pp. 127–30.

[77] Friedman's lack of immediate results in convincing fellow economists has been blamed on his early habit of extreme aggressiveness in debate. But as Milton Viorst has noted, "If he was once considered a pushy Jewish kid from New Jersey, [Friedman] is now acknowledged to be unfailingly thoughtful and courteous. Desisting from the technique of withering insult, he couches his arguments . . . in the most sweetly reasonable terms, though without ever sacrificing a cutting edge." (Milton Viorst, "Friedmanism" *New York Times Magazine*, 25 January 1970, p. 83.) Paul Samuelson paid tribute to Friedman's powers of persuasion by remarking that "I would bet that *any* two persons in the same room with Milton Friedman for ten minutes will come out on the same side, at least temporarily." *Milton Friedman and Paul A. Samuelson Discuss the Economic Responsibility of Government*, p. 36.

August 1978 meeting of the American Economic Association. Most of these doyens indicated that they had retreated from a belief in activist economic policies. There was a growing recognition among them, as well as among the younger "rational expectationists," that government intervention not only does not deliver the desired results but also imposes tremendous costs. There was a general disillusionment with government and what was felt to be an unconscionable tax burden which it imposed. In addition to this pragmatic attitude, Dean reported that the change in mood toward policy nihilism was a result of

> . . . the steady gains made by Chicago-style economic philosophy, roughly coinciding with the progress of Milton Friedman's career, and the far friendlier reception of his ideas since inflation has become of major and worldwide concern.[78]

---

[78] James W. Dean, "The Dissolution of the Keynesian Consensus," *The Public Interest*, Special Edition, 1980, p. 30.

15

CONCLUSION

Those intrepid enough to write a volume summarizing the policy controversies that divide contemporary economists are surely free of any obligation to provide a guide to the future. At least we have resisted mightily our recognition of this duty. A chapter titled, "What of the Future?," would doubtlessly lend a proper air of contemplativeness to the study and provide a (short-run) reputation for profundity to its authors. But such prognostication is not for us. The history of economics suggests prudence in this regard. The questions of when and how the next revolution in economic thought and policy will come about are best left to the future to decide. Our excursion is over. It remains only to see where we are.

The Economic Revolutionaries

The doctrine of the need for an activist government to control economic affairs was constructed upon the rubble of the neoclassical structure. The demolition of the House of Marshall was carried out, in the main, by Thorstein Veblen, A. C. Pigou, E. H. Chamberlin, and John Maynard Keynes. These writers stressed the existence of consumer irrationality, divergencies between private and social costs, the wastes of competition, and the inadequacy of aggregate demand under laissez-faire. So the chief pillars of Alfred Marshall's temple were undermined: the economic man, the quantity theory of money, Say's Law, and the unmitigated benefits of competition. These doctrines together had provided the intellectual gantry for a laissez-faire economic policy.

The New Economics

Alvin Hansen's work carried on the attack in two areas: first, he helped bring the Keynesian message to America and taught it to the generation of students at Harvard who were to help form the economic policy of post-World War II America. His second and less influential effort came late in his career when he began to speak out on questions that arose in the wake of Veblen, Pigou, and Chamberlin: What are the implications of the abrogation of consumer sovereignty and the existence of advertising and product differentiation? In answer, he developed in embryonic form some of the themes that were later fully developed in the work of his colleague, John Kenneth Galbraith. One of Hansen's most brilliant pupils, Paul A. Samuelson, was to replace Hansen as the leading teacher of the young people who would eventually inspire macroeconomic policy. His best-selling introductory textbook reached more tyro economists than had any such book before. In it, the Keynesian system was reduced to precise arithmetic and geometry so that the elements of the analysis and its policy suggestions could be grasped by the undergraduate. In his more arcane contributions, and at the suggestion of his mentor Hansen, he combined the Keynesian multiplier with the accelerator into an elegant mathematical model that gave a theoretical underpinning to the business cycle and stimulated much work in the development of growth models. Furthermore, his interests were catholic. He fashioned from the Pigovian analysis of externalities and public goods, the logical analytics supporting a theory of government expenditure. And in his more "popular" moods, he spoke out on policy questions, particularly those regarding discretionary monetary and fiscal policy to control employment and the price level, lending his prestige to specific recommendations.

The contributions of Abba P. Lerner to economic thought and policy in America should be appreciated at least as much as those of Hansen's and Samuelson's. Lerner's functional finance analysis provided a neat set of directions for use with Keynes's monetary and fiscal tool kit. With Lerner's functional finance rules in front of him, the policymaker could, in a moment, tell what is needed in the event of any contingency from inflation to unemployment. Unfortunately, as it later turned out, the two extremes were not mutually exclusive. And so Lerner, in conceding the inappropriateness of his instruments for attacking the new inflation of the late 1950's, developed his theory of sellers' inflation and suggested remedies.

Playing to a much larger audience than the American Economic Association, John Kenneth Galbraith became the most noticed of social critics. His brilliantly sophisticated cynicism and writing style, with which he satirized the "conventional wisdom," gave a voice to those who inarticulately sensed a malaise in an opulent society. Galbraith's Veblen-like concern with consumer irrationalities and the technological imperatives of the second half of the twentieth century suggested new meanings in the patterns of industrial organization that far transcended Chamberlin's concerns. What's more, his association with famous movie stars, artists, and political figures, and his widely publicized leisure class postures, provided the economics profession with a public celebrity that lent it glamour. Even the most hopeless drudge of an academic scribbler could derive positive externalities generated by Galbraith's fame.

The New Neoclassicism

When Alfred Marshall, in an uncharacteristic moment of despondency over the vitality of his contributions, expressed his fear that his *"Principles* will be waste paper" in 50 years, he could not have foretold his good luck in having men of the calibre of Knight, Simons, and Friedman to carry on. Frank Knight completed the neoclassical structure with his analysis of the role of profit in economic life. In doing so, he provided a formidable armor for protection against the attacks on consumer sovereignty. More important, he firmly grasped the nettle offered by Pigou's charge of "market failure" under laissez-faire by showing the importance of clearly defined property rights in a neoclassical framework. This contribution provided the battleground for future campaigns over the issue of the necessity of government intervention to reconcile the divergencies between private and social costs. In addition, he was Hansen's counterpart at Chicago, where he stimulated his colleagues and students to accept a largely free market philosophy that ran counter to the trend of the times.

Knight's colleague, Henry Simons, provided the ideological bearings for the counterattack on Keynes and Hansen. His stress on the rule of law rather than authorities in economic affairs and his brilliantly reasoned defense of a positive program for a laissez-faire society inspired many disciples.

By far the most influential of these has been Milton Friedman. Friedman donned the white robes of science to demonstrate the singular relevancy of neoclassical economics for contemporary problems. Friedman amassed empirical evidence to demonstrate the inappropriateness of much economic policy that had been promoted by the new economics, and he carried the main burden of the new neoclassicism's counterattack. Pragmatists like Samuelson and Lerner were met on their own ground by an economist of at least equal brilliance and persuasiveness. If a refurnished and reformed market economy survives the onslaught of the new economics, much of the credit will go to Friedman and the new neoclassicism. As Veblen said in another context at the end of his *Theory of Business Enterprise*: "Which of the two antagonistic factors may prove stronger in the long run is something of a blind guess; but the calculable future seems to belong to the one or the other."

AFTERWORD

The Academic Scribblers after Twenty-Five Years

William Breit and Roger L. Ransom

The Academic Scribblers was first published in 1971. A revised edition appeared in 1982. In the concluding chapter to both editions we wrote:

> Those intrepid enough to write a volume summarizing the policy controversies that divide contemporary economists are surely free of any obligation to provide a guide to the future. . . . [S]uch prognostication is not for us. The history of economics suggests prudence in this regard. The questions of when and how the next revolution in economic thought and policy will come about are best left to the future to decide. Our excursion is over. It remains only to see where we are.

During the years that have passed since we penned those thoughts, it has become increasingly clear to us that we need make no apology for our stubborn refusal to resist the pull of prognostication. It is one thing to observe where we are; it is quite another to divine the future. The Duchess of Windsor—a woman who convinced Edward VII to renounce the throne of England to marry her—is credited with having once remarked that "one cannot be too rich nor too thin." We would add to this aphorism only the words: "nor too prudent."

So here we are in the world of 1998, rapidly approaching the millennium. The economists included in *Scribblers* had their greatest impact during the half-century from 1930 to 1980. Given the momentous events that have occurred since that period, it would be astonishing indeed to discover that changes in economic thought in the last two decades of the twentieth century would not require us to revise significantly were we to attempt a completely new edition of this work. Yet, after rereading the 1982 edition, what pleases and surprises us is how few alterations we would be tempted to make to our discussion. Times have changed, yet the issues that were at the core of the debates carried on in the 1950s through the 1970s remain as challenges facing our economy today.

That is not to say the interpretation of the economic arguments of our "scribblers" might not be improved and embellished by placing them in the context of the 1990s. Two kinds of amendments suggest themselves. First, some economic problems have become less serious than they seemed fifty years ago, while others have become more pronounced. These differences should be noted. Second, some economic scholars have come upon the scene whose powerful theorizing has changed the way we think about certain policy issues that seem particularly crucial today. These new scribblers would require some attention.

A striking example of the first kind of revision would be the disappearance of the problem of "stagflation," which played such a large role in our discussion of economic policy a decade and a half ago. High levels of inflation accompanied by deep and persistent levels of unemployment was the most worrisome economic problem of the 1970s and early 1980s. The Keynesian nostrums seemed impotent in the face of this phenomenon, and it was during this period that monetarism and rational expectations came to dominate macroeconomics policy discussions. The Phillips Curve tradeoff between inflation and unemployment, so prominently emphasized in our chapters devoted to Samuelson, Lerner, and Friedman has in recent years given way to a period of unprecedented low levels of unemployment accompanied by price stability. Compared to the Hobson's choice facing economists and policymakers wrestling with price stability and unemployment in the middle of the century, politicians and academics of the 1990s have their cake and eat it too!

Accordingly, macroeconomists turned their attention during the late 1980s to a new problem: growing budget deficits and the accompanying increase in the national debt. A thoroughgoing revision would need to devote considerable attention to the controversy among economists over the question of the burden of public debt and the significance and implications of growing deficits that defied political demands that they be reduced. Such analysis would of necessity involve scrutiny of the dispute among scholars over the effects of deficits. Here there would doubtless be some disagreements within the ranks of those we characterized as the "New Neoclassicals." Nor could we fail to note that those we classified as the "New Economists" would hold less firmly to strongly held Keynesian positions concerning the benign effects of budget deficits—although here too, there has been controversy within the ranks. And it would be noted that toward the end of the 1990s the problem of budget deficits suddenly became the quaint problem of what to do about possible budget surpluses.

A second example of the changing nature of economic problems would be the ways in which economists view labor markets. It had become apparent for some time that neither the classical assumption of competitively determined wages nor the Keynesian assertion that wages were "rigid" provide useful insights to explain the behavior of wages and employment in the economic environment of large firms and powerful unions. In the 1980s a new approach, called "internal labor markets," evolved. The stability of wages, prices, and employment within the industrial sector is explained by emphasizing the *continuity* of labor contracts rather than stressing the *inflexibility* of labor contracts associated with labor unions. This view of labor markets also addresses other issues at the center of economic policy today: health care, retirement, and economic security as workers grow old. Other problems that moved to the forefront of study during the past two decades are those of growing income inequality, job insecurity, and inner-city poverty. Our revised *Scribblers* would have to follow these developments—a path that would surely lead us back to the basic question of whether economic security is a public or private good. On that question the dispersion of opinion both within and between the various "schools" of economics remains high.

A distinguishing feature of *Scribblers* in both editions was an emphasis on the importance of style and personality to be, as we put it, "ultimately decisive in the art of persuasion." This is why in-depth discussions of various theories and policy debates were surrounded by biographical sketches of the main characters. These detailed pen-portraits were not provided simply as amusing anecdotes about the lives of scholars. We were convinced that biographical data can bring the reader closer to identifying with a scholar's vision, thereby allowing a deeper understanding of his or her ideas. A completely rewritten edition could continue this emphasis. As explained below, however, this approach would have greater difficulties in an era of extreme specialization and narrow focus on technique that have come to characterize the work of most of the leading scholars in economics today.

The first two editions examined those American economists who had or were likely to have influence on economic policy in the latter half of the twentieth century. To place their ideas into perspective, it was necessary to recognize the importance of their predecessors in Great Britain and the United States who gave shape to the thought of our own times. Whereas most historians of economic thought saw John Maynard Keynes as the sole figure shaping modern economic thought and policy, we stressed the importance of Thorstein Veblen, A. C. Pigou, and Edward Chamberlin—in addition to Keynes—as exemplars of economic revolutionaries who undermined the hegemony of the Neoclassical model of economics (which we represented through Alfred Marshall's *Principles*). Our story was told in terms of powerful and individualistic thinkers who took their lead from these intellectual giants of an earlier period. These figures were Alvin Hansen, Paul Samuelson, Abba Lerner, and John Kenneth Galbraith, and we designated their contributions under the rubric *The New Economics*. The revolutionary impact of this new way of thinking brought forth—as revolutions in intellectual thought invariably do—a counterattack in the form of three powerful thinkers whose ideas we labeled *The New Neoclassicism:* Frank Knight, Henry Simons, and Milton Friedman.

When we were asked to bring out a revised version of *Scribblers* in 1982 we concluded "with some surprise not unmixed with relief" that no single figure had come on the scene who had achieved influence in so many areas of economic discussion as had the personalities in the first edition. But we were careful to note that "there are some scholars within hailing distance of greatness in that regard who, in a few more years, might earn a niche in our gallery." A few more years have passed. Whom might we include in another edition?

Here we must proceed with caution. Although a number of the younger generation of economists have made significant contributions to our understanding of the economy, we believe that no single figure has yet emerged to take a place alongside the greats of the first two editions. But have we overlooked an obvious contender?

A conspicuous place to look for candidates to be inducted into our pantheon of thinkers would be a list of Nobel laureates in economics over the past two decades. Here we would find strong confirmation that the ideas we highlighted in earlier editions of *Scribblers* were, indeed, the foundation for much of what would follow. James Tobin [1981], Robert Solow [1987], and Franco Modigliani [1985] are Neo-Keynesian laureates who pioneered macroeconomic models of economic growth, saving, and investment. The New Neoclassicists have also been well represented by Nobel committee selections. George Stigler [1982] was recognized for his work on markets; Gary Becker [1992] for extending the logic of markets to the study of discrimination, marriage and the family, and education. James Buchanan [1986] laid the groundwork for the development of the field of public choice economics; while Ronald Coase [1991] did the same for the study of law and economics with his work on property rights. Some of these scholars—all of whom are in roughly the same generation as the writers we selected to be in earlier editions of *Scribblers*— would surely merit entry into our arcade of distinguished economists. Some of their work is discussed in chapters in *Scribblers* mainly devoted to others.

The theoretical basis of policy early in the next century will be shaped by debates among the new generation of economists. The counterattack of the New Neoclassicists made substantial inroads into the dominance of Keynesian thought—particularly among young scholars. "By about 1980," Alan Blinder wrote in 1988, "it was hard to find an American academic macroeconomist under the age of 40 who professed to be a Keynesian." Much of the credit for this remarkable change in macroeconomic views can be attributed to the success of the rational expectations model propounded by Robert

Lucas, who became a Nobel laureate in 1995. Colleagues such as Thomas Sargent and Robert Barro have helped popularize this model which, as we noted in the chapter on Milton Friedman, challenges the efficacy of traditional Keynesian fiscal policy. Yet the debates on macroeconomic policy are far from over. A group of "new" Keynesians, led by men such as Alan Blinder, Paul Krugman, Joseph Stiglitz and Lawrence Summers continue to uphold the legacy of Keynes in modified versions. A freshly minted *Scribblers* would have to address this continuing debate among this new generation of protagonists.

Even this cursory review of potential nominees suggests that a newly revised *Scribblers* would involve opening up new wings of our "gallery of economists" to deal with the work of new entrants. Their number alone would make it difficult to maintain the pedagogical clarity with which we presented the paradigms championed by only a few prominent people three decades ago. But space is not our only problem. If the list of Nobel laureates confirms our judgment of choices in the 1970s, it also reveals a significant change over the past four decades in the way that economists analyze and discuss economic theory. Our approach in *Scribblers* stresses the importance of how economists communicate among themselves and with people outside the profession. Economists have increasingly relied on mathematics as the "language" with which to communicate their ideas to an audience. This is hardly a new phenomenon; in his *Foundations of Economic Analysis,* Paul Samuelson sought to break with the "imprecise" literary tradition of earlier generations of economists and employ mathematical models to demonstrate the validity of economic propositions. The list of Nobel laureates underscores the extent to which mathematical economics has risen to the forefront of economic research.

The most significant development of mathematical economics has been the emergence of *general equilibrium theory* which, in addition to the work of Paul Samuelson, was pioneered by Nobel laureates such as Kenneth Arrow [1972], Gerard Debreu [1983], and Maurice Allais [1988]. Over the same period the field of *econometrics*—the empirical study of economic problems using increasingly sophisticated statistical models—has flourished in economics departments throughout the country. Jan Tinbergen, one of the pioneers of economic analysis, shared the first Nobel Prize in 1969. Subsequently the committee has recognized the econometric work of Wassily Leontief [1973], Tjalling Koopmans [1975], Lawrence Klein [1980] and Trygve Haavelmo [1989]. More recently, the emphasis on mathematical models has been accompanied by greater attention to *applied* aspects of economic theory that has produced a narrowing of focus for the prize. In the 1990s the Nobel selection committee has recognized a variety of researchers in applied economics for their efforts to develop theories of market information; determine conditions of equilibrium in non-market situations; predict prices in financial markets; and use the powerful tool of game theory to explain and predict the pricing, advertising and output strategies of large business firms.

An essential element in the pedagogy of our presentation of economic theories in *Scribblers* was to identify broad theoretical themes that formed the basis for debates that shaped the theoretical foundations of economic policy. The movement away from that breadth takes the theoretical debates among economists away from the realm of policy and the "real world." Moreover, the use of mathematical and econometric models severely restricts the audience and in fact leads to disillusionment and cynicism among graduate students. A recent survey by Arjo Klamer and David Colander examined the views of graduate students enrolled in six elite economics programs. The responses to their survey revealed that "problem-solving abilities and mathematical excellence are far more important to success [in the graduate programs] than knowledge of the economy and ability to do empirical research"—an indication that students observe what makes a successful economist. Yet the survey also strongly suggests that the students "resist the identification with engineers and do not like the preoccupation with techniques in graduate school and in the literature. They want more ideas, more policy relevance, more discussion of the fundamental assumptions, and more serious consideration of alternatives." The result of this apparent contradiction, Klamer and Colander suggest,

> . . . is a definite tension, frustration, and cynicism that, in our view, went beyond the normal graduate school blues. There was a strong sense that economics was a game and that hard work in devising relevant models that demonstrated a deep understanding of institutions would have a lower payoff than devising models that were analytically neat; the façade, not the depth of knowledge, was important. This cynicism is not limited to the graduate school experience, but is applied to the state of the art as they perceive it.

The economist who was "most respected" by students in the Klamer and Colander survey was John Maynard Keynes. He was respected for "his ability to make a radical departure from past history and his scope of vision." Keynes wrote at a time when the very foundations of a free society were being threatened. Partly because of what he perceived as the urgency of the situation, Keynes wrote *The General Theory* with a style that was polemical; included reasoning that at times bordered on carelessness; and made empirical statements that were not supported by careful research. He wanted to send a strong message to a large audience and the impact of the book cannot be denied. All of the thinkers we examined in this volume make their mark by the boldness with which they challenged and redefined the way one looks at "the economic problem." It is surely a measure of their success that for the past decade and a half no one has emerged to once again challenge the basic parameters by which we economists conduct our thinking. The absence of bold new approaches may also measure the degree to which events over the last quarter of the twentieth century have not produced challenges as severe as those facing an earlier generation of economists. It remains to be seen whether the collapse of the Soviet Union and the emergence of a global economy will elicit bold new approaches in the twenty-first century.

For all of these reasons, a totally new *Scribblers* would be a difficult—perhaps a Herculean—task to undertake. We would be less than candid with the readers of this edition if we did not confess that the chore would be particularly difficult for us because we share a rather strong sense that the changes in economic research over the past two and a half decades have taken the economics profession away from where we would prefer to have seen it go. The focus of interest of many of the new economic stars has become narrow to the point where a totally new edition of this study would probably need to proceed under the rubric of specific topics rather than complete chapters devoted mainly to individual economists themselves.

But in doing so much would be lost. In looking back over this book we feel proudest of our attempt to humanize the great economists. To a large extent our study is personality driven. The economic writings of scholars necessarily reflect their authors' reaction to the world in which they live and take their being. The greatest of them cause us to see economic phenomena as they see them, creating those economic enclaves we recognize as "schools of thought": classical, neoclassical, Marxist, institutionalist, Austrian, Keynesian, monetarist, rational expectationist, supply-sider, public choice theorist, and new institutionalist. Each of these approaches has had powerful leaders whose personalities (reflected in their teaching and writing styles) created or refined a distinct version of a world in which others have come to live. Therefore we continue to believe that biography is an essential tool, not only to seize and hold the attention of readers, but to help us understand the economists themselves.

This study of the great contemporary economists from 1930 to 1980 in terms of revolutions and counterrevolutions in thought suggests the possibility of methodological renewal. In a reaction against the sterility of the "technique for technique's sake" training in graduate school, it is likely a new generation of intellectual entrepreneurs will emerge whose wide-ranging interests and powerful persuasive skills will inspire lesser scholars to follow them. The great academic scribblers of the recent past will surely have their successors.

NAME INDEX

SUBJECT INDEX